Ideas in Action

Ideas in Action

Political Tradition in the Twentieth Century

Stephen Eric Bronner

ROWMAN & LITTLEFIELD PUBLISHERS, INC.
Lanham • Boulder • New York • Oxford

ROWMAN & LITTLEFIELD PUBLISHERS, INC.

Published in the United States of America
by Rowman & Littlefield Publishers, Inc.
4720 Boston Way, Lanham, Maryland 20706

12 Hid's Copse Road
Cumnor Hill, Oxford OX2 9JJ, England

British Library Cataloging in Publication Information Available

Library of Congress Cataloging-in-Publication Data

Bronner, Stephen Eric, 1949–
    Ideas in action : political tradition in the twentieth century
Stephen Eric Bronner.
        p.   cm.
    Includes bibliographical references.
    ISBN 0-8476-9386-4 (cloth : alk. paper). — ISBN 0-8476-9387-2
(paper : alk. paper)
    1. Political science—History—20th century.   I. Title.
JA83.B689   1999
320'.01—dc21   98-52021
                                                    CIP

Printed in the United States of America

♾ ™ The paper used in this publication meets the minimum requirements of
American National Standard for Information Sciences—Permanence of Paper for
Printed Library Materials, ANSI Z39.48–1992.

In memory of my grandfather, Julius Tiefenbronner

Contents

Preface

Politics is not a self-evident enterprise—or, at least, not any more. Conflicts are generated not merely by different material interests but also by different value systems. Making sense of these divergent norms, and the ways in which they intersect with material interests, is the province of political thought. Its importance is often underplayed. But its debates resonate everywhere. They illuminate the character of our society and our time. Enough books deal with the exclusively Western canon of political theory; others offer insights into various contemporary trends. No book has sought to provide an overview of the major political traditions of the twentieth century, however, let alone interpret them with an eye upon their practical impact.

Ideas in Action is an attempt to fill the gap. Undertaken from the standpoint of intellectual history with a political intent, informed by a concern with the social implications of epistemological assumptions, it highlights the friction between theory and practice. It confronts the past and, ultimately, calls for a new perspective with which to greet the future. Including every political tendency and dealing with every political thinker of the century would, of course, have been impossible. Perhaps some discussions should have been lengthened and others shortened: the decision was ultimately always made with respect to how well a particular thinker illuminates the tradition in question. Attentive readers will also surely note the lack of sustained discussion of religions themes, psychoanalysis, and the connection between literature and political thought. The reason is simple enough: the object of scrutiny here is normative political theory; to investigate the impact upon it of other disciplines would have been a very different undertaking.

This book employs the notion of tradition as its organizing principle. Fusing theory with practice, generating its own project, its reconstructed notion of tradition prevents either reducing ideas to their sociological context or considering them in transcendental terms as part of a preordained metaphysical canon. The unity of the work is self-evident: the parts, which follow one another in roughly chronological order, are built around certain themes, and the chapters deal with distinct traditions. The work is synthetic in its attempt to develop the conversations within political theory and between political theory and politics.

It also walks a fine line between a survey text and a scholarly monograph, and perhaps inevitably, on occasion, it leans unfavorably toward one side or the other. It seeks to be fair to the great theorists of our time. But it makes no claim to objectivity. There is no need: political theory is an inherently normative enterprise, and reasoned debate lies at its core. The character of this work and the purpose informing it are clear enough. It judges different political ideas in relation to different political undertakings and their relevance, whether explicit or implicit, for developing a progressive politics in the present. The point, after all, is to emphasize the salience of political theory rather than simply anoint yet another set of "classics." Thus, while the expositions of different tendencies and works are, I hope, balanced, my voice is partisan, and my own political standpoint is apparent throughout.

Many friends and colleagues contributed their efforts to this book. John Ehrenberg, Michael Forman, Kurt Jacobsen, and Manfred Steger spent much time with the manuscript. Their insights and criticisms surely made it better. I would also like to thank Farid Abdel-Nour, Pedro Caban, Anand Commissiong, Susan Craig, Christian Fenner, Judith Grant, Douglas Kellner, Christine Kelly-Filkohazi, Elizabeth Kelly, Eduardo Mendieta, and Linda Zerilli for their perceptive comments on chapters dealing with their particular areas of expertise. Without Jennifer Knerr, my editor at Rowman and Littlefield, this project would never have reached fruition, and I genuinely appreciate the efforts of my copy editor, Katherine Kimball. Finally, in closing, let me once again express my gratitude to Anne Burns, my wife, for everything.

Stephen Eric Bronner
New York City, 1998

Times pass, and were they not to pass, it would be grave for those who do not sit at the golden tables. Methods become exhausted, impulses give out. New problems arise and demand new remedies. . . . Nothing arises from nothing, the new emerges from the old. Yet it is indeed for that very reason still new.

Bertolt Brecht

Prologue

◆━━━━◇

Tradition, Interpretation, Commitment

T he past is not mechanically divided from the present like the mark-
ings on a clock. Ideas build upon ideas, thinkers upon thinkers,
books upon books. Traditions and interests conflict, coalesce, and
fall apart once more. Amid the seeming chaos, however, politics retains its
intellectual canon; it is taught in classes, it socializes students, and it provides the sanctioned alternatives for thinking about practice. There is also
something inherently useful, almost self-evidently important, about becoming acquainted with the great minds of the past. But the established canon
of political thought is tottering. None of its representatives could possibly
have anticipated the dramatic events of the twentieth century, let alone
Auschwitz or the gulag, the allure of totalitarianism, or the concerns of the
new social movements and the struggles of non-Western peoples. Political
thought can no longer simply rely on the religious or transcendental assumptions underpinning its classical heritage. New traditions have appeared
with novel combinations of norms, divergent interests, and emergent existential forms of self-identification.

These traditions rest on more than the repetition of claims, common symbols, or rituals; they are not invariant, and they do not simply sanction innovations by making reference to precedent. They often begin with mutually
exclusive assumptions, and they are not always compatible. They generate
conflicts; and, especially given the narrowing of contemporary political dis-

course, highlighting what is distinctive about them is probably more important than ever before. Consensus is the death of political theory, the continuing salience of which rests upon its ability to foster real, if reasoned, debate. Neutrality offers no challenge to the assumptions taken for granted by the various traditions; it contests repression as little as it fires the imagination. The need to choose ineluctably makes itself felt. The purpose of political theory becomes clear: it introduces criteria with which to judge the character of given traditions, their assumptions, and their ability to deal with actual political events.

This requires a form of reflection that is reducible to the concerns of no particular tradition while also capable of calling each into question. Such reflection must prove "critical" in character. It must navigate between two poles. It can identify itself neither with empirical "problem solving," which makes no reference to normative concerns, nor with the simple proclamation of ideals divorced from an analysis of the obstacles preventing their realization. The former would turn political theory into a branch of public administration; the latter would provide it with an impotent autonomy. A critical form of reflection has no alternative; it must posit an "emancipatory interest."[1]

Political theory should never serve as the handmaiden of political practice. But it also should never simply sever its ties with history. It would thereby deny the obvious, relegate its insights to the realm of metaphysics, and—most importantly—truncate its ability to illuminate reality. It is more urgent than ever to recognize or, better, to draw the implications of what John Maynard Keynes simply took for granted:

> The ideas of economists and political philosophers, both when they are right and when they are wrong, are more powerful than is commonly understood. Indeed, the world is ruled by little else. Practical men, who believe themselves to be quite exempt from any intellectual influences, are usually the slaves of some defunct economist. Madmen in authority, who hear voices in the air, are distilling their frenzy from some academic scribbler of a few years back. . . . Soon or late, it is ideas not vested interests which are dangerous for good or evil.[2]

---

1. Jürgen Habermas, *Knowledge and Human Interests*, trans. Jeremy J. Shapiro (Boston: Beacon, 1971), 301 ff.

2. John Maynard Keynes, *The General Theory of Employment, Interest, and Money* (New York: Harcourt Brace, 1936), 383–84.

Even the most scholarly forms of political theory, whether consciously or unconsciously, offer a response to events and stand in some relation with actual politics. Hannah Arendt looked back longingly to the *polis* and, following the Hungarian uprising of 1956, embraced the notion of a workers' council or democratic soviet.[3] But no less than when expressing her admiration for the "anti-federalists" of the American Revolution,[4] or direct participation over institutional accountability, she never dealt with any of the constraints limiting the decentralization of authority or the actual problems associated with it: coordination, patronage, provincialism, the adjudication of grievances, the impact of markets, and the like. Influenced by her experience with totalitarianism, suspicious of the bureaucratic state and the effects of a newly emerging consumer society, she believed politics was losing its substance. Arendt sought to render politics autonomous and preserve it from infringement by instrumental interests. Her philosophical response to history was to identify politics with "speech" and a "self-exhibition" among equals rather than with the economic or bureaucratic concerns of the state and its institutions.

Attempts of this sort to divorce political theory from the workings of "politics" or the struggle for power, whatever their sparkling intellectual value, undercut the salience of the general enterprise. The attempt to combat contemporary politics with classical philosophy proved both hopelessly abstract and counterintuitive. Liberalism and Marxism and fascism were suddenly deemed antipolitical. It did not matter that these forms of political theory most directly informed the mass struggles of our century. They were condemned for their collusion with the state, their anti-participatory character, and their suspension of the categories most appropriate to political theory.[5] It was the same with thinkers like Marx, even though his work constituted a landmark in political theory and directly influenced the political commitment of millions.[6] "Real" politics would now concern itself less with

3. Hannah Arendt, *The Human Condition: A Study on the Central Dilemmas Facing Modern Man*, 2d ed. (New York: Doubleday, 1959), 194.

4. Hannah Arendt, *On Revolution* (New York: Harcourt and Brace, 1963).

5. Sheldon Wolin, *Politics and Vision: Continuity and Innovation in Western Political Thought* (Boston: Little, Brown, 1960), 286 ff.

6. Marx is seen as expressing a "belief in the ultimate futility of politics. At its very worst . . . political action might pervert human affairs; at its best, it could only register social reality, but in no sense could political action supply a creative direction." Quoted ibid., 415–16.

issues of power and interest than with what is "general and integrative to men, a life of common involvements."[7]

This negative view of political power is not confined to one philosophical perspective. Advocates of critical theory like Max Horkheimer and Theodor Adorno also occupied themselves with the increasing dominance of instrumental reason. At least, however, they were consistent. Ultimately they withdrew the idea of resistance from political theory altogether and identified it with theology and philosophical aesthetics respectively. It is the same with many proponents of postmodernism for whom the only value remaining for philosophy is "play" or game strategies. That perhaps marks an advance. The major influences on political theory in the United States following World War II largely remained content with juxtaposing an indeterminate and anachronistic idea of politics against the reality of politics and then mistook the idea for the reality.

THEORY AND PRACTICE

History made this possible. Totalitarianism left an ineradicable mark on intellectual life. Reality had seemingly betrayed any notion of reason that, in keeping with Hegel, identified freedom as its goal. Totalitarians had transformed philosophy into ideology, and the only logical response by democrats seemingly involved separating genuine politics from its involvement with masses, parties, and states. It perhaps only made sense that political theory in the United States, the homeland of pragmatism and the bastion of individualism, should have proved particularly suspicious of all systematic philosophical approaches as well as the snares of an increasingly bureaucratic mass society: instrumentalism, political interest, ideology, and—above all—power.

But healthy suspicion should not turn into avoidance. Mainstream political theory in the United States is still trying to ignore the fact that politics today is mass politics. Over the past fifty years, its principal practitioners have either arbitrarily redefined politics or simply retreated from the determinate context in which action is defined and contingency is structurally constituted. This process began in response to the cold war and the rise of the culture industry, with its emphasis upon consumerism and rejection of

---

7. Ibid., 433–34.

"ideological" involvement. It also, however, was influenced by the emergence of seemingly dangerous new trends in political science.

Especially in the United States during the 1950s and 1960s, and more recently in Europe, many considered it necessary to defend political theory against a behaviorist onslaught.[8] The value-free and "nonideological" presuppositions of scientific reasoning, its pragmatic and "falsifiable" character, appeared to offer a sharp rebuke to the metaphysical dogmas of totalitarianism. Various forms of political theory, however, criticized the attempt to extend the methods of the natural sciences into society. They legitimately castigated the advocates of behaviorism for their refusal to deal with the basic speculative questions inherited from the past. They were appalled by the way in which scientific reason was turning into what David Hume termed "a slave of the passions" and a servant of established interests.

Some deplored the apparent connection between the transformation of politics into a set of techniques and the rise of civic apathy. Others were concerned with the ways behaviorism uncritically reflected the values of existing institutions and undercut the force of the imagination. There was great power in the classical assault on the new scientism. Nevertheless, there was also a way in which the response of normative political theory to behaviorism was exaggerated and self-defeating.

Perhaps the definition of politics offered by Harold Lasswell, the important behavioralist and pluralist, is too narrow: politics must surely involve more than a description of "who gets what, when, how."[9] But when such issues are completely ignored, when political theory simply turns its back on the structural imbalances of power, when it rejects the need for any objective referent or partisan commitment to actual movements and interests, the salience of the undertaking and its identity become increasingly questionable. The approach employed by mainstream political theorists did not help matters. They resolved only to draw the wagons ever tighter and to increasingly occupy themselves with the "idea" of politics as it appears in the "conversation" among the "master thinkers"—the "great men" of political theory—who constitute a predetermined "canon" beyond time and space.

Despite McCarthyism and the civil rights movement, the cold war and the emergence of a "Third World," the 1950s and early 1960s is generally

8. John Gunnell, *The Descent of Political Theory* (Chicago: University of Chicago Press, 1993).
9. Harold Lasswell, *Politics: Who Gets What, When, How?* (New York: McGraw-Hill, 1936).

considered an apolitical period, and during this time political theory plunged into the *text*. It was not alone. Similar tendencies made their appearance in a variety of other fields. Literature departments, for example, witnessed the emergence of the "new criticism" of Northrop Frye, with its rejection of all external ideological and sociological influences upon the work. French intellectuals like Jean-Paul Sartre or members of the German Group 47, which included figures like Günther Grass and Alfred Andersch, may have spoken about engagement. But the popular mood in both countries opposing commitment—encompassed in the German phrase, "without me" *(ohne mich),* that became a slogan for the time—was more telling.

Political theory did not remain immune from these developments. Its canonical writings came to be seen ever less in terms of the context in which they arose; even where this concern surfaced in the form of a rather conservative sociology of knowledge, moreover, any political purpose was usually expunged. It became far more important to illustrate how a particular author "understood" himself or herself. According to Leo Strauss, perhaps the preeminent representative of this position, it is only through the texts of those classical authors engaged in the ongoing "conversation" over issues like "virtue" or "the good life" that the discipline of political theory has "understood" itself.[10]

The conversation, of course, remains hopelessly abstract. It also makes as little sense to consider a work in terms of how an author has "understood" himself or herself, when the text is the only point of reference, as it does to reduce a work to the sociological context in which the author grew to maturity. The former generates an idealistic mode of subjectivism that banishes history and its interests in favor of an imaginative reconstruction of the text. The latter fosters an empiricist or objectivistic form of materialism, readily apparent in the magisterial *History of Political Theory* by George Sabine, that reduces the text to its context: the "anticipatory" content of the work, its enduring appeal, its transcendent elements, all vanish in favor of the ways in which it reflects certain social interests.

Both approaches reify the work. The textual approach simply presupposes its classical character and consigns it to a museum of the mind: the work is preserved from the mob and kept ready for yet another Talmudic exegesis by yet another academic "aristocrat" of the future. The contextual

---

10. Leo Strauss, *Liberalism, Ancient and Modern* (Chicago: University of Chicago Press, 1995).

approach, by contrast, transforms the work of political theory into an object of purely historical interest; its salience is always undercut and its specificity is obscured.

A work is reducible to neither its text nor its context. To ignore either is to undermine the political relevance of the given theory. But it is also insufficient merely to emphasize the "interplay" between the two. This evades the conceptual problem of elucidating how the interplay is achieved. Indeterminacy and arbitrariness thereby gain a new foothold. Situating the text within the context from which it emerged, and wherein it is being read, thus becomes a matter of some importance. Such an undertaking will call for dealing with the *horizon*—not only of theory but also of practice—in which new worldviews have been created and old ones have been revised.[11] It will indeed involve introducing the category of tradition but also providing it with a new and more flexible connotation.

THE ABSTRACT AND THE CONCRETE

Tradition brings meaning into the world. It is neither simply an intellectual, historical, nor social construct. Tradition also harbors a political dimension. Even when traditions are analytically constructed without reference to history, whether wittingly or unwittingly, they connect certain understandings of the ideal with the real, knowledge with interest, and theory with practice. Tradition, in this way, is always concrete. Especially in the United States, however, it has been left hanging in the abstract by the most influential representatives of contemporary political theory. It is usually employed either to organize a canonical group of thinkers engaged in a "conversation" about similar ideas or to categorize an ongoing or "genealogical" reproduction of interests. Textualists identify it with transcendent values devoid of material concerns, and contextualists view it in terms of material concerns devoid of transcendent values. Defined by what they oppose, once again, two methodological perspectives dominate the current interpretive discourse.

The canonical perspective lifts tradition beyond material interests, move-

---

11. Hans-Georg Gadamer, *Truth and Method*, trans. Garrett Barden and John Cumming (New York: Seabury, 1975); Terence Ball, *Reappraising Political Theory* (Oxford: Clarendon, 1995).

ments, or ideological aims. Such a stance is predicated on the belief in what Karl Jaspers, the mentor of Leo Strauss, termed a "perennial philosophy" whose "traces" or "ciphers" (*Chiffren*) are in need of constant reinterpretation, even though they manifest themselves in the great works of every civilization and unite them.[12] There is no articulated "system" for philosophy, there is only "philosophizing." But the classical bias is evident from the start: the future always, and inevitably, lies in the past. It is the same, interestingly enough, in the genealogical understanding of tradition. The approach itself stems from Frederick Nietzsche,[13] who employed it to illuminate how the interest of the "herd" actually underpins all moral systems. His aim was to confront all generally accepted normative assumptions in the name of a new stance whereby those capable of mastering their "will to power" could finally engage in a radical "transvaluation of values." This critical moment of the genealogical approach is reflected, whether consciously or not, by numerous thinkers of very different political and theoretical persuasions.

Sir Karl Popper, a liberal, could find the rudimentary assumptions of the "closed society" in Plato and could argue that they were carried over into the present through the pseudodemocratic radicalism of Jean-Jacques Rousseau and, most crucially, the historicism of G. W. F. Hegel and Karl Marx.[14] A far more radical thinker like Michel Foucault, however, also explicitly employed the genealogical method in any number of wide-ranging sociological investigations through which either historical or anthropological interests in domination become apparent.[15] Conservative thinkers from the time of Edmund Burke and Joseph de Maistre have generally made reference to

12. Karl Jaspers, *Philosophy*, trans. E. B. Ashton (Chicago: University of Chicago Press, 1971), 3:113 ff.

13. Frederick Nietzsche, *Beyond Good and Evil: Prelude to a Philosophy of the Future*, trans. Walter Kaufmann (New York: Vintage, 1966). The best general statement of Nietzsche's views is provided in his "Twilight of the Idols," in *Twilight of the Idols and The Anti-Christ*, trans. R. J. Hollingdale (New York: Penguin, 1968).

14. "[Plato's] theory of the best or most ancient state . . . treats its human cattle exactly as a wise but hardened shepherd treats his sheep; not too cruelly, but with proper contempt." Karl R. Popper, *The Open Society and Its Enemies* (Princeton: Princeton University Press, 1950), 55.

15. Michel Foucault, "Nietzsche, Genealogy, History," in *Language, Counter-Memory, Practice: Selected Essays and Interviews*, ed. Donald F. Bouchard, trans. Donald F. Bouchard and Sherry Simon (Ithaca: Cornell University Press, 1977); Michel Foucault, *The History of Sexuality, Vol. 1, An Introduction*, trans. Robert Hurly (New York: Random House, 1978).

the baneful elements of human nature in developing their arguments; insofar as ideas are often reduced to hidden drives and complexes, Freudians have also contributed to the genealogical undertaking. But whether this takes place from the conservative, liberal, or radical perspective is epistemologically irrelevant. The assumptions remain the same.

Even criticism of mainstream ideas about tradition generally accepts the prevailing paradigms and skirts what is at stake. It is insufficient simply to emphasize the fact that a multiplicity of conversations, rather than one single dialogue, constitutes the history of political theory.[16] Other objections are more sophisticated but just as limited. Traditions, for example, are often seen as breaking down through the force of compromise: its advocates are condemned to lose control over its terminology or identifiable concerns.[17] Analytic definitions of tradition, however, are as worthless as attempts to identify it with a certain kind of "speech praxis."[18]

Traditions are forged from a given complex of ideas and goals, material interests and institutional strategies, as well as divergent styles and constituencies. Each has its normative features and practical interests. Each also retains an existential dimension and thereby provides a mode of self-definition in relation to others. Tradition is, in short, different from the way in which metaphysicians, positivists, and phenomenologists conceive it. It can evidence various conflicting tendencies or subtraditions. But it is inherently informed by a *project*, an expressly political commitment, to transform its ideas into reality. Future forms of political theory, if they seek to remain relevant, must more self-consciously focus upon the role of traditions and their projects: the ideas they have utilized, the institutional constraints they have navigated, and the material interests they have embraced.

Employing the notion of tradition politically is impossible without making reference to the particular project. Making reference to a project, in turn, presupposes a particular standpoint for explaining reality and the manner in which it is constituted. The motivation for political practice, which derives from the project, is also the basis for the hermeneutic character of tradition. The project retains a transcendent component even as it ren-

16. J. G. A. Pocock, *Politics, Language, and Time: Essays on Political Thought and History* (Chicago: University of Chicago, 1989), 17.

17. Jeremy Waldron, *Liberal Rights: Collected Papers, 1981–1991* (New York: Cambridge University Press, 1993), 35 ff.

18. Matthias Bolhlender, *Die Rhetorik des Politischen: Zur Kritik der politischen Theorie* (Berlin: Akademie, 1995), 233 ff.

ders determinate the residue of the past, the prejudices and hopes, in the work of every thinker.

Walter Benjamin suggested, in this vein, that every document of civilization is simultaneously a document of barbarism.[19] And he was correct. Traditions of political theory are, after all, sustained by genuine problems and exigencies pertaining to political practice. The realm of freedom they project is always contaminated by the realm of necessity they confront. Traditions and subtraditions thrive insofar as social, economic, institutional, psychological, or anthropological obstacles inhibit the realization of particular interests and norms. The willingness to engage these unresolved and pressing problems is what determines whether any given tradition will remain a dynamic force or whether it will instead become a matter of purely academic interest. Therein alone lies its ability to develop and progress.

PAST AND FUTURE

Tradition need not lead to viewing the new in terms of the old. It is not inherently connected with nostalgia for a bygone past in which the exploited and oppressed knew their place. Tradition exists in the present and often opens new possibilities for the future. Marxism was not buried with Marx, conservatism did not end with Jacob Burckhardt, and liberalism continued to develop after Herbert Spencer. The changes within these modes of thought were, moreover, not simply incremental or predicated on acceptance of the fundamental assumptions behind the original paradigm. New traditions are constantly in the process of being formed and refashioned by new constituencies with new ideological and political interests.

Tradition defines the terms, or mediates the context, in which the "conversation" between thinkers occurs. It always takes place through, between, and within traditions. Tradition alone makes it possible to grasp the diverse empirical forms taken by political theory in this century. It is useless to simply list the multitude of approaches taken by a multitude of thinkers. An organizing category is necessary to make sense of trends within the discipline. Compared with more mainstream approaches, however, this category cannot be divorced from the material world of interests or the historical

19. Walter Benjamin, "Theses on the Philosophy of History," in *Illuminations*, ed. Hannah Arendt, trans. Harry Zohn (New York: Schocken, 1969), 256.

conditions in which it assumes value. The use of the category implies an approach willing to deal with the form and the content, the ideals and the interests, the strictures and the compromises, within a certain common undertaking in theory and practice.

Tradition need not subvert a critical approach to the past in the manner of hermeneutical thinkers like Hans-Georg Gadamer. Quite the contrary. Ironically, those thinkers usually seen as constituting the canon are often those whose insights retain a critical edge. They also usually best exemplify the concerns of given traditions in conflict or the transition from one period into the next. Not every thinker fits neatly into one tradition or another; Alisdair MacIntyre can be seen as a conservative or a communitarian; Che Guevara can be seen as a traditional communist or a new representative of postcolonial thought, or both. The danger in employing tradition as a category is that the specific contributions of particular thinkers can become lost, and there is always an element of subjectivity in determining its applicability. But that is equally the case with mainstream approaches that emphasize either the text or the context.

There is no substitute for the thinkers themselves. But the category of tradition makes it possible to distinguish between those who are more and less important.[20] It makes clear how given thinkers offer nodal points, or determinate conceptual contributions, for its unique development and also how they enable it to face particular historical problems of political practice. With political theory, no less than with art, tradition also illuminates the ways in which the truth content of a movement need not necessarily culminate in the greatest works. It makes room for the study of other less recognized authors and works as well. This is the way in which tradition offers a horizon for inquiry. It mediates between text and context even as it serves as a corrective for those concerned exclusively with either one.

Tradition fits the thinker into history. Imaginative linkages between authors and new interpretations are always possible: traditions can be invented for scholarly or academic purposes with no real relation to events, self-evident influences, or genuine trends. No thinker is reducible to the traditions with which he or she is associated in the popular imagination. If history is not defined by dialectical "necessity," however, neither is it simply defined by contingency. Accident does not explain why some thinkers, like

20. Theodor W. Adorno, *Aesthetic Theory*, trans. C. Lenhardt (London: Routledge and Kegan Paul, 1984), 36 ff.

Voltaire and Immanuel Kant, have overwhelmingly been appropriated by progressive political movements whereas others, like Nietzsche and Martin Heidegger, have primarily been embraced by political movements of the right, even if their roles can change when considered in terms of cultural movements or particular artistic genres like poetry and painting. Situating these thinkers within particular traditions of theory and practice, under any circumstances, provides an insight.

Employing the category of tradition fruitfully depends upon viewing the diverse trajectories of ideas in relation to the profound material changes the world has experienced in the twentieth century. There are reasons why liberalism, conservatism, and anarchism were already losing their appeal prior to the outbreak of World War I. There are also reasons why their roles became even more tenuous during the interlude between the wars when, whatever the principled republicanism of social democracy, the now discredited mass movements of fascism and communism dominated the political scene. There is similarly nothing accidental about the growing lack of faith in modern notions of progress and instrumental reason or the Western vision of the state and economic development during the latter part of the century. World War II and the shock of the concentration camps, the experience of imperialism, and the new awareness about racism and sexism gave rise to new movements and new ways of thinking. Critical theory, postmodernism, and an explosion of ideas from the formerly colonialized territories sought to confront these developments, while a spate of "new social movements" attempted to build the identities of previously excluded social groups and to question the institutional assumptions of traditional political action.

There is, arguably, a pressing need for the invention of new traditions. But there should be no mistake: establishmentarian forms still remain dominant and provide the points of reference. Conservatives now offer a new mixture of cultural elitism and the free market. Socialism is in flux. New forms of fascism have surfaced in Austria, France, and elsewhere. Even communism is still alive in the states of the former Soviet Union, and its partisans are desperately groping for values. Greater diversity seems to exist than ever before. But there is a more conformist side to this intellectual flowering. All political actors now seemingly embrace the liberal capitalist state. It is even tempting to speak about the "end of history" as the twentieth century draws to a close.

Thinking of this sort, however, subverts the recognition of what is really new; a utopian impulse still lingers. History has not died. The "best" life still preoccupies us. What Ernst Bloch termed an "anticipatory consciousness" still generates the need to formulate the connection between institutional constraints and the concrete possibilities for expanding the realm of freedom. Tensions between states are taking new forms, and distinguishing between the different expressions of liberal capitalism is becoming a matter of ever greater importance. New concerns generated by environmentalism and scientific development have entered the popular consciousness, and old solutions are no longer adequate to deal with them.

The world is growing smaller while the chasm between rich and poor is growing larger. Transnational organizations are on the rise even as ethnic consciousness is producing ever greater fragmentation. A cosmopolitan sensibility is becoming ever more necessary; a new internationalism looms on the horizon. Giving it shape while forging more liberating and more encompassing traditions is the challenge awaiting the political theory of the next century. Tradition has for too long been in the hands of traditionalists. It has dynamic cosmopolitan and radical internationalist possibilities. These are the issues the following pages seek to address.

PART I

ENVISIONING DEMOCRACY

1

The Dilemmas of Democratic Theory

Democracy has a complex history. It has been claimed by movements and ideological traditions of various political stripes. Over the last quarter of a century, however, democracy has appeared ever less as an object of determination and contention in the struggle between different traditions. The collapse of teleology and the inability of fascism and communism to generate a viable alternative to the liberal capitalist state has given the concept an appeal even its supporters would not have expected in the 1920s and 1930s. Democracy has taken on a life of its own. Every other book on politics has democracy in the title, and there is hardly an article in which the author does not immediately proclaim his democratic convictions. Democracy has become a tradition in its own right, a form of political self-identification, and the object for a self-defined area of inquiry known as democratic theory.

There is something in democratic theory for everyone. Liberal rationalists like John Rawls have furthered the development of democratic ethical inquiry. Communitarians like Charles Taylor have deepened the discussion about multiculturalism and provided new insights into the nature of solidarity and the self. Rational choice theorists, following Mancur Olson, have indicated the debilitating effects on democracy of differentiated information costs and elite groups unified with regard to their particular interests. Democratic theory has also attracted thinkers, like Jürgen Habermas, steeped in the tradition of critical theory. Conservative anticommunists and fanatical believers in the free market have justified their politics in terms of democratic values, and even anarchists, whatever the standing of their original political project, can identify themselves as proponents of democratic theory.

Democratic theory has helped inspire an attack upon dogmatism and self-righteousness. Its unswerving emphasis upon public deliberation and participation, its eclecticism and contempt for "systems," has produced a new concern with participation and a new appreciation of "difference." Its assault upon the ideologies of the past has sought to provide a practical response to an increasingly inhospitable climate for the propagation of progressive ideas. The invocation of "democracy" has seemingly generated the prospect of consensus, recognition, and legitimation. Nevertheless, in the process, it has been turned into an all-encompassing concept.

Democracy has become the answer to every question and the solution to every problem. Its critical edge has been lost. Structural imbalances of economic power and the requirements for their transformation have almost disappeared from its theoretical discourse. Institutions have been ignored in favor of a nearly exclusive concern with "movements" or "the people" or the "practice" of citizens in a "democratic community." Democratic theory has become "pragmatic." But, ironically, there is little urgency for dealing frankly with pragmatic issues: the cut-throat competition for scarce resources among the different "movements," the various alternatives for organizing "the people," and the institutional constraints on "practice." Raising such concerns might inhibit the respectability of the new undertaking. The demand for concreteness when dealing with the actual pursuit of democracy would certainly threaten the perilous quest for consensus.

Liberalism, communitarianism, conservatism, and anarchism all have fundamentally different understandings of democracy. Each has a rich tradition, and each deserves consideration in its own right. But there is a current attempt under way among many thinkers to subordinate the heritages of these diverse tendencies and enter into a new discourse. The move has not been entirely satisfactory, to put it mildly. The supposed political and philosophical breakthroughs made by democratic theory are, indeed, far less certain than most would care to admit. Its "rationalist" or liberal wing still judges reality without reference to its historical constitution, and attempts to identify democracy with some form of discourse ethic still leave it divorced from instrumental issues, existing power relations, or the ways in which agendas are actually set. "Communitarian" forms of democratic the-

ory have not moved much beyond Alexis de Tocqueville and Emile Durkheim in dealing with either the threats posed by modernity for a democratic
politics or the ubiquitous extension of the commodity form and instrumental reason; its proponents are still unable to articulate any objective criteria
for making judgments between traditions. Conservative advocates of democratic theory still remain fearful about their economic privileges and the excesses of reform, even if they no longer necessarily embrace the more aristocratic sorts of elitism from times past; and anarchists remain concerned with
direct democracy beyond any serious consideration of institutions, structures of constraint, or broader forms of economic planning. It is indeed no
longer clear against whom the proponents of democratic theory are actually
arguing or just whom they are trying to convince of what.

Heinrich Mann was surely justified in saying about what was perhaps his
finest novel, *The Small Town* (1909), that it resonates with the "noble song
of democracy." Populist in tone, republican in spirit, this work offered a
utopian critique of the authoritarianism and elitism underpinning Wilhel-
mine society; its radical political purpose was unequivocal in the context. In
the 1960s it was also surely legitimate for thinkers like Paul Goodman and
Christian Bay to employ "democracy" against a conservative mainstream
opposed to civil rights, a liberal establishment wary of increased participation from various new social movements, and an orthodox left still grap-
pling with communism. But those times have passed. The basic assumptions
underpinning the democratic idea—the belief in autonomy and reciprocity,
constitutionalism and popular sovereignty, civil liberties and an independent judiciary, majority rule and respect for minorities, regular elections
with competing parties—are accepted virtually across the political spectrum
in the advanced industrial societies. Socialists now always identify themselves as social democrats; former communists, for their part, call themselves democratic socialists; conservatives present themselves as fundamentally committed to democratic ideals; and even right-wing authoritarians
now use the language of democracy. Only on the most extreme fringes of
modern political life are there political figures willing to argue on principle
against the liberal rule of law and for class privilege, racism, or dictatorship.

There should be no misunderstanding. It is perfectly sensible to call a
broader political movement "democratic" or "progressive." But it is another matter for individuals participating in such a movement to abandon
their unique traditions. This only dampens discourse within the movement,
creates confusion over goals and principles, undermines a sense of history

and political identity, and inhibits the ability of partisans to push the broad movement in any particular direction. But then, again, democratic theory was not created to foster genuine political engagement in the first place. Its indeterminate notion of democracy has nothing to do with political parties, ideologies, movements, or struggles; it really involves nothing more than a purely philosophical attempt to supplant older traditions of liberalism and socialism, republicanism and anarchism, communitarianism and conservatism. The legacies of the postwar consumer society, the cold war, and the reaction against ideological commitment make themselves felt. Democratic theory privileges no constituency and no interests. Its usage often rests on the attempt to abolish traditional distinctions between left and right.

Interestingly enough, of course, the rise of democratic theory and the attack on the distinction between left and right took place precisely during the time in which conservatism was launching its international assault on all progressive movements. It is also not as if a new bipartisan fusion of ideological extremes has taken place. Quite the contrary. Political choice is increasingly becoming circumscribed between one party intent on devastating the disempowered and another content with neglecting them. The proletariat may have vanished, but capitalism remains, and those who should be providing a structural critique and a structural response have gone into hiding. A counterpunch was necessary. But "democratic theory" has retreated into a neutral corner. It has offered nothing to counter apathy among the young and complacency among the old; it has offered nothing to reinvigorate the natural base for progressive movements; it has only tepidly protested handing the ideological agenda to the right.

The left has been losing the battle of ideas. No version of democratic theory has provided new ways of illuminating structural imbalances of power; none has offered a new or compelling critique of totalitarianism; and none has dealt with the terms in which a confrontation with the genuine remaining enemies of democracy can take place. Conservatives have clearly been setting the institutional agendas, in part, because they rely on their values and they make reference to their traditions: they trumpet democracy even as they embrace atavistic cultural ideals and the unhampered freedom of the market. Their opponents, however, have chosen a different strategy. Too many liberals and socialists have embraced a pragmatic, "postliberal" and "postsocialist" form of democratic theory in which their genuine ideals are veiled and their actual traditions are obscured.

The new popularity of the term *democracy* has, of course, enabled many progressives in the United States to more fully appropriate a homegrown tradition that stretches back from the New Left over John Dewey to Abraham Lincoln and Thomas Jefferson. But it has also facilitated a new "pragmatic" identification with the dominance of the United States in a postcommunist world—and with a clear conscience. European thinkers now cross the Atlantic in search of intellectual inspiration and, from a somewhat more cynical perspective, new visions of a new "bipartisan" and "nonideological" stance. Its political justification, however, is never really made clear. Against which antidemocratic forces and against what uniquely antidemocratic, rather than antiliberal or antisocialist, groups or coalitions they define themselves is never made explicit. It is seemingly enough that "democracy" cast an aura of legitimation over its partisans in an era when the collapse of communism has tainted everything connected with socialism and even liberalism has become a suspect term.

Figures like Jürgen Habermas and Adam Michnik now insist that among the values embraced by progressive political movements of times past, only "democracy" retains its relevance. In principle, however, a commitment to democracy need require support for neither internationalism nor economic justice. Enough genuine democrats embrace nationalism. Enough also embrace the self-regulating market. Nothing indicates any common agreement on most basic values, criteria of judgment, or policy implications by the partisans of democratic theory.

Consider social justice: Robert Nozick argues that state intervention into the economy undercuts liberty and human dignity, whereas Joshua Cohen and Joel Rogers argue the opposite. Consider the understanding of politics: John Rawls relies on Kant and the utilitarians to emphasize the liberal primacy of process over substantive ends, whereas Michael Sandel and Amitai Etzioni rely on the presuppositions of Edmund Burke and Alexis de Tocqueville to emphasize the primacy of voluntary associations and civic virtue for democratic life. Consider nationalism: Jürgen Habermas emphasizes the importance of "constitutional patriotism," Richard Rorty privileges "ethnosolidarity" and a "civilized indifference" to the culture of others. Consider internationalism: weak calls for a "new" cosmopolitanism combat the most provincial forms of localism in what still remains a completely underdeveloped discourse.

Exponents with particular views of democracy can, of course, always claim their opponents are not "really" democratic and that existing forms are not "genuine" or—less charitably—that they do not conform to their definition. But this is as silly as historical materialists ahistorically obsessing over what Marx or Lenin or Trotsky "really" meant. Seeking a general theoretical definition simply by looking to historical cases is equally useless, because the application of a theory is always different in different circumstances. No empirical expression of democracy can exhaust the phenomenon. Its existential and political meanings derive only from those very different traditions of theory and practice whose salience is contested by the proponents of democratic theory.

Deciding which understanding of democracy is "more democratic" is possible only by making reference to the general context in which the struggle for democracy takes place, the agents carrying on the struggle, and the assumptions whereby the determinate meaning of the concept is projected into the future. And this makes democracy different from terms like socialism, communism, fascism, liberalism, feminism, nationalism, or even various religious beliefs. Socialism has certain variants, for example, but its basic commitment to republicanism, social justice, and internationalism makes the concept easily comprehensible. It is the same with communism, given the basic belief of its various supporters in the dictatorship of the proletariat, the vanguard party, and democratic centralism. Even with fascism, whatever the fuzziness of its categories and its often polemical usage by antifascists, its character is still relatively clear.

No less than democracy, of course, these ideologies have been qualified in any number of ways and even combined with one another in the most bizarre manner. Their radical thrust has often been tempered. Arguably, they also stand in danger of losing their intellectual vigor and their ability to inspire commitment. But democratic theory was supposed to constitute an advance on the past. None of the other theories, moreover, was employed primarily to foster an illusory consensus. All of them highlight, whether implicitly or explicitly, a particular constituency or a certain tradition. All of them make reference to a unique historical legacy of theory and practice: a more or less coherent body of ideas and a movement, or set of movements, associated with certain clearly distinguishable demands and goals. That is not the case with a vague and indeterminate notion of democracy or a fashionable democratic theory confused with respect to its intellectual tradition and lacking any connection with a genuine movement.

Democratic theory has not overcome the vagaries or intellectual problems attendant upon other traditions. It also does not offer what some have called a "new language" for the left. Its concerns should now supposedly involve the development of a program composed of particular issues upon which all progressives can agree without reference to "first principles" or ideology. Without criteria, and a general perspective for making political judgments, however, it remains unclear what issues deserve inclusion in a general program: the result ultimately becomes nothing more than a hodge-podge, once again, incapable of inspiring any loyalty to any organization or vision. It also apparently does not matter that the "left" in the United States has been talking the language of democracy, working on single-issue coalitions, and seeking a consensual "nonideological" program since the close of World War II. The fact of the matter is that the "language of democracy" has projected consensus and produced marginality.

And the reasons are clear. Every movement relies on issues; but every successful movement also relies on an overriding ideology capable of pulling together diverse values. Interest groups are often a source of power for the disenfranchised; but their bureaucratic structure also generates a concern with autonomy rather than coordination with other groups. Single-issue coalitions are essential for bringing about change, but they also foster internecine competition over scarce resources. Different interests within the broader "movement" have, in short, been pitted against one another, and the whole of the left has become less than the sum of its parts. The "new language" has not dealt with these problems, and as for the new issues, again, the "new language" remains quite old fashioned in its concern with health care, day care, higher wages, and campaign finance reforms. There is, of course, nothing wrong with proponents of democratic theory supporting these demands: they are, indeed, of crucial importance. But there is something wrong with the pretense that something new is being put on the table. Demands of this sort are holdovers from the liberal and socialist movements. There is nothing to indicate that the new language of democratic theory has moved beyond these traditions in practice let alone resolved the philosophical conflicts between them.

It may have made sense in the past to posit a fundamental antagonism between democracy and capitalism. But this is surely no longer the case: democracy and capitalism have become self-reinforcing in the popular imagination. Support for the free market is often justified in terms of its efficiency and as a means of evidencing consumer preferences in a noncoercive manner. But it is also justified in terms of principle: capitalism is seen as anchoring freedom, and the market as a bulwark against the intrusions of the bureaucratic state. Historically, in fact, the labor movement was labeled antidemocratic precisely because its partisans were seen as seeking to interfere with the individual's "right" to property. It is possible, of course, to counter the formal and market-oriented view of personal liberty by insisting upon the "right" to a job or even the substantive importance of a guaranteed income. Making reference to democracy does not help resolve the issue. Social ends conflict in accordance with different understandings of personal liberty, and the same is true of "rights."

Democracy has historically been understood as a political notion based on some fairly simple assumptions. It retains a belief in majority rule coupled with institutional protections for the minority. It privileges the peaceful adjudication of collective decisions; it projects the fullest participation of the interested parties and the greatest possible accountability of the institutions involved in the process. Unfortunately, however, the relatively simple understanding of democracy becomes contorted and confused once other progressive values are smuggled into its definition. This should offer a clue to the problem. "Liberty is liberty," Isaiah Berlin once wrote, "not equality or fairness or justice or culture or human happiness or a quiet conscience." It is the same with democracy. Democracy is democracy: it is not commensurate with socialism or internationalism or constitutionalism; it does not offer existential security or religious certainty, and it does not exhaust utopia. The elastic expansion of "democracy" to include a host of other commitments and concerns has turned a critical concept into a catchphrase. It has obscured qualitative differences between political traditions. Perhaps worst of all, however, it has diverted thinking away from the prerequisites for political action in the name of countless purely discursive, categorical, or plainly dogmatic definitions and justifications of the democratic idea.

A commitment to democracy *can* foster a commitment to socialism or internationalism. But that need not be the case. Karl Marx was well aware of the ways in which the imperatives of formal and substantive democracy can conflict. A flat tax is democratic, for example, insofar as it is formally egalitarian and simultaneously undemocratic insofar as it substantively favors the wealthy. It is possible simply to designate as democratic only those programs capable of satisfying the criteria of both formal and substantive democracy, but this would call into question any program whose benefits are specific to the working class, women, or minorities. The situation is no different with respect to internationalism, given the different the democratic or nondemocratic understandings of national self-determination and cultural autonomy. The only way in which the commitment to democracy can further the commitment to socialism or internationalism is by making the connection between them explicit. The more vague and indeterminate the connection between them, the more "democracy" is used to dismiss other concepts and the more eclectic and incoherent become the politics its proponents can embrace. Thus, ironically, the extent to which democracy breaks its bonds with particular traditions of theory and practice is the extent to which its critical edge becomes blunted.

Democratic theory is also permeated by presumptions about the supposedly always latent will to participate. Motivation is ascribed to the logical perception of arbitrary forms of injustice or repressed material interests. It remains questionable why public participation is somehow more rewarding than private pursuits and also whether it is not more important to stress the need for rendering institutions accountable to other institutions. Extending participation and individual rights, in any event, need not necessarily lead to constriction of the power exercised by capitalist elites. The principal factor in motivating public participation has always been ideology: the overriding framework in which injustice is understood, material demands receive their justification, and a positive alternative is generated with which to contest the status quo. Unfortunately, however, that is precisely what democratic theory has been unable to provide.

"Speaking truth to power" is one thing; looking in the mirror, identifying with a history and a distinct set of values is another. The struggle for democracy was shaped by traditions with other normative concerns and commitments. Without articulating those other concerns and commitments, in this age, too, the calls for democracy will ring hollow. Its theorists, however, remain committed to a quest for "consensus" that has confused, sanitized, and ultimately demoralized the left. The consequence of this situation has become all too clear. The partisans of democratic theory usually have little unique to say about politics, privilege no particular constituency or interests, and therefore should not be surprised when no one listens.

The time has come for progressives to reflect anew upon those traditions of theory and practice in which democracy receives its distinct determinations. Such a move might help them confront a growing political identity deficit among young people. It might lead them to contest an ideological situation in which democracy has been politically emasculated. It might indeed force them to resurrect the critical character of the democratic idea and finally offer the public a sense of its real meaning.

2

✦━━━✦

The Liberal Heritage:
Individualism, Dialogue,
Universalism

iberalism was once a revolutionary phenomenon. Through its precepts, its primarily bourgeois supporters of the seventeenth and eighteenth centuries identified their interests with those of "the people,"
by which most meant or implied not merely those of common birth but also
the excluded and the disinherited. John Locke and Adam Smith, Jean-
Jacques Rousseau and Thomas Jefferson, Voltaire and others envisioned a
new world in which the arbitrary authority of the church and an arrogant
aristocracy would cease to exist; a world in which reason and democracy
would temper provincial ethnic and religious hatreds between states and
races; a world of unfettered freedom, without radical differences in the distribution of wealth, in which an individual might better his lot through hard
work and without fear of obstruction by the state.

The constitution was the jewel in the crown of this new world. The individual would be no longer an object of domination but rather a subject
vested with rights: a citizen. Reciprocity, rather than artificially imposed
forms of hierarchy, would define the formal relations between individuals.
Each would become part of an undertaking intent on constraining the arbitrary exercise of power under the liberal idea of the "rule of law." Thus, in
a sense, it is legitimate to maintain that the creation of a constitution did

"not just mean [changing] the mode of domination. It [was] tantamount to the creation of a new universe."[1]

The monarchical state was the principal object of democratic transformation during the classical age of liberalism. And the commitment to political egalitarianism under the rule of law, whatever the material inequities generated by the new market economy, allowed for a rising bourgeoisie that would equate its interests with those of humanity. This changed during the revolutions of 1848. In that year throughout Europe the liberal bourgeoisie confronted the aristocratic supporters of the Restoration, who sought to roll back the ideals of the French Revolution one last time.

Europe resounded with the call for a *république démocratique*. But the liberals retreated when working people, especially in Paris, sought to radicalize the slogan and demanded a *république démocratique et sociale*, which would also mitigate the inequities of the market and institutionalize what Louis Blanc called "the right to work." Especially with the rise of a mass-based social democratic labor movement, which sought universal suffrage and thereby threatened private property, liberals realigned themselves with the aristocratic enemies of the original revolution and helped repress the new uprisings. Their own political power was crushed, but the market was saved.[2]

This schizophrenia on the part of liberals during the second half of the nineteenth century, and during the years leading into World War I, helps explain the profound contradictions of their doctrine and the incoherence with which its tenets were often expressed. Its democratic features contracted as the radical promises projected by Enlightenment thinkers like Gotthold Lessing, Denis Diderot, and Thomas Paine vanished in favor of the visions developed by racists with a heart of gold, like Rudyard Kipling; social Darwinists, like Herbert Spencer or William Graham Sumner; staunch nationalists with a rationalist bent, like Max Weber; imperialists with a belief in civil liberties, like Randolph Churchill; and even monarchists with a critical spirit, like Friedrich Meinecke or the young Thomas Mann. By the second half of the nineteenth century, especially in Europe, liberalism had become the ideology of the bourgeois gentleman.

---

1. Ulrich Preuss, *Constitutional Revolution: The Link between Constitutionalism and Progress*, trans. Deborah Lucas Schneider (Atlantic Highlands, N.J.: Humanities Press International, 1995), 6.

2. Karl Marx, "The Class Struggles in France, 1848 to 1850," in Karl Marx and Frederick Engels, *Selected Works* (Moscow: Progress, 1969), 1:186 ff.

It was difficult for the liberal not to expect an extension of civil rights to all citizens—or at least to male ones—sooner or later. [Liberalism] had achieved its most spectacular economic triumphs and social transformations by systematically opting for the individual against the institutionalized collectivity, for market transactions (the "cash nexus") against human ties, for class against rank hierarchy, for *Gesellschaft* against *Gemeinschaft*. It had thus systematically failed to provide for those social bonds and ties of authority taken for granted in earlier societies and had indeed set out to and succeeded in weakening them. So long as the masses remained outside politics, or were prepared to follow the liberal bourgeoisie this created no major political difficulties. Yet from the 1870s onwards it became increasingly obvious that the masses were becoming involved in politics and could not be relied upon to follow their masters.[3]

European and American liberalism developed differently. In a sense, the adaptive and experimental qualities of American liberalism, its inherently critical character, derived from the fact that it never had to contest a feudal order. Liberalism in the United States was born free, and its advocates were never in chains. In Europe, however, the situation was different. Its proponents had struggled from the beginnings of the modern state; and, following the revolutions of 1848, liberalism made peace with the status quo. Its original internationalism was now belied by an ongoing, and quite general, support for imperialism. Its principled commitment to civil liberties was belied by opportunistic support for the monarchical regimes dominating the continent. Its belief in equality was confined to the state, at best, and belied by the existence of extreme class divisions. Liberalism, in short, became identified with "bourgeois" interests. It now served merely as a legitimating ideology.[4]

Benedetto Croce and Giovanni Gentile sought to give the rationalist elements of the liberal idea a romantic and vitalist twist precisely in order to contest its identification with bourgeois interests and a crumbling "center" in the Italy of the early twentieth century. It was ultimately a defensive action. Liberalism rested on an idea of liberty, and the promise of history it-

---

3. Eric Hobsbawm, "Mass Producing Traditions: Europe, 1870–1914," in *The Invention of Tradition*, ed. Eric Hobsbawm and Terence Ranger (New York: Cambridge University Press, 1983), 268.

4. Harold J. Laski, *The Rise of European Liberalism* (New Brunswick, N.J.: Transaction, 1996).

self, building on Hegel, was its "story."[5] The idealist interpretation of liberalism rendered any material preoccupations with progress or any commitment to the market secondary to its potential to expand the experience of freedom. Its "spirit" of liberty, dynamic and irreducible to any set of institutional arrangements or interests, had become primary. Liberty is its own end; it never goes in search of employment, for, in the famous phrase, "it employs itself."[6]

Using Hegelian language, this attempt to expand experience is what makes "the real rational"—if only for the time being. Liberty always exists in action; and insofar as it constantly seeks to enlarge the lives of people and expand or intensify their experience, it is capable of contesting existing legal arrangements in a democratic society and confronting the abuses of power in an authoritarian one. This noninstitutional interpretation of liberty and history as its story, of course, tended to obscure the distinction between the existential and the political as well as that between the self and society. Its emphasis on the rationality of the real seemingly justified the brief flirtation of certain Italian liberals, like Gentile, with the nascent fascist state led by Benito Mussolini.

But there was also a different interpretation of Hegel available to liberals. The nineteenth-century English liberal philosopher, T. H. Green, would appropriate from Hegel his belief in the ability of the state to realize, or further, the idea of freedom. The state in question was, of course, seen as subordinate to the rule of law and the preservation of property. Bureaucratic action, however, could mitigate the disastrous impact of industrialization upon the working masses: it appeared obvious to Green that the Hegelian idea of freedom had been truncated when the majority of the population was unable to exercise the rights or fulfill the obligations of citizenship because of their miserable economic conditions.[7] The state could even act in their behalf. State action need not interfere with personal liberty, as traditional liberals like Locke and his followers believed. Improving the eco-

5. Benedetto Croce, *History as the Story of Liberty*, trans. Sylvia Spirgge (New York: Meridian, 1955).

6. Benedetto Croce, "Justice and Liberty," in *My Philosophy: Essays on the Moral and Political Problems of Our Time*, trans. R. Kilbansky (New York: Collier, 1949), 101.

7. T. H. Green, *Lectures on the Principles of Political Obligation and Other Writings*, ed. Paul Harris and John Morrow (New York: Cambridge University Press, 1986).

nomic situation of the workers would, in fact, enhance liberty by, in Green's famous phrase, "hindering the hindrances to the good life."

World War I exploded the fantasy: it spurred the creation of a new interventionist state, but it also ushered into being a society that would become unkind to liberalism and its unique emphasis upon the individual. National economies everywhere began experiencing dramatic deficits in production, raw materials, and labor power. The market alone could not handle the demands of this first "total war," in which imperialism played such a vital role. Administrative planning became a priority among all its major participants. New developments in mass media complemented the increasingly conformist character of mass production. New commercialized forms of culture profoundly transformed the once vibrant sphere, and the state engaged in what the great French liberal historian, Élie Halévy, called "the organization of enthusiasm."[8]

The assault on traditional liberal principles was profound. Even in the aftermath of the conflict, however, little change in liberal political theory occurred. Its proponents generally retained their traditional belief in free trade, colonialism, and the minimalist state essentially intent on protecting the public welfare and ensuring the rights of individuals to engage freely in business and public affairs. Liberals prided themselves on their pragmatism and their willingness to compromise. Nevertheless, their political weakness in Europe during the next decade derived largely from their hyperpragmatism and their inability to deal with the polarized atmosphere born of the new mass politics and the economic problems raised by a new era.[9]

Liberals had always feared the radicalism of the burgeoning social democratic labor movement on the continent, and some, like T. H. Green and John A. Hobson, realized that the theory must begin to meet the challenges posed by a burgeoning new phase of capitalism. But it was in America, arguably, that the initial theoretical changes in liberalism took place. Progressivism, whose most important theoretical work was probably *The Promise of American Life* (1909) by Herbert Croly, sought a mass following. It also incorporated the idea of state action, along with many demands originally raised by the labor movement. The electoral importance of progressivism dissolved with the failed presidential run of Robert LaFollette in 1928,

8. Élie Halévy, *The Era of Tyrannies*, trans. R. K. Webb (Garden City, N.Y.: Doubleday, 1965), 284.
9. Karl Polanyi, *The Great Transformation: The Political and Economic Origins of Our Time* (Boston: Beacon, 1944), 237 ff.

whom the communists refused to endorse, but its general theory would influence the new developments in American liberalism of the 1930s.

Massive economic upheaval, radical unionism, and perhaps even the fear of revolution created a situation following the Great Depression in which the old commitment to individualism became tempered by a new identification with the administrative state. The earlier preoccupation with the free play of market forces gave way before policies designed to stimulate demand and provide a safety net for working people. The previous emphasis upon purely formal freedoms was balanced by a new concern with substantive equality. The New Deal was the result—the American variant of the socialist program promulgated by the antifascist "Popular Front" in Europe.

Continental liberals never really adapted. They remained as they had always been: committed to civil liberties and markets. They sought to occupy the middle ground not merely between communism and fascism but also between social democracy and both totalitarian movements. Representing the interests of big business, and particularly those sectors intent upon free trade, they were resigned to the lack of a mass base. Their political activity was essentially no different from that still carried on by continental liberal parties—a politics predicated on brokering between other mass parties and intent upon serving, crudely speaking, the interests of enlightened capitalists.

The new republican regimes of the 1920s promised liberty and democracy. But they were introduced by the socialist labor movement rather than by liberals. European liberals were "pragmatic," and the masses sensed their lack of conviction; German intellectuals like Mann and Meinecke were known as "skeptical republicans" *(Vernunftrepublikaner)* less committed to the Weimar Republic than resigned to its existence. European liberals also did not play a major role in the struggle against fascism or the postwar reconstruction; and in the United States, the pivotal role played by liberals in pursuing the Vietnam War, and their inability to combat the assault upon "big government" and "welfare dependency" by the forces of Reaganism, increasingly left the philosophy bereft of political support.

History and politics would thus prove less important than metaphysics and epistemology in articulating the importance of the liberal heritage as the 1970s turned into the 1980s. It also makes sense that the philosophy of Immanuel Kant should have taken center stage. The universal subject, formal egalitarianism, due process, individual rights, reciprocity, and a discursive notion of truth became the core categories for liberal political theory. But they were generally developed without reference to action or program. Their emancipatory and critical qualities first made it possible to illuminate the tension existing between the reality of democracy and its motivating ideals. Ever more surely, however, this critical stance transformed itself into a new preoccupation with the "hypothetical" preconditions for a liberal politics.[10] Jürgen Habermas, indeed, would take his place at the forefront of this new trend.

Born in 1929, Habermas grew up under the Nazi regime and then studied critical theory with Max Horkheimer and Theodor W. Adorno. Perhaps for biographical reasons, the Enlightenment and the liberal tradition held an enormous appeal for Habermas. He was indeed skeptical, from the very beginning, about utopianism as well as particularist criticisms of reason and science. His concern with justifying normative claims in the name of furthering a liberal democratic politics, which ultimately put Habermas at odds with the thinking of his teachers,[11] connects his earliest work with his most recent. His first major book, *The Structural Transformation of the Public Sphere*,[12] for example, places a marked emphasis upon the existence of an arena, a public sphere, which protects the individual from the state and allows political grievances to be raised. Indeed, even if advanced industrial society has undermined that sphere through its monopolistic "culture industries," his work highlights the vision of a public realm predicated on the unfettered exchange of ideas as well as a healthy respect for the intelligence and moral capacity of everyday citizens.

Habermas never identified freedom with the subjectivity of the subject. He instead always emphasized, following Kant, the existence of a common emancipatory purpose for knowledge: a "generalizable interest." He would initially maintain that the determination of such an emancipatory interest in any specific instance would presuppose a form of "undistorted communication."[13] An example of such communication occurs in the discourse between psychoanalyst and patient insofar as both seek to free the patient

10. Jeremy Waldron, *Liberal Rights: Collected Papers, 1981–1991* (New York: Cambridge University Press, 1993), 55 ff.

11. Jürgen Habermas, *The Philosophical Discourse of Modernity: Twelve Lectures*, trans. Frederick Lawrence (Cambridge: MIT Press, 1987), 106 ff.

12. Jürgen Habermas, *Strukturwandel der Öffentlichkeit: Untersuchungen zu einer Kategorie der bürgerlichen Gesellschaft* (Berlin: Luchterhand, 1962).

13. Jürgen Habermas, *Knowledge and Human Interests*, trans. Jeremy J. Shapiro (Boston: Beacon, 1971), 214 ff.

from unconscious or unexamined problems. Only by positing a notion of "undistorted communication" and the existence of individuals capable of employing rationality, Habermas would claim, is it possible to comprehend the distorted forms of communication employed by the culture industry and the existing political process. Yet he was not completely convinced.[14] Neither the generalizable interest nor the notion of "undistorted communication" could explain their own genesis. They contested a degraded reality. Nevertheless, they lacked criteria for their own validation and, under those circumstances, it would prove impossible to justify other normative truth claims.

Habermas could have chosen to analyze the conditions and institutions hindering the formation of emancipatory interests and the realization of an undistorted form of communication in terms of a critical theory of society. But this would obviously have prevented him from anchoring his theory, or grounding it, in strictly philosophical terms. His other option was to take an analytic approach, anchor his concepts, and separate his philosophical endeavor from issues dealing with interest, power, and the like. He made his choice. The need to validate claims and make them intelligible would subsequently lead Habermas toward a "linguistic turn." He would speak out consistently on issues ranging from the attempts by ultraconservatives like Ernst Nolte to turn their backs on the German past in the "historians' controversy" to the integration of Europe. But his later philosophical work would primarily concern itself with showing how language implicitly seeks consensus with respect to our common problems and that criteria exist within language itself for resolving them.

Issues concerning the structural imbalances of power in our society, the setting of agendas for discourse, and the character of interest formation faded into the background. But Habermas anchored the liberal understanding of democracy in a notion of "communicative competence," itself grounded in a "universal pragmatics."[15] Communication is seen as inherently presupposing a formal egalitarian recognition of others, a willingness to justify positions in a rational spirit based on good will, and an implicit commitment to ultimately accept the better argument beyond any specific set of material or instrumental interests. Habermas finds universal criteria

---

14. Ibid., 301 ff.
15. Jürgen Habermas, *Moral Consciousness and Communicative Action*, trans. Christian Lenhardt and Shierry Weber Nicholson (Cambridge: MIT Press, 1990), 43 ff., 116 ff.

for the validation of claims within the presuppositions for meaningful communication. And this, he believed, makes his philosophy "postmetaphysical," in contrast with earlier thinkers of the idealist tradition intent on finding a transcendental foundation for their normative concerns. Those who deny the premises for meaningful communication will in practice, according to Habermas, necessarily find themselves in a state of logical contradiction with their purportedly democratic aims.

The idea of politics constituting a "city in speech," where the "passions" and the "interests" are mitigated by the force of reason and persuasion, goes back to Plato. But there is something tautological in the formulation offered by Habermas. Those unconcerned with democracy are never unafraid of standing in contradiction with themselves. The discourse ethic indeed preaches only to the converted; and in the expulsion of instrumental or material concerns from the universal pragmatics, the defenders of liberal democracy are left without any conceptual way of dealing with their enemies.

Immanent critique of the sort employed by Habermas has proved a powerful weapon in the battle against mystification and injustice. Martin Luther King Jr. often juxtaposed racism in the United States with the ideals articulated in the Declaration of Independence. The concern was concrete, and it involved instrumental interests. Habermas also wishes to confront the inequalities of modern life with the egalitarian postulates on which communication is based. But his approach is metaphysical and indeterminate. It ultimately turns into a purely scholastic enterprise directed against what has become an essentially sterile tradition of analytic linguistic philosophy in the United States.

Politics drops out. There is no point of practical reference nor any possibility of immanently dealing with instrumental interests, institutions, and power from within the theory itself. Translating the democratic implications of the discourse ethic into practice against those who would oppose them thus becomes impossible. Habermas's "linguistic turn" highlights an enduring element in the liberal tradition: its emphasis on persuasion over coercion and the justification of claims over their dogmatic assertion. But the basic inadequacy of the theory remains. A genuinely "postmetaphysical" philosophy must begin with neither the deconstruction nor the reconstruction of "truth," or even the criteria for its validation, but instead with the specification of those material conditions that inhibit and best foster its quest.

Karl Jaspers, one of the most important figures in the history of existential philosophy, sought to reaffirm the values of liberalism amid the rubble of postwar Germany and with an eye toward the failure of the Weimar Republic. Kant had noted that the perfect republic was one in which even devils could coexist. But the inherently imperfect character of democracy, the lack of assurances attendant upon maintaining it, had been glaringly validated by events. Under extreme circumstances, Jaspers believed, democracy may even have to become "intolerant of intolerance itself."[16] There is no philosophical move, political trick, or institutional mechanism for sustaining a democratic order. It lacks any ultimate grounding or foundation. But this only begs the question. In terms of what does it become possible to adjudicate between interests and place priority upon one set of values rather than another? Karl Jaspers called for faith in democracy, a refusal to deduce a course of action from any particular creed, and a willingness to rationally develop a common insight from existing material interests.[17] His recourse to faith, however, seems at odds with the emphasis on reason. The existential attempt to rehabilitate liberalism fails.

Liberal rationalism would become increasingly intent on eliding existential concerns while affirming the need for a belief in first principles. Alienation from practice only aggravated the desire to ground liberalism in theory. And, clearly, the most dominant figure in this enterprise would become John Rawls. *A Theory of Justice*, his classic work, essentially seeks to ground intuitively attractive notions of social justice in a framework of rational consent whose validity no reasonable person could reject. The foundation for this enterprise was the hypothetical "original position" in which individuals are stripped of their material interests and history in order to illuminate the moral values any self-interested person would accept. The logic is not dissimilar to what Thomas Hobbes employed in viewing the interest in survival as the precondition for the pursuit of all other interests. The result is a maxim whereby social policy is judged in terms of whether it favors the least advantaged member of society.

In the "original position," where each is cloaked by a "veil of ignorance" and no one knows what social situation he or she retains, it would seem a matter of prudent self-interest for each to embrace this maxim. The "difference principle" assumes that social and economic inequalities are arranged so that they can be expected to serve the advantage of everyone with posi-

---

16. Karl Jaspers, *The Future of Mankind*, trans. E. B. Ashton (Chicago: University of Chicago Press, 1958), 295.
17. Ibid., 265.

tions and offices open to all. The utilitarian self-interest in security becomes bound with the commitment to reciprocity on which ethical rationalism is founded. Rawls attempts to unify the two most profound philosophical strains of liberalism without relinquishing its traditional emphasis on the individual or due process. Therein lies his notable contribution. Nevertheless, from the first, the character of the undertaking is clear: it seeks to render the political world intelligible by reducing it to philosophical categories.[18]

In a sense, Rawls sought in *A Theory of Justice* to deal with the gulf between metaphysics and history. A new moral constructivism, which initially appeared in a later set of essays,[19] came to define his next work, *Political Liberalism*. The point increasingly became one of emphasizing the "political" over the "metaphysical" character of the argument and building upon the ability to confront the social system without invoking transcendental assumptions. His maxim and the various principles related to it would increasingly find their grounding in various intuitive understandings of what constitutes a good society and in the customs and assumptions underpinning a constitutional order.[20]

The purpose of political philosophy, according to Rawls, is to clarify this consensus and uncover new ways of resolving basic questions in a mutually acceptable way. It must seek to show why certain ways of arranging institutional forms are more appropriate than others for realizing democratic values such as liberty and equality. This is possible only by making reference to tradition and those provisionally fixed convictions wherein such an arrangement, or a given notion of justice, can make sense to the public at large.

Fairness remains tied to the refusal to prejudge conflicting and even incommensurable conceptions of the public good. The "original position" and the "difference principle" remain what they were. All of this, however, now receives a foundation in what he terms an "overlapping consensus." And this is precisely what undercuts the practical relevance of the theory developed by John Rawls. The invocation of the "original position" and the

---

18. Benjamin R. Barber, *The Conquest of Politics: Liberal Philosophy in Democratic Times* (Princeton: Princeton University Press, 1988), 54 ff.

19. The most important of these is John Rawls, "Justice as Fairness: Political Not Metaphysical," *Philosophy and Public Affairs* 14 (Summer 1985): 223 ff.

20. John Rawls, *Political Liberalism* (New York: Columbia University Press, 1992).

"veil of ignorance" turns every issue into one of distribution; the "difference principle" generates implications amenable to the thinking of republicans and democrats, statists and antistatists, cultural radicals and cultural conservatives. The theory is obviously antifascist and anticommunist. Nevertheless, the entire enterprise ultimately comes down to grounding the philosophical categories of liberty in the already constituted tradition of constitutional democracy.

Questions related to the inability of the original theory to confront structural imbalances of power, the role of markets, and the contradictions of the production process remain unanswered. It is even impossible to determine who is the most disadvantaged when divergent interests come into play between the drug addict, the poorest-paid worker, the farmer, and the young "welfare mother." Rawls seeks to please all in theory and, in the process, pleases very few in practice. His thinking may ultimately even sacrifice what is most important about political liberalism: its ability to contest traditionally undemocratic societies and champion the introduction of liberal ideas where they are not in existence.

Liberalism is rooted in representative institutions predicated on formal reciprocity among citizens, regular elections, checks and balances, an independent judiciary, and—above all—guarantees of civil liberties. It begins with the assumption that personal conduct, unless explicitly prohibited by law, is a matter of preference and is best left to the individual. The genuine contribution of liberal rationalism lies in its ability to recognize the practical impossibility of resolving disputed religious, philosophical, or moral issues according to substantive and particular notions of the good. Such a stance, however, calls for an institutional standard of judgment that is irreducible to any of the interests involved. Such was the original starting point of the liberal theory of the state in which, no matter how uneasily, the public was separated from the private sphere. The possibility of democracy, its ability to constrain arbitrary power and to further diversity, depends precisely on its refusal to compromise its insistence on the primacy of due process and procedure in the name of substantive identifications with one particular notion of the good over another.

Liberals have clearly allowed themselves to be backed into a corner by communitarians and postmodernists regarding their commitment to diversity and pluralism. The more reactionary critics of liberal republicanism understood their convictions regarding the need for diversity, even if only on the basis of competing parties with competing ideas, and condemned them for it. There was never a question for liberals of whether diversity should exist. It was rather a matter of whether it *could* exist without reference to the universal principles underpinning the "process" of democracy and the liberal rule of law.

The very idea of a public sphere presupposes the existence of diversity and pluralism, and the structural expression of this conviction receives explicit articulation in the emphasis upon "faction" by federalist supporters of the United States Constitution like James Madison. This concern was then carried over into the future. Lord Acton coined the famous phrase, so profoundly liberal in conviction, that "power corrupts and absolute power corrupts absolutely." His point was, course, that only pluralism and factions intent on competing for power could mitigate the otherwise unqualified authority of the state. Indeed, seeking to temper the nationalist intolerance arising during the last part of the nineteenth century, he could also note that "the combination of different nations in one State is as necessary a condition of civilized life as the combination of men in society."[21]

Pluralism is as much a part of the liberal tradition as civil liberties. Sir Isaiah Berlin, a genuinely liberal critic of liberal pretensions and a pluralist critic of communitarian relativism, was correct when he noted that not all the supreme values pursued by mankind are necessarily compatible: there are no "true" answers to the central problems of life. His pluralistic liberalism is skeptical of all-embracing truths, and its sense of tolerance reaches back to Montaigne. It militates against eschatology, utopia, a belief in technocratic solutions to every problem, and the pursuit of a single value against all other values. It also places liberal thinking in conflict with the basic assumptions underpinning a *philosophia perennis*.[22] Berlin's form of thinking assumes that positive and negative understandings of liberty can collide with one another and that either can clash with the commitment to equality.[23] "Rights" also can come into conflict, and the solution of the problem of which takes primacy will involve a political choice. The answer can never be given in advance.

---

21. Lord Acton, "Nationality," in *The Nationalism Reader*, ed. Omar Dahbour and Micheline Ishay (Atlantic Highlands, N.J.: Humanities Press International, 1995), 113.

22. Isaiah Berlin, *The Crooked Timber of Humanity: Chapters in the History of Ideas*, ed. Henry Hardy (New York: Vintage, 1992), 8.

23. Isaiah Berlin, "Two Concepts of Liberty," in *Four Essays on Liberty* (Oxford: Oxford University Press, 1969), 118 ff.

The world that we encounter in ordinary experience is one in which we are faced with choices between ends equally ultimate, and claims equally absolute, the realization of some of which must inevitably involve the sacrifice of others. Indeed, it is because this is their situation that men place such immense value upon the freedom to choose, for if they had assurance that in some perfect state realizable by men on earth, no ends pursued by them would ever be in conflict, the necessity and agony of choice would disappear, and with it the central importance of the freedom to choose.[24]

Such a stance can, arguably, lead to relativism. But "grounding" rights in language, or abstractions like "solidarity," does not help matters: "That we cannot have everything is a necessary, not a contingent truth."[25] It is sufficient to posit the possibility of "intercommunication" between cultures and, simultaneously, to recognize that making good upon its cosmopolitan and internationalist implications must involve highlighting the fairness of the process over the commitment to any particular social value other than the constraint upon arbitrary power. That is all we have.

But perhaps it is enough. The degree to which private interests and prejudices are identified with public ones is the degree to which society works in favor of the powerful. The incursion on universalist assumptions, which are implicit in the liberal rule of law, is precisely what has always allowed for the exercise of arbitrary power. The constraint of arbitrary power is indeed the basis of liberalism and its great promise for democracy. It is mistaken to identify liberalism solely with the market or to reduce its formalistic concerns to abstractions from everyday life. Its inherently critical quality can also turn it into more than a middle ground between socialism and conservatism.[26] Its idea of liberty is dynamic, and it calls into question the practices carried on in its name. Such was the reason for the institutional attraction of liberalism to the proponents of women's suffrage around the turn of the century, the partisans of the civil rights movements in the 1950s, those in the streets seeking the abolition of communist authoritarianism in 1989, and the majority of those among the exploited and excluded. Every attempt to identify justice with fairness, for this reason, must presuppose the notions of reciprocity and tolerance implicit in the liberal worldview from its very inception.

---

24. Ibid., 168.
25. Ibid., 170.
26. Immanuel Wallerstein, *After Liberalism* (New York: New Press, 1996).

Liberalism has triumphed insofar as most contemporary thinkers in advanced industrial society embrace the liberal rule of law and its emphasis upon process. The real difference exists less between liberals and their "democratic"—either communitarian or postmodern—critics than between those in each camp who support or reject, seek to radicalize or to minimize, the traditional liberal aim of establishing a level playing field conducive to letting the most productive qualities of individuals flourish. Most liberals essentially believe in a liberal society committed to encouraging economic ambition, individual choice, social mobility, and meritocracy.[27] But this lukewarm set of commitments says nothing about whether substantive equality is really the aim of formal equality. It is in making this choice that liberalism will either further a new form of international socialist commitment or identify itself with the privilege, exploitation, and traditionalism of the status quo.

---

27. Alan Ryan, *Liberal Anxieties and Liberal Education* (New York: Hill and Wang, 1998).

3

The Communitarian Idea: Solidarity, Pragmatism, Particularism

Communitarianism is a particularly sophisticated response to the crisis of liberalism arising in the last two decades of the twentieth century. Its proponents span the ideological spectrum. Some focus on the need for voluntary associations in contrast with state-sponsored programs. Others continue to recognize the importance of state intervention as they emphasize the need for diversity and the irreducible experiences of different cultures. But whatever the differences between its major representatives, mirroring the aim of democratic theory in general, communitarianism seeks to overcome traditional distinctions between liberal and conservative or left and right.[1]

All communitarians are concerned with the loss of public participation in the political process and of what Niccolò Machiavelli originally termed civic virtue and Charles-Louis Montesquieu later understood as political virtue: that is, love of *la patrie*. The expression of this loss can take numerous forms ranging from a decline in voter turnout and an apparent lack of "trust" in government to the decrease in the size of unions, parent-teacher associations, and the Boy Scouts. Communitarians contend that the quality of pub-

---

1. Bruce Frohnen, *The New Communitarians and the Crisis of Modern Liberalism* (Lawrence: University of Kansas Press, 1996), 8 ff.

lic life and the performance of democratic institutions are profoundly affected by the degree of civic engagement by the citizenry.[2] They have illuminated the tension between social needs and private interests, along with the primacy accorded "government" compared with voluntary associations born of neighborhood involvement. They fear the growth of an impersonal bureaucratic state machine and seek legitimation for the existing order, even if they do not necessarily sanctify tradition per se. They deplore the corrosive effects of individualism, and they question the seemingly abstract universalist propositions of philosophical rationalism, with its emphasis on "rights." Indeed, especially in the modern era, communitarians have sought to emphasize the increasingly forgotten substance of liberal democracy.

Liberalism was initially identified with the creation of a new "public sphere." Against the courts of kings, the elitism of the aristocracy, and the dogmatism of the church, its partisans placed a new emphasis on a public realm of free discussion and prized the common sense—or what Thomas Paine understood as the use of "public reason"—of the individual to render judgments and adjudicate grievances. Multiple newspapers, the town meeting, and other cultural forms contested the alienated and cumbersome power of the burgeoning state apparatus. Democracy is considered less in terms of institutions and formal procedures than as a culture and a form of practice. It is, in short, understood as emanating from a particular form of community. Concern over the status of the "community," however, did not originally derive from a preoccupation with democracy. Quite the contrary. Preoccupation with the "democratic" community, in fact, is relatively recent, and its theoretical expressions still show the effects of a more reactionary lineage. It was, indeed, not merely Marx who was aware that under capitalism, "all fixed, fast-frozen relations, with their train of ancient and venerable prejudices and opinions, are swept away, all new-formed ones become antiquated before they can ossify. All that is solid melts into air [and] all that is holy becomes profaned."[3]

Communitarianism retains romantic roots, and many of its supporters, past and present, were preoccupied with the heartlessness of modern society. Those originally concerned with preserving an organic community, especially on the political right, also generally exhibited doubts about the abil-

2. Robert D. Putnam, *Making Democracy Work: Civic Traditions in Modern Italy* (Princeton: Princeton University Press, 1993).
3. Karl Marx and Frederick Engels, "The Communist Manifesto," in Marx and Engels, *Selected Works* (Moscow: Progress, 1969), 1:111.

ity of the market and its "invisible hand" to transform the economic war of each against all into a paradise of social harmony. They were appalled by the ways in which tradition, religion, and myth were increasingly seen as little more than inhibitions on material progress rather than the glue with which society was spiritually held together. They also despaired over the tendency of the burgeoning democratic state to emphasize the need for reciprocity among indeterminate "citizens" rather than the unique cultural experiences of a "community of the people" *(Volksgemeinschaft)*.

Certain important contemporary communitarians still look to premodern and hierarchical forms of social organization with a nostalgia similar to that of Rousseau and Burke. They believe that the self-interested individualism and factionalism, the secularism and instrumentalism, fueling modern society will render its normative conflicts incapable of rational or peaceful solution.[4] Even the most conservative of these contemporary communitarian thinkers would disavow any connection with fascism or its ideology. Nevertheless, interestingly enough, that very idea created enormous mischief in the aftermath of World War I, when the preoccupation with "community" took particularly authoritarian and reactionary forms.

A longing for solidarity arose in response to four years of trench warfare. The "community," whether defined in terms of class or nation, was believed to have been "betrayed" or "stabbed in the back." Fascists held to these views in the extreme. Even many moderates, however, could note with dismay that the new parliamentary republics of Central Europe, with their emphasis on formal process, pluralistic interests, competitive political parties, and separation of powers, were generating fragmentation and paralyzing the "national will." The organic whole was seemingly succumbing to its mechanical parts. Liberal and socialist ideas were seen as undermining the existential bonds of community through, respectively, their universalist notions of citizenship and class politics. The point was instead to understand society as a unique living entity with its own peculiar and distinct culture as well as its own peculiar and distinct prejudices. Relativism lay at the core of the communitarian undertaking from its very inception. Only from such a perspective could its exponents privilege the nation over the state and the person over the citizen.

Talk about the need for "rootedness" and the "loss of the soul" *(Entseelung)* generated by the alienating effects of modern society virtually domi-

---

4. Alisdair MacIntyre, *After Virtue* (London: Duckworth, 1981), 52 ff.

nated the intellectual discourse of Europe through "life-philosophy" *(Lebensphilosophie)*, ultranationalism, Zionism, existentialism, and even much of the avant-garde, whose primary opponent was modernity itself. Max Weber envisioned a "disenchantment of the world" and a society in which, with the original spirit of enlightenment "irretrievably fading," there would remain only "specialists without spirit, sensualists without heart."[5] Emile Durkheim, arguably the most profound if unacknowledged influence on modern communitarianism, had noted even earlier that the inevitable collapse of traditional society would result in an increasing sense of existential hopelessness, or *anomie*, though he kept open the possibility that new institutions—like unions—might yet deal with the crisis.

For political theory, however, the increasing power of the communitarian idea as a response to the crisis of modernity was perhaps best expressed by the great liberal historian, Friedrich Meinecke.[6] His monumental work on *raison d'état* suggests that the entire ideological foundation of the modern state is predicated on a tautology and, with genuine regret, reaches the conclusion that its legitimacy as well as the only justification for its preservation derives from its ability to protect and maintain the unique cultural "community" on which it was based. The logic of this idea, whether consciously or unconsciously, would help lead intellectuals of great stature on one side of the trenches in World War I to sign public declarations rejecting the superficial notions of "civilization" fostered by France during the Enlightenment in favor of the "deeper" German notion of "culture" *(Kultur)*.

Contemporary communitarians, of course, emphasize tolerance and are wary of attempts to export any specific ideology or institutional form of politics. The best among them recognize the costs of such undertakings, and they retain a legitimate fear of imperialist cultural or political practices.[7] Thinkers like Michael Walzer are concerned with strengthening the conditions for civilized conduct within and between groups, and their commitment to the values of liberal democracy is real.[8] But this does not change matters: communitarianism militates against a fundamentally critical per-

---

5. Max Weber, *The Protestant Ethic and the Spirit of Capitalism*, trans. Talcott Parsons (New York: Scribner, 1958), 182.
6. Friedrich Meinicke, *Machiavellism: The Doctrine of Raison d'Etat and Its Place in Modern History*, trans. Douglas Scott (Boulder: Westview, 1984).
7. Michael Walzer, *Spheres of Justice: A Defense of Pluralism and Equality* (New York: Basic Books, 1983).
8. Ibid., 17 ff. and passim.

spective. And so, from within a consistently communitarian logic, the relevance of liberal principles for groups elsewhere necessarily depends upon the existence of already constituted democratic societies. This truncates the ability of communitarianism to contest social orders with profoundly authoritarian and antiliberal traditions. There is, at best, a false assumption that the ideological as well as the practical problems with liberal state building have been solved. The critique of imperializing arrogance, at worst, turns against itself.

Pluralism is similarly a fundamental concern, especially for communitarians on the left, and the emphasis placed upon the "shared meanings" within a community as the point of departure for political action is an attempt to secure it.[9] Rousseau recognized that those committed to practical political change must make reference to the habits and customs, the ingrained sentiments and values, of a particular nation. Politics assumes primacy over philosophy; it becomes less the attempt to impose "rational" principles upon a historical context than the pragmatic willingness to further given ends within a set of objective constraints.[10] The attempt to reduce philosophy to politics, however, is as misguided as the attempt to reduce politics to philosophy. What meanings are really "shared" remains open to question: a conflict can also always exist between the larger community and certain of its parts. This becomes clear when the racial history of the United States, specifically, that of the former states of the Confederacy, is considered, for even with the best of will there are no criteria by which to decide whether to privilege a national or a local community. The problem is only compounded by the more conservative tendency within contemporary communitarianism to identify with the "neighborhood" and anachronistic notions of the "family" and to attack divorce and avoid dealing with the implications of homosexuality on a host of "shared meanings."[11] Indeed, for all the talk about pluralism and tolerance by such communitarians, quite traditional assumptions too often emerge concerning "the right kinds of citizens" necessary for a "healthy liberal democracy."[12]

There is no eliding the paucity of formal criteria within communitarian-

9. Ibid., 272 ff.
10. Benjamin Barber, *Strong Democracy: Participatory Democracy for a New Age* (Berkeley: University of California Press, 1983).
11. William A. Galston, *Liberal Purposes: Goods, Virtues, and Diversity in the Liberal State* (Cambridge: Cambridge University Press, 1991), 222.
12. Frohnen, *The New Communitarians and the Crisis of Liberalism*, 42 ff.

ism for determining which traditions are legitimate and which are not. There is also too little recognition regarding the bureaucratic mechanisms and formal rules—the legal structure—needed to guarantee pluralism and the "rights" of each.[13] The costs are obvious. Either an undefined notion of stability arbitrarily justifies privileging some traditions and meanings over others, or all traditions necessarily assume validity in their own right. The choice is meaningless. The door opens for the introduction of provincialism, what Richard Rorty enthusiastically termed "ethnosolidarity" from the left, and what has been called "ethnopluralism" among the European conservatives, as well as an assault on cosmopolitan ideals and human rights.[14]

Solidarity is the central concern. But communitarians or particularists make it too easy for themselves. Solidarity is not necessarily a form of identification between equals within a community with shared values and the like; it can also manifest itself through identification with a leader among equals who, though they live within a community of shared values, cannot identify with one another for any number of reasons. Such was the case with Ghengis Khan and the Mongols, and so was it also the case, whatever the obvious differences, with Josip Broz Tito and the citizens of what was once Yugoslavia.

Particularism, voluntarism, localism, and populism are inherent expressions of the communitarian undertaking beyond any political distinctions between left and right. Thomas Jefferson and Alexis de Tocqueville share these values with any number of profoundly reactionary and irrationalist thinkers. What differentiates them is only, and crucially, the type of community they envision and the context from which their thinking derives. Authoritarian and racist forms of the communitarian impulse were largely discredited with the defeat of fascism, even though they have recently reappeared in Bosnia and elsewhere. Virtually all European communitarians of the modern era, for this reason, look to the United States, whose most important representatives of this philosophical trend—ironically—find their thinking entangled with the very liberalism they seek to oppose.[15]

This becomes evident even in the work of perhaps the greatest modern

---

13. Amitai Etzioni, *The Spirit of Community: The Reinvention of American Society* (New York: Simon and Schuster, 1993), 266.
14. Note the discussion in Richard Rorty, *Contingency, Irony, Solidarity* (Cambridge: Cambridge University Press, 1987), 190 ff.
15. Will Kymlicka, *Liberalism, Community, and Culture* (Oxford: Oxford University Press, 1989).

philosopher from the United States, the innovative exponent of pragmatism, John Dewey.[16] His commitment to the liberal rule of law, his belief in the value of due process and civil liberties, is apparent in any number of ways, including his activity in the international commission demanded by Leon Trotsky to judge the validity of the incredible charges levied against him by Stalin in the 1930s. As a communitarian, however, Dewey was concerned with the increasingly bureaucratic character of the constitutional state and its formalistic understanding of democracy. Therein lies the core of what would become his critique of liberalism and, whatever the important role played by certain of his pragmatist followers, also the New Deal.

Dewey considered it illegitimate simply to identify democracy with any state system or with any set of formal procedures, even those predicated on the liberal rule of law. Government is, for him, merely a mechanism for securing the effective operation of democracy, and bureaucracy often threatens its real purpose: participation.[17] The genuine context for assuring the possibility of democratic action, the possibility for making ideals such as equality and liberty concrete, derives from the "community," and, indeed, Dewey actually defines democracy as "the idea of community life itself." Equality must mean more than the "mechanical identity," or interchangeability, of citizens within a parliamentary state, and liberty can only remain abstract if it is defined in terms of autonomy from all social ties or as the simple affirmation of individualism.

Individuals are the socialized products of groups with their own unique history and interests. Dewey considers it necessary to recognize them as such and simultaneously to understand them less as empirically distinct parts of an additive or mechanical sum than situated expressions of an organic whole. The democratic community is irreducible to its constitutive parts, even while it recognizes these parts in their singularity. Only in a community, for this reason, can the communication between different interests take place through which the public can genuinely define its interests. There is a sense, of course, in which the word *community* takes on two different meanings: the universal, wherein criticism can come from anyone within the human "community," and the particular, in which such participation is constricted. The former definition is perhaps necessary for any conception of

16. Robert B. Westbrook, *John Dewey and American Democracy* (Ithaca: Cornell University Press, 1993).
17. John Dewey, *The Public and Its Problems* (New York: Henry Holt, 1927).

critique or nonarbitrary determination of truth, whereas the latter alone can guarantee the existential benefits generally associated with the "community."

A divorce between theory and practice is built into the indeterminacy of the concept. There is also a profound tension, perhaps even a mutually exclusive character, between these two understandings of community. But there are other problems as well. In a sense, the discursive community supplants the institutions by which criticism is guaranteed. The community takes over certain functions of the state, even though the illegitimacy of the "community" among its constituents, itself predicated on shared customs and habits, is presupposed. The procedure for adjudicating interests becomes less a matter of concern than the substantive discussion over their character.

The ability to articulate those interests and reflect upon them, however, is seemingly what modern life undermines. As a consequence, according to Hannah Arendt, politics is in danger of losing its deeper meaning. The "social" character of modern life, the willingness of politics to entangle itself with the all-pervasive power of money, has already undermined what was previously understood as the distinction between the private and the public realms.[18] The private now either defines the public or, in the case of authoritarian forms of collectivism, is invaded by it. The lines dividing public and private, in any event, have become blurred by the emergence of a hybrid notion of "society."[19] No longer is it possible to consider politics as a realm of "self-exhibition" among equals who, spared from the routine drudgery of labor, have the time to cultivate the persuasive power of speech. Genuine politics has disappeared, along with any direct interchange among citizens concerned with existential and normative rather than purely instrumental issues. Alienation is the result of a world in which the bureaucratic state, the "rule of nobody," has supplanted the Greek *polis*.

But there are problems both with this nostalgic view of politics and with the values supposedly crucial for a viable public life. It is surely the case that modernity has tended to make private life a matter of public concern. But if this is debilitating—as it is, for example, when the private lives of presidents become matters of public debate—it is surely invigorating for political dis-

---

18. Hannah Arendt, *The Human Condition: A Study on the Central Dilemmas Facing Modern Man*, 2d ed. (New York: Doubleday, 1959), 68–78.
19. Ibid., 38.

course when formerly private issues, such as incest and spousal abuse, become public concerns. The line legitimately demarcating public and private may not be as blurry as it is often assumed to be: the ability to grieve an arbitrary exercise of power, the assault on the human dignity of an individual, must be a matter of public concern, whereas what does not speak to such an arbitrary and nonconsensual employment of power and resources deserves to remain private. Such an essentially liberal understanding of the difference between public and private, however, necessarily contests the communitarian need to externalize private virtues, if not interests, in a local communal arena.

Assumptions of this sort help explain the inability of communitarian critics to offer any serious positive program for a new enlivened public sphere. They also make it possible to ignore the manner in which a "tyranny of intimacy" has become paramount.[20] Self-exhibition is indeed less consigned to the past than it is a seminal feature of contemporary public life. Social meanings are constantly seen as generated by the "feelings" of individuals. Just this preoccupation, in fact, helps generate the illusion that power becomes more accountable the smaller and more intimate the scale. It does not matter that the lack of impartial and impersonal forms of public scrutiny is precisely what creates the patronage and sinecures traditionally associated with small-town politics.[21] It also does not matter that actual local politics is obsessively instrumental in its content and concerns. The myth prevails. Community must become a weapon not merely against society but also against the state.

Nowhere does this become more apparent than in the communitarian preoccupation with voluntary associations lauded so famously by Alexis de Tocqueville. The diminishing support for civic activity is seen as reflecting a more general degeneration of "trust" in the community.[22] Causes for the degeneration of public life are usually seen as including the movement of women into the labor force, new forms of social mobility, democratic transformations, and the technological transformation of leisure.[23] But this is

---

20. Richard Sennett, *The Fall of Public Man: On the Social Psychology of Capitalism* (New York: Vintage, 1978), 338 ff.

21. Grant McConnell, *Private Power and American Democracy* (New York: Vintage, 1968), 3 ff.

22. Francis Fukuyama, *Trust: The Social Virtues and the Creation of Prosperity* (New York: Free Press, 1995).

23. Robert Putnam, "Bowling Alone: America's Declining Social Capital," *Journal of Democracy* 6, no. 1 (January 1995): 68, 74–75.

merely empiricism at its worst. Daniel Bell may have intelligently seen that capitalism fosters a self-interested consumerism, which in turn undermines the competitive values for further economic growth.[24] The inability of other communitarians to deal with structural factors of this sort, however, helps explain the general paucity of serious proposals and the unwillingness to illuminate problems embedded in the culture of capitalism itself. Especially their programmatic statements usually resonate with platitudes highlighting the need for "trust" in authority, a new emphasis on "self-reliance," and the inherent connection between them.

Any number of sophisticated communitarian thinkers have, of course, identified the source of contemporary alienation in the tendency of liberalism to define the individual as a universal and indeterminate, ahistorical and interchangeable, entity without obligations to what exists prior: that is, the "community."[25] It inherently presupposes a free and rational subject abstracted from any contingent circumstances and "unencumbered" by emotional attachments to any particular tradition or group. Such is the foundation for the liberal emphasis upon inalienable rights, an impartial judiciary, and a belief in the ability of individuals to decide their own ends as well as those of the society in which they live without predetermined notions of what the "good life" actually entails. These thinkers have also noted that liberal philosophical presuppositions regarding the "self" deprive concrete individuals of their "authenticity,"[26] their traditions, the categories with which to make sense of history, and the basis for any emotional attachment to the community in which they live.[27]

Communitarians believe that liberalism, precisely because of its existential inadequacies, also fails to make sense of either everyday morality, with its historically situated allegiances of political life, circumstances wherein the interests of the community demand expression, or, given its universalist and imperialist ambitions, the need for group rights with regard to threatened cultures like that of the Eskimos. Such political inadequacies within

24. See Daniel Bell, *The Cultural Contradictions of Capitalism* (New York: Basic Books, 1984).
25. See Michael Sandel, "The Procedural Republic and the Unencumbered Self," *Political Theory* 12 (February 1984).
26. See Charles Taylor, *The Ethics of Authenticity* (Cambridge: Harvard University Press, 1991); and Seyla Benhabib, *Situating the Self: Gender, Community, and Postmodernism in Contemporary Ethics* (New York: Routledge, 1992).
27. Charles Taylor, *Sources of the Self: The Making of Modern Identity* (Cambridge: Harvard University Press, 1989).

the liberal worldview are seemingly what require correction by the communitarians. But most people suffering an injustice, whether at the hands of strangers or members of their own community, have sought to justify their position to outsiders in everyday life.[28] It is also possible that the degree to which rich and binding communal ties exist can prove the degree to which provincialism and intolerance also exist. The case of Salman Rushdie, whose criticisms of Islam in *The Satanic Verses* led Iran to offer a bounty for his murder, illuminates the tension between the spirit of liberal democracy and the spirit of community. It is inadequate, both morally and practically, simply to maintain that the two are culturally "different" without rendering a judgment.

And there should be no mistake: the refusal to render a normative judgment between contending cultural or ideological practices is itself a form of judgment. This becomes evident, if perverse, from a communitarian standpoint with respect to the lack of "reasons" as to why even democratic nations should have offered "foreign aid" or, arguably, should have opened their borders to Jewish exiles from Nazi Germany.[29] Solidarity is a function solely of the particular community. It is not a matter of "human rights" or abstractions about what "people" might share in common. It is, in general, enough to idealize the sense of "belonging" and mutual support a given "community" provides for its members. Thus, the degree of consistency or radicalism of any particular communitarian way of thinking is the degree to which it gives terms like *common humanity* as minimal a meaning as possible.

There is, of course, a certain arrogance within liberalism, manifest in its individualism, its skepticism, its secularism. Liberalism has also often been used to justify imperialism. But when this has occurred, it has usually taken place in terms of its commitment to free trade rather than in terms of its "rule of law" or its belief in extending a single procedural rule for rationally adjudicating grievances;[30] nationalist aspirations, or communitarian con-

---

28. "The view that justification runs out where the sharing of traditions ends . . . seems especially troubling given that the modern world makes us especially susceptible to the good or ill of the physically and culturally distant." Samuel Assefa, introduction to *A Political Morality of One's Own: A Critique of Contemporary Particularist Thought* (Buffalo: Prometheus, forthcoming).
29. Consider the implications of the arguments developed by Michael Sandel, *Democracy's Discontent: America in Search of a Public Philosophy* (Cambridge: Harvard University Press, 1996), 17 ff.
30. Walzer, *Spheres of Justice*, 17 ff. and passim.

cerns with validating one "way of life" against another, have been far more powerful ideological forces with respect to fueling policies of war and imperialism. Finally, given the acceptance of certain requisite political notions like the rule of law and the integrity of the individual, it is somewhat questionable whether the reform of liberalism to meet "group concerns"—if these involve a contestation of liberal assumptions concerning individual rights—can take place from within liberalism itself.

Communitarians feel that formal equality now must make reference to the "particular." The issue of *recognition* becomes paramount. Will not a Jew suffer if he or she feels impelled to close his or her shop on Saturday when the law states that all shops must be closed on Sunday? Perhaps. But it is also possible to conceive a situation in which the liberal state simply allows each to take a day of rest when he or she wishes. Is it necessary to consider AIDS in terms of a particular policy problem primarily perceived as connected with the gay community, or might it not make more sense to deal with the issue in terms of a new and more radical, universal, notion of catastrophic health care? Should the law recognize the particularity of Mormons when it comes to matters of polygamous marriage, or might it not make more sense for the state to abjure making any moral determinations on what constitutes marriage altogether?

Communitarians in general, and conservative communitarians in particular, often ignore the role that state policies can play in generating participation. It is simply not true, as Michael Sandel might claim, that liberalism denies the possibilities of mutual attachments and "solidarity"; its terms, however, are not predefined with respect to tradition and uncritically accepted cultural mores. Participation was actually never greater in the United States than during the 1930s and the 1960s. Assault on the interventionist state and on the organs of political participation from below, ranging from community groups to unions, also has historically occurred in concert. It is necessary to draw the consequences. In seeking to overcome self-interested forms of particularism, or individualism, communitarianism actually fosters a plethora of voluntary organizations, each concerned with its own agenda, which must compete for time, members, and resources. Indeed, the problem has never been lack of participation in voluntary organizations, whose efficacy is actually fostered by an interventionist social agenda, but rather the manner in which bureaucratic norms and various external forms of deference and hierarchy pervade the thousands of voluntary organizations working on an incredible range of issues.

Civic associations ranging from the American Legion to the PTA have generally been fostered—rather than retarded—by state intervention, regulatory agencies, wars, and other events of national significance. It is simply an avoidance of real issues to claim that localism and particularism must anchor any public philosophy capable of addressing the loss of autonomy and the community.[31] Erosion of "trust" has indeed been impelled in the United States less by "apathy" or "bureaucracy," as communitarians claim, than by what has become the most unequal division of wealth in the industrialized world,[32] coupled with various other structural factors. These include a political life increasingly stripped of ideological debate, riddled with corruption, and distorted by the undue influence of money on elections as well as a set of culture industries intent on fostering an obsession with "scandal."

But there is still something else. Many critics have pointed out the authoritarian implications of linking a critique of moral decay with calls for the reaffirmation of traditional values stemming from religion or "the community." Women, minorities, homosexuals, and dissidents indeed have no historical reason whatsoever to trust the innate tolerance of a "community" rather than the rule of law enforced by a liberal state. Communitarians ignore the obvious: the initial purpose of the liberal state was to guarantee the preservation of a community in which diversity is possible and grievances can be adjudicated peacefully. They are also unwilling to draw the consequences of their own position. If the liberal state really enervates communal feeling then it would make sense for communitarians to call for rolling back the various bedrocks of purely procedural justice like the separation of church and state as well as what have become fundamental entitlements. But there is hardly a respectable communitarian of either the left or the right willing to take such a stand. The critique of liberal foundations in theory is coupled with their acceptance in practice.

Few communitarians would deny the need to oppose certain practices demanded by certain religious communities, such as forced cliterectomies or the torturing of animals, which fundamentally militate against the spirit of autonomy and a democratic order. Prudence also calls for certain forms of compromise with established traditions; society cannot rest simply on pro-

---

31. See Jean Bethke Elstain, *Democracy on Trial* (New York: Basic Books, 1996).

32. It is estimated that 1 percent of the population in the United States owns 48 percent of the national wealth, while the bottom 80 percent owns only 6 percent. Edward N. Wolff, *Top Heavy: The Increasing Inequality of Wealth in America and What Can Be Done about It* (New York: New Press, 1996), 11.

cedural rules or on the most dogmatic distinctions between the state and the private beliefs of its citizens. Pragmatism and flexibility indeed mark much of modern communitarian theory. But, for all that, the historical connection between communitarian concerns and movements of the right is neither simply arbitrary nor contingent. Calling into question the universalistic and rationalistic presuppositions of the Enlightenment can have dangerous implications. It is what makes communitarian themes so easily susceptible to manipulation by the supporters of chauvinism, war, and imperialism. The recourse to "civic religion" and mythical symbolism may reflect the longings repressed by a secular world or what have been called "the habits of the heart."[33] But the search for emotional attachment obviously undermines the ability to engage in "a relentless critique of everything existing."[34] The critical spirit hands itself over to faith. That is why, especially in periods of crisis, "If there is such a thing as a dialectic of the heart then it is surely more dangerous than a dialectic of reason."[35]

33. Robert Bellah et. al., *Habits of the Heart: Individualism and Commitment in American Life* (New York: Harper and Row, 1985).

34. Karl Marx, "Letter to Arnold Ruge, September 1843," in *Writings of the Young Marx on Philosophy and Society*, ed. Loyd D. Easton and Kurt H. Guddat (New York: Doubleday, 1967), 212.

35. Helmuth Plessner, "Die Grenzen der Gemeinschaft" (1929), in *Gesammelte Schriften* (Frankfurt am Main: Suhrkamp, 1981), 5:12.

4

The Conservative Disposition: Custom, Stability, Markets

Conservatism is often viewed as a simple reaction against either reform or revolution. But it is clearly more than that. Conservatism is a worldview based on the desire to maintain what has been in the face of what will be. Interestingly enough, of course, this betrays its distinctly modern character, and indeed conservatism emerged as a political phenomenon only in response to the revolutionary upheavals of the seventeenth and eighteenth centuries. The recognition that things can be different, that there is no longer a divine and immutable order, is precisely what distinguishes conservatism from the "traditionalism" dominant in non-Western and premodern societies. This is not to deny the importance of religion, symbol, and myth for conservative thought, let alone the value attributed to prejudice by any number of thinkers.[1] Nevertheless, conservatism is modern insofar as it rests on a reflective commitment to maintain the past.

François de Chateaubriand gave the term its modern connotation. He viewed it as an attempt to "conserve" the complex of customs and habits handed down from generation to generation. For this very reason, however, conservatism is actually predicated less on political than on cultural assumptions and less on explicit philosophical principles than on what Michael Oakeshott termed a "disposition" for pursuing a certain form of con-

---

1. See, e.g., Irving Babbitt, *Democracy and Leadership* (Boston: Houghton Mifflin, 1924), 139–40.

duct, in his classic essay, "On Being Conservative." This piece by one of the leading English thinkers since World War II highlights the propensity to "prefer the familiar to the unknown." It praises the conservative disposition for being unadventurous and predicated on "rational prudence." This disposition greets innovations skeptically and maintains that reformers must bear the burden of proof in showing how the proposed change will be beneficial. "Every change is an emblem of extinction," Oakeshott argues, so conservatives must logically seek to mitigate, if they can, and assimilate, if they must, the new as quickly and painlessly as possible.

In the conservative view, traditions and values are given a value in their own right, and relativism is considered anathema. There is consequently a logic in the emphasis placed by major conservative thinkers like Eric Vogelin and Leo Strauss on the "ancients." These two German exiles, who had such a profound impact on political theory in the United States, gave the great philosophers of the classical and medieval ages new currency even as they sought to preserve the autonomy of political theorizing from the imperializing desires of behaviorism during the 1950s. Their enemy, significantly, is modernity and those thinkers, beginning with Machiavelli, who radically questioned established authority and an immutable social order in which each has his or her place.

The rejection of secularism plays a profound role in modern conservative political theory. Vogelin identified with a Christian–Hellenic view of the world predicated on transcendent truths and bluntly equated any "gnostic"—historicist, scientific, or speculative—criticism of a religiously ordered universe with relativism and ultimately chaos.[2] Strauss never attempted a study of the symbolic structuring of reality on the scale of Vogelin's mammoth *Order and History*. Nevertheless, his values were similar even with respect to the emphasis on those "leaps of being" that his friend considered the foundation for change.

Strauss called upon political theorists, after all, to deal with classic texts less in terms of the relative truth or historical value they represent than as expressions of truth as such. He also viewed the entry of the secular, the critique of the transcendent, as the source of degeneration. Strauss abhorred the decline in "liberal education," by which he meant education in a preestablished Western canon, and the increasing refusal to recognize the "authoritative" voices of the Western political tradition. Such voices are seen as

---

2. Eric Vogelin, *Science, Politics, and Gnosticism* (Chicago: Regnery, 1968).

receiving expression in the "great books" and what he termed the ongoing "conversation" over enduring issues whose incessant examination necessarily places the critic in opposition to the relativizing tendencies of mass culture and mass education. Philosophy is essential for the breeding of a "gentleman," according to Strauss, and conservative political theory must self-consciously strive to create an intellectual "aristocracy within mass society."[3]

The retreat of these European thinkers to the classics of Greece and the Middle Ages indeed renders them irrelevant to the formation of any positive notion of political action. Both stand in coherent relation to Edmund Burke, not merely for his view of society as an organic and hierarchically structured order but also for his concern with maintaining a certain mode of conduct and keeping "the fine draperies of life from being torn asunder." Those draperies, however, come in many styles, and the mode of conduct depends on context. Except in the South, for example, and then only superficially, American conservatism never identified itself with the hierarchical status and religious strictures of a feudal society. The forms taken by conservatism in the United States were different from those it took in Europe. The difference rests on what precisely these various forms of conservatism wish to conserve.

European conservatives in the beginning of the twentieth century were primarily representatives of an aristocracy whose existence and values were forged under feudalism. They were generally supportive of the reigning church, and their nationalism was mixed with attitudes justifying premodern forms of hierarchy. Their philosophical stance, and this is where Vogelin and Strauss fit perfectly, essentially rested on a rejection of everything associated with natural right:[4] rationalism, universalism, empiricism, positivism, and critique. Their philosophical opposition toward the premises underlying every form of thought generated by the Enlightenment translated into a political assault on the idea of the social contract, popular sovereignty, equality, and—perhaps above all—constitutionalism.

Conservatism rested on a romantic conception of the feudal ideal and an aristocratic hierarchy grounded in established religion as the proper response to the crisis of modernity. This self-understanding of the conserva-

---

3. Leo Strauss, *What Is Political Philosophy?* (Chicago: University of Chicago, 1962), 113.

4. Karl Mannheim, "Conservative Thought," in *Essays on Sociology and Social Psychology*, ed. Paul Kecskemeti (London: Routledge and Kegan Paul, 1953).

tive project only made sense, given the existence of so many interlocking dynasties whose histories often stretched back into the impenetrable mist of the past. Amid the carnage of World War I, however, the Austro–Hungarian, Ottoman, Russian, and German empires were cast into what Hegel called "the dustbin of history." Traditional forms of elitism lost their appeal. The aristocracy surrendered its social dominance to "the masses," nationalism became informed by a new sense of "mission," and totalitarian ideology substituted itself for religion. Conservative political theory could offer little in the way of competition to the new totalitarian movements on the right, and it held little appeal for even moderates on the left.

But its intellectual and political representatives adapted well. Conservatives may have opposed all forms of utopianism equally in theory. But in practice they were far more critical of some than of others. There should be no misunderstanding. In the 1920s, it was not a matter of choosing between Stalin and Hitler. And they knew it. The communists were never genuine competitors for power anywhere in Europe after, at the latest, 1923. Virtually everywhere on the continent, the choice was between an authoritarian right committed to antidemocratic and anti-Enlightenment values and republican regimes with a social democratic mass base. Conservative parties overwhelmingly aligned themselves with the former rather than the latter, and, indeed, the same thing occurred in Chile amid the fall of the regime led by Salvador Allende in 1973.

The career of the famous conservative political thinker and legal theorist Carl Schmitt particularly provides an important case in point. Already a well-known representative of the Catholic Center Party in the 1920s, among the most prominent reactionary critics of the Treaty of Versailles and the Weimar Republic, he joined the Nazi Party in 1933. Whether his conversion derived from conviction, a combination of anticommunism and antiliberalism mixed with a traditionalist obedience to authority and a genuine sense of patriotism, or simple opportunism remains an open question.[5] In any event, his conversion reflects a more general trend as well as a more general truth: success for the fascist cause, in Italy no less than in Germany or even Chile, rested as much on a form of legitimation by the conservative establishment as on the effects of economic crisis or even a concrete threat from the far left.[6]

---

5. Andreas Koenen, *Der Fall Carl Schmitt: Sein Aufstieg zum "Kronjuristen des Dritten Reiches"* (Darmstadt: Wissenschaftliche Buchgesellschaft, 1997).

6. Norberto Bobbio, *Ideological Profile*, trans. Lydia G. Cochrane (Princeton: Princeton University Press, 1995), 46 ff.

The transformation of Carl Schmitt from a representative of the Catholic Center Party into a Nazi was fluid and theoretically justifiable in his own terms. He had always been a legal positivist who, following Hobbes, believed that all notions of right depended upon the will of the existing state power. And, indeed, his loyalty to the new regime never wavered: he praised the murderous purge of Hitler's best friend, Ernst Röhm, and the "revolutionary" leadership of the "brown shirts" *(Sturmabteilung)* in 1934 during what became known as "the night of the long knives";[7] he endorsed the "purging of the Jewish spirit" from the national life of Germany; and he justified German imperialism, or a theory of *Grossraum*, by pointing to the Monroe Doctrine.

In defining politics as the determination and struggle between "friend" and "foe"[8]—a definition that stands fully within a conservative understanding of a uniquely national notion of tradition—Schmitt engaged the state in a continual fight against "enemies." Indeed, without such an engagement, the state would lose its legitimation. Thus politics, for this conservative, is not war by other means, as it was to an older conservative like Karl von Clausewitz: rather, it can employ the same means. There is ample justification for the state to find and then eliminate ever new "enemies," either at home or abroad. Schmitt is admittedly uninterested in the "prudence" demanded of the sovereign by Hobbes and the type of mechanical "balance of power" advocated by Machiavelli. Schmitt demands dynamism from the state rather than security. He is also completely unconcerned with guaranteeing the existence of a private realm or the possibility of expressing particular interests. The state evidences the "will" of the populace, the general will, by definition; its ability to make a "decision" must remain unencumbered either by checks and balances or by any moral postulate underpinning the liberal rule of law. The state is involved in struggle, its purpose is struggle, and its "destiny" is struggle. Schmitt is probably the only conservative to forward a genuinely political theory stripped of cultural predilections. Nevertheless, it is something hard for many more traditional conservatives to fathom.

Gone is the complacency, the aristocratic refinement, the organic understanding of tradition, so crucial for other forms of conservatism. The inabil-

---

7. Charles Bloch, *Die SA und die Krise des N-S Regimes, 1934* (Frankfurt am Main: Suhrkamp, 1970), 96 ff.

8. Carl Schmitt, *The Concept of the Political*, trans. George Schwab (Chicago: University of Chicago Press, 1996).

ity to make a normative judgment on social conflict, which is anchored in the romantic conception of the "organic" state, now gives way to the need to establish the difference between "right" and "wrong."[9] That determination can only be made by the person who exercises power and renders a "decision." Vitalism undermines Schmitt's avowed positivism, and neoromantic assumptions inform his famous critique of political romanticism.

Schmitt's claim that parliamentary democracy is no longer functional in a period of mass democracy should not be taken as serious support for direct or "genuine" democracy. Quite the contrary. "Genuine" democracy was always a ploy, which never received any institutional definition in his thinking, and—in the historical context—it served as an endorsement of the plebiscitary politics employed by virtually every right-wing dictator. Schmitt's contempt for the masses, his rejection of the idea of competing political parties and what are now called "special interests," his traditional anti-Semitism and his vision of an undifferentiated sovereign state, his critique of the liberal rule of law and his refusal to provide any rationalist criteria for resisting authoritarianism, are all part of the European conservative tradition. But his attempt to identify the existing order with the interests of the ruled, his belief in the need for a firm hand to make a "decision" in the—always "extreme"—situation, his antiliberalism and anticommunism, are beliefs shared by virtually all forms of conservatism. His thought evidences no serious concern with contesting the arbitrary exercise of power, and his thinking never really had anything to do with democracy, representative or direct, in the first place. His ideas were used roughly the way they were intended. In any event, they easily serve to justify something far more dangerous than a conservative authoritarian state, namely, fascism or Nazism.

The still pervasive myth that conservatives somehow have clean hands with respect to fascism is historically preposterous. There were some important exceptions, of course, like François Mauriac and Winston Churchill. But it is no accident that conservatism should have suffered so intense a crisis when World War II came to an end. Its intellectual representatives primarily derived from those conservatives now disillusioned with the "conservative revolution," like Ernst Jünger and Friedrich Jünger, or Carl Schmitt; its political supporters drew heavily from the ranks of the failed movements

9. Carl Schmitt, *Political Romanticism*, trans. Guy Oakes (Cambridge: MIT Press, 1986), 116 ff.

of the more extreme right, especially in the new republics of Italy and Germany. Conservatives grew especially bold in France during the beginnings of Gaullism in the aftermath of World War II, and its nativism and authoritarianism became evident in the United States in the form of McCarthyism. It was at this point that conservatives mimicked their liberal opponents and sought to restore their legitimacy by rejecting "totalitarianism," first by equating communism with Nazism and then, during the 1980s, by associating dictatorial regimes of the left, like that of Fidel Castro, with "totalitarianism" and those of the right, like Pinochet's, with "authoritarianism."

Only after World War II, in any event, would conservatives genuinely engage in an attempt to recast their thinking. The romantic nostalgia for the feudal order in Europe is now gone except on the fringes. The market is taken for granted, along with a grudging acceptance of the need for a "democratic" society. Elitism in the United States now defines itself less in terms of positive concerns than against issues like affirmative action, quotas, and multiculturalism. Also, in Europe and especially in Germany, following the reunification of the country, conservatives expressed a new concern with reestablishing a supposedly lost "national identity" and reappropriating traditional populist values in waging an assault on the universalist foundations of liberalism.[10]

Conservatism always showed established religion profound respect. But the new radical forms of religious fundamentalism also evidence a profoundly populist spirit. Such fundamentalism is perhaps the dominant ideological phenomenon of the postcommunist age, and it is inspired by profoundly conservative values. Disdain for "secularism," "hedonism," "decadence," and the demarcation between church and state is common to the movement, beyond the obvious differences between Christians and Moslems, Hindus and Jews. Religious fundamentalism is a movement of the masses. As with the relation between establishmentarian conservatism and the far right, however, it is also indirectly tied to developments occurring within traditional religious organizations and orientations.

Islamic fundamentalism has become the dominant force in the south-central parts of the former Soviet Union; its attraction was strengthened by the continuing economic underdevelopment of the region and the disintegration of secular authority as well as by the success of the revolution in Iran and

---

10. Note the collection edited by Heimo Schwilk and Ulrich Schacht, *Die Selbstbewusste Nation* (Berlin: Ullstein, 1994).

the anti-imperialist struggles waged in the Middle East. An increasingly conservative Catholic Church, which often served as the cultural and political locus of anticommunist resistance, has received new legitimation in Eastern Europe. Conservative religious trends, in short, have mirrored political ones. They too have proved international in character.

As capitalism changed its face toward the end of the 1970s, shifting its emphasis from industrial products like steel to informational systems and computers, progressives were caught unaware. Traditional industrial jobs started to disappear, and, if a minority of highly skilled workers benefited, the majority of unskilled workers did not. International competition became more pronounced as new production techniques were introduced, techniques that generated demands by capital for a reduction in the welfare state even as ever more people became reliant upon it. Resentment and uncertainty grew in response to these developments all along the political spectrum, giving rise to first neoliberalism and then neoconservatism.[11] The initial attempt to scale back the state by neoliberals like President Jimmy Carter ultimately combined with a new form of right-wing politics that had been delegitimated since the close of World War II. These gripped traditional right-wing constituencies: the atavistic sectors of the economy, the provincial communities once insulated from change, religious extremists, and malcontents on the fringes. But there was also a widespread consensus. Indeed, just as conservatives played a prominent role in the rise of fascism, neoliberalism helped shape the victory of neoconservatism.

With communism appearing increasingly sclerotic and without any new ideological alternative on the left, segments of the working class began to express their frustration by turning to the right. An increasingly small skilled male and white labor force thus became pitted by racially charged "wedge issues" against the remainder, whose members would bear the brunt of economic dislocation: women, minorities, and the unskilled. Trade unions declined; capital fled the cities, whose infrastructure fell into disrepair. An attack on the state and its regulatory functions, in short, was already under way as the "free market" ever more surely began to define the economic discourse. Conservatives everywhere began their counterattack on the legacy of the 1930s and the 1960s. They attempted to portray all forms of progressive social policy as futile, self-defeating, and ultimately op-

---

11. See Mark Gerson, *The Neoconservative Vision: From the Cold War to the Culture Wars* (Lanham, Md.: Madison, 1996).

posed to the interests of the oppressed. Welfare and state-sponsored programs like social security supposedly worked against the interests of the disadvantaged;[12] affirmative action undermined the opportunities for people of color; women's liberation militated against the true interests of women. It never occurred to most authors to ask why these reforms were undertaken in the first place; and, even if they admitted some grounds for their introduction, they simply maintained that the improved conditions of these groups now made the reforms irrelevant. This rhetoric of reaction was indeed strikingly successful in its impact on the masses of voters.[13] The new context offered opportunities everywhere for employing nationalism, racism, and an assault on progressive values and policies.

Ronald Reagan certainly made the most of them. His eight years in office led to a transformation of the American economic landscape comparable in effect to the change brought about by Franklin Delano Roosevelt; it has now been estimated that approximately 1 percent of the population garnered more than 60 percent of the wealth produced during the 1980s. There was no "trickle down"; and while the gross national product grew, income disparities widened, and the real wages of average people precipitously declined.[14] Cutbacks in state spending helped hasten an already decaying quality of life in the cities and among minorities. Strong evidence suggests that the majority of voters were less supportive of the new austerity measures than is generally assumed.[15] But this provides an indication less of the cabals by some conspiratorial elite than the lived reality of a new conservative ideology, its ability to override material interests, and the collapse of traditional liberalism.

Conservative trends in the West were only strengthened by events in the former Soviet Union—and vice versa—even though they suffered the same pitfalls in practice. The world watched with joy as an authoritarian state crumbled. Capitalist "shock therapy" and the abrupt introduction of market values were initially greeted with jubilation as any alternative bearing even the faintest connection with the communist past and the "left" stood

---

12. Charles Murray, *Losing Ground: American Social Policy, 1950–1980* (New York: Basic Books, 1984).

13. See Albert O. Hirschman, *The Rhetoric of Reaction: Perversity, Futility, Jeopardy* (Cambridge: Harvard University Press, 1991).

14. Kevin Phillips, *The Politics of Rich and Poor: Wealth and the American Electorate in the Reagan Aftermath* (New York: Random House, 1990).

15. Thomas Ferguson and Joel Rogers, *Right Turn: The Decline of the Democrats and the Future of American Politics* (New York: Hill and Wang, 1986), 11 ff.

discredited in the public eye. But the euphoria dissipated quickly as standards of living plummeted and the impact of an increasingly severe identity deficit gripped the masses. Ultranationalism, ethnic provincialism, and religion rushed to fill the void.

Conservatives never looked back. The defeat of "shock therapy" was never taken seriously. They instead used the events in the East as further legitimation for their assault on the recent past. The collapse of the Soviet Union seemed to justify the old anticommunism. The trauma induced by the Vietnam War, coupled with the collapse of the great protest movements, had produced a sense of moral malaise. Suspicion of the welfare system, fueled by affirmative action,[16] expanded, and taxes rose. All of this combined to generate a new feeling of disillusionment with the past. The liberal worldview of the 1930s began to totter as its opponents called for an uncompromising assault on the counterculture of the 1960s and eventually on the welfare state itself. A new admiration for what has been termed the "possessive individualism" of seminal liberal thinkers[17] and praise for its market-oriented economic principles became fused with an equally new recognition of populist and religious themes under the rubric of "family values."

These two dominant subtraditions of American conservatism had long opposed one another despite their common commitment to anticommunism. They threaten indeed to oppose one another again over the state, the market, and the imposition of cultural values. Conservatives placing primacy on an unfettered capitalism, like Milton Friedman, had little other than ideological use for tradition and, in principle, were willing to let the market, rather than any commitment to existing customs and mores, dictate the national posture toward issues like drugs and prostitution. Populists have always been communitarian, sometimes even nativist, and Christian in their religious orientation. They have also been historically critical of the "eastern establishment" and all foreign influences. Each of these two trends sought to "conserve" a different aspect of the American heritage.

The classical liberal vision has informed the United States since the founding of the country.[18] With its emphasis on *laissez-faire* and civil liberties,

---

16. Alba Alexander, Stephen Eric Bronner, and Kurt Jacobsen, "Affirmative Action Politics," *Critical Sociology* 23, no. 13 (1997): 85 ff.
17. Crawford Brough Macpherson, *The Political Theory of Possessive Individualism* (Oxford: Oxford University Press, 1962).
18. Louis Hartz, *The Liberal Tradition in America: An Interpretation of American Political Thought since the Revolution* (New York: Harcourt and Brace, 1955).

with its radically anticommunitarian values, its conservative offshoot traditionally appealed to the economic interests of big business as well as political libertarians like Senator Barry Goldwater, who headed the Republican presidential ticket in 1964. Its early advocates included essayists like Paul Elmer More, who liked to claim that "the rights of property are more important than the right to life"[19] and defended the great trusts against the demands of the burgeoning union movement. In the 1970s, however, with far greater sophistication, Robert Nozick undertook a defense of the minimalist state and the inviolability of private property in accordance with the idea of "voluntary consent" underpinning the social contract. Neither social utility nor "fairness" are seen as adequate for legitimating the intervention of the state in the economy, because state intervention can only result in the violation of individual rights.[20] The ethical priority accorded property rights over the demands of social utility is never fully justified, and the argument steps behind the thinking of Milton Friedman who, also combining a normative with a utilitarian argument, maintained that the unhampered exchange of goods and services on the free market underpins political democracy. Friedrich von Hayek and Ludwig von Mises had indeed already gone so far as to claim that any incursion of the state into the workings of the free market will necessarily result in a dangerous step along "the road to serfdom."[21]

Conservatism built on such "possessive individualism" lacked a genuine mass base until its antistatist views gained new legitimacy with the economic developments of the 1970s and the fall of communism in the 1980s. Its identification with elite interests was obvious, and its advocates were branded as intellectuals and representatives of corporate interests by supporters of the other powerful trend within American conservatism. Nevertheless, this second "populist" subtradition had little to offer on the intellectual or even the programmatic level.

Its thinking, if not its high-tech form of organization, harked back to the "know nothing" movement of the nineteenth century and the type of Bible Belt dogmatism associated with the Scopes "monkey trial" of the 1920s.

---

19. Paul Elmer More, "Property and Law," in *The Portable Conservative Reader*, ed. Russell Kirk (New York: Penguin, 1996), 442, 445.

20. Robert Nozick, *Anarchy, State, and Utopia* (New York: Basic Books, 1974).

21. Friedrick A. von Hayek, *The Road to Serfdom* (Chicago: University of Chicago Press, 1976); Ludwig von Mises, *Epistemological Problems in Economics*, trans. George Reisman (New York: NYU Press, 1981).

Laced with anti-Semitism and racism and steeped in anticommunism and manifold fears of international conspiracy,[22] perhaps best exemplified by the supporters of Senator Joseph McCarthy during the late 1940s and early 1950s,[23] it was nourished on contempt for the capitalistic "eastern establishment" and "Washington" politicians. Conservative populism always retained a certain grassroots organizing capacity; its modern incarnation, the Christian Coalition, can be viewed as a type of new social movement directed against everything associated with the 1960s: feminism and abortion, civil rights and affirmative action, secularism and sexual freedom, multiculturalism and the new immigrants.

Reaganism fused, even if uneasily, possessive individualism with right-wing populism. The philosophical expression of this fusion was "neoconservatism." Driven by an attempt to extend anticommunism into antisocialism and then antisocialism into antiliberalism, this new political perspective called for (a) giving "government" back to the people by attacking "bureaucrats" and "politicians"; (b) dismantling the welfare state and calling for increased military expenditures; (c) proclaiming the virtues of a new nationalism and combating the supposed preoccupation with "special interests" like women, unions, minorities; and (d) attacking the concerns of feminism and the new social movements in the name of traditional values like "family" and "religion."

Journals like *Public Interest,* edited by Irving Kristol and Daniel Bell, and *Commentary,* edited by Norman Podhoretz, played a crucial role in formulating the new doctrine of neoconservatism. Both were appalled by what Norman Podhoretz termed the "virulent hostility" of an intellectual minority from the 1960s toward the capitalistic ethos embraced by the majority of Americans; it was the same with other neoconservative thinkers like William Bennett.[24] The support of this minority for affirmative action and the welfare state was seen as militating against American individualism; their multiculturalism and sympathy for the Third World were understood as undermining inherited Western values; and their leftism was viewed as directed against not only capitalism but also the struggle against communist totali-

---

22. Richard Hofstadter, *The Paranoid Strain in American Politics and Other Essays* (New York: Knopf, 1966).

23. Michael Paul Rogin, *The Intellectuals and McCarthy: The Radical Specter* (Cambridge: MIT Press, 1967).

24. William Bennett, *The Devaluing of America: The Fight for Our Culture and Our Children* (New York: Summit Books, 1992).

tarianism in the cold war. The supporters of the "adversary culture" became viewed as the "enemy," and what was called the "silent majority" during the Nixon administration, the "friend."[25]

Neoconservatives stand squarely in support of "traditional American values" even as they ignore the increasing disparities in income distribution. They inveigh against declining "morals" without mentioning the "possessive individualism" generated by the economic system in which they believe. They speak of American responsibilities abroad even while many of them call for withdrawing from the United Nations. They deplore rising crime and they oppose gun laws. They praise the land of immigrants and they call for shutting down immigration. They thump their chests over the freedoms enjoyed in the United States, but they are homophobic, and they consistently subvert the separation between church and state. Their intolerance poisons the cultural atmosphere, and their actions undermine faith in the democratic process.

Neoconservatives are their own worst adversaries. They have little use for the aristocratic elitism of Oakeshott,[26] the medievalism of Vogelin, or the classicism of Strauss, which stand essentially opposed to the populist and capitalistic values of contemporary American conservatism. Still, neoconservatives have made good on the ideological and practical possibilities for political action. Through hard work at the grass roots and genuine organizational skill, through a willingness to infuse political action with genuine ideological conviction, they have—for better or worse—set the agenda in the United States as the century draws to a close.

---

25. Norman Podhoretz, "The Adversary Culture and the New Class," in *The Bloody Crossroads: Where Literature and Politics Meet* (New York: Free Press, 1986).

26. See Irving Kristol, "America's 'Exceptional' Conservatism," in *Neoconservatism: Selected Essays, 1949–1995* (New York: Free Press, 1995).

5

The Anarchist Impulse: Localism, Participation, Autonomy

narchism is based on a profoundly uncompromising vision of freedom. It is, for this very reason, a river with many tributaries. Anarchism has often been associated with the rejection of all constraint
and every notion of reciprocity. But that is true only of certain tendencies
within the broader tradition. One such subtradition is the radically individualist and culturally experimental anarchism whose most famous philosophical representatives include Arthur Schopenhauer, Max Stirner, and
Friedrich Nietzsche. Twentieth-century modernism, with its great avant-
garde movements like expressionism, futurism, dada, and surrealism, was
deeply influenced by this particular understanding of anarchism. With its
equation of freedom with license and its emphasis on the creative moment
of destruction, however, the mass appeal of such "salon anarchism" was
obviously limited.[1] Its precepts opposed the unyielding emphasis on community, equality, and democracy underpinning the various forms of political
anarchism.

Pierre-Joseph Proudhon, Louis-Auguste Blanqui, and Prince Mikhail Ba-

---

1. A more modern version, which retains far greater appeal, is often termed "lifestyle" anarchism. Note, for a critical analysis, Murray Bookchin, *Social Anarchism
or Lifestyle Anarchism: The Unbridgeable Chasm* (San Francisco: AK Press, 1995).

kunin were the great names of political anarchism during the first part of the nineteenth century, and their adherents once constituted an important tendency in the labor movement. But the tradition harbors antitheoretical, and sometimes even anti-intellectual, elements. Basic beliefs are often held in the manner of a faith. This was true indeed even for the greatest intellectual representatives of anarchism. All identified democracy, for example, with the direct participation of the populace over all social institutions. All considered power inherently evil. All rejected the state and electoral activity. All were suspicious of grand theories and "intellectuals," and all were prone to conspiracy theories. All spoke to the poor rather than to any particular class. All essentially believed in the latent goodness of those whom Rousseau called the "simple souls" and criticized the decadence of "civilization." All believed in the revolution as a self-generating phenomenon intent on contesting hierarchy and bureaucracy. All denied any compromise with the existing order, and most were sectarians.

The Paris Commune of 1871 remains perhaps the decisive experience for the anarchist tradition, and the followers of Proudhon, Blanqui, and especially Bakunin were its heroes. These included the painter Gustave Courbet, the feminist revolutionary Louise Michel, and the writer Jules Vallès. Anarchists constituted the opposition to Karl Marx and Frederick Engels in the First International, and they were primarily responsible for orchestrating this great experiment in democracy. With its vision of a free federation of totally autonomous neighborhood communities and its commitment to equality and tolerance, the Paris Commune essentially informed the tradition of anarchism well into the twentieth century.[2] Its defeat and the wholesale murder of its supporters essentially ended the First International and crippled the labor movement in France. The center of activity for what would become the new Second International in 1889 shifted to Germany. Its members emphasized political parties over unions, electoral activity over abstentionism, republicanism over calls for the abolition of the state, and Marxism over anarchism. A rapidly growing proletariat, whose representatives despised the *Lumpenproletariat* and whose enemies included the peasantry, emerged as the focus of this new labor movement. Anarchists like Domela Niewenhuis from the Netherlands, Errico Malatesta from Italy,

---

2. A more sober perspective is provided by Franz Borkenau, "State and Revolution in the Paris Commune, the Russian Revolution, and the Spanish Civil War," *Sociological Review* 29, no. 41 (1937): 41–75.

Louise Michel from France, and Gustav Landauer—later savagely executed for his role in the Bavarian Soviet of 1919—initially sought to participate in the Second International. They also looked to the Paris Commune for inspiration when they opposed the central resolution of the new organization, calling upon member parties to "make full use of political and legal rights in an attempt to capture the legislative machine." This is where the line was drawn. The radicals were defeated at the Zurich Congress of 1893 and expelled from the International in 1896.[3]

Anarchist practice in the 1880s and 1890s was highlighted by the "propaganda of the deed," which made for excellent literary material in the critical novels dealing with anarchism written by artists like Ivan Turgenev and Fyodor Dostoyevsky, and the assassinations of figures like President William McKinley. Revolutionary theorizing was irrelevant for those like Sergei Nechayev, whose insistence on acts of terror and on the existence of a broad network of small groups of individuals throughout Russia temporarily seduced even Bakunin. The end justified the means: the tradition informing tightly organized revolutionary groups like the German Red Army Faction of the 1970s and 1980s, and other fanatical sects of the present, maintains that acts of terror undertaken by committed people light a revolutionary spark among the masses. But "propaganda of the deed" has rarely worked. And the boldest forms of anarchist theory in the 1880s and 1890s recognized that. Their commitment to action almost completely unencumbered by theory now began to generate its opposite: the development of theory unrelated to action.

The thinking of Peter Kropotkin, who became the preeminent anarchist theoretician in the aftermath of the Paris Commune, is a case in point. Born into a noble family and educated as a physical geographer, well traveled and an outstanding essayist, Kropotkin sought to provide a scientific foundation for the anarchist belief in what he would later term "mutual aid," the principle by which free societies could evolve without any form of centralized constraint.[4] The Paris Commune obviously informed his vision. All values, institutions, and systems inhibiting the development of this capacity in human

---

3. Julius Braunthal, *History of the International*, vol. 1, trans. Henry Collins, Kenneth Mitchell, and Peter Ford (New York and Boulder: Praeger and Westview, 1980), 242–54.

4. Peter Kropotkin, *Memoirs of a Revolutionist*, ed. James Allen Rogers (New York: Doubleday, 1962); and Peter Kropotkin, *Mutual Aid: A Factor of Evolution* (London: Freedom Books, 1987).

beings constituted the enemy. Capitalist preoccupation with profit would give way to a new political economy dedicated to equalizing toil and meeting the needs of the poorest elements; reliance on the state would disappear in favor of "decentralism"; pacifist attitudes would provide a substitute for violence in the relations between people; and all forms of privilege, with their egoistic foundations, would erode through a new educational process intent on fostering individual responsibility for the common good.

Such was the vision of Peter Kropotkin. He favored a strain of anarchism indebted to the Enlightenment. He was a scientist and an idealist, an intellectual and an activist. His aim was a new and more radical form of democracy, which appeared to receive expression in the rise of "soviets" following the Russian Revolution of 1905. His theory involved an extension of the liberal understanding of freedom and an ethics predicated on the Kantian attempt to link means and ends: a peaceful society could only be achieved by peaceful means. Nevertheless, although he said much about ends, he said less about the means by which anarchists might contest existing institutional constraints.

Others sought to rectify the problem. A more ominous form of anarchism emerged around the beginning of the twentieth century in which ends were collapsed into the means: spontaneous action by the masses would overthrow the existing order and unleash the tendencies for the new one. Intent on responding to the hegemonic commitment to parliamentarism and reformism by the socialist movement, Georges Sorel articulated this perspective in a sensational set of writings.[5] These works evidenced a voluntaristic rejection of determinism and rationalism, an emphasis upon the creative power of the irrational, and finally an insistence upon the "myth" of a general strike as the pragmatic way to inflame the imagination of the masses. Action for its own sake and political purpose, the irrational and the instrumental, combine. It would be the same with the various forms of a newly emerging fascist theory, many of whose intellectual representatives admired Sorel.

The "myth" of the mass strike was, for Sorel, no better than any other myth capable of generating solidarity between the masses and setting them in motion. A nation under siege might serve just as well. This myth, in fact, helped lead Gustave Hervé and certain other anarcho-syndicalist leaders

---

5. Georges Sorel, *Reflections on Violence*, trans. T. E. Hulme (New York: Collier, 1950).

into enthusiastic support of France in World War I. It was the same in Italy, where F. T. Marinetti and the futurist avant-garde celebrated the outbreak of war even as a formerly ultra-left socialist by the name of Benito Mussolini and his followers began embracing an even more vehement form of militaristic nationalism. The war seemed to confirm the anarchist view that society did not conform to rational laws, and it gave a particular twist to the belief that convention merely constrained the natural impulses of the masses. This strain of right-wing anarchism was marked by a rejection of humanism and the Enlightenment and intoxicated by the irrational and the lure of adventure, and it would prove both morally debilitating and politically dangerous for the movement.[6]

But there should be no mistake: most anarchists, like Erich Mühsam and Gustav Landauer, remained true to the pacifist streak within the theory and opposed the war.[7] With the Russian Revolution, however, things were different. American anarchists like Emma Goldman initially extended their support,[8] and a burst of revolutionary enthusiasm by brilliant young European anarchists like Victor Serge and Augustin Souchy greeted it.[9] Certain anarchists played an important role during the "heroic years" of the revolution and the terrible civil war waged by the Bolsheviks against the "whites." Others sought a more independent path. In the Ukraine, for example, Nestor Makhno led a militant group of anarchists in expropriating aristocratic estates and creating, in the spirit of the Paris Commune, anarchist communities, each composed of a few hundred people.[10] These anarchists understood the exigencies of an emergency situation in which a clear-cut choice seemed necessary and the existence of a new regime, with untold possibilities, was being imperiled by the most reactionary forces, with external support. But they brooked no compromise with their principles once the emergency had passed. Anarchists in general would become increasingly

---

6. Note some of the futurist essays in F. T. Marinetti, *Marinetti: Selected Writings*, ed. R. W. Flint, trans. R. W. Flint and Arthur Coppotelli (New York: Farrar, Straus and Giroux, 1972).

7. Augustin Souchy, *Erich Mühsam: Sein Leben, sein Werk, sein Martyrium* (Reutlingen: Trotzdem, 1984).

8. Emma Goldman, *Living My Life* (New York: Da Capo, 1931).

9. Victor Serge, *Memoirs of a Revolutionary*, trans. Peter Sedgwick (Oxford: Oxford University Press, 1963), 59 ff.; Augustin Souchy, *Reise nach Russland 1920* (Berlin: Klaus Guhl, 1979).

10. Note the manifestos collected in *The Anarchists in the Russian Revolution*, ed. Paul Avrich (Ithaca: Cornell University Press, 1973), 128 ff.

disillusioned with communist authoritarianism, and their support for the revolution effectively ended with the repression of the Kronstadt Soviet in 1921.

Anarchism became increasingly marginal. Support for the Industrial Workers of the World diminished in the United States, even though the political trial of Sacco and Vanzetti became a *cause célèbre* during the 1920s. It was the same in France, and in Germany it was even worse. Only in the least economically developed nations did anarchism retain a certain appeal. It maintained a certain influence in Italy and even more so in Spain, where its partisans gained such fame during the tragic years of civil war.[11] It took the form of the *kibbutzim* in Israel, and Martin Buber, a leading figure in the Zionist movement and a major philosopher of existentialism, was correct in viewing this radical understanding of the commune as a way of rejecting the trends by which society was being assimilated by the state and attempting to recreate the authentically human interconnections between people undermined through the industrialization process.[12] Nevertheless, with the arguable exception of the United States, anarchism in the more economically advanced nations could offer no concrete theoretical or practical opposition to either the social democratic or the communist wings of the labor movement.

Underground groups persisted, and terrorists bandied about its slogans in the 1950s. Only in the 1960s, however, would anarchism experience a certain resurgence among students and intellectuals in Europe and the United States. Works by the "situationists" were embraced by the *gauchistes* and the *enragés* of the French student movement in 1968, and they also gained a certain cult following elsewhere. Depicting a world in which the spectacle has substituted itself for reality, wherein "revolutionary theory is now the enemy of all revolutionary ideology *and knows it*,"[13] Guy Debord called for an unrelenting commitment to invert what Marx called the "inverted world" of the commodity form. He and his comrades raised once again the vision of the Paris Commune, the councils, and the rejection of centralized authority. Committed to exploding conformity, puncturing the illusions of the culture industry, and appropriating work time for leisure, they reinvigo-

11. Murray Bookchin, *The Spanish Anarchists: The Heroic Years, 1868–1936* (San Francisco: AK Press, 1998).

12. Martin Buber, *Paths in Utopia*, trans. R. F. C. Hull (Boston: Beacon, 1958), 139 ff.

13. Guy Debord, *The Society of the Spectacle* (Detroit: Black and Red, 1983), 122.

rated the anarchist tradition and attempted to fuse its individualist with its communitarian strains in a new mode of activism.

Others had tried this before. Emma Goldman had always called for "educating the individual," and her anarchism always had a profoundly libertarian streak. An advocate of gay and abortion rights, a staunch critic of the church and communism, Goldman had opposed bourgeois convention in all its forms long before World War I. But her emphasis on the solidarity necessary for realizing her vision of an emancipated anarchist community, which she inherited from Kropotkin, oscillated with her commitment to the unhampered expression of individual desires, for which she was indebted to Stirner and Nietzsche.[14] The lack of fit between these two elements of her theory did not undermine its influence. Quite the contrary. Goldman anticipated many of the gender issues raised by feminism, and her opposition to hierarchical and bureaucratic forms of organization influenced both the form and the content of what would become known as the new social movements.

Anarchists have generally been considered sectarians. They have often been depicted as simple terrorists and as the enemies of parliamentary democracy. And, with respect to many tendencies within the tradition, this depiction is accurate. Especially when anarchy has had ideological roots in the masses of peasants and workers, however, anarchists have acted in solidarity with others. During the Spanish civil war, anarchists chose to support the existing republic, which had been created in 1931, and even ran in the parliamentary elections. The conflict in Spain, no less than in the Russian civil war, called for a clear-cut choice.[15] The republic had never gained the support of the Catholic Church, the military, the aristocracy, or the reactionary peasantry and many among the middle classes. Under the leadership of Generalissimo Francisco Franco, with promises of support from Hitler and Mussolini, the army staged a revolt in 1936, which sparked what would become a horrible civil war. Anarchists, communists, liberals, socialists, and Trotskyists responded by joining together to defend the republic in a Span-

---

14. Emma Goldman, *Anarchism and Other Essays* (Atlantic Highlands, N.J.: Humanities Press International, 1996).

15. Henry Pachter, *Espagne, 1936–1937: La guerre dévore la révolution* (Paris: Spartacus, 1986); Burnett Bolloten, *The Spanish Revolution: The Left and the Struggle for Power during the Civil War* (Chapel Hill: University of North Carolina Press, 1979).

ish version of the Popular Front. The Spanish civil war evokes images of unity on the left.[16] Nevertheless, that unity was short lived.

Conflicts over economic policy, politics, and foreign policy quickly undermined the coalition. Anarchists and Trotskyists, who wished to carry forward a political revolution and economic collectivization of the countryside while fighting the civil war, found themselves confronting an alliance of communists, social democrats, and bourgeois republicans, all of whom opposed that undertaking, if for different reasons. This intractable division within the antifascist camp soon led to violence. The economic and military support rendered by the Soviet Union had made the communists dominant within the Popular Front alliance. They offered a rallying point for those made fearful by the extremism of the anarchists. The communists unleashed a vicious propaganda assault. Then, in 1937, their forces massacred the anarchist revolutionaries at the Battle of Barcelona and thereby sealed the fascist victory.

The communists would capitalize on their role in the struggle. They would emphasize the willingness of the Soviet Union to reject the "neutrality" practiced by Western democracies and support the Spanish republic. They legitimately highlighted the selflessness and bravery of the International Brigades primarily organized by the Communist International. They would point to their pragmatic antifascism in the Spanish civil war as a prelude to their alliance with the Western democracies in World War II. But they ignored the terror practiced by their secret police in Spain, the purely tactical character of their commitment, and the wholesale slaughter of their anarchist rivals. Nevertheless, the persecution suffered by the anarchists does not simply translate into an endorsement of their policies.

Anarchist politics was fueled, as usual, by a mixture of revolutionary romanticism and simple voluntarism. Even many anticommunist opponents of Franco considered their policies self-defeating: they probably scared away many potential moderate supporters; they surely added to the economic chaos; and, in calling for a radically democratic and nonhierarchical army, they may have created disciplinary problems at the front. They also perhaps made support from abroad even more difficult to gain; and they added grist to the propaganda mill of the reaction. But for all that, the anar-

---

16. Note the classic work by George Orwell, *Homage to Catalonia* (New York: Harcourt and Brace, 1952), 64 ff.

chists fought bravely, and they delivered a number of important victories. No economic program would probably have had much chance of success; and the anarchist project at least gave the masses a direct material stake in the success of the antifascist enterprise. It is also highly doubtful whether any set of policies would have convinced the Western democracies to intervene in the conflict. Franco's victory had far less to do with the anarchist program than with a host of other external factors. And, whatever the faults in their program, the Spanish anarchists offered a radical alternative to communist totalitarianism. They sought to make the ideal of a "classless society" concrete in a way never attempted before. This becomes clear in the famous description of Barcelona, which was under the rule of the anarchists, rendered by George Orwell:

> It was the first time I had ever been in a town where the working class was in the saddle. . . . Every shop and café had an inscription saying that it had been collectivized; even the bootblacks had been collectivized and their boxes painted red and black. Waiters and shop-walkers looked you in the face and treated you as an equal. Servile and even ceremonial forms of speech had temporarily disappeared. . . . The revolutionary posters were everywhere, flaming from the walls in clear reds and blues that made the few remaining advertisements look like daubs of mud. Down the Ramblas, the wide central artery of the town where crowds of people streamed constantly to and fro, the loudspeakers were bellowing revolutionary songs all day and far into the night. And it was the aspect of the crowds that was the queerest thing of all. In outward appearance it was a town in which the wealthy classes had practically ceased to exist. Except for a small number of women and foreigners there were no "well-dressed" people at all. Practically everyone wore rough working-class clothes, or blue overalls or some variant of the militia uniform. All this was queer and moving. There was much in it that I did not understand, in some ways I did not even like it, but I recognized it immediately as a state of affairs worth fighting for.[17]

No less than in the case of the Paris Commune or the soviets organized in Russia during the revolutions of 1905 and 1917, Barcelona under the anarchists projected a society free from coercion. Individuals were seen as capable of governing themselves and exercising their responsibility to the community without reference to the disfiguring influence of private property or

---

17. Ibid., 4–5.

an alienated bureaucracy. With the creation of a mass society dominated by the bureaucratic politics of the state and increasingly complex forms of capitalist production, however, this goal has increasingly become less important than the striving to achieve it. Or this is at least the position, the most coherent and nonsectarian position, reached by Augustin Souchy, one of the major representatives of this tradition.

Souchy devoted his long life to anarchism. In the beginning, he too believed in the absolute character of the "revolution." Before his death, however, this grand old man of European anarchism ultimately recognized its limits. In his autobiography,[18] Souchy expresses his pride in the great revolutionary commitments and the experiments undertaken by the anarchists in Russia and Spain. In the last analysis, however, he is even more proud of the way in which many anarchist concerns have found their way into contemporary discourse: the critique of the centralized state, the assault on technological progress, the idea of participatory democracy, the connection between the personal and the political, the creation of a new culture of freedom. Souchy would always see authority and freedom as mutually exclusive. The choice is still "between" them. Therein lies the uncompromising element within anarchism in general. Either autonomy is surrendered, in which case subordination of the individual to any form of government is possible, or all governments must be considered as illegitimate institutions whose commands must be judged and evaluated before they are obeyed.[19] The aim is obviously to set private interest aside, pursue the common good, and create an association that maximizes the autonomy of each. But that only begs the question: is it possible to organize the undertaking without hierarchy or an organization capable of enforcing its principles?

An affirmative answer is predicated on a rejection of the values and alternatives structured within the given institutional system or context. Anarchist thinkers like Murray Bookchin raised the specter of environmental devastation long before it was popular and radically linked the common understanding of technological progress with bureaucratic hierarchy. Few have been as radical in calling for the creation of "eco-communities" in which a new interaction between the collectivity and nature is reflected in

---

18. Augustin Souchy, *"Vorsicht: Anarchist!" Ein Leben fur die Freiheit: Politische Errinerungen* (Frankfurt am Main: Suhrkamp, 1977).

19. Robert Paul Wolff, *In Defense of Anarchism* (New York: Harper Torchbooks, 1970), 18.

the equality of participation by all members.[20] It is also undoubtedly the case that small groups of politically unaffiliated individuals, often living a collective existence and seeking to attack racism and sexism in everyday life,[21] have taken it upon themselves to shut down nuclear plants, counter neofascist rallies, endorse alternative forms of medicine, and protest vivisection and the mass torture of animals. Sometimes their demands are self-serving, as in the case of squatters, and anarchist demonstrations have often bred violence. But there is no question that these primarily young people, committed to anarchist principles of association, have often seen what their more establishmentarian critics have ignored. They have raised public awareness about any number of issues, and the cynicism occasioned by some of their demands often says more about the prejudices of their opponents than the naïveté of their own beliefs.

The radical vision of participatory democracy, in a sense, defines the anarchist project. It assumes that change must occur outside the confines of the capitalist economy and the state bureaucracy. Grassroots movements therefore take precedence over the search for legislative solutions to existing social problems. Change must occur at the base: autonomy can not be commanded. The emphasis upon decentralization and participation, libertarian principles and contempt for hierarchy, has provided anarchism with a bold response to the problem of alienation and a radical understanding of democracy. Eugene Debs, an anarcho-syndicalist and socialist, who was among the leaders of the Industrial Workers of the World, put it succinctly in one of his speeches: "I don't want you to follow me or anyone else. If you are looking for a Moses to lead you out of the capitalist wilderness you will stay right where you are. I would not lead you into this promised land if I could, because if I could lead you in, someone else would lead you out."[22]

This uncompromising emphasis upon direct democracy, however, can often prove self-defeating. It can fragment national or international responses to powerful business concerns; it can also blind supporters to the ways in which setting priorities and efficiently employing resources in com-

---

20. Murray Bookchin, *The Ecology of Freedom* (Palo Alto, Calif.: Cheshire, 1982).

21. George Katsiaficas, *The Subversion of Politics: European Autonomous Movements and the Decolonization of Everyday Life* (Atlantic Highlands, N.J.: Humanities Press International, 1997).

22. This quotation is taken from the touching depiction of Debs in the novel by John Dos Passos, *The 42d Parallel* (Boston: Houghton Mifflin, 1946), 29 ff.

plex industries may simply not prove conducive to localized control. The market and the state have become the only practical alternatives for more or less rationally coordinating the needs of local units in the modern world. Because market decisions are ultimately predicated on autonomous choices, which preclude the accountability of individuals and institutions to the larger society, the only real alternative to state regulation becomes no regulation at all. As a consequence, the anarchist form of organization, committed to the abolition of private property in theory, becomes subservient to market forces in practice.

Anarchists emphasize the inherent desirability of direct participation; indeed, they view it as the primary end of political action and a good, perhaps even the ultimate good, in its own right. Rendering social institutions accountable to the public through various representative organs, however, is an equally sensible goal. In a way, of course, participation and accountability presuppose one another. But there is also a sense in which the uncompromising anarchist emphasis on direct participation or "unitary" democracy conflicts with an "adversary" understanding of democracy predicated on the primacy of institutional accountability.[23] Emphasizing the need for "balance" obviously avoids what is truly at stake: it is necessary to privilege either accountability or participation, constitutionalism or spontaneity, liberty or democracy.

The New England town meeting, no less than the Paris Commune and the workers' council, serves as an example of unitary democracy, in which participation assumes primacy over accountability. Either institution, in order to function effectively, assumes a commonality of interests between equal individuals, an absence of fundamental conflicts, and a direct encounter between them in the formulation of policy. These assumptions are precisely what render issues of institutional accountability basically irrelevant. As soon as they are questioned, however, an "alienated" form for adjudicating grievances becomes necessary. To protect the interests of each in some degree, this institution must stand removed from all. The degree is, of course, open to debate. Introducing "secondary associations" might mitigate the now alienated relationship between individuals and the new institution, between the market and the state, between the desire for participation and the need for accountability. But even this would not solve the basic

---

23. Jane Mansbridge, *Beyond Adversary Democracy* (Chicago: University of Chicago Press, 1983).

problem. Alienation is not susceptible to quantification or compromise. Once participation becomes a matter of degree, democracy turns into a system of constraint. This indeed was precisely the point made by the most impressive representatives of the anarchist tradition.

The problem with the anarchist conception of politics is not the belief that small islands of genuine democracy can overcome structural imbalances of power in the society at large. It is not simply that plans for coordinating localities have remained vague at best. It is not that anarchists have valorized the local and ignored the penchant for provincialism, patronage, and corruption. And it is not their inability to deal with the manner in which decentralization on the political level strengthens the centralizing power of capital or their refusal to see the implications of a situation in which capital is becoming more mobile and workers are becoming less so. It is something else, something more damaging and more dogmatic: it is the assumption that participation is the essence of democracy, a good unto itself, or as Hannah Arendt might say, a way of making us human.

But, in fact, it is entirely legitimate to consider politics, and especially democratic politics, less as a demand for constant involvement or participation than as a way of liberating individuals for other more pleasurable pursuits. Anarchists of the salon, perhaps, are always ready to admit this. It is another matter, however, for political anarchists. Their theory romanticizes politics, and it refuses to recognize the profoundly boring character of real, everyday, distributional issues, especially on the local level. Privileging adversary forms of democracy, rendering political institutions accountable to the public, inherently presupposes a certain resigned acceptance of this state of affairs. It assumes, for better or worse, an alienation that anarchist proponents of unitary democracy and direct participation oppose on principle. Adversary democracy and the preoccupation with accountability necessarily focus on routine, whereas unitary democracy and the emphasis on participation presuppose an ongoing enthusiasm founded on an unqualified civic virtue. This indeed is what makes for the impracticality of anarchism and, perhaps especially among the young, its continuing allure.

PART II
CHANGING THE WORLD

6

The Masses in Motion

S ocialism, communism, and fascism were the great mass movements of
this century among the Western nations. They secured the loyalty of
millions and offered their followers a new revolutionary vision of the
future. Each had its distinct form of political theory and its major intellectual representatives. These were not, by and large, professional philosophers. But they made political theory meaningful in a profoundly direct way.
They wrote for a broad international audience, and there was no ambiguity
about the values they embraced. Metaphysical questions were important to
intellectuals in these movements. Controversies abounded over issues of historical agency, teleology, ethics, and the like. Nevertheless, of principle concern were problems connected with practice: the role of the political party,
the character of the state, and the nature of the enemy.

Political theory drew upon these movements; it became invigorated by
them and, in turn, invigorated them. Socialists like Jean Jaurès, Rosa Luxemburg, Carlo Rosselli, and others offered new insights into their tradition
and the struggle against war, imperialism, and authoritarianism. They gave
an activist stamp to democracy, they linked it with internationalism and
economic equality, and they offered a legacy other movements and programs like the Popular Front and the New Deal would employ. Communists
like Vladimir Ilyich Lenin, Antonio Gramsci, Josef Stalin, and Mao Tse-
tung gave concrete meaning to the idea of revolution, created a new form
of party and state, presented themselves as a new moral force, brought the
economically underdeveloped world into the center of progressive discourse, and fostered the hope of modernization without regard to human

costs. Fascists like Maurice Barrès, Benito Mussolini, José Antonio Primo de Rivera, and Adolf Hitler sought to obliterate the Enlightenment legacy, to inspire the masses with discipline, vitality, chauvinism, and often racism, and to exterminate their enemies with a ferocious cruelty. These thinkers were all political actors, and the movements they represented were intent on changing the world.

In the profession of political theory, however, none of these theorists is taken very seriously. It is as if theorists and theories capable of gripping the masses are somehow beneath scholarly consideration. Socialism is usually disregarded as an empty dogma, even though its partisans founded the modern welfare state. Its theory is mostly viewed as "economistic" and "antipolitical," though it inspired the democratic politics of the millions who served as the principle bulwark against European totalitarianism. A cursory understanding of Lenin or Hitler is, by the same token, generally considered sufficient for understanding the thinking of the two great totalitarian movements of our time. The theories of these mass movements are usually identified with either the cynical "pursuit" of purely practical aims or outrageous utopian visions. There is little interest in what these movements accomplished, the problems they confronted, or the intellectual traditions they generated. Even worse, there is little concern with how and why these movements and ideas should have gained such popularity and loyalty among ordinary people.

During the last quarter of the nineteenth century and the years preceding World War I, socialism seemed the force of the future. Communism and fascism, however, also had their origins in the prewar era, though they would gain a foothold among the broader masses only in the aftermath of the conflict. The times were marked by the emergence of urban life and the growth of the bureaucratic state, monopoly capitalism and imperialism, nationalism and militarism. They were distinguished by the political decline of the old aristocratic elites, a new uncertainty on the part of precapitalist classes like the peasantry and the *Mittelstand*, vacillation by the bourgeoisie, rumblings on the fringes of political life by alienated groups like the *Lumpenproletariat*, and the entry of the working class into the social and economic life of nations.

Each of these new movements—socialism, communism, and fascism— would uniquely express a distinctly new form of mass politics, and each of them would seek to make good on the interests of different combinations of these classes and groups. The new mass movements would compete vehe-

mently with one another in the aftermath of the war, and they would casti-
gate one another in theory beyond any occasional compromises in practice.
Each would view itself as revolutionary, and each would seek to transform
what it considered structural imbalances of economic and political power.
The battle between them was neither illusory nor superficial. It would in
many lands ultimately define the conflict between republicanism and totalitarianism.

Marxism was embodied in the social democratic labor movement from
the last quarter of the nineteenth century to the Russian Revolution of 1917.
Its members considered themselves the legitimate heirs of the Enlightenment
legacy. They were the acknowledged advocates of internationalism, political
democracy, and economic justice. Under the banner of orthodox Marxism,
indeed, social democracy grew steadily from a sect numbering thousands
into an international enterprise numbering millions. It soon became the fast-
est-growing movement on the continent; its triumph appeared inevitable to
both friends and opponents, and, especially on the broad left, it dominated
political discourse at the beginning of the twentieth century.

Revolution had a clear and distinct meaning. Socialists generally understood it as having two stages: the bourgeois and the proletarian. Only the
first, especially for those movements existing under monarchical regimes,
was of relevance: the second played no practical role whatsoever. Socialists
disliked speculative talk about the "future state" *(Zukunftsstaat)*. It is often
forgotten that the socialist labor movement on the continent was mostly
forced to organize under monarchies rather than bourgeois republics and in
societies without strong democratic traditions where the aristocracy and
feudal traditions still played an important role. Early socialists sought a
"bourgeois republic" with full civil liberties wherein workers could press
their interests and seek a fair adjudication of their grievances. Just such a
republic—with social democracy dominating the life of the nation—was
generally what they politically identified with the "dictatorship of the proletariat" as against the economic "dictatorship of the bourgeoisie."

Workers anywhere prior to World War I would indeed have been repulsed
by the claims of modern conservative and postmodern thinkers alike with
respect to the supposedly antidemocratic character of Marxism. For the millions of workers suffering under autocracy, or the social democratic activists
who forged them into the first genuinely mass democratic parties on the
continent, its democratic message was obvious. The republicanism of these
social democratic parties, as will become evident, fit well with their commit-

ment to "orthodox Marxism." It was never totalitarian or antidemocratic in its original deterministic and positivistic version. Quite the contrary. The guarantee of a steadily growing proletariat justified the republican ideals advocated by the labor movement: social democracy would "inevitably" become the political preference of the great majority of society; and under a republican form of government, it would ultimately realize a "socialist" alternative to the status quo.

Although revolutionary in word, however, the labor movement was basically reformist in deed. Its "embourgeoisement," or integration, into capitalist society had begun long before World War I. But the outbreak of hostilities radicalized the trend. Socialist parties with their working-class base supported their nation-states in the conflict; and in its aftermath, with the collapse of the great continental empires, they became the pillars of a new republican establishment. Socialists were immediately charged with class treason by the militant left for having led workers to the slaughter, even as the militant right attacked them for their lack of nationalist and imperialist enthusiasm. The idea of bringing about a "proletarian" revolution and a "communist" society ever more surely faded from view as socialists identified themselves with the new democratic welfare state.

Other classes, however, were less inclined toward democracy, and the new regimes of the 1920s and 1930s were mostly unstable. Social democracy found itself paralyzed; it would remain caught between a radical rhetoric and a conciliatory practice. Only in the aftermath of World War II, with the introduction of the Marshall Plan and the start of the cold war, would social democracy finally resolve the contradiction by shedding all revolutionary pretenses, rejecting Marxism, and defining itself as a national party rather than an organization of the working class.

But for all that, social democracy consistently resisted the totalitarian temptation; it remained true to its original republican commitments and the humanistic values dominant on the left in the years preceding World War I. Perhaps for this very reason, it never touched the hearts of the new generation, or the significant part of this generation, which had formed quite different values in the years of slaughter. Great writers of the most diverse political persuasions—Henri Barbusse, Bertolt Brecht, Ernest Hemingway, Ödön von Horváth, Ernst Jünger, Ignazio Silone, Thomas Mann, and others—gave them artistic expression. The new generation felt angry, and it had grown hard. Its members were ill suited for everyday life, and, perhaps to compensate, many of them inclined toward apocalyptic visions of the fu-

ture. The war had made them critical of individualism and democracy, reform and compromise, rationalism and humanism. They believed that either
their class or their nation had been betrayed by the prewar establishment.
This generation may have initially felt itself "lost." Except for politically
marginal bohemians and intellectuals, however, its members soon enough
found a home. Indeed, this generation of the trenches fueled the new totalitarian movements of the 1920s.

Both communism and fascism had a military vision of the political party,
identified their party with the state, relied upon a "cult of the personality,"
and ruled through a mixture of propaganda and terror. Both employed
masses to exterminate masses. The ideological inspiration for the two movements, their political theory, was surely different. Their members died fighting one another in the streets and, later, on the battlefields. But the political
structure of their party organizations, their police states, and their styles—
their paranoia, their music, their uniforms, their parades, their conventions—were remarkably similar. Both were sons seeking vengeance on the
father.

Communism first became widespread as a designation of political identity
around the time of the Russian Revolution, when Lenin sought to differentiate his movement from social democracy. Communists and socialists profoundly disagreed over the proper interpretation of Marxism, the stage theory of history, the nature of the party, the role of democracy, and the
meaning of socialism. The socialist labor movement was always a libertarian movement *(Freiheitsbewegung)*. But the communists were far more dramatic in their opposition to the war, their support for revolutionary struggle, and their use of symbolism. It was the same with the fascists and the
more traditional nationalists. Fascists were not simply, or even primarily,
opposed to the communists: their principle enemy was also the social democrats. They were the original disciples of Karl Marx, and they constituted
the majority among the "Reds." They were the real "traitors" who had
given Germany its "stab in the back." They were supposedly behind the
signing of the hated Treaty of Versailles, with its onerous reparations and
its admission of German guilt for the war. They were the "November criminals" who, in collaboration with the war profiteers, had created the Weimar
Republic. Fascists everywhere fused xenophobia with imperialist ambitions.
They lionized the state and idolized their leader. Terror was both a means
and an end. They mesmerized the masses, radically transvalued existing val-

ues, and ultimately employed racism in a way unimaginable to earlier conservatives.

Hardly anywhere in the 1920s or 1930s, however, was the political choice one between communists and fascists; it was almost always a matter of choosing between a republican regime with a social democratic base and an authoritarian regime with a fascist base. The old-fashioned conservatives knew this; and the communists knew it, too. That indeed was why, already under Lenin, they refused to offer support for "bourgeois democracy" and why, later, the communists could identify social democracy first with the "left wing" of fascism and then as its "twin brother." The fascists, for their part, despised those who refused to draw the consequences attendant upon the decay of the German community *(Volksgemeinschaft)* and who merely sought to reinstate some version of the past. They looked backward to a mythical Teutonic state, and they embraced a modern paganism.

Communism and fascism challenged the style of the old order—its pragmatism, its humanism, and perhaps above all its understanding of historical change. The totalitarians brought a new vitality to bear against their older rivals. Neither communism nor fascism had any use for universal ethical values or an "agent" of revolutionary transformation constrained by "objective conditions." It is true, of course, that many of the worst crimes perpetrated by the communists were justified by reference to "historical necessity"; and the *Führer* always spoke of "destiny." With respect to communism, however, "necessity" was actually never anything more than an excuse, and with respect to fascism, "destiny" was only what the leader wanted it to be. These movements in their most radical phases, and with respect to their most radical policies, never exhibited a sense of the way reality and ordinary morality might limit ambitions and goals. Their leaders and parties ultimately believed, whatever the tactical retreats and opportunistic compromises, that they could bend history to their will.

Fascism and communism were infused with a profound form of organizational voluntarism. Both ideologies, of course, were critical of the individual and individualism, and an authoritarian bureaucracy channeled their energies. But material constraints were taken into account only in the abstract. The state embodying the national community took precedence over the economy, and the needs of the party, identified with the choices of its leader, dominated the more routine bureaucratic concerns of the state. Fascism and communism undercut the common belief that the philosophical rejection of objectivity, determinism, and structural constraints somehow constitutes the foundation of liberation and the opposition to totalitarianism.

"Objectivity," determinism, and structural constraints were precisely what communism and fascism, albeit in different ways, refused to accept. Mussolini spoke of "Italian mathematics," and Hitler spoke of "Jewish physics," in the same way that Stalin—if not Lenin—spoke of "bourgeois" and "proletarian" science. Fascism and communism both placed primacy on the ability of the political party to overcome any limits set by economic conditions. Neither the "final solution" initiated by Hitler nor the purges of Stalin are comprehensible from the perspective of imperatives imposed by war or the economy. Fascist and communist radicalism both pitted the will against history. Their organizational commitment to revolutionary voluntarism indeed links totalitarian political philosophies beyond the more obvious differences between them.

Absolute power and the ultimate elimination of private life, the creation of a "new man," were the goals of both communism and fascism. There is a sense in which each offered an "ideology of adolescence"; and, especially among older comrades, ideology became mixed with lots of old-fashioned corruption. But in both cases, ideology played an important role, and its goals were revealed over time. Both movements evidence elements of continuity and discontinuity. Lenin was not Stalin, and Stalin was not Castro. But the communist enterprise always rested on the identification of the "true" interests of the working class and the peasantry with those of the "vanguard" party and the interest of the party with those of the state. There was never a place for countervailing institutions or checks and balances and, for this reason, never a place for criticism of party dictates from outside its confines. And so, although not every form of communist rule became totalitarian, all would still prove authoritarian.

That was indeed also the case with fascism and its various manifestations. The basic values and beliefs were there from the beginning: hatred of the Enlightenment legacy, preoccupation with the great man and the exercise of arbitrary power, moral cynicism and anti-intellectualism, racism, anti-Semitism, and the use of scapegoats. Nevertheless, differences present themselves within the tradition. The Action Française of Charles Maurras lacked the revolutionary fervor associated with the new totalitarian state of Mussolini, who, in turn, was never able to command the degree of obedience received by Adolf Hitler. Fascism and Nazism subsequently stand in roughly the same relation to one another as Leninism does to Stalinism. The former was the source of the latter, and yet, in qualitative ways, the latter differed from the former. The fascist project, just like the communist, was transformed over time from an ideologically informed authoritarianism into a new form of totalitarianism reserved for very few regimes.

Communists now lack both a revolutionary form of political organization and a utopian vision. And it is the same with the fascists—almost. In Austria, in France, in Italy, and elsewhere on the Continent, they have mixed their traditional xenophobia with a new commitment to the free market, traditional values, and religion. Fascists have refashioned themselves in a way that the communists have not. They too now seek power through electoral means; there are no paramilitary organizations; and there is little emphasis upon a "leader principle" *(Führerprinzip)*. Communism and fascism have, in short, both become forms of practice in search of a theory. Their apocalyptic visions are gone, along with their uniforms, at least for the moment.

7

Socialism: Marxism, Republicanism, Reformism

S ocialism incarnated the hopes of the labor movement everywhere
when the twentieth century began.[1] The defeat of the Paris Commune
called for new tactics, and the burst of industrial modernization,
which shifted the locus of socialist mobilizing efforts eastward from France,
demanded a theory capable of gleaning the implications of these new developments. Organization of a class rather than spontaneous action among the
poor, creation of a mass party rather than a vanguard, and employing the
ballot rather than the barricade would constitute the new tactic: Germany
would emerge as the beacon of the new Second International, and Marxism
would serve as the theory informing the new socialism.

Marxism served as the "objective" or "economic" foundation for the
"subjective" democratic and political outlook of the labor movement. It
was positivistic, deterministic, and teleological. But it also served the interests of party regulars. Functionaries, bureaucrats, and career politicians of

---

1. The following works offer an instructive general background to the history of
socialism: Wolfgang Abendroth, *A Short History of the European Working Class*,
trans. Nicholas Jacobs et al. (New York: Monthly Review, 1972); Carl Boggs, *The
Socialist Tradition: From Crisis to Decline* (New York: Routledge, 1995); Julius
Braunthal, *History of the International*, 3 vols., trans. Peter Ford, Kenneth Mitchell,
John Clark, and Henry Collins (New York and Boulder: Praeger and Westview,
1980); James Joll, *The Second International, 1889–1914* (New York: Harper, 1966);
and Donald Sassoon, *One Hundred Years of Socialism: The West European Left in
the Twentieth Century* (New York: New Press, 1996).

what had become a mass movement were content with its slow and peaceful growth as predicted by the theory. Legendary party leaders like Victor Adler and August Bebel, who respectively dominated the Austrian and German labor movements, could champion Marxist orthodoxy precisely insofar as it presented the fall of the existing order as "inevitable" and simultaneously insisted on postponing the revolution until "objective conditions" were appropriately "ripe." There is indeed a danger in ignoring the ideological function of Marxism: it inspired workers, it gave them a sense of dignity and purpose, it fostered solidarity, and above all, it made sense of the world for them. Its teleological vision of the future indeed justified the sacrifices they would make in the present.

Marx can, of course, be read in many ways. Even during the "golden age" of Marxism,[2] which lasted roughly from the 1880s until 1914, its orthodox version spawned a number of rich debates. In terms of literary criticism, Franz Mehring published his classic *The Lessing Legend*, and Georgi Plekhanov provided new sociological interpretations of French drama;[3] Max Adler sought the roots of Marxism in the idealist tradition;[4] Paul Lafargue, the son-in-law of Marx, highlighted the need for free time in his pamphlet, "The Right to be Lazy";[5] and Otto Bauer dealt with the connection between federalism and nationalism.[6] Rudolf Hilferding argued against the belief in an inevitable "breakdown" of the economic system, recognized the new interventionist possibilities of the state, and emphasized the primacy of circulation over production in what he would ultimately term "organized capitalism."[7] Debates raged over the relation between law and society, the character of socialist ethics, class consciousness, and a host of other issues.

---

2. Leszek Kolakowski, *Main Currents of Marxism*, trans. P. S. Falla (Oxford: Clarendon, 1978), 2:1 ff. and passim.

3. Georgi V. Plekhanov, "Die französische dramatische vom Standpunkt der Soziologie," in *Marxismus und Literatur*, ed. Fritz Raddatz (Hamburg: Rowohlt, 1969), 1:160 ff.

4. Max Adler, *Kausalität und Teleologie im Streite um die Wissenschaft* (Vienna: Wiener Volksbuchhandlung, 1904).

5. Paul Lafargue, "The Right to Be Lazy," in *The Essential Works of Socialism*, ed. Irving Howe (New Haven: Yale University Press, 1986).

6. Otto Bauer, *Die Nationalitatenfrage und die Sozialdemokratie* (Vienna: Wiener Volksbuchhandlung, 1907).

7. Note the classic study, which formulates these trends, by Rudolf Hilferding, *Finance Capital: A Study of the Latest Phase of Capitalist Development*, ed. Tom Bottomore, trans. Morris Watnick and Sam Gordon (London: Routledge and Kegan Paul, 1981); also see F. Peter Wagner, *Rudolf Hilferding: Theory and Politics of*

For all the controversy, however, social democracy was the single vehicle for the realization of the Marxist vision. It was the sole object of loyalty, and its brand of Marxism offered a form of concrete hope, for the vast majority of the working class in the decades prior to World War I; it engaged a mass constituency in political action like no movement before it. That has changed. Marxists may still employ the dialectical method to confront the mistaken claims of the theory and the perverse practices undertaken in its name. But they have been unable to deal with the dissolution of the original connection between theory and practice. The integration of the social democratic labor movement and the collapse of the communist alternative, the explosion in competing views and the increasingly esoteric commentaries, the multiplication of sects claiming to speak in its name, and its linkage with any number of other "isms" reflect the inability of Marxism to still inform a unified movement of working people with clear and recognizable aims.

Its original normative purposes have become distorted. The contemporary preoccupation with the abolition of alienation,[8] and other utopian concerns raised in the famous *Paris Manuscripts of 1844*,[9] had negligible practical appeal for the labor movement. The current dislike of "science" and "systems" by "Marxists" would have amazed its partisans. The philosophical superiority of Marxism, indeed, was seen as resting on its ability to illuminate actual conditions as well as the concrete possibility for their transformation. No major intellectual or practical representative of the Second International would have questioned its radical democratic message or utopian content. All of them also envisioned a profound transformation occurring in the wake of socialism. New sensibilities and new possibilities, new values and new priorities, would define what Oscar Wilde, in the title of a beautiful and moving essay, would call "the soul of man under socialism."[10] Marxist teleology was understood as a materialist reinterpretation of Enlightenment assumptions about progress; and, perhaps more importantly,

Democratic Socialism (Atlantic Highlands, N.J.: Humanities Press International, 1996).

8. See Istran Mezáros, *Marx's Theory of Alienation* (London: Merlin, 1970); Bertell Ollman, *Alienation: Marx's Conception of Man in Capitalist Society* (Cambridge: Cambridge University Press, 1971).

9. Karl Marx, *The Economic and Philosophic Manuscripts of 1844*, ed. Dirk J. Struik, trans. Martin Milligan (New York: International, 1964).

10. Oscar Wilde, "The Soul of Man under Socialism," in Howe, *Essential Works of Socialism*.

socialism was understood as fulfilling the democratic promises betrayed by the bourgeoisie.

Jean Jaurès made this view explicit in his mammoth *Socialist History of the French Revolution* as well as in other shorter works like "From the Rights of Man to Socialism."[11] A legendary orator and a genuine civil libertarian, a pacifist and an internationalist, Jaurès was the virtually undisputed moral leader of the French labor movement for more than twenty years. He was a leading figure in the Dreyfus affair, a thinker who helped introduce German idealism into the world of French socialism, and his assassination in 1914 abolished the last great hope of resistance to the burgeoning imperialist conflict. A certain Jacobin influence becomes evident in his preoccupation with the "new army," the citizen militia; and Jaurès was certainly no pillar of philosophical "orthodoxy." But he exemplified the socialist commitment to republicanism, with its emphasis on institutional accountability and the integrity of the individual. His was indeed a pluralist understanding of socialism in which "the splendor of wealth will make manifest the victory of right, and joy will be the radiance of justice."

The widespread repression occurring in the wake of the Paris Commune only highlighted the lack of democratic values and the power of monarchical regimes almost everywhere in Europe. With the failure of the revolutions of 1848, in fact, the bourgeoisie retreated from its earlier radical political commitments. Monarchs dominated the continent; and for the labor movement, especially where a strong capitalist class and democratic traditions were lacking, it became more a matter of envisioning a "bourgeois" revolution than a socialist transformation. In most countries, for this reason, the fledgling social democratic movement of the nineteenth century shouldered a dual burden.[12] It was called upon to simultaneously champion the particular economic interest of its proletarian constituency with respect to issues of economic justice and the universal political interest in a republican form of government. The first was considered conducive to reform, the second was not, and therein lay the basis for what would become the initial tension between radicals and reformers with respect to their notions of the socialist undertaking.

But this does not change the basic point. From the beginning, supporters

---

11. Jaurès, "From the Rights of Man to Socialism," in Howe, *Essential Works of Socialism.*

12. Stephen Eric Bronner, *Socialism Unbound* (New York: Routledge, 1990), 2 ff. and passim.

and enemies of the labor movement alike understood socialism as intertwined with republicanism.[13] "Orthodox Marxism" justified this connection. Some might argue that the emphasis upon republicanism by social democrats was predicated on a "revision" of Marx and the original intentions of his theory. But even if that were the case, such "revisionism" was surely no greater than that undertaken by the Bolsheviks. After all, following the seizure of power in 1917, Lenin and his followers were primarily engaged in securing their ideological identity against the vast majority of workers committed to European social democracy and those thinkers most associated with "orthodox Marxism," like Karl Kautsky.[14]

Kautsky, often called the pope of Marxism, was a prolific writer of great range. His interpretation gripped the masses during the last quarter of the nineteenth century and defined the way in which Marx was popularly understood. Kautsky portrayed history as a series of stages in which the newest would arise only when economic forces could no longer expand within the old political and ideological framework. These economic forces, in turn, were defined by class conflict, which would necessarily take different forms in different economic systems. Class conflict under capitalism was seen primarily as revolving around the increasing antagonism between those who buy "labor power" and those who sell it—the bourgeoisie and the proletariat. Competition among the former would produce an ever greater concentration of wealth along with ever more efficient production, based on the introduction of technology and the elimination of jobs, or "living labor." The bourgeoisie would grow smaller and richer, and the proletariat, fueled by the erosion of premodern classes like the peasantry and the petty bourgeoisie, would grow larger and poorer. Supply would outstrip demand, and a "falling rate of profit" would produce one increasingly severe "crisis" after another. Capitalism was thereby condemned to create its own "gravediggers" and "objectively" or "inevitably" generate a proletarian revolution of the great majority. This indeed would make it different from all revolutions of the past.[15]

"Economism" of this sort obviously implied that any revolutionary trans-

---

13. Braunthal, *History of the International*, 1:242, 3:503.

14. Massimo Salvadori, *Karl Kautsky and the Socialist Revolution, 1880–1939*, trans. Jon Rothschild (London: New Left, 1979); John H. Kautsky, *Karl Kautsky: Marxism, Revolution, and Democracy* (New Brunswick, N.J.: Transaction, 1994).

15. Karl Kautsky, *The Class Struggle (Erfurt Program)* trans. William E. Bohn (New York: Norton, 1971).

formation of the given order would have to await the point in time when the proletariat dominated society. It would then usher in a new republican order and ultimately create the conditions for a second "socialist revolution." The view fit perfectly with the interests of activists intent on building a mass-based organization, and Kautsky caught the mood when he defined social democracy as "a revolutionary organization that does not make revolution." Orthodox Marxism sought to prevent the type of "voluntarism" associated with the Paris Commune and what would become the Bolshevik seizure of power in 1917. But its teleology did not produce fatalism or passivity on the part of the masses, as so many mainstream representatives of contemporary political theory would suggest. Quite the contrary.[16] It offered workers an existential meaning for their bleak lives even as it seemingly explained the remarkable growth of social democracy from a sect of thousands into mass movements of millions virtually everywhere on the continent.

Kautsky knew it. He was adamant in his insistence on the role of class consciousness, which he identified with commitment to the social democratic party apparatus, and he never wavered in his republican beliefs. He also provided a visionary framework for the new society.[17] The problem with his work was of a different sort. None of it dealt with the tactics necessary for consummating the conquest of power. In a way, however, this failing was understandable. It reflected the constraints faced by all the major social democratic parties in the historical situation prior to World War I. In spite of their extraordinary growth, which seemingly justified their belief in Marxism, they were nonetheless always left too small to rule democratically and too large to embark on a revolutionary adventure.

Rosa Luxemburg refused to accept these alternatives.[18] A former protégé of Kautsky and a fervent apostle of internationalism, always critical of the

16. An analogous connection exists between the revolutionary impact of puritanism and the motivations for action produced by predestination. See Michael Walzer, *The Revolution of the Saints: A Study in the Origins of Radical Politics* (Cambridge: Harvard University Press, 1965).

17. Karl Kautsky, *The Social Revolution*, trans. A. M. Wood and May Wood (Chicago: Samuel A. Bloch, 1910).

18. See Stephen Eric Bronner, *Rosa Luxemburg: A Revolutionary for Our Times*, 3d ed. (University Park: Pennsylvania State University Press, 1998); Paul Fröhlich, *Rosa Luxemburg: Her Life and Work*, trans. Johanna Hoornweg (New York: Monthly Review, 1972); J. P. Nettl, *Rosa Luxemburg*, 2 vols. (New York: Oxford University Press, 1966).

bureaucratic tendency in the labor movement, her notion of socialism underscored the transformation of workers from "dead machines" into the "free and independent directors" of society as a whole. This stance, in turn, called upon the party to foster the "self-administration" of the working class itself and intervene in the "objective" process of capitalist development. It indeed led her to call upon Germany to create its own version of the Russian Revolution of 1905, in her finest work of political theory, *Mass Strike, Party, and Trade Unions* (1906).[19]

A series of spontaneous strikes among workers, which began in the Baku oil fields in 1902, had gradually moved westward. They generated new experiments with the "soviet," itself patterned on the Paris Commune, as well as new calls for a legislature (*Duma*), a republic, and the institution of the forty-hour workweek.[20] Luxemburg went to Warsaw and participated in the revolutionary events. There she experienced firsthand the innovative possibilities of the masses in democratically organizing their milieu even where they were not the majority. The "mass strike" appeared as a way to overcome the "artificial" bifurcation of the economic struggle of the unions from the party's commitment to a revolutionary politics. Action of this sort, she believed, would generate a new organizational dialectic whereby the party would heighten the revolutionary "friction" between classes and ultimately foster the need for a republic as well as ever more radical forms of democratic participation.

Her critique was directed less against the theory of the social democratic movement than against its practice. She did not privilege the party organization, which helps explain her relative lack of political influence, but instead placed primacy on the revolutionary consciousness of the working class. For this very reason, however, her views tended to scare off potential allies of more moderate political persuasion; and indeed, in the aftermath of the mass strike in Russia during 1905, European social democrats encountered electoral setbacks. Dedicated party activists were appalled, and Karl Legien, the leading unionist in the German movement, loudly proclaimed that the "mass strike is mass nonsense." Tensions began to grow even among the majority of the party, whose commitment to Marxism and revolution had almost immediately placed them in opposition to a steadily growing right-

---

19. Rosa Luxemburg, *The Mass Strike, the Political Party, and the Trade Unions*, trans. Patrick Lavin (New York: Harper and Row, 1971).
20. Leon Trotsky, *1905* (New York: Pathfinder, 1967).

wing coalition of genuine reformers, provincial nationalists, simple oppor-tunists, and antitheoretical bureaucrats. These tensions boiled over in 1910: the result was a split in which the enemies of both "revolutionary" factions were left with what would become an ever firmer grip on organizational power.[21]

Karl Kautsky and his supporters would occupy the "center" of the social democratic movement. They advocated neither political confrontation with the state nor an exclusive emphasis upon reforms. They were content to re-main in the "opposition," to wait for the "laws" of capitalist development to fulfill themselves and to let conditions become "ripe" for revolutionary action. Orthodox Marxism could, in short, offer little more than patience, or what Kautsky termed a "strategy of attrition."[22] The party would strengthen the proletarian commitment to a future revolution even while, in the present, everyday activity would revolve around realizing reformist demands. Theory and practice, ends and means, thereby increasingly stood in danger of losing any plausible connection with one another.

This chasm had, arguably, already emerged in the Erfurt Program of 1889. The founding document of the German Social Democratic Party (SPD), which served as an inspiration for virtually every other European so-cialist organization, had two distinct parts: the first explicated the character of orthodox Marxism and the "inevitable" collapse of capitalism through "natural necessity," the second anticipated the modern welfare state with a set of reformist demands ranging from better working conditions to a free burial. Only the first part was revolutionary; the second was reformist. The first part was written by Kautsky, and the second by his closest friend, Edu-ard Bernstein.[23]

Exiled to England for his political work, originally a staunch advocate of orthodox Marxism and a close friend of Frederick Engels, Bernstein would remain a socialist until the end of his life. He was proud of the social demo-cratic labor movement and the gains it had achieved. His concern, in con-

---

21. Carl E. Schorske, *German Social Democracy, 1905–1917: The Development of the Great Schism* (New York: Harper, 1972), 88 ff.

22. Karl Kautsky, *The Road to Power* (Atlantic Highlands, N.J.: Humanities Press International, 1994); note also the excellent discussion by John Kautsky, *Karl Kautsky*, 97 ff.

23. Peter Gay, *The Dilemma of Democratic Socialism: Eduard Bernstein's Chal-lenge to Marx* (New York: Collier, 1970); Manfred Steger, *The Quest for Evolution-ary Socialism: Eduard Bernstein and Social Democracy* (Cambridge: Cambridge University Press, 1997).

trast with Rosa Luxemburg, was with the theory of the movement rather than its practice. Already during his stay in England, he had become skeptical about the predictive power of Marxism under new conditions in which capitalism had apparently stabilized. Old friends suggested that Bernstein keep his reservations to himself. With great political acumen, for example, Ignaz Auer wrote to him, "My dear Ede, what you want is not something which one *decides* upon, not something that one *talks* about, but something that one does in practice."[24]

Bernstein feared, however, that the ongoing commitment to an anachronistic theory would ultimately impede the practical development of the movement. A genuinely materialist theory must respond to new conditions, and for this reason, he believed, his "revision" of Marxism actually stood in the original spirit of the enterprise. The "critical" use of Marxism, its employment as a method over and beyond the specific claims and predictions made by its author, begins with the set of articles written by Bernstein in 1898.[25] Indeed, with their assault on the assumptions underpinning Marxist orthodoxy, they created a sensation.

Bernstein began with the revolutionary teleology predicated on the growth of the industrial working class. And here there should be no misunderstanding: although Marx and his followers defined the working class in structural terms, as the class which sells its labor power, they also assumed its members would share the same empirical interests. The structural and empirical understanding of class converged during the "second industrial revolution" of the nineteenth century in the proletariat. But Bernstein saw new developments taking shape. He concluded that the working class was becoming stratified, the industrial proletariat was not growing, and wages were rising. Capital was also apparently not concentrating itself in ever fewer hands, a middle class was emerging, and credit was mitigating the crisis character of capitalism.

Bernstein had little use for "metaphysical" discussions about the structure of capitalist society or the production process without reference being made to empirical reality. If the industrial proletariat was not expanding, if other classes were indeed growing, then the "inevitable" proletarian revolution anticipated by Marx was clearly no longer on the agenda. It would become

---

24. Eduard Bernstein, *Ignaz Auer* (Berlin: Dietz, 1907), 63.
25. Eduard Bernstein, *The Preconditions of Socialism*, ed. and trans. Henry Tudor (Cambridge: Cambridge University Press, 1993).

the work of a minority and necessarily result in authoritarianism. For Bernstein, no less than for the majority of his orthodox Marxist opponents, this was not an option. But, in contrast with Kautsky and others, Bernstein was willing to draw the consequences. Economic reform would displace the goal of political revolution, and the commitment to democracy, even under authoritarian and exploitative conditions, would take precedence over socialism. Compromise with nonproletarian classes was seen as having become unavoidable; if only for this reason, social democracy would have to jettison orthodox Marxism and its revolutionary "cant." Socialism would now have to "evolve" within capitalism. "The movement is everything," according to what would become the oft-quoted phrase of Bernstein, "the goal is nothing."

In "Social Reform or Revolution?" (1899),[26] Luxemburg countered by claiming that credit would not eliminate the crisis character of capitalism, that the expected concentration of capital was taking place, and that Marxist teleology retained its legitimacy. Fearing that an unrestricted politics of class compromise could justify any choice by the party leadership and shift power to the trade unions, she also argued that there were limits to reform; that trade unions could never govern the actual level of wages or resolve the basic contradiction between social production and private appropriation of wealth that defines the capitalist production process. Then too, even regulating wages and working conditions depended upon political power; without a political revolution, she argued, the reforms granted under one set of conditions could be retracted under another. A simple emphasis on economic reforms would thus result only in a "labor of Sisyphus." Indeed, without an articulated socialist "goal," she believed, the SPD would increasingly succumb to capitalist values and so surrender its sense of political purpose.

The debate shook the party to its foundations. As the decades passed, however, the instrumental or pragmatic standpoint grew so hegemonic that contemporary social democrats now often identify it with the very movement their predecessors, like Eduard Bernstein, had originally sought to transform. The last association of social democracy with Marxism was finally sundered with the fall of Guy Mollet in France and the Bad Godesberg Program of 1959, whereby German social democrats transformed their or-

---

26. Rosa Luxemburg, "Social Reform or Revolution?" in *Rosa Luxemburg Speaks*, ed. Mary-Alice Waters (New York: Pathfinder, 1970), 33 ff.

ganization from a class party into a catch-all "party of the people" *(Volks-partei)*. Ironically, the very preoccupation with economic interests for which Marxism has been so soundly criticized—though not, interestingly enough, by Bernstein himself—would become the mainstay of reformist practice. Instrumental politics and "pragmatic" compromise would ever more surely define the politics of the labor movement; and beyond the legislated reforms, the result has been an erosion of *élan* as well as a debilitating identity crisis.

The father of "revisionism" may have anticipated, even if only dimly, the possible consequences of his original undertaking. The writings of his later years were marked by a concern with the identity of the movement and the ethical character of socialism.[27] Even his earlier work never really captured the provincial mood of the bureaucrats and nationalists dominating the "reformist" coalition within German social democracy. They had always distrusted Bernstein the intellectual and the committed socialist. They liked only his empirical critique of Marxist teleology and its "metaphysical" claims. They sensed that its employment of instrumental reason, grounded in the "pragmatic" need for compromise, could secure them from the ethical or structural—the "naive" and "utopian"—concerns of their radical critics. They indeed successfully turned Bernstein's critique of Marxist metaphysics into a critique of normative thinking as such. That was surely not Bernstein's intention. But this does not change the dynamic unleashed by his work.

It would take time for this dynamic to gather strength. A first step was taken by supporting the war effort in 1914 and another in the aftermath of the conflict, when, fearing the prospect of a soviet-style revolution, social democrats in Germany and elsewhere essentially compromised with reactionary forces—the army, the imperial bureaucracy, the industrial bourgeoisie—in order to crush the workers' uprisings, like the Spartacus Revolt of 1919, in which Rosa Luxemburg was murdered, along with a spate of other revolts elsewhere on the continent.[28] During those years social democracy

27. Note the excellent collection edited and translated by Manfred Steger, *Selected Writings of Eduard Bernstein, 1900–1921* (Atlantic Highlands, N.J.: Humanities Press International, 1996).
28. F. L. Carsten, *Revolution in Central Europe, 1918–1919* (Berkeley: University of California Press, 1972). Also note the outstanding study by Sebastian Haffner, *Failure of a Revolution: Germany, 1918–1919*, trans. George Rapp (Chicago: Banner, 1986).

lost its radical aura among the more militant if not among the more staunch supporters of the status quo. The old form of orthodox Marxism continued to serve as its guiding spirit. Its practice, however, became ever more estranged from its revolutionary theory.

Social democrats sharply criticized the increasingly authoritarian character of the Russian Revolution of 1917, although they opposed all attempts to suppress it, and Leon Blum was correct in noting the "moral incompatibility" between what would become the two parties of the working class. The Russian Revolution ultimately illuminated precisely what socialism was *not* in the minds of the founders of the social democratic labor movement. Nowhere does this become more apparent than in the legendary pamphlet on the Russian Revolution by Rosa Luxemburg.

Written while she was in jail for opposing World War I, just before her tragic death during the German revolution of 1919, it decries the dictatorship of a clique and identifies a genuine "dictatorship of the proletariat" with the radical application of democracy, the abolition of all class privileges, and the creation of a new and invigorated public sphere. The working class must participate directly in building a new society; otherwise, authoritarianism will take on its own dynamic: it will spread from the constitutional assembly to the soviets to the entire society. The choice was clear-cut: democracy or dictatorship, the rule of a class or the rule of a clique, a vibrant pluralism or a deadening conformism. Controversy and public debate indeed retained a value in their own right. Thus, Luxemburg could proclaim, "Freedom is only and exclusively freedom for the one who thinks differently."[29]

The war had tumbled the reigning dynasties in imperial Germany, Austria-Hungary, Russia, and Turkey. The "revolution" was seen by most social democrats, if not by Rosa Luxemburg herself, as having been accomplished, in the form of the new republics led by them. For a variety of reasons, however, these states lacked ideological legitimacy,[30] and social democracy suffered the consequences. The movement was criticized on the left for compromising its principles, leading its proletarian constituency to the slaughter, and then integrating itself into the "bourgeois" state. But it also stood discredited in the eyes of moderates for its socialist commitments and

---

29. Rosa Luxemburg, "The Russian Revolution," in *Rosa Luxemburg Speaks*, 389.

30. Arthur Rosenberg, *Geschichte des Weimarer Republik* (Mannheim: Europäische, 1961).

castigated on the far right for its republicanism and its half-hearted support of the war effort. European social democracy found itself increasingly on the defensive and in search of allies. The need became ever greater after Hitler took power in Germany and the possibilities for a "popular front" presented themselves in France in the early 1930s.

Compromise and ideological flexibility were demanded in order to forge an antifascist program capable of appealing to a coalition of diverse class forces and diverse class interests. A Popular Front composed of liberals, social democrats, and communists won the French elections of 1936, which resulted in the institution of the forty-hour workweek and the right to collective bargaining, along with a host of other reforms. In Spain, partisans of the Popular Front defended the country's republic against the forces of reaction led by Generalissimo Francisco Franco. The coalition ultimately fell apart owing to fear of more radical reforms by the liberals and the dogmatism of the communists. But its commitment to republicanism and radical economic reform, its coalition of democratic forces led by the working class, made it perhaps the last movement reflective of the spirit inspiring the original labor movement and its particular brand of orthodox Marxism.[31]

As for the social democratic labor movement, which drew support from the majority of the working class, its political theory during the years surrounding the Popular Front became ever more preoccupied with solidifying the connection between socialism and liberalism. Carlo Rosselli indeed made this explicit.[32] A guiding force of Italian social democracy and a leader of the Italian antifascist movement in exile, he fought for the loyalist cause during the Spanish civil war before his assassination at the hands of Mussolini's henchmen in France. But the importance of Rosselli extends beyond his personal bravery and the symbol of antifascist resistance he presented. His work theoretically broke the bond between Marxism and socialism, which had been inherited from the last quarter of the nineteenth century, and it reasserted the moral character of the socialist undertaking against the ethical relativism and authoritarianism of the communists. Rosselli emphasized the importance of parliamentarism and compromise. But he also highlighted the role of values like "justice and liberty," which served as the name of the important antifascist group he helped found during the 1930s, along

---

31. Stephen Eric Bronner, *Moments of Decision: Political History and the Crises of Radicalism* (New York: Routledge, 1992), 57 ff.

32. Carlo Rosselli, *Liberal Socialism*, ed. Nadia Urbinati, trans. William McCuaig (Princeton: Princeton University Press, 1994).

with ideals, like the "classless society," capable of inspiring the labor movement.

According to Rosselli, however, no ideal could justify incursions on the liberty of individuals or the liberal rule of law. Means would have to stand in a coherent relation with ends, and freedom could no longer take shelter in dialectical sophistry. Therein lies the core of his social democratic politics. In this respect, again, the Popular Front provided the moment of decision. Leon Blum, its leader, whose long career as a socialist activist began during the Dreyfus affair, had previously distinguished between the "exercise" and the "conquest" of power.[33] The distinction may well have been purely ideologically motivated, a bow to orthodox Marxists within the French socialist movement, from the beginning. The conquest of power was never a realistic possibility. The army would have surely turned against the Popular Front under any circumstances; its electoral majority was not overwhelming; and none of its organizational participants was ready for civil war. But the fear of sacrificing republican principles was also crucial in leading Blum to jettison any attempt at transforming the "exercise" into the "conquest" of power. It had indeed become a matter of securing the connection between liberalism and socialism.

The "liberal socialism" of Carlo Rosselli and Leon Blum harked back to Jean Jaurès. It reflected the democratic spirit of the Popular Front, which involved more than a simple list of discrete reforms, and it anticipated the worldview often associated with political figures like Pietro Nenni, Willy Brandt, Olof Palme, Norberto Bobbio,[34] and a host of other noncommunist socialist intellectuals.[35] All these thinkers considered socialism both an idea and a movement of the masses. But it has clearly lacked a radical élan since the 1930s. Various attempts were made after World War II to reinvigorate the old vision with a concern for egalitarian forms of socialized planning, more participatory forms of democracy, and a "concrete internationalism."[36] Nevertheless, they all floundered on the reefs of the cold war.

---

33. Note the classic biography by Jean Lacouture, *Leon Blum*, trans. George Holoch (New York: Holmes and Meier, 1982), 173 ff.

34. Norberto Bobbio, *Which Socialism?: Marxism, Socialism, and Democracy*, trans. Roger Griffen (Minneapolis: University of Minnesota Press, 1979).

35. Erich Fromm, ed., *Socialist Humanism: An International Symposium* (New York: Doubleday, 1966).

36. Note, in particular, the work originally published in 1947 and written by Richard Lowenthal under the pseudonym Paul Sering, *Jenseits des Kapitalismus: Ein Beitrag zur sozialistischen Neuorientierung* (Bonn: Dietz, 1977).

Especially in retrospect, there was little choice for the movement other than to identify itself with the West in its struggle against communism. In the process, however, socialism was increasingly used to justify establishmentarian institutions and policies: its claims on the imagination of the young, the idealistic, and the militant grew increasingly less secure. Few important advances in political theory took place, and the great debates between figures like Eduard Bernstein and Rosa Luxemburg vanished into the mist of the past. The mass base of social democracy remained the working class, which never did politically constitute itself as the great majority of society; but the former sense of identity withered as the movement turned into just another variant of liberal reformism. It has indeed become fashionable for social democrats to speak about a "third way" between socialism and capitalism following the electoral victory of Tony Blair in England and other social democratic triumphs in France, Germany, and elsewhere in 1997 and 1998.[37] But, ultimately, this "third way" has little new to say:[38] it accepts the market and seeks to mitigate its excesses through the state when necessary, but with more concern for capitalist efficiency and the responsibility of the individual than before. Its partisans speak of invigorating the "community" and attacking bureaucracy; but there is little more involved than the traditional reformist emphasis upon "partnership" between the private and public sector undertaken within the ideological framework developed by Margaret Thatcher and Ronald Reagan. Proponents of the "new labor" pride themselves on their pragmatism and on their rejection of "grand plans." They have little use for the old symbols and old solutions, such as nationalizing inefficient industries. They have indeed been unable to contest the sense of drift so apparent in the social democratic movement, let alone deal with what has become an ideology of reformism predicated on a virtually unqualified willingness to compromise.

This ideology is not a product of some new commitment to "market socialism,"[39] which seeks to further socialist ends by employing the state and other public associations to mitigate the debilitating effects of the free market, or socialist debates over the role of the state current in the 1970s and

---

37. Tony Blair, *New Britain: My Vision of a Young Country* (Boulder: Westview, 1997).

38. Anthony Giddens, *The Third Way: The Renewal of Social Democracy* (London: BPI, 1998).

39. See *Market Socialism: The Debate among Socialists*, ed. Bertell Ollman (New York: Routledge, 1998).

1980s. A preoccupation with economic reform was dominant within the proletarian labor movement from the beginning; the attempt to offer a wholesale political alternative was consummated when social democracy identified itself with the new republics of the 1920s and 1930s, and the cultural enterprise was never even fully articulated. Ideals and values have indeed become more important for invigorating socialism as its technocratic and pragmatic qualities have asserted themselves in the postwar era.

The erosion of socialist values within the socialist movement was a predominant concern of Henry Pachter.[40] A communist during the 1920s, a social democrat in the 1930s, he participated in the antifascist struggle in Germany, Spain, and France before emigrating to the United States, where he became a noted historian and political scientist. Pachter saw the basic problem of postwar social democracy in its instrumentalism and its preoccupation with the technical aspects of instituting and legislating reforms. By the same token, however, he knew that the old labor movement—its style, its propaganda, its proletarian class base—had become a relic of the past. Pachter was among those engaged in developing new forms of socialist theory to meet the new problems of a new "postindustrial" economy. He emphasized the need to instill a new commitment to reduce the workweek, equalize the burden borne by the least dignified forms of labor, champion ecological concerns, and foster cosmopolitan values. But it was for him also a question of reaffirming the central premise of the original undertaking. Socialism *is* the resistance against all forms of class domination and the whip of the market, according to Pachter, and it is the opposition against every attempt to transform human beings into a "cost of production." Socialism is therefore not equivalent with a set of institutions, policies, or systematic principles. It is a quest for freedom, which always stands in an asymptotic relation to reality.

The most pressing problem for socialists is the impossibility of any longer presupposing the moral impetus to engage in the creation of what Alec Nove called a "feasible socialism" or, for that matter, any other libertarian kind. There is no teleology, or science, or "dialectic," that assures an emancipatory outcome to current affairs. The inherent connection between the expansion of capitalism and the development of its gravediggers has been

---

40. Especially note the essays, "The Right to Be Lazy," "Freedom, Authority, Participation, and "The Idea of Progress in Marxism," in *Socialism in History: Political Essays of Henry Pachter*, ed. Stephen Eric Bronner (New York: Columbia University Press, 1984), 3 ff. and 36 ff.

broken: classes have given way before interest groups, and the old models are no longer appropriate for a new reality. Political organizations of labor are becoming a dim memory, though perhaps the memory might prefigure struggles more advanced than those of the moment. But faith in the emancipatory possibilities of the future, or belief that the dialectic will somehow reassert itself, is simply inadequate. It has become necessary to admit that socialism can exist today only as an ethic or a regulative idea.

An inherently contingent commitment alone underpins the struggle for what André Gorz once called "non-reformist reforms": changes that speak to the character of society, its structural imbalances of power, and the genuine empowerment of workers. Ultimately, if socialists are to reclaim their project, they must begin without the comfort of teleology, the security of reformism, or the belief in clearly defined institutional models. Even with the new economic crises that are emerging toward the very end of the twentieth century, whatever the increasing imbalances of power and maldistribution of income, the socialist project is more fragile than ever before. Its partisans must subsequently begin more soberly, more modestly, and with a different form of commitment. They must indeed begin with the assumption that "One cannot have socialism. One is a socialist."[41]

---

41. Henry Pachter, "Aphorisms on Socialism," in *Socialism in History*, 331.

8

Fascism: Irrationalism,
Reaction, Apocalypse

W orld War I was a "total war." The lines blurred between state
and market, man and material, education and ideology, administration and politics, individual and mass. Respect was fostered
for those in command or, better, those capable of making a "decision," and
the world was divided into "us" and "them." Fascism transformed the reality of "total war" into a new vision of the "total state," and it injected this
vision with a new set of anachronistic ideological impulses.[1] Its worldview
attracted those soldiers with nationalistic inclinations who saw World War
I as the defining event of their lives. It justified their hatred of the "defeatists" and traitors—liberals, socialists, communists, and Jews—who had either robbed them of their victory or bargained it away. It exalted those who,
amid the bloodshed and the drudgery, the sacrifice and the heroism, felt they
had experienced a higher form of solidarity.

Fascism surely offered itself as a solution for the economic chaos, the class
conflict, and the decline of authority in the aftermath of World War I and
during the turbulent 1920s. It relied on an authoritarian state; it trumpeted
its expression of a national will; it castigated the deviant; and it always

---

1. General treatments are provided by Walter Laqueur, *Fascism: Past, Present,
Future* (New York: Oxford University Press, 1996); Roger Eatwell, *Fascism: A History* (New York: Penguin, 1995); Ernst Nolte, *Three Faces of Fascism: Action Française, Italian Fascism, National Socialism*, trans. Leila Vennewitz (New York: Signet,
1965).

found a "scapegoat." Especially in ideological terms, fascism was never really about the need for "law and order." Quite the contrary. It was about the arbitrary exercise of power and the attempt to keep the excitement of the populace at a fevered pitch. It lauded action for its own sake; it fostered war for the sake of war and death for the sake of death. It was predicated less upon a coherent form of thought than on a feeling for action; less upon a set of particular instrumental interests than on a call for purposeless sacrifice; less upon a commitment to ideas than to myths; less upon a reasoned patriotism than on an emotive xenophobia; less upon reason and the intellect than on experience and intuition.

Ernst Bloch liked to recall the words of a young Nazi: "One does not die for a program that one understands, one dies for a program that one loves."[2] These words provide a key for understanding the appeal of fascism. Its sources, arguably, appear in the very beginnings of civilization:[3] the cult of the leader, fear of the foreign, surrender of the self, the exaltation of the irrational, and even anti-Semitism retain an anthropological quality. But then, as Nietzsche put it, those who see similarities everywhere really do not see very well. Fascism requires a certain degree of technological development; it requires a bureaucratic state; it requires, above all, masses. Fascism would indeed make use, far better use than its competitors, of the new possibilities for propaganda and terror with an eye on what the Belgian politician and thinker, Henri de Man, called "massification" *(Vermassung)*.[4]

Fascism is ultimately a modern phenomenon; it assumes the existence of what it wishes to obliterate. Its vehemence derives from its contempt for modernity with its various philosophies of the "cash register." It condemns liberalism and socialism, rationalism and materialism, for draining a people of its vitality and its will to power. It has no use for personal liberty; it despises the idea of equality; and it scorns any universalist notion of fraternity. Indeed, just as the avant-garde composer in Thomas Mann's *Dr. Faustus* made a pact with the devil to "take back" Beethoven's Ninth Symphony, fascism made a commitment to obliterate the most progressive legacy of the Enlightenment and the French Revolution.

The "age of reaction" against the democratic revolutions, which ranged

---

2. Ernst Bloch, *Erbschaft dieser Zeit* (Frankfurt am Main: Suhrkamp, 1973), 65.
3. Note the classic analysis by Max Horkheimer and Theodor Adorno, *Dialectic of Enlightenment,* trans. John Cumming (New York: Herder and Herder, 1972), 3 ff.
4. Henri de Man, *Vermassung und Kulturverfall* (Bern: Francke, 1970).

from the seventeenth into the nineteenth century, is subsequently often seen as the genuine source of fascism. And there is some truth to this. Its most important representatives, like J. G. Hamann and Joseph de Maistre,[5] already evidence many of the core concepts. The anti-Semitism, the irrationalism, the chauvinism, the organic view of society, the emphasis upon community, and the fear of modernity are all there. Reactionary conservative and romantic ideology of this sort, in fact, often blends with fascism; its proponents were people of the right, and, when a choice between socialism and fascism presented itself in practice, they usually chose the latter. But there is a mistake in taking this too far and interpreting the influence of older theoretical traditions too mechanically. This romantic reaction against everything connected with 1776 and 1789 was fundamentally inspired by its faith in the Catholic Church and its hierarchical vision of an ordained feudal order. It was an appeal for the elite to unite against a rising democratic and socialist tide rather than a call for the masses to awaken. It was conservative, in the original sense of the word, rather than revolutionary.

Fascism took over the assault on the Enlightenment generated by the reactionaries of the nineteenth century. But the original counterrevolution would only gradually become revolutionary. This development was nourished by the ungraspable *élan vital* of Henri Bergson,[6] the nonobjectifiable "will to power" of Nietzsche, the new elitism expressed by Vilfredo Pareto and Gaetano Mosca,[7] the "cult of the self" inaugurated by Barrès, the "social Darwinism" of liberals like Herbert Spencer, the vision of a cosmological racial struggle articulated by Houston Stewart Chamberlain in his bestselling *The Foundations of the Nineteenth Century* (1900),[8] and the explo-

---

5. Isaiah Berlin, "The Counter-Enlightenment," in *Against the Current: Essays in the History of Ideas*, ed. Henry Hardy (New York: Penguin, 1979); and "Joseph de Maistre and the Origins of Fascism," in *The Crooked Timber of Humanity: Chapters in the History of Ideas*, ed. Henry Hardy (New York: Vintage, 1992). Also see Isaiah Berlin, *The Magus of the North: J. G. Hamann and the Origins of Modern Irrationalism* (London: John Murray, 1993).

6. Note the general worldview presented in Henri Bergson, *An Introduction to Metaphysics: The Creative Mind*, trans. Mabelle Andison (Totowa, N.J.: Littlefield, Adams, 1965).

7. Vilfredo Pareto, *The Rise and Fall of Elites* (New York: Arno, 1979); Gaetano Mosca, *The Ruling Class*, ed. Arthur Livingston, trans. Hannah D. Kahn (New York: McGraw-Hill, 1939).

8. For a general overview of the intellectual context, see Henry Pachter, "Irrationalism and the Paralysis of Reason: The Festering Sore," and "Aggression as Cultural Rebellion: The German Example," in *Weimar Etudes* (New York: Columbia University Press, 1982).

sive *ressentiment* from atavistic classes whose interests opposed both the bourgeoisie and the proletariat.[9] With their vitalism and intuitionism, their contempt for metaphysics and positivism, these intellectual trends were seen as constituting a new philosophical approach, which reflected certain ideological elements propagated by a new set of burgeoning political movements. The ideology was reflected in the emergence of a new authoritarian—and often anti-Semitic—populism that sought to present itself as an alternative to both capitalism and socialism or what was traditionally labeled "left and right."[10] This new protofascist politics indeed was evidenced by the Christian social movements of Adolf Stocker in Germany and Karl Lueger and Georg Ritter von Schönerer in Austria, as well as—the most intellectually respected—the Action Française in France.

The origins of the French movement lay with those who had supported the failed military coup against the Third Republic by General Georges Boulanger in 1889 and, perhaps even more importantly, the resolute anti-Semites, disgruntled by the outcome of the infamous Dreyfus affair, which had torn the nation apart in the years between 1894 and 1899.[11] A military court had condemned Captain Alfred Dreyfus, the only Jew on the French General Staff, to Devil's Island for betraying military secrets to Germany. Perjured testimony, concocted evidence, a plot to conceal the identity of the real traitor, and a military cover-up took place. The "affair" took the form of a mystery thriller, and it was fueled by the fears and hatreds generated during the Franco–Prussian War. A certain segment of the labor movement led by Jules Gusede, a crude orthodox Marxist convinced that the controversy was a "bourgeois" affair, sought to remain aloof. Nevertheless, it soon became apparent that the fate of Dreyfus was connected with the future of the French state and society.

Two sides squared off against one another. Liberals and socialists op-

---

9. Max Scheler, "On the Phenomenology and Sociology of *Ressentiment*," in *Ressentiment*, ed. Lewis A. Coser, trans. William W. Holdheim (New York: Schocken, 1961).

10. Zev Sternhell, *Neither Left nor Right: Fascist Ideology in France* (Berkeley: University of California Press, 1986), 25–26 and passim.

11. Note the outstanding study by Jean-Denis Bredin, *The Affair: The Case of Alfred Dreyfus*, trans. Jeffrey Mehlman (New York: George Braziller, 1986), and the excellent documentary history provided by Louis L. Snyder, *The Dreyfus Case* (New Brunswick: Rutgers University Press, 1973); for the cultural climate and the tone of the anti-Dreyfusard ideology, see *The Dreyfus Affair: Art, Truth, and Justice*, ed. Norman L. Kleeblatt (Berkeley: University of California Press, 1988).

posed a conservative establishment grounded in the military, the church, and precapitalist classes. It is indeed difficult to imagine today the manner in which the trial divided France: only the histories of the event and the novels by Marcel Proust and Anatole France serve to remind us. A single innocent man, unjustly convicted and suffering a host of tortures on Devil's Island, galvanized a nation. Childhood friends like Emile Zola and Paul Cézanne, the great painter, split over the "affair." Anti-Semitic mobs staged riots. Governmental cabinets fell, and, in the end, a majority of those on the General Staff committed suicide following publication of "J'Accuse," by Zola, and then "Les Preuves" (The Proofs), by Jaurès, and the vindication of Dreyfus.

The Action Française was born, in response to these developments, on June 20, 1899. Many students of fascism tend to underestimate its mass base of support and its importance for the formation of a fascist ideology. The movement was, however, far more than a pressure group or a sect. It was among the most consistent and bellicose antagonists of the Third Republic in France. It was indeed a signal source of support for establishmentarian conservative political parties during the 1920s and 1930s. But it also tacitly supported ultraright and genuine terrorist groups like the Cagoule or Le Faisceau, organized by one of its former leaders, Georges Valois, against the antifascist Popular Front. It helped push the country to the brink of civil war during the 1930s, and, following the defeat of the French Republic by the Nazis in 1940, it became an important bulwark for the collaborationist Vichy regime.

And what was true of its practice was mirrored in its theory. The identification of the Action Française with the Catholic Church, its monarchist inclinations, and its aristocratic elitism may seem to place it less within the fascist or even protofascist than within the right wing of the conservative camp. But the distinction here is illusory. The Action Française's commitment to violence was part of its origins; its members were constantly in search of a charismatic leader; its supporters were imbued with the anti-Semitism of Edouard Drumont, whose major work, *France under the Jews* (1886), would run into its two-hundredth edition by 1914; its "integral nationalism" was populist in tone; its hatred of everything associated with the Enlightenment was always coupled with the vision of a martial authoritarian state; and it was informed by an obsessive desire for a war of "revenge" against Germany, even if its members later liked to shout the slogan, "Better Hitler than Blum!" Indeed, if the major political figures of French fascism in the 1930s were primarily renegades from the socialist and communist movements, like Marcel Déat and Jacques Doriot, its ideology was actually forged from the protofascist writings of Charles Maurras and, perhaps of even greater interest, Maurice Barrès.[12]

A well-respected novelist and polemicist with friends across the political spectrum, Barrès derided "intellectuals" for their critical rationalism and liberal universalism during the Dreyfus affair.[13] And, in a way, his critique was legitimate. Intellectuals like Emile Zola and Jean Jaurès could decry the injustice accorded Dreyfus—the Jew—because they placed reason above experience, evidentiary truth above tradition, and human rights above the exigencies of any particular national "community." This attempt to anchor justice in the liberal rule of law and a universalistic notion of subjectivity, however, was precisely what Barrès and his supporters rejected. They saw ideas and subjectivity "rooted" in an organic community. These right-wing intellectuals, of course, actually stood in no closer connection to the "people" than their Dreyfusard opponents—and probably less so. But this was not the point. They painted intellectuals as "abstract," inherently divorced from "real life," and as "individualists" ignorant of what was truly decisive: the nation as a source of existential unity for its "people."

The most famous novel by Barrès, *The Deracinated*, indeed sought to show the implications of what has been called "integral nationalism," the unique experience of life generated by different "nations," and the impossibility of any mutual understanding between the French and the Germans. It suggested not merely the need to explode universal abstractions in the name of experience but also the need to cultivate the sources of that experience in terms of national myths and traditions. Barrès considered universal ideals inherently abstract and misguided, and he believed that the intellect had, at best, only a secondary place in the lived life of a "people." Thus, he could write in *Scenes and Doctrines of Nationalism*:

---

12. Note the illuminating exchange between Maurice Barrès and Charles Maurras, *La République ou le roi: Correpondance inédite, 1883–1923* (Paris: Plon, 1970).

13. "The term 'intellectual' appears to originate from the pen of Clemenceau in an article in *L'Aurore* of January 23, 1898, as a collective description of the most prominent Dreyfusards. The new term was promptly taken up in a pejorative sense of unscrupulousness and irresponsible disloyalty to the nation by Maurice Barrès in *Scènes et doctrines du nationalism* (Paris, 1902), p. 46 (where incidentally even the un-French quality of the word itself becomes part of the accusation)." J. P. Nettl, "Ideas, Intellectuals, and the Structures of Dissent," in *On Intellectuals*, ed. Philip Rieff (New York: Doubleday, 1969), 87.

Truth is not something to be known intellectually. Truth is finding a particular point, the only point, that one and no other, from which everything appears to us in proper perspective. . . . I must settle myself at that point which my eyes take as their own so that it is the past centuries which form my vision; that point from which everything is seen through the eyes of a Frenchman. The totality of these proper relationships between given objects and a given subject, the Frenchman, that is French truth and French justice. And pure nationalism is simply the discovery of that point, searching for it, and when it is found, holding fast to it and receiving from it our art, our politics, and the manner of living our life.

This anti-intellectual evocation of intuition, this dogmatic fusion of subjectivity with the national community, would ultimately play a profound role in the thinking of every major fascist philosopher. It certainly exists in the writings of José Antonio Primo de Rivera, leader of the Spanish fascists known as the Falange,[14] who fought against the loyalist supporters of the existing republic when a bloody civil war began in 1936. A man of supposedly extraordinary charm and a brilliant speaker, son of a former dictator of Spain and a genuinely dashing political figure, Primo de Rivera was the most fiery presence among the truly banal authoritarians led by Generalissimo Francisco Franco. His capture, trial, and execution, in 1936 at the age of thirty-nine, at the hands of the enemy was catastrophic for his movement.

Primo de Rivera offers perhaps the most vitalistic, if not the most radical, interpretation of fascism as a revolutionary doctrine. His writings exist mostly in the form of speeches and short polemical essays. But this does not take away from their value. Primo de Rivera believed that politics must speak to the "deeper liberty of man" and the emotional bond tying together the people of a nation. Membership in the *patria* or the *Vaterland*, or whatever, is a matter of blood and sensibility. Fascism declines to offer a program or concrete solutions to concrete problems, and its partisans must show themselves ready to "suffer death and carry out hard missions" precisely for reasons and aims in which they have "no interest at all." Struggle assumes an independent value. There is no talk of privileges, and there is no talk of profit. But there is talk of "national destiny." Fascism speaks of sacrifice for an indefinable goal, renunciation of the self, and the liberating experience of violence.

14. Stanley G. Payne, *Falange: A History of Spanish Fascism* (Stanford: Stanford University Press, 1961).

This extreme voluntaristic impulse both informs and complements the more realistic and organizational form of thinking in the work of Benito Mussolini.[15] The future *duce* had begun as a man of the socialist left, the friend and protégé of the legendary Angelica Balabanoff,[16] who would later serve as secretary of the Communist International in 1920 before quickly returning to her socialist roots. Mussolini became the editor of the most important paper of the Italian Socialist Party, *Avanti*, in 1912 at the age of twenty-nine, and when the war began in 1914, he was one of its young luminaries. Mussolini was another superb orator and an intellectual of sorts, with fine prospects, and it remains an open question whether he moved to the right out of revolutionary principle or simple opportunism. It was probably a combination of both.

What Norberto Bobbio calls the "forces of the irrational" played a part in the thinking of the far right in Italy.[17] An admiration for war and "living dangerously" intersected with the revolutionary ambitions of those syndicalists, inspired by the writings of Georges Sorel, who formed the "fascists for revolutionary action" (Fasci di Azione Rivoluzionaria) in 1914. They sought to foster unity in support of Italian intervention in the war, and they gained the support of various ultranationalist militarists like the poet–politician Gabriele D'Annunzio, who saw war as a purifying "bloodbath," as well as avant-gardists with a syndicalist streak, like Fillipo Marinetti and the Futurists;[18] it was indeed from these cultural figures that Italian fascism would inherit the straight-arm salute and the black shirt.

Italian radicals of the far right also sought to overcome the nostalgic identification with the humanism and cosmopolitanism of the Renaissance in favor of a ruthless antihumanism supposedly more conducive to a dynamic and technologically advanced society. Commercialism and materialism, rationalism and pacifism, generated scorn on the part of Giuseppe Prezzolini and Giovanni Papini, along with the intellectuals who published in journals like *Leonardo* and *Lacerba*. It also became clear to many left-wing socialists

15. Christopher Hibbert, *Il Duce: The Life of Benito Mussolini* (Boston: Little, Brown, 1962).

16. Angelica Balabanoff, *My Life as a Rebel* (Bloomington: Indiana University Press, 1973), 44 ff. and passim.

17. Norberto Bobbio, *Ideological Profile of Twentieth-Century Italy*, trans. Lydia G. Cochrane (Princeton: Princeton University Press, 1995), 33 ff.

18. Note the collection entitled *Marinetti: Selected Writings*, ed. R. W. Flint, trans. R. W. Flint and Arthur Coppotelli (New York: Farrar, Straus and Giroux, 1972).

like Roberto Michels that social democracy would never make a revolution. This would later turn him into an ardent supporter of an Italian fascist dictatorship; his famous formulation of the "iron law of oligarchy" was indeed initially intended as critique of the bureaucratic reformism practiced by the socialist labor movement.[19] Surely, in the same vein, Mussolini became convinced that the socialist movement, with its retrograde humanism, was not making the most of the political opportunities presented by the outbreak of World War I.

The first program of his new Fasci di Combattimento of 1919, essentially forged from war veterans contemptuous of democracy and fearful of Bolshevism, was eclectic and opportunist. Its tone was populist; it called for the abolition of the monarchy and the confiscation of church property; and it was explicit in its desire to overcome the traditional distinctions between left and right in the name of a new revolutionary posture. Mussolini sensed the limits of a working-class stance in a relatively undeveloped nation riven by regional differences with a large peasantry, an influential aristocracy, and an omnipresent Catholic Church.[20] Nevertheless, he saw the value of a "vanguard" party and gradually grasped the idea of identifying it with the state.

The new totalitarian state would ultimately create the nation, according to Mussolini, by "conferring volition" and making people aware of their "moral unity." He opposed the established practice among democratic political parties of *transformismo*, with its coalition building, logrolling, and attempts to integrate ideologically driven movements. Mussolini condemned instrumental politics for diluting the national will. His new form of state would, by contrast, inherently incarnate the will of the people; indeed, "outside of it no human or spiritual values can exist."

And so, if only for this reason, loyalty must prove unconditional. The interests of the nation-state must transcend those of political parties and private persons. It must integrate all particular interests even as it must bind capitalists and trade unions within a "corporatist" system. Everything, in-

---

19. Robert Michels, *Political Parties: A Sociological Study of the Oligarchical Tendencies of Modern Democracy,* trans. Eden Paul and Cedar Paul (New York: Free Press, 1968).

20. These same issues would ultimately receive theoretical articulation, albeit from a very different political perspective, by Antonio Gramsci, in *Selections from the Prison Notebooks,* ed. and trans. Quintin Hoare and Geoffrey Nowell Smith (New York: International, 1971), 44 ff. and passim.

deed, gains definition from the state; "thus understood, fascism is totalitarian, and the fascist state—a synthesis and a unit inclusive of all values—interprets, develops, and potentiates the whole life of a people." The state takes on a personality; its demands must be met with utmost speed and, if necessary, utmost ruthlessness; it necessarily requires a leader, whose "decision" *is* that of the state and who is therefore accountable only to his own "will."[21]

Mussolini did not become *Il Duce* right away.[22] He identified himself as a monarchist when he took power, and, as late as 1928, he forged a concordat with the Catholic Church. He played off the "chieftains," known by the Ethiopian word *ras*, of different regions within his own party against one another for years. His power was initially constrained, and he proceeded carefully; his intrusion into the public sphere was relatively limited, his secret police relatively constrained, his use of propaganda relatively primitive; his foreign policy was bellicose in word and, except for his invasion of Ethiopia in 1938, generally cautious in deed. He chose his "scapegoats" as circumstances dictated: it was first the "Reds," then the Freemasons, and only in the late 1930s—when Mussolini finally fell under the spell of Hitler—the Jews. Mussolini called his state "totalitarian," but it was only, if the word fits, authoritarian.[23]

Then again, the totalitarian state is never totalitarian enough. Fascism generates its own dynamic. Arbitrariness always seeks to render itself absolute. Early authoritarian forms of fascism, whatever their totalitarian self-image, were capable of turning into something qualitatively even more oppressive: prisons became concentration camps, prejudice became transformed into obsession, the cult of the leader metamorphosed into deification, imperialism turned into the dream of world conquest, genocide was unleashed in an entirely new way, and anti-intellectualism gave way before insanity. This was the point at which fascism became truly totalitarian and at which, in the form of Nazism, it attempted to fulfill its most irrational impulse.

Probably no state has ever been so identified with its leader as Nazi Ger-

21. Benito Mussolini, *Fascism: Doctrine and Institutions* (New York: Howard Fertig, 1968).
22. Gaetano Salvemini, *The Origins of Fascism in Italy*, trans. Roberto Vivarelli (New York: Harper and Row, 1973), 330 ff.
23. Edward Tannenbaum, *The Fascist Experience: Italian Society and Culture, 1922–1945* (New York: Basic Books, 1972).

many was with Adolf Hitler.[24] He was born in the small Austrian town of Braunau in 1889, and he was eighteen when he came to Vienna. There, he absorbed the anti-Semitic nationalism of Georg Ritter von Schönerer, who coined the unifying slogan, "Germany belongs to the Germans," and admired the cult of personality surrounding Karl Lueger. Hitler developed an intense hatred of the liberals and socialists, cosmopolitans and literary modernists, so dominant in the life of the multicultural capital of Austria during the prewar years.[25] Ultimately, he could not find a place in this setting. Hitler failed in his attempt to become a painter; bereft and alone, he drifted around the city without purpose or ambition. World War I came as a godsend. Hitler was decorated with the Iron Cross for bravery, and he became a corporal; ironically, he was prevented from rising higher in the ranks because of what was perceived as a lack of leadership skills. Under any circumstances, however, he experienced the loss of the war as a trauma.

Peace found Hitler without prospects or hopes. He raged against the "defeatists," the "profiteers," and the socialist leaders of the new Weimar Republic or, as they were generally known on the far right,[26] the "November criminals." He was in the same situation as he had been when the war began, except that he was now living in Munich. That city was, perhaps even more than Vienna, a crucible of left-wing radicalism and cultural modernism. Its spirit was exemplified by the ill-fated Bavarian Soviet, whose leaders were now mostly forgotten figures like the great humanitarian socialist Kurt Eisner and the radical avant-garde playwright Ernst Toller.[27] The movement was crushed by the protofascist Freikorps, composed of former soldiers like Hitler, with the support of anachronistic classes like the peas-

---

24. Important biographies include Allan Bullock, *Hitler: A Study in Tyranny* (New York: Harper and Row, 1962); Phillippe Burrin, *Hitler and the Jews: The Genesis of the Holocaust*, trans. Patsy Southgate (London: Arnold, 1977); Joachim Fest, *Hitler*, trans. Richard Winston and Clara Winston (New York: Harcourt, Brace, 1974); Konrad Heiden, *Der Führer: Hitler's Rise to Power*, trans. Ralph Mannheim (Boston: Beacon, 1944).

25. Note the essays included in *Vienna: The World of Yesterday, 1889–1914*, ed. Stephen Eric Bronner and F. Peter Wagner (Atlantic Highlands, N.J.: Humanities Press International, 1997).

26. Kurt Sontheimer, *Antidemokratisches Denken in der Weimar Republik: Die politischen Ideen der deutschen Nationalisten zwischen 1918 und 1993* (Munich: Nymphenburger, 1968).

27. Stephen Eric Bronner, "Persistent Memories: Jewish Activists and the German Revolution of 1914," *New Politics* 5, no. 2 (Winter 1995): 83–94.

antry and the petty bourgeoisie. Eisner was killed,[28] Toller was imprisoned, and other political artists, like Bertolt Brecht and Lion Feuchtwanger, moved to Berlin. Munich lost its position as the cultural center of Germany; it was left in the grips of reaction, and its politics exemplified what would become an ever stronger right-wing threat to the Weimar Republic.[29]

Anti-Semitism, xenophobia, ultranationalism, authoritarianism, and provincialism were all in the air. Right-wing politicians sprang up all over Munich, the most prominent among them unquestionably General Erich von Ludendorff. Ludendorff had served as the principal commander of the German army during World War I, and, notoriously, he was among the first to propagate the legend that the country had lost the war because it had been "stabbed in the back" by "defeatist" and "alien" elements on the home front. Hitler, just as after his discharge in 1920, joined what would soon become the German National Socialist Workers' Party (NSDAP), and the former corporal immediately showed his talent as an organizer and as orator on the streets and in beer halls. He soon came to dominate the organization, and he made contacts among the industrialists, disaffected elements of the army, and various cultural circles. His appeal must have been extraordinary, for almost instantaneously Hitler became a leading figure on the far right. By 1923, in fact, he felt his support strong enough to ally himself with Ludendorff in staging what became known as the Beer Hall Putsch. The attempt failed, and after a sensational political trial in 1923, Hitler was convicted of treason and sentenced to only three years in jail.

While behind bars, fearing the future and contemplating suicide, Hitler wrote his only sustained political work in the form of a self-serving autobiography, *Mein Kampf*. Its blurry neoromanticism merges with a megalomaniacal decisionism; its social Darwinism justifies racial elitism; its anti-intellectualism fosters xenophobia; and its unlimited belief in imperialism is propelled by memories of the "brotherhood of the trenches." It offers the vision of a racially pure people unified under an authoritarian state and identified with a single leader committed to regaining the dominant position

---

28. Werner Maser, *Der Sturm auf die Republik: Frühgeschichte der NSDAP* (Düsseldorf: Econ, 1994), 14 ff.; a superb literary portrait of the cultural reaction in Munich during this period is provided by Lion Feuchtwanger, in *Erfolg* (Frankfurt am Main: Aufbau, 1988).

29. Eugene Davidson, *The Making of Adolf Hitler: The Birth and Rise of Nazism* (London: Macmillan, 1977), 150 ff.

of Germany in the world by any means necessary. It already makes evident what would become the guiding slogan of the "New Germany": "One People, One Leader, One Empire" *(Ein Volk, Ein Führer, Ein Reich).* The great man finds his master race, and the people exemplifying this race retains a "moral right to engage in colonial politics." The calls for law and order in the name of a "return to normal life," skillfully employed later against the "Reds," appear impelled by something very different. Hitler saw the disjunction between the politician and the theorist, the practitioner and the visionary, and in *Mein Kampf* he evidences a desire to overcome it: "For if the art of the politician is really the art of the possible, the theoretician is one of those of whom it can be said that they are pleasing to the gods only if they demand and want the impossible. . . . In the long periods of humanity, it may happen once that the politician is wedded to the theoretician."[30]

Mein Kampf is a poorly written work, illogical in its argumentation and haphazard in its construction, infused with paranoia, megalomania, and visions of contemporary "decay" and future destruction. It substitutes a pathos-laden *Weltanschauung* infused with a pathological anti-Semitism for any genuine political theory, and its populism is opportunistic from the very beginning. The very title of the Nazi party—the German National Socialist Workers' Party—reflects the opportunistic attempt to appeal to conservatives, nationalists, socialists, and communists. And the same holds true for the book. It is far less concerned with presenting a program than venting hatred against the "system" and its "degenerate" supporters. Hitler's autobiography manifests a paranoic quality. But it is mixed with shrewd political insight. He notes how a future political victory will rely less on a coup than on using a mass movement to turn democracy against itself. Much has also been made of Hitler's perception regarding the future possibilities of mass media, his understanding of propaganda, and the role of the "big lie." His most important tactical insight, however, was informed by his pathology. Others had pitted fascism against the ideas of liberalism and Marxism, the values of cosmopolitanism and humanism, the interests of capitalists and "Reds," and the "defeatists" at the homefront as well as "the war criminals" who had signed an ignoble peace treaty and created a new republican state. Hitler was the first politician, if not theoretician, to portray his enemies in a single image: that of the Jew.[31]

---

30. Adolf Hitler, *Mein Kampf,* trans. Ralph Mannheim (Boston: Houghton Mifflin, 1971), 212.

31. Note the seminal study by Saul Friedländer, *Nazi Germany and the Jews: The Years of Persecution, 1933–1939* (New York: Harper Perennial, 1997).

Absolute power demands an absolute enemy. Therein lies the essence of totalitarianism. It dramatizes the fundamental conflict, explicitly formulated by Carl Schmitt, between "friend" and "enemy." The victim now deserves the hunger, the sores, the lice, the blows, the excrement, and the arbitrary introduction of death. Stalin and Mao consistently redefined the "enemy": there was always a new conspiracy being launched against the regime by a new group of plotters. In Nazi Germany, however, the enemy remained constant. It was the Jew. The Jew was biologically and cosmologically the incarnation of evil, and his or her existence created a situation in which the refinement of sadism could take on its own logic. This is where the insane medical experiments come into play, the euthanasia, and the regularized forms of degradation practiced in the concentration camps.

Nazi practice was shaped by its racialist ideology. In 1942, just after Hitler had opened a second front against the Soviet Union, he gave official sanction to the "final solution" of the Jewish "problem." This program of annihilation transformed the concentration camps into death camps and identified the regime with an exercise of arbitrary power previously unknown and unimagined.[32] The war against the Jews was pursued neither for instrumental gain nor military advantage. It was undertaken instead for ideological reasons. The extermination of the Jews was indeed only the preamble: gypsies, Slavs, homosexuals, and others would follow. Hannah Arendt saw the matter clearly when she wrote:

> Violence has always been the *ultima ratio* in political action and power has always been the visible expression of rule and government. But neither had ever before been the conscious aims of the body politic or the ultimate goal of any definite policy. For power left to itself can achieve nothing but more power, and violence administered for power's (and not for the law's) sake turns into a destructive principle that will not stop until there is nothing left to violate.[33]

Nazism was totalitarian in its attempt to empty the world of people and people of their individuality. It was the unremitting assault on the Other and, simultaneously, the expression of self-hatred; it was the fulfillment of

---

32. Eugen Kogon, *The Theory and Practice of Hell: The German Concentration Camps and the System behind Them*, trans. Heinz Norden (New York: Berkeley, 1975).

33. Hannah Arendt, *The Origins of Totalitarianism* (Cleveland: Meridian, 1951), 137.

the arbitrary use of power advocated by the initiators of fascism. Nazism was the ideology, paraphrasing T. S. Eliot, of hollow men. This indeed is what made it the quintessential symbol of evil for a century not lacking in competitors for that honor.

The 1930s still weighs like a nightmare on the living, and understandably so. The past decade of the century has not been kind. Skinheads desecrated hundreds of synagogues in Europe, racism remains a cancer in the United States, and "ethnic cleansing" in the former Yugoslavia elicits memories of an even darker time. Pogroms have been recorded in Rumania. Street gangs recall the Brownshirts elsewhere in Eastern Europe. *The Protocols of the Elders of Zion* sells briskly not only in the Baltic states but also in the United States, both among the extremist "militias" in the western part of the country as well as among supporters of the Nation of Islam in the ghettos of the inner cities. Anti-Semitic organizations like L'Oeuvre Française still catch the public eye, and roaming groups of thugs obviously remain dangerous, especially when, as in cities like Dresden and Leipzig, their assaults on immigrants are given tacit and sometimes even explicit support by the police and the populace. But current estimates are that hard-line advocates of the far right explicitly indebted to the prewar movements number only a few thousand, if that, in most nations of Western Europe. They are a lunatic fringe, without serious institutional influence, condemned from all sides. The real enemy today is different: it is neofascism.

Neofascism also has its history.[34] After World War II, many former fascists and former Nazis sought to reconstitute their movements and ideas.[35] Following his release from prison, the important British fascist, Oswald Mosley, became the driving force behind "Eurofascism," though the political attempt to create a type of "fascist international" quickly came into conflict with the xenophobic ideology underpinning the entire enterprise. Paramilitary organizations were also formed, along with networks of right-wing sympathizers, publications, pressure groups, and parties of various kinds, whose most important representative was probably the Italian Social Movement (MSI), created in 1946, which would profoundly inspire later fascist developments in Italy.

---

34. Eatwell, *Fascism*, 245 ff.; Laqueur, *Fascism*, 93 ff.
35. Note the excellent collection of writings by postwar fascists in *Fascism*, ed. Roger Griffith (New York: Oxford University Press, 1995), 315 ff.

There were also theorists. Julius Evola, perhaps the most important fascist philosopher of the postwar society, liked to bemoan the loss of a warrior–priest society. Leon Degrelle, the former leader of the Belgian fascists known as the Rexists, waxed poetic from his Spanish exile about the ideals of the past. Numerous other dissident fascists like A. K. Chesterton, Gerhard Frey, Ernst Niekisch, and a host of others wrote about the way their ideals had been betrayed. Marshal Philippe Pétain, even today, has his following. Nevertheless, these were all men of the past.

Younger fascists like Alain de Benoist and the intellectuals associated with the French New Right have sought to engage in a "cultural war" against the loss of identity—or "difference"—attendant upon an imperialistic "Coca-Cola culture" and the creation of new international institutions. More innovative types have also attempted to link ecological concerns about preserving the environment with racist concerns about preserving the "nation." Ernst Nolte initiated a major debate in an attempt to relativize the Holocaust,[36] and other less respectable scholars associated with the *Historical Review* have gone even further.[37]

Some contemporary fascists still harken back to the lessons of Mussolini, if not Hitler. They still inveigh against declining "morals" and "alien" elements. They still advocate the constriction of civil liberties, the repression of "particular interests," and a variant of "integral nationalism." They condemn feminism; they remain homophobic; and they still offer a scapegoat, albeit the outsider or the immigrant rather than the Jew. Their intolerance toward multiethnicity still contaminates cultural life, and they undermine faith in "politicians," if not yet in democratic government.

There is a temptation to draw parallels with earlier times. But it is misguided. The world has become different from what it was in the 1920s and 1930s. The labor movement no longer poses the same threat, economic conditions are radically different, and the "culture industry" has made it increasingly difficult to insulate a nation for purposes of indoctrination or even to identify a single enemy in the manner of times past. Especially in the Western democracies, if not in nations like Yugoslavia, fascism has lost its

36. Note the collection entitled *Forever in the Shadow of Hitler? Original Documents of the "Historikerstreit": The Controversy Concerning the Singularity of the Holocaust*, trans. James Knowlton and Truett Cates (Atlantic Highlands, N.J.: Humanities Press International, 1993).
37. Deborah E. Lipstadt, *Denying the Holocaust: The Growing Assault on Truth and Memory* (New York: Plume, 1993).

legitimacy amid the ashes of Auschwitz. The new movements of the far right have had to temper their rhetoric, change their tactics, and moderate their goals. They no longer speak of war or imperialist expansion. They no longer present themselves as revolutionary. They no longer employ the cult of the leader or paramilitary organizations.

Neofascists may cynically use the rednecks and Neanderthals in the streets, but they disavow them later. They may secretly hold democracy in contempt, but they call themselves "republicans" or even "liberals" and refuse any explicit endorsement of dictatorship. They remain racists, but they shy away from rigid ideological doctrines to support their views. They oppose "politics" and "politicians," but they take pains to appear "reasonable." Neofascists, at least for now, remain content to play power broker. They have no other choice. The Austrian Freedom Party of Jorg Haider may lead a government following an electoral victory. But nothing suggests that the extreme right can actually seize absolute power in a major European state. A greater danger indeed has become the potential impact of neofascism on the respectable establishment. The most pressing problem is the influence that organized and well-financed right-wing movements exert on mainstream conservative parties whose more reactionary factions may actually have helped legitimate the activities of the far right in the first place.

Mainstream political figures who once stood in support of strengthening the European Community now, ever more frequently, employ organicist notions of integral nationalism to denounce its imperializing ambitions. Attempts in Germany to insulate the *Volkstaat* from the Nazi past, attempts to exclude the children of Moroccan parents from French citizenship by supplanting the "law of the soil" with the "law of blood," and the racist immigration policy advocated by the English Tories are often nothing more than establishmentarian attempts to integrate, or pacify, more extreme sentiments. The far right has obviously had a profound impact on shaping both the foreign and domestic policy of Benjamin Netanyahu and his Likud government, and Yasir Arafat has had to deal with terrorist organizations like Hamas. Vehement rhetorical and sometimes physical assaults on immigrants have become part of the European landscape, and in the United States, the Reverend Louis Farrakhan has had a genuine influence on African American politics. It is even worse in France. Once respectable figures like Valéry Giscard d'Estaing of the moderate Union for French Democracy have actually spoken of an Arab "invasion," and Gaullists like Jacques Chirac, who previously decried the "smell" stemming from an "overdose" of immigrants, are now challenged for their "moderation" in fighting the "immigration lobby" and the forces of "cosmopolitanism" by Jean-Marie Le Pen and the National Front.[38]

But these are not the only political forms in which neofascism can present itself. Especially in certain Islamic nations, but also among groups on the far right in the United States and elsewhere, it cloaks itself in religious garb. "Clerical fascism" was already identified as a possibility in the 1920s with the attempt by certain organized groups to merge their Catholic beliefs with a commitment to the New Rome. Its religious underpinnings, of course, make fundamentalism irreducible to conventional notions of fascism or neofascism. But the "elective affinity," to use Max Weber's term, between fundamentalism and authoritarianism is pronounced. The two share a similar notion of community, and fundamentalism offers, perhaps, an even more powerful form of existential self-definition. Fundamentalism is also always a movement of the masses, and it retains a profound disdain for the Enlightenment political legacy. Above all, however, it rejects modern individualism and, most importantly, any genuine encounter with the Other. There is indeed little exaggeration in the claim that "it is impossible for fundamentalists to argue or settle anything with people who do not share their commitment to an authority, whether it be an inerrant Bible, an infallible Pope, the *Shari'a* codes in Islam, or the implications of *halacha* in Judaism."[39]

Fundamentalism is among the dominant ideological phenomena of the age, and its authoritarian, or neofascist, implications for world politics are enormous. In the West, however, neofascism remains a movement on the defensive. Its intellectual representatives are unimpressive: there is no one with the stature of an Ezra Pound or a Carl Schmitt. Its leaders lack the daring and the flamboyance of their predecessors. Its ideology consists of little more than fear: fear of immigrants, fear of open borders, fear of international organizations, fear of cultural change. Its message is provincial: immigrants cost jobs, international organizations threaten identity, and the decline of religion creates a decline in public morals. As for the past, it remains stuck in their throats. The neofascists can neither swallow it down nor vomit it up. And that will always prove their undoing.

38. See Michalina Vaughan, "The Extreme Right in France: 'LePenism,' or the Politics of Fear," and Douglas Johnson, "The New Right in France," in *Neo-Fascism in Europe*, ed. Luciano Cheles et. al (London: Longman, 1991).

39. Martin E. Marty, "Fundamentalism as a Social Phenomenon," *Bulletin of the American Academy of Arts and Sciences*, no. 42 (1988): 22.

9

Communism: Revolution, Dictatorship, Totalitarianism

W orld War I produced the "great betrayal." In 1914, outside of Italy, social democratic parties everywhere endorsed the bellicose policies of their particular nation-states. Roughly the same coalition of bureaucrats, nationalists, and rank opportunists had everywhere traditionally supported imperialism and economic protectionism. They believed war would give social democracy the chance to cement a "partnership" with their governments and enter the world of "real politics." The explosion of hostilities put prior commitments to internationalism, democracy, and economic justice on hold in favor of a new "civil truce," or class alliance, with the bourgeoisie and the existing regime usually ruled by the aristocracy. Rosa Luxemburg was correct when she predicted the new "partnership" would become a sham, social democracy would lose its independence, and the proletariat would pay a high price for the compromises undertaken by its representatives.[1]

There is a sense, of course, in which social democracy found itself presented with a fait accompli.[2] Committed activists and intellectuals were ini-

---

1. Rosa Luxemburg, "The Junius Pamphlet: The Crisis in the German Social Democracy," in *Rosa Luxemburg Speaks*, ed. Mary Alice Waters (New York: Pathfinder, 1970); also, note the response by V. I. Lenin, "On The Junius Pamphlet," ibid.

2. Stephen Eric Bronner, *Moments of Decision: Political History and the Crises of Radicalism* (New York: Routledge, 1992), 15; Eric Hobsbawm, *The Age of Extremes: A History of the World, 1914–1991* (New York: Vintage, 1996), 22 ff.

tially left in a quandary when the war broke out: support would invite the cry of hypocrisy; neutrality or passivity would produce charges of vacillation; and radical opposition would bring on shouts of treason and sectarianism. Most of the major figures associated with social democracy were skeptical about the war. Some gave their support because of their fear of Russian absolutism and its imperialist ambitions; others feared having their domestic organization crushed by the introduction of emergency decrees at home. But history has little use for excuses. The Second International collapsed, along with the "iron unity" of the working class: the principled commitment to pacifism, democracy, and noninterference in the national affairs of member parties, ironically, had made the organization incapable of assuring compliance with its dictates.

As the years passed, as the corpses mounted, a new communist movement—a "wind from the East"—swept away the militants of the left disillusioned with social democracy.[3] They looked with wonder to Lenin, who had transformed a small sect into a world-historical revolutionary force.[4] They understood his emphasis on discipline and his unsentimental bearing. They identified with his mixture of intransigence and pragmatism. They applauded his willingness to offend even the left wing of international social democracy when, in 1914, he called upon the workers of the world to turn the international conflict among nations into an international class war. They agreed with his explanation of the war as having been generated by imperialist competition over colonies among nations under the sway of finance capital and with the connivance of a social democratic "labor aristocracy." They admired his bold claim that the revolution would occur "at the weakest link in the chain" and the daring he showed in making good on his

3. Different perspectives on the general history of the movement are provided by Franz Borkenau, *World Communism: A History of the Communist International* (Ann Arbor: University of Michigan Press, 1962); Stephen Eric Bronner, *Socialism Unbound* (New York: Routledge, 1990), 76–126; Fernando Claudin, *The Communist Movement: From Comintern to Cominform*, 2 vols., trans. Brian Pearce (New York: Monthly Review, 1975); Arthur Rosenberg, *A History of Bolshevism* (Garden City, N.Y.: Doubleday, 1967); and Bertram D. Wolfe, *Three Who Made a Revolution* (Boston: Beacon, 1955).

4. Works of general interest include Angelica Balabanoff, *Impressions of Lenin*, trans. Isotta Cesari (Ann Arbor: University of Michigan Press, 1968); Neil Harding, *Leninism* (Durham: Duke University Press, 1996); Leon Trotsky, *Lenin: Notes for a Biographer*, trans. Tamara Deutscher (New York: Putnam, 1971); and Dmitri Antonovich Volkogonov, *Lenin*, ed. and trans. Harold Shukman (New York: Free Press, 1994).

prediction. Workers now saw an alternative to social democracy in the form of the new "communist" movements whose name reflected a reassertion of the revolutionary ideals originally associated with the writings of Marx and Engels.

Leninist political theory mixed organizational authoritarianism with voluntarism from the very beginning. It was born in 1902 with the split in the Russian Social Democratic Party between the Mensheviks, who wished to import the democratic structure of European socialist parties, and the Bolsheviks, led by Lenin. This latter group of younger activists essentially believed that the political repression and economic backwardness of the Russian empire rendered a social democratic mass party along European lines impossible. Inspired by the more radical elements of Jacobinism, along with the uncompromising voluntarism of figures like Louis-Auguste Blanqui, Lenin and the Bolsheviks originally advocated the transformation of Russian social democracy into a "vanguard party" whose military structure would enable it to operate underground and effectively organize the interests of both a tiny working class and a huge peasantry. The ostensible purpose for this new form of party organization was to realize the democratic aims of orthodox Marxism under radically different circumstances or, putting it in slightly different terms, organizing the popular will to action. Indeed, Lenin's classic text of 1902, "What Is to Be Done?," made clear that this undertaking should leave the party accountable to neither class and should subordinate the quest for immediate economic reforms to the ultimate concern with political revolution.

"The actuality of revolution," the attempt to place revolution on the historical agenda as a practical reality, was the guiding principle behind Lenin's thought.[5] He was concerned not merely with power for his "vanguard" but with an international assault on capitalism and imperialism. His radical purpose was less to establish "socialism in one country" than to foster revolution throughout the world under the aegis of the new communist international. His critique of reformism had both a practical and a theoretical dimension. Economic reform for the proletariat would obviously prove difficult to achieve in an industrially backward society where peasants, whose interests were often radically different from those of workers, constituted the vast majority. Lenin maintained the need for reforms but only in-

---

5. Georg Lukács, *Lenin: A Study on the Unity of His Thought*, trans. Nicholas Jacobs (Cambridge: MIT Press, 1970), 11.

sofar as they would help foster the revolutionary spirit of the movement. The problem was nonetheless obvious. The ability to recognize the need for revolution already presupposed a high level of political development. Economic exploitation alone, according to Lenin, would not produce revolution; it was rather a matter of building the consciousness necessary for bringing it about. "The history of all countries," according to Lenin, "shows that the working class, exclusively by its own effort, is able to develop only trade union consciousness."[6]

The party must step into the breach. Composed of "professional revolutionary intellectuals" capable of preserving the vision of a revolution from the temptations posed by reform, the "vanguard party" would have to bring workers an understanding of their political mission from "outside" their ranks. Organized in military style, along the principles of "democratic centralism," the feelings of members in local cells would rise up the ladder of party councils and organs until the "central committee" issued a decision, which all cells would have to support in public. A radical division was, from the very start, seen as existing between those outside and those inside the organization. The party incarnated the possibility of socialism, the "true interests" of the working class, and any criticism, first from outside and then from inside its ranks, evidenced only "false consciousness." Leon Trotsky was prophetic when he stated, in 1902, that Lenin's theory comes down to this: the party will substitute itself for the class, the central committee will substitute itself for the party, and ultimately a single dictator will substitute himself for the central committee.

Lenin never argued the matter in philosophical terms, but the logic of his thinking called for the vanguard party to supplant the working class as the vehicle or "agent" for realizing the teleological aims of Marxist theory. There was a basic sense in which he no longer considered it possible for workers to know their own interest. This distinguished him from the other main figures in the social democratic movement. Lenin exhibited none of the humanism or principled commitment to liberal values associated with figures like Karl Kautsky, Eduard Bernstein, Jean Jaurès, and Rosa Luxemburg. All of them were intellectuals, most came from bourgeois circumstances, and Kautsky himself recognized the primacy of the political party in forging the movement. None of these social democrats, however, was

---

6. V. I. Lenin, "What Is to Be Done?" in Lenin, *Selected Works* (Moscow: Progress, 1970), 1:143.

quite as willing as Lenin to draw the organizational, voluntaristic, and sectarian consequences of the claim made in *The Communist Manifesto* that a revolution could only occur once a certain segment of the ruling class had "broken off" and joined the exploited in its quest for power.[7]

Lenin made the seizure of state power, the creation of a "dictatorship of the proletariat," into the priority of the socialist movement. Although prior to 1917 he was a staunch advocate of a "two-stage" theory of revolution whereby a "bourgeois" phase would have to precede the "proletarian" transformation, his thinking reflected a new notion of organization as well as the voluntaristic longings for action of the exploited in an economically underdeveloped situation. Orthodox Marxism could only call for patience, and that was obviously insufficient. Trotsky had already come to terms with this dilemma in 1905 with the help of Alexander Helphand (also known as Parvus). To justify radical political intervention in the tumultuous events of that year and the attempt to create new organs of popular democracy, Trotsky,[8] the brilliant leader of the St. Petersburg Soviet, and his friend Parvus,[9] a close associate of Rosa Luxemburg, developed the notion of the "permanent revolution."[10]

The basic idea was simple enough: it was both possible and necessary to fuse the two stages of the revolution into one process. France had experienced a bourgeois revolution in 1789 without a fully developed bourgeoisie, and so logically, in nations like Russia, there was no reason the first stage of the revolution could not be pushed into the second, proletarian, stage, even where a proletariat did not constitute the majority of society. In this way issues of revolution became less a matter of "ripe" economic conditions

7. "A small section of the ruling class cuts itself adrift, and joins the revolutionary class, the class that holds the future in its hands. . . . [But, in contrast to Lenin, for Marx and Engels, the Communists] do not form a separate party opposed to other working-class parties. They have no interests separate and apart from those of the proletariat as a whole. They do not set up any sectarian principles of their own, by which to shape and mould the proletarian movement." Karl Marx and Frederick Engels, "The Communist Manifesto," in Marx and Engels, *Selected Works* (Moscow: Progress, 1969), 1:117, 19.

8. Isaac Deutscher, *The Prophet Armed: Trotsky, 1879–1921*; *The Prophet Unarmed: Trotsky, 1921–1924*; and *The Prophet Outcast: Trotsky, 1929–1940* (New York: Vintage, 1965).

9. Z. A. B. Zeman and W. B. Scharlau, *The Merchant of Revolution: The Life of Alexander Israel Helphand (Parvus)* (New York: Oxford University Press, 1965).

10. Leon Trotsky, *The Permanent Revolution and Results and Prospects* (New York: Pathfinder, 1977).

than of political will. Neither Trotsky nor Parvus, who later drifted away from the movement, ever contemplated the need for a new form of political organization by which the general will of various exploited classes might receive expression. This was, of course, precisely the purpose of the "vanguard party" introduced by Lenin.

Trotsky and Parvus both shied away from its authoritarian implications. The Russian Revolution, however, was not originally predicated on authoritarian principles. The first upheaval took place in February 1917. A "provisional government" promised "bourgeois" democracy in the form of a new constituent assembly, which would undoubtedly have marginalized the proletarian parties by others grounded in the peasantry and the existing order; Lenin responded by employing the more radical democratic slogan of "All power to the soviets." His famous pamphlet, "State and Revolution," published after the communist seizure of power in November 1917, emphasized the manner in which class interest, rather than commitment to any particular governmental form, is alone crucial for a revolutionary perspective, and he called for "a state which is no longer a state in the proper sense of the word."[11] The soviets never ruled Russia, and as early as 1905 Lenin was skeptical about their actual utility. But support for them was a useful means for the Bolsheviks to challenge the provisional government in the name of a "dictatorship of the proletariat and peasantry." The first stage of the revolution was pushed into the second stage, the revolution became "permanent," and many believed it was possible for an authoritarian party like the Bolsheviks and a democratic institutional form like the soviets to coexist.

The civil war between partisans and enemies of the revolution destroyed that possibility, if it ever truly existed in the first place, but even many anarchists initially felt ethically called upon to support the Reds against the reactionary Whites. It only made sense for Lenin to have embraced the "permanent revolution" and the talents of Trotsky, who, for his part, decided to join the Bolsheviks as a member of the Central Committee in 1917. Events dictated their new alliance as a utopian halo of radical democracy and solidarity was cast over the revolution during its early "heroic" phase.

The Russian Revolution was a world historical event. It was greeted by revolutionary uprisings throughout Europe. These failed, and by 1923 the Soviet Union was clearly on its own. Internationalism made way for a new nationalism among communists everywhere, focused on the "homeland of

---

11. V. I. Lenin, "The State and Revolution," in Lenin, *Selected Works*, vol. 2.

the revolution." But this expressed something more. The revolution had proved itself successful in the least developed, rather than the most developed, capitalist nation. It was carried out in a society dominated by peasants, rather than workers, and in an empire renowned for its repression of national minorities. It ever more surely symbolized an anti-imperialist revolution carried out in the name of the right to national self-determination, and it reflected what would become the last great shift in the locus of revolutionary action to the underdeveloped nations.

"Imperialism: The Highest Stage of Capitalism,"[12] which was undoubtedly Lenin's finest theoretical effort, brought the masses of the colonized world into the center of the revolutionary discourse. Lenin understood imperialism as arising from an organizational restructuring of capitalism in which banks and "finance capital" dominated other sectors of the economy. This development rendered production more efficient and, in turn, made the export of an overproduced surplus necessary. Competition for colonies among advanced or hegemonic nations was a logical consequence. "Superprofits" would accrue from them, by which it would become possible for the imperialist state to "buy off" its working-class parties with social welfare policies. Short-sighted prospects for economic reform would subsequently defuse long-term revolutionary commitments. Exploitation would become concentrated in the colonies, and indeed a "labor aristocracy" would actually benefit from the sufferings of the truly "wretched of the earth." As for the party in the colonial setting, without an indigenous working class or bourgeoisie, it would have to organize as a national coalition against the "imperialist" aggressor in the first phase of the revolution and only then take the next revolutionary step: the party must, in short, lead the struggle against imperialism before connecting it with the struggle against capitalism.[13]

"Imperialism: The Highest Stage of Capitalism" assumes that the drive for colonies is an economic necessity rather than a political choice; it dismisses the possibility of "socialist imperialism"; it ignores the extent to which trade still mostly occurs between the advanced nations; it mistakenly identifies imperialism with the last and "highest" phase of capitalism; and it offers a basically polemical view of the "labor aristocracy." But it also

---

12. Lenin, *Selected Works*, vol. 1.
13. For a more extensive interpretation of the pamphlet's explanatory power, see Bronner, *Socialism Unbound*, 116 ff.

serves as a plausible explanation for a number of historical developments from a very new perspective. This interpretation of events shows the genesis of World War I in terms of an intrinsic connection between militarism, imperialism, and capitalism. It explains why Western working-class political parties should have supported their nation-states in World War I. It gives a reason why revolution occurred not in the advanced capitalist nations but rather in Russia, at the "weakest link in the chain." It indeed also suggests that, in an underdeveloped territory, the party must make the revolution "permanent" and ultimately link the national struggle against imperialism with broader international concerns.

Lenin's *Imperialism* and Trotsky's theory of the "permanent revolution" together provide a viable way of understanding the Russian Revolution from within Marxist theory. But the perspective they offer undercuts the philosophical coherence of the doctrine. The Marxist feminist and antiwar activist, Clara Zetkin, put this plainly when, in 1917, she offered the following justification for the communist revolution: "The Russian proletarians and peasants are ripe for revolution and for the seizure of power because they want the revolution and state power and they are not afraid to fight for it."[14] Such a stance, of course, has nothing to do with Marxism. Social democratic defenders of Marxist orthodoxy, indeed, immediately noted the lack of material conditions for a successful revolutionary enterprise, and they saw this at the base of the communist recourse to terror and authoritarianism.

Thus, Antonio Gramsci was not alone in viewing the Russian Revolution as a revolution "against *Capital*."[15] Born a hunchback in Sardinia in 1891, profoundly influenced by the writings of Croce and Antonio Labriola, Gramsci began his political work in the socialist movement. But the future author of the legendary *Prison Notebooks*, written while he was incarcerated by Mussolini's regime,[16] became disillusioned with its economic determinism and its rigid view of historical stages. Furthermore, in contrast with

14. Clara Zetkin, "The Battle for Power and Peace in Russia," in *Selected Writings*, ed. Philip S. Foner (New York: International, 1984), 140.

15. Antonio Gramsci, "The Revolution against *Capital*," in *Selections from Political Writings, 1910–1920*, ed. Quintin Hoare, trans. John Mathews (New York: International, 1977), 36.

16. See Carl Boggs, *The Two Revolutions: Gramsci and the Dilemmas of Western Marxism* (Cambridge, Mass.: South End, 1984), 37 ff. and passim; Giuseppe Fiori, *Antonio Gramsci: Life of a Revolutionary*, trans. Tom Nairn (New York: Schocken, 1970); and James Joll, *Antonio Gramsci* (New York: Viking, 1978).

the majority of social democrats, Gramsci welcomed the Russian Revolution, along with its original slogan, "All power to the soviets."

He sought to introduce both into Italy in the aftermath of World War I during the strike wave of the early 1920s in Turin and other parts of what would become the industrialized "Red belt" of the North. But the experiment failed, and Gramsci began a period of reflection. He came to see the source of the problem in the existence of what Lenin had originally termed "uneven development," the backwardness of southern Italy, and the cultural constraints on political action. Gramsci recognized the manner in which exploitation and the existing state apparatus rest upon cultural institutions like the Catholic Church and that an assault upon the "hegemony" of the existing order would demand a more radical set of counterhegemonic educational commitments by a vanguard willing to act as a "modern prince" in bringing revolution to the whole of Italy.[17]

Gramsci built on Lenin's voluntarism, radicalized it, and arguably even gave it a democratic twist. But for all that, Gramsci never criticized the terms under which the Third International was formed in 1920. He was a proponent of Lenin's famous "Twenty-one Points,"[18] by which all groups wishing to participate were called upon to accept the "vanguard" form of party organization and their subordination to the dictates of the Communist International. Gramsci's preoccupation with the "national road" to socialism, in fact, led to his endorsement of Stalin, and his idea of "socialism in one country," against the revolutionary internationalism of Trotsky. There is indeed a sense in which Gramsci's death in 1937 occurred just in time to preserve his fame.

Gramsci's work is composed primarily of fragments. Confined in prison and constrained by censors, forced to contemplate the failure of the communist movement and the triumph of fascism in Italy, he became ever more removed from the momentous controversies in the Soviet Union. His writings never dealt rigorously with the inherent tension between party and soviets. He never became an advocate of civil liberties or made an appropriate connection between liberalism and socialism. Most unfortunately, however,

---

17. Note Gramsci's famous reinterpretation of Machiavelli in Antonio Gramsci, *Selections from the Prison Notebooks*, ed. and trans. Quintin Hoare and Geoffrey Nowell Smith (New York: International, 1971), 123 ff.

18. V. I. Lenin, "First Congress of the Communist International: Theses and Report on Bourgeois Democracy and the Dictatorship of the Proletariat," in *Selected Works*, 3:150 ff.

he did not foresee the dangers in the new form of historical voluntarism through which socialism would ultimately become identified with industrialization, and the Bolsheviks would be forced to "create the conditions needed for the total achievement of their goal."[19]

But what was the goal? The economic backwardness of the new state was undeniable. Lenin himself admitted on numerous occasions that the Soviet Union would be lucky if it entered the stage of "state capitalism" in the near future. The best for which the revolutionary masses could hope was a transformation of precapitalist conditions under state direction. But this would put the communists in the embarrassing position of having to create *artificially* the benefits of economic progress offered by capitalism without providing any of the political liberties associated with "bourgeois democracy." The only way to deal with the problem was to identify socialism with modernization *tout court*. Each step toward modernization would subsequently need to become redefined as a step toward socialism.

Teleology, in this way, became a directly political issue. It alone imbued the party with its historical "privilege," and it generated extraordinary loyalty and devotion on the part of the organization's supporters. The agent of a utopian future should not feel itself constrained by the morality of its "class enemy." The enormity of the revolutionary task facing the "vanguard" was seen as justifying the suspension of traditional ethics.[20] Normative judgment became subordinated, as a principle of political theory, to the demands of "necessity." And the party alone could define what was necessary. The Russian Revolution ironically, invalidated the teleological theory its defenders now employed to justify their actions. Communist sophistry justified the most bestial acts and the worst mistakes of the leadership.[21] The party always knew better, or so its supporters thought. "The party has a thousand eyes," wrote Bertolt Brecht in *The Measures Taken*, "we have only two."

Much has been written about the connection between Lenin and Stalin. The leader of the Russian Revolution had listed any number of possible successors other than Stalin in his famous "last testament": Leon Trotsky, Grigory Zinoviev, Nikolai Bukharin, Georgi Pyatakov, Lev Kamenev, and Josef Stalin. The first and most logical candidate to inherit Lenin's mantle would

19. Gramsci, "The Revolution against *Capital*," 36.
20. Note the discussion in Georg Lukács, "Tactics and Ethics," in *Political Writings, 1919–1929*, ed. Rodney Livingstone, trans. Michael McColgan (London: New Left, 1972), 6 ff.
21. Maurice Merleau-Ponty, *Humanism and Terror* (Boston: Beacon, 1969).

be tried in absentia and then murdered in Mexico by an agent of the Comintern; the others would be officially killed by the last and, at the time, least famous of the group. Lenin himself and his various successors might have undertaken very different programs and policies in areas ranging from the use of terror to cultural affairs. But the crucial point is that only the party was in the position to make such decisions. Lenin had no use for civil liberties. He was an advocate of state terror. He banned all "factions" within the Communist Party, and he destroyed all potentially countervailing institutions before his death. Admittedly, he considered many such measures "temporary." Nevertheless, even if the possibility need not have become reality, his theory and practice set the stage for the totalitarian regime that later emerged.

Lenin had brought Stalin into the inner circle of the party. His protégé had fought as a guerrilla when the Georgian Communist Party was underground; he had shown great administrative skill when Lenin named him general secretary; and he had written an important work on nationalism and the nationalities, commissioned by Lenin himself. Their sensibility and level of intellectual sophistication were assuredly different. But their basic views on the importance of modernization, the primacy of the party, and the national question were in accord when Stalin took over the reigns of power.[22] There should be no misunderstanding: Lenin had become concerned over the growing bureaucratic petrification within the party. Many of his remarks indicate a belief on his part that the terror, and perhaps even the dictatorship of the proletariat, was a temporary expedient. But he never recognized the imperatives of a bureaucracy to stabilize itself and grow larger. He never understood the need for democratic accountability or the importance of institutional checks and balances. The dying man, in short, offered no solutions to the governmental problems facing the Soviet Union; with respect to the question of international revolution, it had ceased to be a real possibility even before his death. Lenin himself had, indeed, already begun to speak of "socialism in one country."

The "dictatorship of the proletariat" would remain, as Stalin put it, "un-

---

22. Noteworthy biographical works include Helene Carrere d'Encausse, *Stalin: Order through Terror* (New York: Longman, 1981); Isaac Deutscher, *Stalin: A Political Biography* (New York: Oxford University Press, 1949); Leon Trotsky, *Stalin*, ed. and trans. Charles Malamuth (New York: Grosset and Dunlap, 1941); and Robert C. Tucker, *Stalin as Revolutionary, 1879–1929: A Study in History and Personality* (New York: Norton, 1973), and *Stalin in Power: The Revolution from Above, 1928–1941* (New York: Norton, 1990).

restricted by law and based in force."[23] No institutional or legal checks should curtail its power, and no institutional or legal protection would exist for minority views. The purpose of the dictatorship was still to crush the resistance of its enemies and consolidate the gains of the communist revolution.[24] Calls for its abolition were still tantamount to treason. A new society was still on the agenda. But the utopian glow had begun to fade. Alternative perspectives glimmered: Trotsky sought to reignite the prospects for international revolution and "workers' democracy," Bukharin wished to modernize in a more gradual way, and there were even suggestions calling for communists to embrace the idea of a "democratic dictatorship" and "bourgeois reforms" in their foreign policy.[25] As the Soviet Union sought to industrialize at breakneck speed during the late 1920s and 1930s, however, the totalitarian logic introduced by Lenin intensified. The country turned inward, its organizational style changed, its vibrant cultural life withered, and it began to generate a new conformity beyond what Lenin or the rest of the early Bolsheviks had ever imagined. The "transitional state" now sought to make itself permanent through an arbitrary and all-encompassing terror intent on forging history beyond any given set of constraints: its all-powerful police was now used to settle grudges, buttress a new "cult of the personality," and hide massive miscalculations in foreign policy and domestic planning.

There is little sense in speaking of political theory under Stalin. Dialectical materialism was designed and redesigned to meet the requirements of policy decisions already undertaken, even as it became the ritual catechism and the official state philosophy.[26] Marxism simultaneously became relativistic and absolute. Its critical edge was eliminated. It was no longer a question of propositions or concepts. Marxism came to mean "nothing more or less than the current pronouncement of the authority in question."[27] The idea of a better tomorrow was, of course, never repudiated. But, in fact, ever more extreme forms of voluntarism in practice produced ever more arbitrary forms of voluntarism in theory. The radical purposes for which the move-

23. See Josef Stalin, *Foundations of Leninism* (New York: International, 1939).
24. Lenin, "The State and Revolution," 299.
25. Georg Lukács, "The Blum Theses, 1928–1929," in *Political Writings, 1919–1929.*
26. The most sophisticated interpretation from within the communist camp was by Henri Lefebvre, *Dialectical Materialism*, trans. John Sturrock (London: Jonathan Cape, 1968).
27. Leszek Kolakowski, *Main Currents of Marxism*, trans. P. S. Falla (Oxford: Clarendon, 1978), 3:4.

ment originally fought—an end to the state, an end to capitalist exploitation, an end to violence, an end to egoism—became increasingly irrelevant.

The "vanguard" form of organization never had much appeal in the
West; it always attracted only a minority of the working class. It was the
same with Leninism. Western communist parties were rigidly devoted to the
soviet line, and there was little room for philosophical ingenuity. The situation was somewhat different in Eastern Europe. Many remembered the
cowardice of the Western democracies at Munich, and the Soviet Union was
originally greeted by the populace of many states as their liberator from the
Nazis. Attitudes changed, of course, as potential allies were turned into sat-
ellite nations. Few serious intellectuals had much use for the "science" of
Marxism–Leninism. Given the dominant discourse, however, it only made
sense that thinkers in the Eastern bloc should have sought to mitigate the
rule of arbitrary power through innovative interpretations of Marx and especially his humanistic *Paris Manuscripts of 1844.*

This was the case with the Hungarian Petöfi circle composed of Georg
Lukács and various of his students who insisted upon the need for democratic reform before the uprising of 1956. Adam Schaff and Leszek Kolakowski in the Poland of the 1950s used Marx to reintroduce a more liberal
and democratic way of thinking about socialism. Others, like Jacek Kuron
in the 1960s, looked to Rosa Luxemburg for inspiration. Also in Yugoslavia, during the 1960s, the "Praxis group" attempted to highlight the experience of alienation as well as the existential concerns of individuals in calling
for a humane order capable of furthering the ideals of freedom.

None of these new undertakings, however, was inspired by Leninism.
They served instead as a reaction against it. Only in the formerly colonized
territories were there genuine innovations in communist theory after World
War II. The vanguard had great appeal for movements seeking to throw off
the yoke of imperialism. That only made sense. Possibilities for organizing
the masses were nonexistent, and the liberal rule of law was not in effect.
Effective popular protest generally demanded a Leninist form of organization beyond questions regarding the specific ideology of the movement. The
emphasis placed on the party by Lenin, however, also made possible the
substitution of the peasantry for the proletariat as the primary agent of revolutionary transformation. This would indeed generate even more radical
forms of voluntarism, among whose most important theoretical and practical representatives is Mao Tse-tung.[28]

---

28. Biographical works include Eric Chou, *Mao Tse-tung: The Man and the
Myth* (New York: Stein and Day, 1982), and Ross Terrill, *Mao* (New York: Harper
and Row, 1980).

Mao Tse-tung, the most important figure in the history of Chinese communism, had learned much from the failed policy of 1927–28 in which Stalin had radically misjudged the potential for a revolutionary uprising, mistakenly insisted upon the need to organize workers in cities like Canton, and miscalculated the interests and the possibility of an "anti-imperialist" alliance with Chiang Kai-shek.[29] Communists were slaughtered by the thousands during this fateful incident. Mao Tse-tung retreated and, with the few remaining troops, undertook the famous three-thousand-mile "long march" into the countryside. With iron discipline he organized the peasantry along the way. Primacy was placed on a new class, and with its support, Mao led a national coalition against the Japanese invasion of 1938 until, with the close of World War II, he successfully turned his guns against Chiang Kai-shek and his noncommunist allies. They withdrew to the island of Taiwan following the communist victory in 1949.

Mao would, indeed, fuse a particularly authoritarian notion of the vanguard with a particularly arbitrary interpretation of the general will. His seminal essay of 1957, "On the Correct Handling of Contradictions," emphasizes that the issue is no longer merely one of class war. New forms of conflict now demand the attention of the state identified with the party. Contradictions exist between "ourselves and the enemy and [also] among the people themselves," which manifest themselves as either "antagonistic" or "nonantagonistic" and therefore demand different responses with respect to the use of coercion as against persuasion. Agitated by the specter of the Hungarian uprising of 1956, however, the Chinese communist leader immediately noted that one form of contradiction can turn into the other. The validity of the terminology is not the issue. It is rather that Mao never supplies any viable criteria for distinguishing between these two forms of contradiction. The decision regarding whether a contradiction is antagonistic or nonantagonistic—like all decisions—ultimately falls upon the party. And there is no possibility of appeal.

Therein lies the real legacy of Leninism. It was never a question of this or that tactical maneuver: the sectarianism of the 1920s, which led to disaster in Germany, the introduction of an antifascist "popular front" in the 1930s, which was marked by communist irresponsibility virtually from the beginning, or the last call for a "historic compromise" by Eurocommunists seek-

---

29. For an excellent account of this complicated event from the "inside," by the wife of an important Comintern agent of Stalin, see Margarete Buber-Neumann, *Von Potsdam nach Moskau: Stationen Eines Irrweges* (Berlin: Ullstein, 1990), 154 ff.

ing to escape the electoral ghetto of the opposition in France and Italy in the aftermath of 1968.[30] These policies have nothing to do with principle: they were pursued in the name of "national interest," and the change of line, every change of line, was philosophically buttressed by teleology. Leninism is not identifiable with this or that policy pursued by this or that regime or party in this or that country. It is predicated instead on a shift of historical agency from the class to the party, an unyielding moral commitment to the vanguard, and a blindness toward institutional dynamics.

Leninism is, strangely enough, a product of faith; it presupposes a faith in the revolutionary character of the party beyond any particular policy it might support or any particular class interest it might momentarily espouse. The party or the state is the agent of history, the vehicle for emancipatory change, beyond empirical proof. This indeterminate teleological perspective justifies divorcing the party from its connection with any class, socialism from liberalism, nationalism from internationalism, and—more generally— means from ends. Leninism is ultimately the inversion of Marxism. It no longer presupposes a proletarian majority; its notion of governance no longer builds on the democratic legacy of the revolutionary bourgeoisie; its logic no longer assumes that revolution will occur where capitalism is strongest and most fully developed; rather, it anticipates the revolution where capitalism is weakest and most undeveloped.

Leninism is ultimately a form of revolutionary romanticism. And the crisis always comes when the romantic must face reality: objective conditions always reassert themselves. The more voluntarist the enterprise and the more economically underdeveloped the nation in which the revolution takes place, the more authoritarian will the party become and the more will it employ human beings as material resources in its quest to modernize. Leninism offered the world the first "proletarian revolution," and it became a model for many of the great movements for national self-determination. But the model was rotten from the beginning. Indeed, if voluntarism is the soul of Leninism, authoritarianism is its legacy.

---

30. Carl Boggs, *The Impasse of European Communism* (Boulder: Westview, 1982).

PART III

RECLAIMING SUBJECTIVITY

10

The Liberation of Subjectivity

Totalitarianism is a term now mostly overused on the right and underemployed on the left. It is quite different from more traditional variants of authoritarianism in both form and content. Totalitarianism presupposes the attempt to monopolize every possible influence on the behavior of individuals. It can perhaps never completely succeed in eliminating freedom, just as no regime can ever completely succeed in actualizing it. But the totalitarian regime comes close in fulfilling its ideological purpose. It abolishes any separation of powers, and it breaks down all institutions capable of deflecting the power of the state and its leader: the media, the church, the union, the school, the family, the neighborhood bar. It fosters an "authoritarian personality" by atomizing individuals, alienating them, and thereby fueling their ultimately devastating emotional identification with the leader. The system depends upon masses for the murder of masses. It is not the work of a clique. The extermination of millions, the participation of millions more in that extermination, the historically innovative use of propaganda and the use of terror as a tool of policy, its monopoly over media and its myriad political and social organizations, its judiciary and its value system are not simply separable from the lived life of the community. Ethical disorientation indeed becomes a fundamental aim of totalitarian politics.

New ways of thinking seemed imperative in the later part of the twentieth century: existentialism, critical theory, and postmodernism followed one another in gaining popularity among the broad intellectual public. Each was committed to reaffirming the subjectivity of the subject, the uniqueness and integrity of the particular, against all metaphysical and teleological definitions. Each pitted the individual against bureaucracy and instrumental forms of rationality; and, with ever greater vehemence, each engaged in an assault upon established authority in the name of personal experience. Engagement, utopia, and universalist ethics lost their appeal. A grudging acceptance of liberal institutions may ultimately have made itself felt: new realms of experience arose, previously excluded groups entered the scene, outworn conventions came under attack, and traditional forms of politics were called into question. Nevertheless, ultimately, the new subjectivism left progressive forces ideologically fragmented and without any genuine moral claim on the conscience of the exploited.

Reclaiming subjectivity produced a flight from the concrete: solidarity and freedom ever more surely became divorced from issues of agency, coordination, and program. Rationalization turned into the enemy of freedom, and progress into its opposite. And perhaps that only made sense. Enlightenment notions of human perfectibility could now only appear as perverse fantasies; Hiroshima indeed offered a different *telos* for humanity or the "bourgeois subject" of progress. As for the proletariat, the "revolutionary subject" of Marxist theory, its invincibility had initially been called into question with the triumph of fascism; its "mission" had already been dramatically compromised by the nightmare in the Soviet Union; and nowhere was its "revolutionary privilege" any longer taken for granted in practical terms. Finally, with respect to the "empirical subject," things were even worse. The individual felt dwarfed by the bureaucratic apparatus and the new forms of mass murder undertaken both on the battlefield and at home among the civilian populations. The liberation of Auschwitz left a terrifying incomprehension in its wake; and with the uncovering of the gulag in the Soviet Union, the individual subject appeared bereft and forlorn within what Daniel Rousset first called a "concentration camp universe."

Writing in the aftermath of the Nazi defeat, at the height of the cold war, Albert Camus and Jean-Paul Sartre captured the mood of the age. World War II had turned them and a generation of intellectuals from bohemians into advocates of antifascist solidarity. With their emphasis on subjectivity and the absurd, responsibility and freedom, individuality and solidarity, they skyrocketed to fame. Each went from highlighting the individual experience of subjectivity to engaging in political action. But, whereas Camus was unconcerned with the effect of any criticism upon the Soviet Union in its battle with the Western democracies, Sartre was fearful of giving ideological support to the imperialist nations. The former saw solidarity in terms of support for the exploited and persecuted individual, beyond any ideology or cause, the latter understood it in terms of an *engagement* with a given movement fighting another movement. The moralist found himself isolated in what would become the anti-imperialist war in Algeria, the realist increasingly sacrificed his critical stance as a partisan of the left. The famous debate of 1952 between Camus and Sartre highlighted questions dealing with individual responsibility, political commitment, and intellectual authenticity in a particularly radical way. It would prove probably the most important controversy of the postwar period.

As *engagement* was being debated by intellectuals, however, politics was losing its militant style, and class consciousness was on the wane. An economic prosperity in the United States and Western Europe, which previously would have been unimaginable, along with the blossoming of the "culture industry" reinforced this apolitical trend. The qualitative difference between Nazism and Stalinism vanished for the majority within the Western nations. Appalled at the excesses recently committed in the name of ideology and fearful of what in the United States was called "McCarthyism," a war-weary continent turned inward. "Politics" would undoubtedly continue, but this time, as the Germans put the matter, it would carry on *"ohne mich"* (without me).

Nazis and Stalinists had innovatively and ruthlessly employed propaganda to consolidate their political power. With the rise of Hollywood and increasing production costs, however, the market in democratic societies appeared to be producing the same conformist end, even if through more gentle and seemingly apolitical means. "Culture" was indeed becoming monopolized by huge business concerns intent upon nullifying once radical or utopian ideas while simultaneously maximizing their profits by directing their goods to the lowest common intellectual denominator.

With the expansion of the standardizing "instrumental" form of reason employed by the culture industry, "authentic" experience was seemingly being undermined, and normative claims upon the system were seemingly losing their salience. Bureaucracy blossomed in all spheres of life. As the cold war settled into place, its antagonists ever more surely defined their concerns in terms of national interests, and each ever more surely sought to resolve its problems by administrative or bureaucratic means. Many on the left began to speak of "convergence"; those on the right celebrated what the important social theorist, Daniel Bell, termed "the end of ideology."

Oppression continued, of course, but the old "agents" of liberation lost their mystique. Communism had never been a serious option for Western nations, and, whereas social democracy was identifying itself with the Western welfare state, unions now purged of their more radical elements were turning the working class into just another interest group in the United States. As for Marxism, the previously hegemonic ideology of the working class, its grip on the major labor parties and the masses was slipping. It began shattering into a host of competing sectarian or purely academic interpretations in the West; in the East, its inability to make good on its utopian claims produced both resentment and cynicism.

Only within the colonized territories, where revolutionaries sought to capitalize on the postwar weakness of their imperialist masters, was there a ray of hope. New movements arose whose members were committed to the idea of national self-determination as well as what would become the subsequent quest for cultural recovery. But these movements could not alleviate the sense of broader teleological loss for the working classes, and they provided no new models for advanced industrial society. The individual was still left without existential comfort, without certainty about the future, and without purpose for his or her sacrifices. The subject was thrown back on his or her subjectivity, and this subjectivity, in turn, appeared in danger of nullification by what was considered an all-encompassing instrumental rationality. It was clearly time for theory to concern itself with the excluded possibilities of "progress," the moment of authentic experience, and the limits of establishmentarian politics and its lack of an emancipatory cultural dimension.

Critical theory and poststructuralism, no less than existentialism, sought to contest this new world of what Herbert Marcuse called "one-dimensional man." Each would constitute a distinct tradition intent on liberating subjectivity from any particular organizational affiliations or commitments. Each would help reshape the discourse of politics, sociology, literary criticism, media studies, psychoanalysis, linguistics, and the scientific method. From the standpoint of political theory, the trajectory exhibited by each is remarkably similar. Each would increasingly surrender its originally more political preoccupations in the name of more metatheoretical concerns. Each would see its notion of emancipation become increasingly indeterminate and sometimes, from a progressive standpoint, even politically suspect. Each would compromise its ability to make sense of structural imbalances of power in the name of cultural concerns or grander philosophical ambitions.

Critical theory is perhaps the most rigorous and self-contained of these three traditions. Many see its sources in cultural modernism and the writings of Nietzsche. But critical theory actually began as an outgrowth of the new "dialectical" undertaking of Georg Lukács and Karl Korsch. Along with Antonio Gramsci, whose influence would take a somewhat different form, these two thinkers were the most important representatives of "Western Marxism." *History of Class Consciousness*, by Lukács, and *Marxism and Philosophy*, by Korsch, both of which were published in 1923, employed the "method" of Marxism to call its practical shortcomings into question. Both books were intent on exploding the identification of Marxism with a finished system and divorcing social theory from its "scientific" pretensions. Their aim was to use the emancipatory ideals projected by Marxism to provide a "critique" of the way it was being politically employed and thereby create a new link between theory and practice. This reliance on the "critical" character of the "method" would indeed become the hallmark of the Frankfurt School.

Opposed to any philosophical system, which is chained to its claims and predictions, critical theory was, from the first, unconcerned with preserving this or that "truth" of Marxism. Appalled by the failings of the Russian Revolution and the growth of fascism and increasingly preoccupied with the barriers to liberation operating in the "superstructure," the Frankfurt School would ultimately revise both the Marxist understanding of capitalism and its theory of revolution. Its members hoped to illuminate those aspects of social reality that Marx and his orthodox followers had previously neglected or played down: the philosophical, psychological, and cultural forms by which the status quo was maintained.

Critical theory would always maintain a nondogmatic perspective sustained by an interest in emancipation from all forms of oppression as well as by a commitment to freedom, happiness, and a rational ordering of society. It would offer a multidisciplinary approach to society based on a combination of perspectives drawn from political economy, sociology, cultural theory, philosophy, anthropology, and history. An antidote to the hegemonic forms of positivism and behaviorism, which accommodate the status quo with their reliance on a purely "instrumental" or mathematical form of reason, critical theory was intent on overcoming the fragmentation endemic to established academic disciplines in order to address issues of common normative interest. Nevertheless, what Jürgen Habermas might term its "emancipatory interest" would become increasingly abstract in its form of presentation and metaphysical in its content.

An emancipatory interest was initially seen as incarnated within the proletariat, whose possibilities were themselves shaped by the "totality" it was intent on transforming. Critical theory had sought to aid this enterprise by fostering a new interaction between empirical research and normative concerns. With the totalitarian degeneration of the new communist state and the integration of the Western proletariat, however, there no longer seemed a "revolutionary subject" adequate for this kind of enterprise. In the shadow of Auschwitz and the gulag, concomitant upon the rise of the "culture industry," the political consciousness and tastes of individuals were increasingly becoming obliterated by the bureaucratic forces of mass society. Critical theory sought to locate the source of this development in modernity itself. The scientific assault upon myth in the Enlightenment was seen as turning upon the emancipatory norms that had guided that assault in the first place. Instrumental rationality was seen as displacing reflexivity to the same degree that technological development was defining progress, a seamless bureaucracy was assuring alienation, and reification was extinguishing any genuine notion of subjectivity.

Critical theory would subsequently seek to break with all forms of instrumental rationality, redefine progress, and reject all bureaucratic forms of social organization. Qualitative differences between regimes vanished, a negative stance emerged toward all systemic treatments of history, and an affirmation of subjectivity took place against the "totality" and against any attempt to give it objective expression. Freedom would now become stripped of its "determinations": reform would evidence nothing other than the integrating power of the "system," and subjectivity would become manifest less through political action than through aesthetic or religious forms of experience. The initial practical ambitions of critical theory gave way before increasingly metaphysical preoccupations.

Aesthetic resistance and sometimes even a certain form of religious experience now appeared as meaningful responses to the "real world." It seemed as if every possibility for authentic subjectivity and liberation was being absorbed by the culture industry. This perspective reflected the pessimistic assessment of traditional politics generally associated with critical theory. But other trends employed this new emphasis on aesthetics and subjectivity in order to justify a new form of cultural transformation with emancipatory forms of solidarity beyond those offered by traditional political parties and institutions. Radical students and intellectuals disgusted with the conformism of the 1950s saw the need for a reinvigorated utopian vision predicated on happiness, creativity, and freedom from convention to contest the motivating ideals of advanced industrial society. This would shape the way in which critical theory was appropriated by intellectuals of the New Left during the 1960s.

This was particularly the case in Europe, though even in the United States, where many of the most important texts would become translated only in the 1970s, thinkers like Erich Fromm and Herbert Marcuse enjoyed a huge following. The method and ideals of critical theory, in any event, fit with the beliefs of many intellectual activists. They were committed to a redefinition of "progress" and a new role for previously excluded groups as well as a "cultural revolution" against the conformity and repressive constraints of "the system." Critical theory may have offered little programmatic direction when it came to the new issues of participatory governance, environmentalism, and the formulation of new ethical norms. Its own shortcomings, in fact, may even have been reflected in the failings of the ultraleft intellectuals: their disregard of organizational issues, their assault on instrumental reason, and even their sectarianism. Nevertheless, there is a way in which critical theory expressed what was best and most intellectually challenging about the movement: its experimental quality, its confrontation with a stultifying form of everyday life, its rejection of the military-industrial complex, its critique of hegemonic ideology, and its cultural pluralism.

A common purpose and a reinvigorated liberalism had informed the civil rights movement and opposition to the Vietnam War in the United States. The "counterculture" resonated with utopian themes. With the collapse of the original movement in the 1970s, however, new suspicions arose concerning the manner in which the particular forms of oppression experienced by groups ranging from people of color to women and gays were being veiled by universalist categories and concerns. New forms of "identity politics" were a response to the disintegration of the civil rights movement, and the promises of modernity became susceptible to a new "postmodern" form of interrogation. There is indeed a sense in which poststructuralism became an expression in theory of this development in practice and a way in which a loosely aligned group of primarily French thinkers—Jean Baudrillard, Gilles Deleuze, Jacques Derrida, Michel Foucault, Jean-François Lyotard, and a number of others—sought to fill the need for a genuinely radical vision.

Postmodernism and *poststructuralism* are often used interchangeably.

The former usually refers to various trends expressive of a new historical phase in which the coordinating structures and universalist assumptions of modernity are no longer valid. The latter usually deals with the methodological ways in which these structures and assumptions are exposed as arbitrary and in the service of a particular form of domination. Neither postmodernism nor poststructuralism should be understood as a unified or coherent doctrine. But unifying themes exist. Virtually all their adherents maintain the need for a historicizing assault upon "essentialist" assumptions and "absolute" claims, all first principles and all utopias, teleology and ethics, idealism and positivism. Virtually all believe the connection between language and words, signifier and signified, essence and appearance, has broken down. Virtually all view any given form of meaning as an artificial social construct and reject the need for "grand narratives." Virtually all believe in the "discursive formation" of phenomena and in the identification of knowledge with power, even as they seek to resist established norms in the name of difference and plurality.

Postmodernism builds upon the extravagant notion of resistance against advanced industrial society, which was fostered by critical theory, and the concern with individual experience highlighted by the existentialists. They take from critical theory the rejection of philosophical foundations and the attack upon reification in the name of what Theodor Adorno termed a "non-identity" between subject and object. They take from existentialism a rejection of metaphysical rationalism, academic philosophy, and the preoccupation with the concrete "situation" within which people define themselves. There is a sense in which the emphasis upon reflexivity by critical theory, and humanistic engagement by the existentialists, recede from the postmodern discourse. The critical encounter with reality and the existentialist attempt to determine authenticity often surrender in favor of a comfortable relativism whose proponents are content to "play" with the rules of any given "game" and show themselves unwilling to engage in genuine self-criticism.

The postmodern world gives the experiential and the subjective center stage. Categories such as the "totality" and the "universal" are seen, following Nietzsche, as harboring nothing more than the interests of particular groups seeking to dominate other groups by identifying their concerns with those of the world at large. Universalistic theories of logic or language, for example, are seen as inherently obscuring or denying the ways in which the discourse of sexism or racism conditions our understandings of women or people of color. Objectivity is an undesirable anachronism. Computer networks and the media are turning the "real" into the "hyperreal." Reality itself is less a given than an artificial social construct, and every boundary, whether between fact and value or between science and metaphysics, is arbitrary. Old-fashioned beliefs in the absolute must now make way for a new relativism in which the viability of the repressed experience or "desire" assumes primacy.

All traditional philosophical undertakings are seen as ignoring the importance of "difference" even as they ultimately deny a given "desire" in order to bolster the status quo and particular forms of domination. Insanity and alcoholism, according to this logic, lose any scientific or medical determination. These categories label certain behaviors as negative and thereby repress certain fantasies or wishes in order to preserve social stability. It is impossible to determine what a person really "is." Or, put another way, any fixed meaning is always "absent." Experience escapes definition and militates against every attempt to objectify it. The liberation of desire from "artificial" social constraints or "hegemonic discourses" is the aim of the poststructuralist enterprise as a new preoccupation with self-definition, or "identity," becomes the political response to the homogenizing ambitions of traditional theory. The finished, the fixed, the consistent, and the systemic are its enemies. Resistance is identified with the response of the particular—of subjectivity—against all attempts to categorize it. The very attempt to regulate, to classify, to organize, produces domination in the more consequent theorists of this tendency. Its radicalism subsequently manifests itself in a challenge to all forms of discursively constructed authority.

Viewing reality as constituted by discourse, and thereby identifying knowledge with power, has its drawbacks. "Culture" simply subsumes all other forms of life, and politics loses its independence and integrity. The indeterminacy of this view makes it impossible to distinguish between the power to persuade and the power to coerce or between metaphysical and physical forms of action. It also becomes impossible to make qualitative distinctions between different kinds of programs, organizations, and regimes. The postmodern attacks on the boundaries separating different spheres of theory and practice leave politics without any form of an objective referent or any ability to speak about determinate imbalances of power. Its rejection of disciplinary boundaries as without philosophical foundations has indeed led postmodernists engaged in the humanities to attempt the deconstruction of scientific and mathematical concepts, which they know nothing about.

The assault on any definition of the "normal" in its more extreme expressions has helped marginalize its more progressive supporters. Its attack on grand narratives has itself taken the form of a grand narrative, and its inability to either situate or judge empirical events in terms of a mediated totality, or what Marx might have called the "ensemble of social relations," has fostered a situation in which entire interpretations can result from reading a snippet of text taken out of context. Its rejection of essentialism and any binding forms of commitment or truth has indeed also tended to turn political theory into just another "language game."

There is clearly a sense in which postmodernism reflects the decay of what was once "the movement" rather than its glory. Its proponents have, often justifiably, inspired outrage and controversy. Judging the phenomenon, however, also calls for understanding the reasons for its popularity. The poststructuralist assault on the absolute claims of the existing order was a protest against all organizational constraints on subjectivity, and it invigorated the radical imagination. Its explosion of any fixed connection between the signifier and the signified made possible radically new and fruitful interpretations of old themes and older texts, the questioning of petrified traditions and musty canons, and a new tolerance for new and diverse forms of cultural practice.

Cosmopolitanism underpinned the assault on the "normal" assumptions of everyday life in the name of various repressed forms of "desire," and a general feeling of reciprocity, whether actually expressed in the theory or not, was presupposed in the positive affirmation of the most diverse forms of identity. It helped lift stigmas from various groups, and it brought to the forefront those excluded from full participation in the life of the community. It provided an impetus to the expression of new experiences of subjectivity, new forms of "identity politics," and—perhaps above all—it forced Western intellectuals to see "difference" in a positive light.

None of these movements was ever really connected with a genuine mass base, and each of them, constituting a general trend, would become ever more detached from real struggles. In seeking to contest finished notions of tradition, fixed notions of totality, they denied tradition altogether and turned the attempt to make sense of a context into a purely arbitrary enterprise. They have been unable to deal with issues relating to production and distribution; they have ignored institutional dynamics; and they have turned the "anticipatory consciousness" into a subjective reflex of desire. In all these ways, to a greater or lesser degree, each has helped undermine what remains of the utopian impulse and the ability to think about the ideological conditions necessary for the creation of a broader solidarity. After its fashion, however, each also sought to free the repressed moment of subjectivity from the clutches of outworn modes of thinking. These movements privileged the moment of resistance as they brought new concerns and previously excluded groups into the limelight. In the dynamic between their excesses and their insights, indeed, lie the dilemmas of progressive politics in our time.

11

Existential Battles: Rebellion, Engagement, Authenticity[*]

Totalitarianism and mass murder created a new concern for the individual and spurred a new interest in "existentialism."[1] The trend initially had gained currency in the 1920s through the works of Martin Heidegger and Karl Jaspers. But its representatives were numerous, and they varied in their methods and conclusions. Few identified with the label, and this only makes sense, since existentialism connotes a preoccupation with individual freedom, authenticity, and the anxiety or guilt surrounding choice in an "extreme situation." Many associated with this general trend, which Georg Lukács bitingly called a form of "religious atheism," saw the world as a desert in which religion had lost its foundation and science could not deal with an increasingly grave crisis of conscience and the spirit. It seemed in the aftermath of World War II as if every absolute had been shattered, meaning had been lost, and a feeling of irremediable despair had arisen. Life had indeed become "absurd."

The term is usually associated with Albert Camus. He was, arguably, the

---

[*]A more extensive discussion is provided in Stephen Eric Bronner, *Camus: Portrait of a Moralist* (Minneapolis: University of Minnesota Press, 1999).

1. F. H. Heinemann, *Existentialism and the Modern Predicament* (New York: Harper and Row, 1953); H. Stuart Hughes, *The Obstructed Path: French Social Thought in the Years of Desperation, 1930–1960* (New York: Harper and Row, 1966); Mark Poster, *Existential Marxism in Postwar France: From Sartre to Althusser* (Princeton: Princeton University Press, 1975); James D. Wilkerson, *The Intellectual Resistance in Europe* (Cambridge: Harvard University Press, 1981).

greatest writer of the immediate postwar period. But he was not its most important philosopher, or political thinker, and he was usually uncertain with respect to the political choices facing him. Yet his story is emblematic of the crisis facing a person of conscience in the aftermath of World War II. And it deserves special attention. His refusal to commit himself to the imperialist practices of the West, the authoritarianism of the Soviet Union, or the use of terror in the name of national self-determination symbolizes the beginning of a dynamic disengagement from organized politics of a traditional sort. It projects a new preoccupation with the sanctity of the individual, a commitment to constitutionalism and human rights, which would ultimately find its fulfillment in the Eastern European revolutions of 1989. His moralism has had a far stronger political staying power than the self-professed "realism" of a far greater philosopher, his rival and contemporary, Jean-Paul Sartre.

Both were changed by World War II. The early defeat of France by the Nazis in 1940 created a short-lived unity between previously conflicting political tendencies ranging from conservatives like General Charles de Gaulle to communists as well as anarchists like Pascal Pia. Even many who were previously nonpolitical found themselves drawn into some form of opposition to Hitler and his puppet rulers of Vichy. Intense, if often short-lived, friendships were forged in cafés, through underground cultural events, and at countless meetings. The years of defeat were the ones in which Camus came to know André Gide, André Malraux, and Arthur Koestler and grew close with figures like Sartre and Simone de Beauvoir. Most of these friendships would sour after the war; understandings of responsibility and solidarity would radically differ. Nevertheless, the bitterness of defeat generated a new sense of community and a hope for the postwar renewal of France from which the legend of the Resistance was born.[2]

The Plague, surely the greatest of the novels written about the Resistance, voiced these hopes. It soon sold more than one hundred thousand copies. The novel was quickly translated into many languages, and it turned Camus into an international celebrity. Ironically, however, it was written before he had committed himself to the Resistance and before he had made his exceptional contribution both as an activist and as the editor of *Combat.* Camus

---

2. See H. Stuart Hughes, *The Obstructed Path: French Social Thought in the Years of Desperation, 1930–1960* (New York: Harper and Row, 1966); and Mark Poster, *Existential Marxism in Postwar France: From Sartre to Althusser* (Princeton: Princeton University Press, 1975).

was living in the Massif Central, far from the fighting, when he composed the work. Camus felt the war as an absence, which is precisely why he deals neither with battles nor the singular acts of wartime heroism but rather with the everyday life of a populace under siege. *The Plague* marks a shift from the attitude of solitary revolt the subject expresses in *The Stranger* and *The Myth of Sisyphus* to the recognition of a human community whose best values are grounded in solidarity.[3]

The Plague crystallized the experience of a generation sick of war, guilty about its early defeat, and suspicious about the future. It is the work in which Camus most clearly pulled together the various themes and images on which his career was built. It most clearly evidences his critique of Christianity, his refusal to love a god who lets the innocent die and who demands unconditional acceptance of the human condition. It exhibits his humanism and provides perhaps the best understanding of his political worldview. The novel reflects the values of the Popular Front and, like so many other works from the 1930s and 1940s, it has no protagonist. It is a work of great humanism and even greater moral simplicity. There are no grand words and no grand gestures. There is, in short, "no question of heroism in all of this. It's a matter of common decency. That's an idea which may make some people smile, but the only means of fighting the plague is common decency."[4]

The Plague is a novel in which freedom contests license. It portrays the existential tension between private and public commitments. Each character has his own worldview. Each makes choices and, with the exception of a collaborator named Cottard, assumes responsibility for those choices. Each has, for this reason, a different version of the events initiated by the plague. According to Camus, however, a "chronicle" is being presented: It begins with rats dying in the town of Oran. They leave the plague as their legacy, and people start becoming incurably ill. The authorities, after first attempting to play down these developments, cling to habit and refuse to accept the evidence of an epidemic. Thus, ultimately, the town is left without any plan for dealing with the emergency.

At this point, however, a motley group of individuals with very different worldviews unites; they form a "sanitation corps" to fight the plague. And

3. Albert Camus, "Letter to Roland Barthes on *The Plague*," in *Lyrical and Critical Essays*, ed. Philip Thody, trans. Ellen Conroy Kennedy (New York: Vintage, 1968), 338.
4. Albert Camus, *The Plague*, trans. Stuart Gilbert (New York: Modern Library, 1948), 150.

their strenuous efforts appear successful. But the novel offers no certainty that the struggle against the plague has ended. Quite the contrary. Resistance does not defeat the plague; it only bears witness against it. The plague seems to subside on its own, and Rieux, who ultimately emerges as the narrator of the novel, ruefully acknowledges to himself "what those jubilant crowds did not know but could have learned from books: that the plague bacillus never dies or disappears for good; . . . and that perhaps the day would come when, for the bane and enlightening of men, it would rouse up its rats again and send them forth to die in a happy city."[5]

Roland Barthes called *The Plague* a "refusal of history." And this is obviously the starting point for any criticism. Numerous critics have also noted that the real nature of fascism is ignored and the battle against an inhuman plague oversimplifies the matter of commitment. There is no reason for anyone to identify with a disease, and violence carried out against a human enemy is very different from the tactics undertaken in fighting the plague. Sartre was correct, in this regard, when he claimed that the conflicts of interest inherent within a concrete "situation" disappear. But, in a way, this critique is external to the novel. It basically attacks Camus for not having written the "realist" or "naturalist" work these critics wanted to read.

The Plague does not pretend to describe the horrors of totalitarianism in systematic fashion, nor is there a reason it should to make its point. Material and instrumental constraints on action are also less the province of an existential tale than the moral conflicts experienced by individuals. Even worse, however, the criticism of Barthes and others like Sartre obscures what is important about the work. It ignores the manner in which this ahistorical novel, paradoxically, offers a historical self-understanding of the Resistance.

Apathy appears as the enemy of subjectivity. Activists in the Resistance saw themselves as engaged in the battle against absolute evil; indeed, men and women of very different creeds united in a common project. Camus glorifies them, and perhaps, in this sense, *The Plague* helped foster what would become the "myth" of the Resistance. But there is also an element of truth in this idealized image. The Manichaean framework of good and evil employed by Camus, in fact, reflects the simplicity, no less than the moral imperative, of choosing between fascism and antifascism. Philosophical excuses for collaborating with the Nazis fall apart. Yet, in contrast with the

---

5. Ibid., 278.

carefully cultivated postwar image of an overwhelmingly popular antifascism, Camus depicts the majority of the populace as apathetic and falling back into a life of habit as the plague runs its course. A certain pessimism concerning the ineradicable character of the plague undercuts the revolutionary optimism in which France found itself enmeshed following the liberation.

Symbolically identifying totalitarianism with a plague, of course, obscures the character of a particular political system. The book perhaps even relativizes Nazism in relation to other forms of tyranny. But this is a double-edged sword. There is nothing xenophobic about the book, and that was important during a time in which anti-German sentiment was particularly strong. Evil has no name, no race, no sex, and no nationality. Camus may have considered it part of the human condition, but he also knew that it could take many forms. His intention was clear: he would refuse to identify any single form of evil "in order better to strike at them all. . . . *The Plague* can apply to any resistance against tyranny."[6]

The subject makes a free choice to resist: he is not under orders from any party. There is not a single communist among the prominent figures in the novel. Rieux, Tarrou, Grand, and Rambert are all liberal humanists; Paneloux is a Catholic. Communists played a prominent role in the French resistance and were part of the common fight against fascism. Camus's decision to omit them was surely purposeful. It was based on what had become a definitive ethical position: "There is no objection to the totalitarian attitude other than the religious or moral objection."[7]

Resistance is the province of the self-conscious subject and, for Camus, solidarity has meaning only insofar as respect for the individual is preserved. Camus had become sick of his age. He was appalled at the thought of untold millions being cynically sacrificed for the utopian dreams of dictatorial regimes. His notion of resistance would extend to all collectivist systems intent on treating the individual as a means rather than an end. Camus was, as a matter of principle, unwilling to countenance the sacrifice of the individual subject for the attainment of transcendent goals. His thinking would ultimately focus on the dangers of revolutionary utopianism and the need to achieve "a rule of conduct in secular life."[8] Rebelling against suffering and

---

6. Camus, "Letter to Roland Barthes," 340.
7. Albert Camus, *Notebooks*, trans. Justin O'Brien (New York: Paragon House, 1991), 2:97.
8. Ibid., 2:10.

seeking to "correct existence" would define his unique brand of existential politics. Such was the message of *The Plague* when it appeared in 1947, when Camus was thirty-four years old.

Understanding postwar Europe is possible only by recognizing the prestige enjoyed by the Soviet Union, particularly in many of the Western countries once controlled by Nazis and fascists. The communist nation was seen, rightly or wrongly, as having supported the Spanish loyalists and opposed the "appeasement" of Hitler. The pact between Stalin and the German dictator, which unleashed World War II and resulted in the dismemberment of Poland in 1939, was perceived by many as a defensive action caused by the vacillation of the democracies. The Soviet Union gained much sympathy for its enormous losses during the war; its citizens epitomized antifascist heroism during the great battle of Stalingrad in 1943, and its Red Army turned the tide against the Nazis. Communists also played a valiant role in the European resistance movements, and their organizations commanded the loyalty of a significant number of workers in France, Italy, and elsewhere in the aftermath of World War II. The Soviet Union was also considered the natural ally of all national liberation movements and the primary opponent of Western imperialism. The future of communism appeared bright, and the "inevitability" of revolution seemed assured.

Exiles and victims obviously knew about the murderous purges of opponents, the concentration camps, the censorship, the constant lying, the egregious policies of the Stalinist regime. There was a sense among many that a communist utopia had become ever more divorced from the bureaucratic police state intent on economic modernization in the present. But the full horror of the "dictatorship of the proletariat," and its sacrifice of millions for the dreams of an egalitarian society, was not fully grasped. Arthur Koestler, with whom Camus enjoyed a tempestuous friendship, vividly crystallized this reality for a broader public in *Darkness at Noon*.[9]

The novel describes a former Bolshevik official existentially coming to terms with his individuality, his previous beliefs and previous actions on behalf of the party, while facing death in a Stalinist prison. The novel created a sensation, and it was instantly condemned by various communist intellec-

---

9. Note also "The Initiates," Koestler's contribution to the famous anticommunist collection, *The God That Failed*, ed. Richard Crossman (New York: Bantam, 1965).

tuals, including, most notably, a different acquaintance of Camus, the important philosopher Maurice Merleau-Ponty. His rejoinder to Koestler, *Humanism and Terror,* essentially justified the authoritarian brutality of Stalinism in terms of "historical necessity" and the difficulties encountered in the march to a communist utopia. He viewed the individual as subordinate to the collective and intentions as irrelevant to the social consequences of actions. Thus, even if the "subjective" criticisms made by Koestler were true, Merleau-Ponty thought it necessary to oppose them because they "objectively" weakened the Soviet Union and strengthened its Western "imperialist" adversaries in a "cold war" whose potential for heating up could produce a nuclear catastrophe.

Camus was caught in the middle. He supported neither the Western imperialist exploitation of colonies ranging from Algeria to Vietnam nor the brutal policies in Eastern Europe practiced by the Soviet Union. Just after the war, in fact, Camus witnessed the bloody repression of the first Muslim uprising in Algeria against imperialist rule. Various conservative cliques both in France and Algeria adamantly opposed liquidating the empire. Governmental cabinet after cabinet was paralyzed, and the intransigence of the right claimed its first victim as the traditional socialist party, the Section Française International Ouvrière, gradually weakened in the face of the Algerian events and its own inability to overcome a mounting set of internal political squabbles.

And so, while the Resistance was fragmenting into communist and Gaullist tendencies, Camus increasingly found himself supporting a form of liberal socialism whose mass base was disintegrating. He refused to identify uncritically with either of the two sides. His concern about the authoritarian cliques surrounding General de Gaulle caused tensions between himself and Malraux. The communists, for their part, deplored his unwavering commitment to civil rights and republican principles.

Camus was increasingly reminded in the postwar era that he had never really articulated a view of engagement, let alone his fundamental criticisms of the communist worldview and its philosophical foundations. *The Rebel* would become his only work of political theory. It fused the personal ethic of lucidity and resistance against the inherent meaninglessness of life, which he had elaborated in *The Stranger* and *The Myth of Sisyphus,* with the notion of solidarity developed in *The Plague.* It proposed a positive political response to an "absurd" existence and a diagnosis of the "pathology" by which the age had come to view mass murder as an acceptable political option. Both aims indeed are encompassed in the title, *L'Homme revolté*, which has a double meaning in French: "the rebel" and "the disgusted or revolted man."

The Rebel is essentially divided into three parts dealing respectively with revolutionary transformation, artistic rebellion, and political ethics. The logic and categories, however, follow directly from *The Myth of Sisyphus*. The individual exists in an "absurd" universe defined by relativism and contingency. Suicide seems the only legitimate response. But that is illusory: suicide is actually nothing other than an acceptance of the absurd and its logic. An affirmation of subjectivity, a genuine rebellion, can alone oppose the notion that "everything is possible and nothing has any importance."[10] Insofar as human life assumes primary value from such a stance, however, suicide becomes as illegitimate as murder. Thus the "limit" on human action: the killing of another person is always wrong unless the murderer is himself or herself prepared to die as well. The murder of the other must be considered from the standpoint of one's own death; such is, indeed, the ultimate meaning behind the famous formulation in *The Myth of Sisyphus*: "There is but one truly serious philosophical problem, and that is suicide. Judging whether life is or is not worth living amounts to answering the fundamental question of philosophy."[11]

Reciprocity among subjects marks the "limit" to rebellion, and it also underpins Camus's belief that murder and suicide are flip sides of the same coin: one must either accept or reject them both. Recognizing this limit, however, does not produce paralysis of the individual will. Rebellion is, for Camus, a product of human nature. It is the practical expression of outrage in the face of injustice by a slave or anyone else who has experienced the transgression of an established limit by the master in any given social situation. The response is a revolt based on the desire to be recognized as a person with dignity and certain basic universal rights: "Rebellion is born of the spectacle of irrationality, confronting an unjust and incomprehensible condition. But its blind impulse is to demand order in the midst of chaos and unity in the very heart of the ephemeral. It cries out, it demands, it insists that the scandal cease and that what has, up to now, been built upon shifting sands should henceforth be founded upon rock."[12]

---

10. Albert Camus, *The Rebel*, trans. Anthony Bower (New York: Vintage, 1954), 5.

11. Albert Camus, *The Myth of Sisyphus and Other Essays*, trans. Justin O'Brien (New York: Vintage, 1955), 3.

12. Camus, *The Rebel*, 10.

Solidarity is implicit in the notion of rebellion. Thus, Camus can make his famous neo-Cartesian claim: "I rebel, therefore, we exist."[13] But too often, the sense of human solidarity and the call for reciprocity inspiring the original enterprise are forgotten. The legitimate goal of countering exploitation is used to justify tactics directly at odds with it.[14] The rebel must, using the phrase of Nietzsche, "transvalue values." He or she must inherently contest the prejudices of the established order and traditional absolutes incarnated in religion. In the twentieth century, however, revolutions have turned history and "reason" into new absolutes, harboring guarantees of a future utopia, in order to compensate for the loss of otherworldly salvation. The "absurd" thereby becomes mirrored in the actions of those seeking to abolish it. The revolutionary is willing to murder all who stand in the way of constructing a just world. The end is seen as justifying the means, and therein, for Camus, lies the "pathology" of modern totalitarianism. It becomes imperative to set and recognize limits.

The rebel must assume that life has intrinsic worth. Otherwise, he or she would not have contested injustice in the first place. The genuine rebel, for this reason, must continually strive to remember what motivated his or her undertaking in the face of political exigencies and the temptation of unethical action against others. "Memory," according to Camus, is the enemy of all totalitarians who, in seeking to break with all of history, transform themselves from revolutionaries into tyrants because they ignore the needs of real living individuals. Denying another's possibility for happiness through murder is legitimate only if one also denies it to oneself through suicide. Murder and suicide, for better or worse, now become conceptually linked. The willingness to exchange one life for another places a limit on rebellion, differentiates it from revolution, and "humanizes" conflict in the face of the bureaucratic murder of faceless millions by totalitarian regimes. The rebel now knows himself or herself in the existential limits he or she accepts or, in short, the degree of tolerance he or she extends to others in pursuing his or her goals.

But is it really the case that because "I rebel, we exist"? Circular reasoning underpins such neo-Cartesian claims. And they appear all the more arbitrary given the philosophical premise that "the first and only evidence that is supplied to me, within the terms of the absurdist experience, is rebellion."[15]

---

13. Ibid., 22.
14. Ibid., 103.
15. Ibid., 10.

Camus knows that not every form of rebellion is justifiable. Neofascists and skinheads also see themselves as engaging in rebellion. But surely Camus would not consider it necessary to first legitimate their initial expression of outrage and only then condemn the exaggerated form their rebellion takes. Enough Nazis and communists were also quite willing to risk death in exchange for the murder of opponents in the brawls and street battles anticipating the rise of Hitler. The problem is obvious: rebellion is, ultimately, identified only with those actions of which Camus approves.

To make matters worse, *The Rebel* reveals nothing new about totalitarianism, and it lacks any practical referent for its metaphysical judgments. No antiauthoritarian movement willing to engage in violence, which includes the antifascist resistance, can begin with the idea of equally exchanging the lives of its partisans for those of its enemies; it must attempt to maximize costs for the enemy and minimize its own losses. Camus is, of course correct in noting the effect of ideology on action and the manner in which revolutions of the past generated organs of terror. But he never deals with the constraints in which such movements operated. He never makes any reference to institutions or interests or possible structural imbalances of power in defining "oppression" or "exploitation." He also never deals with the inherent differences between a theory of revolution and a theory of rule.

All this, however, generally got lost in the emotionally and politically charged climate in which discussion of *The Rebel* took place. Communist hacks blasted it unmercifully. More ominously, conservatives and Catholics applauded Camus for showing how revolutions only produce new hangmen. Camus surely dismissed the criticisms of the communists and deplored the "misunderstanding" of his work by the political right. But even liberal critics, who supported his attack on utopianism and his identification with democracy and the individual, expressed skepticism about his philosophical claims regarding the absolute value of rebellion. Raymond Aron was snide in complementing Camus only for being less of a romantic than Jean-Paul Sartre.[16] Thus, there were already doubts about *The Rebel* even before what would become a bitter debate between friends.

Camus and Sartre, who was eight years older, became friends during the occupation, though they knew of each other's work earlier.[17] Both became

---

16. Raymond Aron, *The Opium of the Intellectuals*, trans. Terence Kilmartin (New York: Doubleday, 1957), 58 ff.

17. Olivier Todd, *Albert Camus: Une Vie* (Paris: Gallimard, 1997), 308 ff., 335 ff., and passim.

famous early in life. But whereas Camus grew up in Belcourt, a working-
class neighborhood in Algiers in extreme poverty, Sartre was part of an
upper-middle-class family in Alsace and a cousin of Albert Schweitzer.
Camus took his degree at the University of Algiers; Sartre studied philosophy at the famous École Normale Supèrieure. Sartre was the leading representative of French existentialism, whereas Camus tried to separate himself
from existentialism and any other "ism." But their work initially dealt with
similar themes: the individual, the absurd, freedom, and responsibility. They
associated with the same people and, following the liberation, contributed
to the intellectual glitter of Paris's Left Bank. Nevertheless, just when
Camus was shifting his focus from individual revolt to the nature of solidarity, Sartre was beginning to incorporate his earlier existential preoccupation
with the unconditional character of individual freedom into what would
gradually become an innovative understanding of Marxism.[18]

By 1952, Sartre and Camus had become rivals. They competed for a similar audience, they chose different political paths following the fragmentation of the Resistance, and they became more suspicious of each other's ambitions. Sartre saw Camus's concern with democracy and limited revolt as
ultimately justifying Western imperialism; and Camus believed his friend
was creating an uncritical "mystique" of the working class. Both were right
in part. Camus never had any second thoughts about his opposition to the
Soviet Union; Sartre, on the other hand, in the context of his break with
Merleau-Ponty, would later say,

> When, about 1950, everything exploded he saw only debris. In his eyes, my
> madness was to hang on to a piece of flotsam while waiting for the rest to re-
> construct the vessel automatically. For my part, I took sides when the left crum-
> bled because I believed its reconstruction was up to us. And certainly not from
> the top, but from the bottom. To be sure, we had no contact whatever with the
> masses, and we were, consequently, without any power. But our job was no
> less clear. Faced with the unholy alliance of the bourgeoisie and the socialist
> leaders, we had no other alternative but to stay as close to the Communist Party
> as possible, and implore others to join us.[19]

---

18. The transitional work, in this regard, is the stunning "Materialism and Revolution," by Jean-Paul Sartre, in *Literary and Philosophical Essays*, trans. Annette
Michelson (New York: Collier, 1962).
19. Jean-Paul Sartre, "Merleau-Ponty," in *Situations*, trans. Benita Eisler (Green-
wich, Conn.: Fawcett, 1966), 202.

Sartre would recognize the need for solidarity, the moment of action, and the willingness of the individual to face necessity and his or her "situation." But he understood all this very differently from Camus. The burgeoning mistrust between Camus and Sartre broke into the open with Francis Jeanson's review of *The Rebel*. It appeared in the legendary journal, *Les Temps Modernes*, founded and edited by Sartre. Camus had apparently asked his colleague to arrange a review, without suggesting any reviewer in particular, and Jeanson had volunteered. The result was not what either Camus or Sartre expected. Rather than treating *The Rebel* tactfully, as he had originally implied he would, Jeanson attacked Camus for his superficial philosophical interpretations of Hegel and Marx as well as his willingness to reject revolution without offering any positive or practical content for his vision of rebellion. Camus was furious. Suspecting that Jeanson was merely acting as the front man for Sartre,[20] he wrote a response to *"Monsieur l'editeur"* entitled "Revolt and Servitude." Camus essentially dismissed Jeanson, implying he was "unworthy" of the assignment to review his book. But he also attacked Sartre, along with the rest of the editorial board, as bourgeois intellectuals and Stalinists unwilling to condemn the concentration camp universe in the Soviet Union.

Sartre responded to Camus in a singularly biting and trenchant polemic.[21] He charged Camus with exchanging his earlier nonconformism and commitment to revolt for a fashionable anticommunism. He presented the willingness of Camus to condemn the excesses of both sides in the cold war as nothing more than a rejection of genuine political "engagement" and an inability to choose between the imperialists and their victims. But there was also a personal attack; and Sartre knew which buttons to push. He castigated Camus for his arrogant treatment of Jeanson, his sensitivity to criticism, his self-professed weariness with politics, and his moral posturing. Indeed, coming from someone who presumably knew Camus well, all this probably carried greater weight with the public than the political arguments.

Each exaggerated the position of the other. Sartre knew that Camus was not some reactionary anticommunist. And, for his part, Camus knew that Sartre was no simple apparatchik. He knew that Sartre had steadfastly re-

20. It is indeed unfair to ignore the differences; see Francis Jeanson, *Sartre and the Problem of Morality*, trans. Robert V. Stone (Bloomington: Indiana University Press, 1980).
21. Jean-Paul Sartre, "Reply to Albert Camus," in *Situations*.

fused to join the French Communist Party and that he had just recently failed in organizing an alternative movement of the left, the Rassemblement Démocratique et Révolutionnaire (RDR), for which Camus himself had campaigned. The ethical division between them occurred over whether the intellectual had an obligation not merely to speak the truth but to do so without reference to context. There was, however, also a practical difference between them, which has been consistently ignored. The issue was not simply whether to support or oppose the communists. It was rather a question of how nonaligned intellectuals should act to foster a progressive politics when the Communist Party tended to poll about 20 percent of the vote and received support from much of the working class, and when a democratic socialist alternative was lacking.

As an existential "revolutionary," Sartre took a "realist" position. He believed "engagement" within a situation was always necessary and considered progressive politics impossible without the Communist Party. The Soviet Union was seen by him as, for better or worse, the only nation willing to identify itself ideologically with revolution; if only for this reason, Sartre endowed it with a certain "privilege" in the cold war. It was a strange position for a "realist" to take, however, because the Soviet Union had not pursued a genuinely revolutionary course since 1923. Thus, even while seeking to foster militancy among the working class, Sartre could never specify how the USSR or its vassal party in France was furthering the revolutionary goal or even social progress.[22] His position was abstract from the start. Raymond Aron was surely correct when he wrote that "the philosopher of liberty never managed, or resigned himself, to see communism as it is."[23]

Sartre's vision of the Soviet Union was still clouded by nostalgia for the "heroic years," the period lasting from 1918 to 1923, when it pursued an ill-fated "offensive" strategy in the international arena and still had a revolutionary mission to accomplish. Sartre was occasionally critical of the Soviet Union; his journal, *Les Temps Modernes*, carried an exposure of the concentration camp system in the USSR, and his *The Ghost of Stalin* was a devastating attack on the Soviet invasion of Hungary in 1956. But his position on the Soviet Union was, from the first, undertaken from the standpoint

---

22. Note the ill-conceived analysis, which even logically justifies Stalinism, by Jean-Paul Sartre, in *The Communists and the Peace*, trans. Martha H. Fletcher (New York: George Braziller, 1968).

23. Raymond Aron, *Memoirs: Fifty Years of Political Reflection*, trans. George Holoch (New York: Holmes and Meier, 1990), 330.

of what Merleau-Ponty properly termed "ultrabolshevism."[24] As the years passed, in fact, Sartre's revolutionary Leninism increasingly merged with a type of radical and even anti-Western Third World populism. By 1968, he had identified himself with the strange and anarchistic version of Maoism popular among certain elements of the far left in France. Discontent with one communist experiment had only led him to the next. Ever more surely, in the name of his "engagement," the "realist" found himself making one unrealistic excuse after another for one Third World "dictatorship of the proletariat" after another. The political judgment of a great intellectual thereby became increasingly compromised, and it has been rendered even more suspect with the collapse of communism.

Nevertheless, Sartre's most important writings remain irreducible to the commitments made by him during the cold war or the Marxism promulgated in either the USSR or China. The philosophical and literary works for which he remains best known were all written before World War II and his "engagement" with politics. A novel like *Nausea*, plays like *No Exit* and *The Flies*, and his major philosophical works like *Being and Nothingness* as well as *Existentialism and Humanism* lack any connection whatsoever with organized politics or political theory. As far as the postwar writings are concerned, with the exception of a disastrous play—*Nekrassov*—and his explicitly polemical works, Sartre never compromised his intellectual independence. His trilogy, *The Roads to Freedom*, remains unfinished precisely because of his inability to decide the future of a major communist character. His famous play, *Dirty Hands*, is less an evocation of communist principles than an example of what Simone de Beauvoir called "the ethics of ambiguity"; and another of his important dramas, *The Condemned of Altona*, actually contains a self-criticism concerning his role in the debate with Camus.

Sartre's unfinished *Critique of Dialectical Reason* was a bold and unorthodox attempt to merge existentialism and Marxism, which the communists condemned as "hopeless idealism": it lacked any sustained institutional understanding of the "political," and its anarchistic strains anticipated the new radicalism of 1968. His multi-volume study of Gustave Flaubert employed Freud in combination with Marxism and existentialism, and like his earlier work on Jean Genet, which the communists detested, it has nothing in common with traditional Marxist forms of biography. The

---

24. Maurice Merleau-Ponty, *Adventures of the Dialectic* (Evanston: Northwestern University Press, 1968).

study of Flaubert introduced new concepts like the *vécu*, or the nonobjectifiable subjectivity of the subject, which establish Sartre's continuing commitment to existentialism. Indeed, until he died in 1980 at the age of sev-
enty-five, he would maintain his affection for the writings of Søren
Kierkegaard.[25]

Camus was surely right, against Sartre, insofar as the Soviet concentration camps constituted an evil in need of unqualified denunciation, especially because they necessarily and inevitably perverted all the ends that the
communists originally sought to realize. His stance on the cold war was
more nuanced, principled, and politically intelligent than that of his adversary. Sartre was also wrong in claiming that only the "engaged" man has
the right to criticize. Such a stance is arbitrary, because no one would make
such a claim for fascism, and circular, insofar as the "privilege" implicitly
accorded the Soviet Union is itself justified only by belief in an unverifiable
teleology. By way of contrast, Camus's emphasis on plausibly connecting
means and ends is fundamental for any form of political ethics under circumstances in which teleological assumptions can no longer be taken for
granted.

Camus was also more prescient than Sartre in seeing authoritarian communism as a moral obstacle for the future of socialism. His unwillingness to
deal with the communists, however, left him without any political strategy
for implementing a democratic agenda. He was content to stand on principle. Camus actually longed for a genuinely republican front capable of opposing both Gaullism and communism, and he received approval for such a
venture from many in the liberal socialist group around François Bondy and
his journal, *Les Preuves*. But no mass base for such a project existed in
France. Raymond Aron correctly noted that in the postwar era, "as a paper
of the Resistance, *Combat* found no place in a regime of parties."[26] That
was probably true of the socialist humanism exhibited by Camus in *The
Rebel*, as well. As a consequence, if the "engaged" man appeared as an ideo-
logue, the moralist found himself increasingly isolated.

Sadly, the two great intellectuals of the postwar era were never reconciled.
Admirers of Camus and Sartre still argue about who "won" the debate. But,
in fact, there was no "winner"—only losers. In very different ways, both

25. Schocken. Note the superb essay of 1964 entitled "Kierkegaard: The Singular
Universal," in Jean-Paul Sartre, *Between Existentialism and Marxism*, trans. John
Mathews (London: New Left, 1974), 141.
26. Aron, *Memoirs*, 156.

ultimately found themselves unable to connect their principles with a viable idea of practice. The debate between them reflects an epoch in which socialists and communists were irrevocably divided. Both movements had compromised their most radical principles and goals in the name of wielding power in a world punctuated by a murderous war just ended and the prospect of a nuclear war always looming on the horizon. Neither the rebel nor the revolutionary could offer a genuinely viable theory of "engagement" or truly adequate solutions for the practical political problems of the time— perhaps because there were none available.

12

＝＝＝＝

Critical Theory: Dialectics, Consciousness, Negativity

C ritical theory is usually associated with the work undertaken by members of the Institute for Social Research in Frankfurt, commonly known as the Frankfurt School.[1] Founded in 1923, the institute became the first formally unaffiliated Marxist-oriented think tank in Europe. Max Horkheimer, Theodor Adorno, Walter Benjamin, Erich Fromm, Leo Lowenthal, and Herbert Marcuse were its most visible associates. Interestingly enough, however, they were not initially its dominant figures. Under the stewardship of its first director, Carl Grünberg, its research program centered around the labor movement, the capitalist economy, and the new experiments with planning in the Soviet Union: its most important intellectual representatives were communist activists and social scientists like Henryk Grossmann, Frederick Pollock, Fritz Sternberg, and Karl August Wittfogel. Their approach was often sophisticated but essentially still traditionally Marxist in its emphasis on political economy.

---

1. See Martin Jay, *The Dialectical Imagination: A History of the Frankfurt School and the Institute for Social Research, 1923–1950* (Berkeley: University of California Press, 1996); Douglas Kellner, *Critical Theory, Marxism, and Modernity* (Cambridge, U.K.: Polity, 1989); Trent Schroyer, *The Critique of Domination: The Origins and Development of Critical Theory* (New York: George Braziller, 1973); Rolf Wiggershaus, *Die Frankfurter Schule: Geschichte, Theoretische Entwicklung, Politisiche Bedeutung* (Munich: Deutsche Taschenbuch, 1988); also see, for a more extensive development of my own views, Stephen Eric Bronner, *Of Critical Theory and Its Theorists* (Oxford: Blackwell, 1994).

Only after Max Horkheimer was named as the new director of the institute in 1930 would the focus shift from the base to the superstructure and from the historical subject of history and class to the imperiled subjectivity of the individual subject.

The term *critical theory* was coined in 1937 after the majority of members of the Institute for Social Research had emigrated to the United States following the triumph of Hitler. It identified its advocates with a rejection of ideology and a willingness to illuminate the interests served by conformist modes of thought from a reflexive standpoint predicated on a commitment to emancipatory norms. But the term *critical theory* was also initially employed as a type of code word, a form of what Adorno called "Aesopian language," which differentiated the work of its exponents from prevailing forms of Marxism. Revolutionary degeneration in the Soviet Union had made the existing orthodoxy unacceptable, and it also would clearly have served as an impediment in an American environment hostile to anything remotely associated with the European "left." Members of the institute needed a new term, and they found one: *critical theory.*

Its roots, however, lie squarely in the "heroic phase" of the Russian Revolution. Indeed, from 1918 until 1921, the possibility of creating a new world seemed to present itself, a radical alternative both to capitalism and to what would later emerge as Stalinism. Critical theory was spawned by a new dialectical form of "Western Marxism" committed to workers' councils, radical egalitarianism, and international revolution. Its most important representatives were Georg Lukács, Karl Korsch, and Antonio Gramsci. Strategic differences between them were real. They were never close friends, and they certainly never constituted a "school." Gramsci would have less of an impact on critical theory, in fact, than on the development of a structuralist form of Marxism and the politics of the new social movements. Nevertheless, he still held certain political and practical concerns in common with Lukács and Korsch.

All three were members of the Communist International, and, for better or worse, their thinking became associated with the call for a revolutionary "offensive" in which uprisings were tried, and failed, in Germany, Hungary, and Italy: Lukács was minister of education in the short-lived Hungarian Soviet of 1919; Gramsci was a prominent figure in the Turin strikes of 1922; and Korsch served as minister of justice in the ill-fated Thuringian Republic of 1923. All three opposed positivism and "objectivism" in favor of a new concern with the idealist legacy and the subjective moment of action. All three refused to identify Marxism with a set of transhistorical truths. All three instead considered it the product of a given phase of historical development and susceptible to becoming an "ideology" in its own right. All three, in short, viewed its practice as inherently open to criticism from the standpoint of its unfulfilled emancipatory norms.

Marxism came to be seen less as a belief in this or that prediction than as a method of analysis.[2] These Western Marxists refused to consider it as a fixed and finished system or as a traditional variant of "science" with neutral criteria comparable to, say, chemistry or physics for evaluating truth claims. They believed, in fact, that Marxism had little useful to say about the natural world, whatever the claims of Engels and the partisans of orthodoxy.[3] Marxism was considered an inherently social theory. Its sphere of relevance was the sphere of "society," and in this sphere, the critique of ideology was as essential as the critique of political economy; it indeed became "essential for modern dialectical materialism to grasp philosophies and other ideological systems in theory as realities, and to treat them in practice as such."[4] Marxism was therefore viewed as a critical worldview capable of comprehending the actions and interests of all classes as well as the way they were being justified within the existing "totality."[5]

Western Marxists were intent upon applying "the materialist method of history to the materialist method of history itself."[6] Only by comparing its historical usage with its emancipatory purpose, its contingent willingness to service certain institutional interests with its ultimate vision of a nonalienated and classless society, would it become possible to keep Marxism from degenerating into yet another "ideology" for stabilizing the status quo. This confrontation of practice with theory, this critique of ideology *(Ideologie-kritik)*, was launched with an eye upon the values of freedom and autonomy as well as the concern for their realization, originally generated by idealism

---

2. Georg Lukács, *History and Class Consciousness: Studies in Marxist Dialectics*, trans. Rodney Livingstone (Cambridge: MIT Press, 1972), 1.

3. "When the ideal of scientific knowledge is applied to nature it simply furthers the progress of science. But when it is applied to society it turns out to be an ideological weapon of the bourgeoisie. . . . It must think of capitalism as being predestined to eternal survival by the eternal laws of nature and reason." Ibid., 11.

4. Karl Korsch, *Marxism and Philosophy*, trans. Fred Halliday (London: New Left, 1972), 72.

5. Note the excellent study by Martin Jay, *Marxism and Totality: The Adventures of a Concept from Lukács to Habermas* (Berkeley: University of California Press, 1984).

6. Korsch, *Marxism and Philosophy*, 92.

and inherited by Marxism. This earlier trend had, after all, identified the problem of philosophy with the establishment of a "realm of freedom."[7] The prime purpose of contemporary thinking was to further the "relentless criticism of all existing conditions" championed by Marx insofar as this world of autonomous and equal subjects had not yet been realized. The critique of ideology fueled by the power of speculative reason, was an essential component of the tradition associated with critical theory from the very beginning.

As one might expect, this form of thinking challenged the stalwarts of orthodoxy in the Comintern. In 1923, when *History and Class Consciousness* and *Marxism and Philosophy* appeared, Marxism was already becoming reduced to quotations exegetically pulled out to justify this or that policy by this or that party leader. The critical and methodological understanding of Marxism posed an obvious threat to the authoritarian unity and dogma increasingly imposed by the Soviet Union upon the Comintern—especially given that the official "line" was changing and that international revolutionary possibilities had petered out by 1923. And so, it is little wonder that while Gramsci was languishing in Mussolini's jail, Lukács and Korsch should have come under attack by Zinoviev in his famous "professors' speech" at the Fifth Congress of the Comintern in 1924.[8] They could either engage in "self-criticism" or face expulsion. Western Marxism effectively came to an end as Lukács retracted *History and Class Consciousness* for its "idealist deviations," Korsch found himself isolated after leaving the movement, and Gramsci died with the implications of his thoughts ignored.

But there were also valid philosophical criticisms of what was common to their approach. The new method lacked criteria for validating its truth claims, and the problem would remain endemic to critical theory down to the present. Its rejection of all ahistorical systems included positivism and symbolic logic, whose notions of validation were obviously inappropriate for a project predicated on speculative reason. The teleological assumptions of "scientific" Marxism, however, were also considered untenable. Although the proponents of Western Marxism may still have envisioned the classless society and a willingness on the part of the proletariat to make good on its revolutionary "vision," they nonetheless laid the basis for an

7. Herbert Marcuse, *Reason and Revolution: Hegel and the Rise of Social Theory* (Boston: Beacon, 1969), 9 ff. and passim.
8. Arpad Kadarky, *Georg Lukács: Life, Thought, and Politics* (Oxford: Blackwell, 1991), 279 ff.

even more radical encounter with determinism and teleology. The proletariat may have had its "privilege," in short, but only insofar as it was capable of thematizing and transforming the relations of capitalist production upon which the existing "totality" rested.[9]

Critical theory gradually withdrew that "privilege": its partisans came to recognize that the revolution was in a state of crisis. Old habits and new forms of oppression were commingling in the Soviet Union, and critical theorists realized, early, that fascism threatened to undermine traditional Marxist assumptions. Without that "privilege," without the assumption that it alone could abolish capitalism and its attendant structures, the proletariat was just another class with just another instrumental interest in the status quo. It was undoubtedly this suspicion that helped lead members of the institute, each after his fashion, to condemn instrumental reason and bureaucracy. There is a sense in which, before the outbreak of World War II, most of them were still looking backward at a "heroic phase" of the Russian Revolution ever more surely vanishing from memory. They emphasized the importance of building a genuinely radical "consciousness" among the proletariat and vanquishing the world of alienation and reification in which workers were treated as nothing more than objects or things.[10] They indeed highlighted the moment of reflexivity embedded in speculative reason.

The aim of critical theory was initially to help make humanity capable of controlling its destiny in a manner consonant with the goals of freedom and autonomy.[11] This was deemed impossible under capitalist social relations where, given the arbitrary manner by which wealth was invested and appropriated, history was made "behind the backs" of its members. In keeping with the Western Marxists, critical theorists were antipositivist, antideterminist, and antisystemic in their thinking. They scorned parliamentary democracy, ignored distributional issues, and basically showed a marked lack of concern with the institutional arrangements of a new order. They also waged an increasingly bitter assault upon alienation and the division of

---

9. Lukács, *History and Class Consciousness*, 52 ff. and passim.

10. It was indeed the inability to recognize the "reification" *(Verdinglichung)* inherent within the capitalist production process, whereby individuals become mere means for the growth and perpetuation of the system, that served as the limit of "bourgeois" thought in terms of its attempt to create a harmonious unity between humanity and its world or, in philosophical terms, between subject and object. Note the seminal essay on the idealist tradition by Georg Lukács, "Reification and the Consciousness of the Proletariat," ibid.

11. Karl Korsch, *Karl Marx* (New York: Russell and Russell, 1938), 157–61.

labor, bureaucracy and reification, in the name of what Marx termed "human emancipation," or the ability of the species to assert its conscious control over all social spheres, and the full flowering of a repressed subjectivity.

Western Marxists of the 1920s anticipated and critical theorists of the 1930s built upon what was revealed in the famous *Paris Manuscripts of 1844* after the manuscript was discovered in the Marx–Engels Archive, smuggled out of the Soviet Union, and finally published in 1932.[12] Both trends were focused on transforming the totality. Their criticisms of the established order were also built upon positive foundations. The inaugural speech given by Max Horkheimer upon assuming direction of the Institute for Social Research in 1930 indeed makes this very clear.[13] He relinquished the prior emphasis upon political economy and the history of the labor movement. He envisioned instead a situation in which the work of his colleagues could aid in the struggle to transform politics, economy, and the psychology of everyday life. It was in this spirit that critical theory emerged from the shadow of Western Marxism.

Horkheimer was the son of a German industrialist. A communist sympathizer in his early years and a philosopher by training, he was also interested in sociology and an astonishingly wide range of other academic pursuits. It was under his leadership that the institute developed the project for which it would become internationally renowned. A highly effective academic entrepreneur, he gathered around him many individuals who would eventually achieve fame in a variety of disciplines, and his speech called for a multidisciplinary program capable of integrating normative inquiry with empirical research.

Critical theory initially distinguished itself less through its contestation of science than with its embrace of *Ideologiekritik*.[14] The idea goes back to Ludwig Feuerbach, who sought to explain religion as the alienated projection of human powers upon a nonexistent entity, which was, in turn, worshiped. Its roots lie perhaps even further back in Kant's attempt to show the

---

12. Note the illuminating review of the *Paris Manuscripts*, after they first appeared, by Herbert Marcuse, *Studies in Critical Philosophy*, trans. Joris De Bres (Boston: Beacon, 1973).

13. Max Horkheimer, "The State of Contemporary Social Philosophy and the Tasks of an Institute for Social Research," in *Critical Theory and Society*, ed. Stephen Eric Bronner and Douglas Kellner (New York: Routledge, 1989).

14. See Max Horkheimer, *The Eclipse of Reason* (New York: Seabury, 1974).

assumptions ignored by David Hume in his assault upon rationality and even in the attempts of Plato to illuminate the self-contradictions of his interlocutors. But the point for critical theory was to show the manner in which existing forms of ideology not only veil certain interests, which Marx had already done, but also inhibit the possibility of imagining an alternative society and radical forms of subjective emancipation. Critical theory would engage in an immanent process: its proponents would develop their own perspectives by calling into question those of its opponents. Thus, they sought to define themselves against the two dominant modes of bourgeois thought, materialism and metaphysics, both of which ignore the subjectivity of the subject and the happiness of the individual.[15]

"Traditional and Critical Theory," by Max Horkheimer,[16] contains perhaps the most comprehensive and systematic statement concerning the multidisciplinary attempts to synthesize philosophy, the social sciences, and an emancipatory political perspective. It starts by demarcating critical theory from both positivism and idealism. Where positivism wishes to exclude normative concerns from social scientific inquiry and idealism shuts itself off from empirical reality, critical theory is willing to undertake the critique of reality in the name of those struggling against its most repressive effects. Each inhibits the attempt to generate solidarity and envision an order intent on emancipating the individual. The "realm of freedom" projected by speculative reason thus becomes the yardstick with which to measure the degree of social rationality or irrationality inherent in any given form of social or political organization.

Critical theory never entertained the idea that freedom is license: its representatives knew too much about the arbitrary exercise of power endemic to totalitarianism. Proponents of critical theory always assumed that a rational ordering of society would, reciprocally and universally, expand opportunities for the exercise of individual autonomy. But this connection with the Hegelian and Marxist traditions was soon shaken by the triumph of Nazism. The importance of this event for the development of critical theory can scarcely be overstated. Because most members of the institute were Jews

---

15. Max Horkheimer, "Materialism and Metaphysics," in *Critical Theory: Selected Essays*, trans. Matthew J. O'Connell et. al. (New York: Continuum, 1982); also see Herbert Marcuse, "Philosophy and Critical Theory," in Bronner and Kellner, *Critical Theory and Society*.

16. Max Horkheimer, "Traditional and Critical Theory," in *Critical Theory: Selected Essays*.

and Marxists, the Nazis, following their seizure of power in Germany, quickly forced the institute and its members into exile. After numerous complications, in 1934 the headquarters for the Institute for Social Research were finally moved from Frankfurt to Columbia University, in New York, which offered office space and institutional support. Upon coming to the United States the institute's members began their inquiry into the roots of fascism and the manner in which socializing institutions induced individuals to accept even the most irrational forms of social and political authority.

All members of the institute were in agreement that fascism had emerged from a capitalism in crisis and that it evinced a new form of the capitalist state. Still, there were sharp arguments over whether the new fascist state was basically autonomous or merely a tool of monopoly capitalist interests. In 1941, Franz Neumann argued that fascism was a form of totalitarian state capitalism.[17] Neumann had been a famous labor lawyer in Weimar Germany as well as an important member of the German Social Democratic Party. In his widely discussed book, he stressed the continuing primacy of the economy over the state in the fascist era. Nevertheless, in opposition to this view, the most prominent economist of the institute, Frederick Pollock, argued for "the primacy of the political" and claimed that the state was assuming power over the economy in the current era of fascism and welfare state capitalism.[18]

Pollock's article exploded any lingering belief in the primacy of the economic "base" over the political and ideological "superstructure," and it established a new framework for the institute's later analysis of the new relations between the state and the economy during the postwar era. State capitalism—in both its "democratic" and "totalitarian" forms—was seen as producing a "command economy" in which the state comes to manage the economy. It follows that capitalism has discovered new strategies to avoid economic crisis, stabilize itself, and prevent the realization of socialism. Thus, Pollock's essay raised new doubts about the revolutionary role of the working class and the validity of classical Marxist theory.

Those convictions were only strengthened among members of the institute as the 1930s turned into the 1940s: the Hitler–Stalin pact of 1939, which unleashed World War II, extinguished the last vestiges of their former

---

17. Franz Neumann, *Behemoth: The Structure and Practice of National Socialism, 1933–1944* (New York: Harper and Row, 1944).

18. Frederick Pollock, "State Capitalism: Its Possibilities and Limitations" in Bronner and Kellner, *Critical Theory and Society*.

ideas about Marxism. Living in the United States, Horkheimer and his friends also became increasingly concerned about the integration of the proletariat into contemporary capitalist societies as well as the extension of instrumental rationality and bureaucracy into all aspects of contemporary life. They worried that new forms of political, social, and especially cultural conformity were becoming institutionalized and that the qualitative differences between different regimes would disappear: the institutions and practices of "advanced industrial society" were seemingly engaged in generating what Horkheimer and Adorno would later call "the totally administered society." Ever more surely, for critical theory, the basic conflict began to pit the "system" against the "individual."

The promise of progress offered by the Enlightenment, with its emphasis upon reason and science, had apparently proved as vacuous as the revolutionary guarantees of Marx. Progress had not produced a more reflective and moral individual or a more peaceful and just world. It had instead resulted in the domination of scientific or instrumental reason, which, in turn, undermined the individual capacity for reflection on both the need and the possibility for emancipation. Modernity was seen as generating a totalitarian world in which the individual was inseparable from the number inscribed on his arm. Progress was seen, in short, as having turned against itself. This was the context in which Walter Benjamin wrote his justly famous "Theses on the Philosophy of History."[19]

Benjamin stood on the margins of the institute. Influenced by the Marxism of Bertolt Brecht and his circle and the works of Jewish mysticism by Gershom Scholem,[20] two incompatible traditions blend in the thinking of Benjamin. It is indeed highly questionable whether the result of his efforts ever culminated in a coherent general theory. But for all that, Benjamin's views on the philosophy of history are extraordinarily provocative, and they evince a particularly radical intention. Progress can no longer be taken for granted, according to Benjamin, and traditional forms of teleology have lost their validity. History is a site of ruins; it must be reconstructed through a form of messianic reflection in which emerges the need to look back in order to move forward. The "end" is less prescribed by science than projected by

---

19. Walter Benjamin, "Theses on the Philosophy of History," in *Illuminations*, ed. Hannah Arendt, trans. Harry Zohn (New York: Schocken, 1969).
20. Note the genuinely remarkable work, *The Correspondence of Walter Benjamin and Gershom Scholem, 1932–1940*, ed. Gershom Scholem (New York: Schocken, 1989).

hope, and it is in terms of this utopian hope that a refashioning of the past, a redeeming of its lost emancipatory moments, becomes possible. The subjective, the contingent, and the voluntary now take on positive philosophical value. It makes no sense to wait for the appropriate time or historical stage. The work of reconstruction can begin at any time. Indeed, such is the meaning behind the famous phrase that every moment is "the strait gate through which the Messiah might pass."[21]

Writing in 1940 as the Nazi war machine blitzed through Europe and the socialist alternative mirrored what it sought to oppose, Benjamin presented the framework for a "negative" philosophy of history. It involved an inversion of the past and the way it was understood. Even high culture was seen by him as cloaking repression; it was always the victors—however barbaric—who wrote history and established systems of thought to legitimate their systems of oppression. Shortly after publishing these theses, Benjamin himself was forced to flee the Nazi occupation of France. He committed suicide on the Spanish border, when it appeared that he would be captured by the fascists, rather than face life in a concentration camp. Ironically, his action helped lead to an opening of the border, and it allowed the rest of his group to escape into freedom.

Walter Benjamin called upon radicals to assert their subjectivity, their repressed dreams and hopes, to transvalue the past and understand history as more than dead time. He saw the past as alive with both unrealized utopian possibilities and untold presentiments of a barbaric future. Every cultural document is for him, in fact, an expression of both civilization and barbarism. And if Benjamin never provides the categories for determining the degree of the mix, his emphasis upon the recollection of past suffering is meant to provide an inspiration for struggle against oppression in the present. The "image of enslaved ancestors rather than that of liberated grandchildren," according to Benjamin, offers the best impetus for emancipation. Utopia becomes intertwined with recovery. This was indeed the context in which he challenged those concerned with emancipatory change to "brush history against the grain."

Nowhere is this attempt more radically undertaken than in *Dialectic of Enlightenment* by Max Horkheimer and Theodor Adorno. Composed under the shadow of Auschwitz, while its authors were living in California, it would mark a new direction for critical theory. Placing the individual at

---

21. Benjamin, "Theses on the Philosophy of History," 264.

the center of a dialectical analysis, contesting accepted understandings of truth, Horkheimer and Adorno forward an anthropological perspective on history in which the instrumental domination of nature ultimately results in expelling freedom from the historical process and threatening the integrity of the subject. Their work emphasizes the debilitating elements of the division of labor, its effects upon the moral capacities of the individual, and the ways in which it contributes to the incessant growth in alienation.

Dialectic of Enlightenment generated a new "negative" form of social thinking. Its analysis of the "culture industry" would transform the discourse on media and society. Its critique of reification would profoundly influence the new social movements by turning the instrumental colonization of everyday life into a political issue. Its anthropological assault upon history would shatter the complacency with which progressives understood their past. Horkheimer and Adorno, for perhaps the first time in the dialectical discourse, question whether the price demanded by all teleological notions of progress is too high. Their epigrammatic style, their bountiful illusions, and the sheer quality of mind informing this book make it a seminal work in the history of twentieth-century philosophy.

Two calamitous wars in the space of roughly thirty years created a deep sense of disillusionment in the postwar era. Subjectivity itself seemed endangered, emancipation was now identified with the status quo, and the moment of negativity had apparently been vanquished. Modernity itself became the culprit, along with its distinct way of thinking lodged in the Enlightenment. Horkheimer and Adorno used the term *enlightenment* in two senses: It was meant to express the most radical vision of a rising bourgeoisie intent on establishing a new production process and solidifying its political control. But it was also seen by them as part of a general anthropological assault on superstition and myth. They surely understood that the scientific demystification of the world was fueled by the norms and goals of freedom and autonomy associated with idealism and its unique form of speculative rationality. With the assumption of power by the bourgeoisie, however, scientific reason was seen as turning upon the speculative intellect and ultimately expelling all normative concerns from the Enlightenment discourse. Criteria for ethical judgment vanished; conscience atrophied; and the power of reflection grew ever weaker. Commodification was extending instrumental reason into every facet of the "totally administered society."

Fascism thereby became a logical outgrowth of liberalism, its opposite, and a modern world in which, as Adorno, put the matter, "the whole is false."[22]

Horkheimer and Adorno personally identified with the reflexivity prized by Enlightenment philosophy and its attack on dogma. In various essays and empirical works, they stressed the importance of democratic as against authoritarian values.[23] They even saw their classic study as a critique of the Enlightenment undertaken in the name of enlightenment itself. But the question here pertains to the dynamic of the theory beyond the intentions of its authors. Their method undermines the ability to draw qualitative political and cultural distinctions, and their "concrete" critique is consequently indeterminate. Focusing simply on the reifying dynamics of instrumental reason obscures the obvious: the triumph of fascism was the result of a conflict between real movements with qualitatively different traditions. Antifascists embraced the Enlightenment heritage, and fascists rejected it; outside of the banal claim that fascism emerged in neoliberal states in the 1920s and 1930s, there is simply no historical validity to the argument that liberalism engendered fascism as its logical consequence.[24] The anthropological attempt of Horkheimer and Adorno to unify qualitatively different phenomena under a single rubric indeed could result only in pseudodialectical sophistry.

Dialectic of Enlightenment set critical theory on a new course. Its orientation would now center around the claim that "the whole is false," and it would highlight the resistance of subjectivity to integration *tout court*. The proletariat is seen as having lost its transformative function, and thematizing the whole must now take a very different form. The Hegelian notion of "totality" subsequently makes way for the notion of "constellation,"[25] a category without fixed mediations or determinations employed to highlight

---

22. Theodor Adorno, *Minima Moralia: Reflections from Damaged Life*, trans. E. F. N. Jephcott (London: New Left, 1974), 50.

23. Most notably, see T. W. Adorno et. al., *The Authoritarian Personality* (New York: Norton, 1950).

24. Also note the essay by Herbert Marcuse, "The Struggle against Liberalism in the Totalitarian View of the State," in *Negations: Essays in Critical Theory*, trans. Jeremy J. Shapiro (Boston: Beacon, 1969).

25. Walter Benjamin influenced the development of this concept, which was originally employed in the essay by Theodor W. Adorno, "The Actuality of Philosophy," *Telos* 31 (Spring 1977): 113 ff.; also see Susan Buck-Morss, *The Origins of Negative Dialectics: Theodor W. Adorno, Walter Benjamin, and the Frankfurt Institute* (New York: Free Press, 1977), 96 ff.

the repressed subjectivity of the subject. The result is something like a montage whose point is to preserve the critical power of reflection without the presumption of being able to define an alternative.[26] It is indeed noteworthy that Adorno should have considered "fireworks" the paradigmatic expression of what is emancipatory in art.

The collaboration of Horkheimer and Adorno marked a distinct shift in the development of critical theory. They ultimately intensified the critique of positivism, with its objective forms of verification, and also existentialism, with its reliance on ontology for formalizing subjectivity.[27] They surrendered their previous attempts to develop a multidisciplinary theory oriented toward the emancipatory transformation of the "totality": they instead became preoccupied with how modernity was rooted in classical forms of domination.[28] They also engaged in a far more radical rejection of systemic thinking than what was previously anticipated: indeed, *Dialectic of Enlightenment* was subtitled "Fragments." Above all, however, they followed Nietzsche in placing the most radical possible emphasis upon the subjectivity of the subject as the locus of freedom.[29]

Critical theory lost its political edge. The new notion of subjectivity hung in the abstract, and the "constellation" lacked any definition. Solidarity turned into a symbolic, metaphysical, or even religious matter.[30] It became impossible to formulate an independent ethic with a cosmopolitan intent or posit an objective referent. The unyielding critique of instrumental reason

---

26. Perhaps the most extraordinary example of a "constellation" occurs in the collection of roughly three thousand quotations, which would then be presented without commentary in order to provide a picture of modernity. Note the legendary, if incomplete, project by Walter Benjamin, *Das Passagen-Werk*, 2 bde., hrsg. Rolf Tiedemann (Frankfurt am Main: Suhrkamp, 1982); also note the outstanding interpretive undertaking by Susan Buck-Morss, *Walter Benjamin and the Arcades Project* (Cambridge: MIT Press, 1991).

27. See Theodor W. Adorno et al., *The Positivist Dispute in German Sociology*, trans. Glyn Adey and David Frisby (London: Heinemann, 1976); Theodor W. Adorno, *Kierkegaard: Konstruktion des Aesthetischen* (Frankfurt am Main: Suhrkamp, 1969); Theodor W. Adorno, *The Jargon of Authenticity*, trans. Knut Tarnowski and Frederic Will (London: Routledge, Kegan Paul, 1973).

28. Note the classic discussion of Odysseus by Max Horkheimer and Theodor W. Adorno, in *Dialectic of Enlightenment*, trans. John Cumming (New York: Continuum, 1972), 43 ff.

29. Jürgen Habermas, *The Philosophical Discourse of Modernity: Twelve Lectures*, trans. Frederick Lawrence (Cambridge: MIT Press, 1987), 83 ff., 106 ff.

30. Max Horkheimer, *Die Sehnsucht nach dem ganz Anderen* (Frankfurt am Main: Fischer, 1970).

also made it difficult to deal with problems concerning "who gets what, when, where, [and] how." Fostering organized political resistance indeed gave way before the more philosophical or aesthetic attempts to ensure the "nonidentity" between subject and object or between the individual and the world.[31]

Other trends within critical theory presented themselves: Herbert Marcuse and Franz Neumann developed projects for a more historical inquiry into the character of social change;[32] Otto Kirchheimer and Neumann himself became leading students of legal theory, political institutions, and the structures of power.[33] Even Adorno would participate in a famous social scientific project concerned with empirically evaluating the "authoritarian personality," though, in keeping with *Dialectic of Enlightenment*, it ultimately suggested that fascism was finding a new home in America, the land of pragmatism and social science; Erich Fromm and Herbert Marcuse, whatever the differences between them regarding their diverse interpretations of Freud,[34] would inspire opposition to the Vietnam War and generate concern with a host of issues ranging from the creation of more participatory forms of governance to the role of what were often called "marginal groups" in advanced industrial society. Both would support the Civil Rights Movement and endorse the presidential campaigns of Eugene McCarthy in 1968 and George McGovern in 1972. Nevertheless, this was not where the

---

31. The tenacity of alienation demands "the continuing irreconcilability of subject and object, which constitutes the theme of dialectical criticism." Adorno, *Minima Moralia*, 246.

32. Herbert Marcuse, *Technology, War, and Fascism*, ed. Douglas Kellner (New York: Routledge, 1998), 93 ff., 191 ff.

33. Note the classic study by Otto Kirchheimer, *Political Justice: The Use of Legal Procedure for Political Ends* (Princeton: Princeton University Press, 1961), and also *Politics, Law, and Social Change: Selected Essays of Otto Kirchheimer*, ed. Frederic S. Burin and Kurt L. Shell (New York: Columbia University Press, 1969); Franz Neumann, *The Rule of Law: Political Theory and the Legal System in Modern Society* (Leamington Spa, U.K.: Berg, 1986); and the brilliant *The Democratic and the Authoritarian State: Essays in Political and Legal Theory*, ed. Herbert Marcuse (New York: Free Press, 1957).

34. The question was basically whether the work of Sigmund Freud should be interpreted as a form of metapsychology capable of informing a new utopian enrichment of Marxism or whether the clinical and practical elements were of primary importance within a project of social transformation; see Herbert Marcuse, *Eros and Civilization: A Philosophical Inquiry into Freud* (New York: Vintage, 1962), 217 ff.; Erich Fromm, *The Crisis of Psychoanalysis: Essays on Freud, Marx, and Social Psychology* (New York: Holt, Rinehart, and Winston, 1970), 1–30.

unique influence or contribution of either the Frankfurt School or critical theory would make itself felt.

Dialectic of Enlightenment had changed the understanding of resistance along with the character of emancipation. Radicalism would ultimately become defined by cultural rather than traditionally political or economic concerns. This ideological shift reflected the growing affluence of advanced industrial society and the disillusionment with its values generated by the new awareness of racism and imperialism. These changes in the meaning of resistance would indeed exercise a profound influence on many intellectuals associated with the New Left.

New concerns, which had been anticipated by critical theory, presented themselves. Its members attempted to deal with the impact of psychological repression, the oppressive character of the nuclear family, the effects of consumerism, and the insidious types of conformism generated by the culture industry. Theorists of the Frankfurt School indeed inaugurated a new discourse about mass communication and "popular culture" in their attempts to analyze the cultural mechanisms through which neocapitalist societies legitimate themselves. They saw the culture industry as engaging in sophisticated forms of ideological manipulation and indoctrination, using "entertainment" to sugarcoat the ideological content of oppression while eroding cultural standards in order to quell any forms of expression capable of contesting the given order. There is an almost obvious sociological truth to many of their claims. Nevertheless, their view of the culture industry also exhibits the same faults as their more directly social theory, owing to its indeterminacy and its willingness to tar all its aesthetic products with the same brush.

Mass culture frequently exhibits socially critical elements and can serve useful political ends; there are, furthermore, surely aesthetic differences between popular comedians like Charlie Chaplin and the Three Stooges. Blithely assuming that "the whole is false" makes it impossible to recognize basic distinctions between works. Such a stance, which emphasizes the ability of the "system" to absorb criticism, also leaves open the matter of whether the effects of a successful reform, or even a television program with a progressive "message," actually changes the system or whether, instead, they are simply nullified and incorporated within it. Issues of this sort and the character of repression, no less than the character of resistance,[35] remain

---

35. Note the unqualified critique of jazz as a simple product of the culture indus-

unresolved. Indeed, whether in terms of cultural or political theory, the new form of what Adorno would later term "negative dialectics" evidenced an increasing emphasis on the experience of subjectivity and an increasing inability to articulate the conditions for solidarity.

Later, after the uproar of the 1960s had died down, Jürgen Habermas attempted to provide a corrective in his two-volume work entitled *The Theory of Communicative Action*. It effectively reveals some of his differences with his teachers and the previous generation of critical theorists. It no longer wages an undifferentiated assault upon the totality, and it no longer assumes that "the whole is false." It evidences a new respect for modernity as well as the normative justification of claims and the positive role of the Enlightenment. His work also indicates some unfinished tasks for the contemporary era.

Habermas provides a critique of the social integration occurring within postliberal societies by highlighting the need to preserve the intersubjective "life-world" from an incursion by the forces of bureaucracy and the market. He calls for inquiry into familial socialization and an assault upon the combined cultural and social forces hindering ego development. He indicates the need for a more qualified confrontation with mass media and mass culture. And, above all, he insists upon recognizing the new potential for protest arising from the new social movements.

There are problems here: the attempt to insulate the "life-world" from bureaucratic infringement can easily reinforce the right-wing attempt to roll back the state in the name of more "voluntary" forms of social action. The emphasis upon "ego development" can easily turn into the call for "moral development" without any practical suggestions for dealing with the corrosive issues of media and mass society. There is also a sense in which Habermas misunderstands the nature of the "new social movements" by primarily identifying them with a middle-class constituency and its concerns. Nevertheless, whatever the limits of the undertaking, Habermas is engaged in an attempt to refashion the enterprise of critical theory by injecting it with a new sense of democratic purpose.

Critical theory was always a grand narrative; its attempts to illuminate the repressed subjectivity of the subject were predicated upon an ability to

---

try capable only of fostering regression, in Theodor W. Adorno, "Perennial Fashion: Jazz," in *Prisms*, trans. Samuel Weber and Shierry Weber (Cambridge: MIT Press, 1983).

totalize the totality; and its surrender of the revolutionary subject was the cause for sobriety and pessimism rather than joy. Critical theorists understood the price of progress, but they knew it was impossible to dispense with the concept. They engaged in a "relentless criticism of all existing conditions," but they did so while opposing relativism and trying to heed the cry of Walter Benjamin to "never forget the best." They called for "the great refusal," but they did so in the name of a repressed form of human solidarity. Critical theory, indeed, currently exhibits only part of its legacy: highlighting the other part, what remains hidden, calls for reappropriating the universalism and commitment to the Enlightenment, the ability to imagine new institutions, and—above all—the concern with politics its most popular representatives seemingly denied.

13

◆━━━◆

Postmodernism and Poststructuralism: Deconstruction, Desire, Difference

Postmodernism is probably the most controversial concept, and poststructuralism is surely the most controversial philosophical approach, of the last quarter of the twentieth century.[1] Its real impact has been shrouded in polemic; its language has been condemned for being impenetrable; its ideas have been castigated for contributing to what Allan Bloom called "the closing of the American mind." And there is no question about it. Postmodernism makes use of the scandalous and the outrageous. It also harbors a debilitating relativism. Its argumentation, couched in notoriously complex prose, is often strangely simpleminded. Still, the "American mind," whatever that might be, was not "closing" because of some postmodern

---

1. Useful introductions are provided by Steven Best and Douglas Kellner, *Postmodern Theory: Critical Interrogations* (New York: Guilford, 1991), and *The Postmodern Turn* (New York: Guilford, 1998); Steven Connor, *Postmodernist Culture: An Introduction to Theories of the Contemporary* (Oxford: Blackwell, 1989); Peter Dews, *Logics of Disintegration: Poststructuralist Thought and the Claims of Critical Theory* (London: Verso, 1987); David Harvey, *The Condition of Postmodernity: An Enquiry into the Origins of Change* (Oxford: Blackwell, 1989); Linda Hutcheon, *The Politics of Postmodernism* (New York: Routledge, 1989).

conspiracy. It was already in the process of being nailed shut by heavy-handed conservative ideologues, and, whatever their other failings, postmodernist thinkers helped keep it open.

Postmodernism generated a plethora of new interpretations of old texts. It breathed new life into the social sciences and the humanities. The canon could now be interpreted from the standpoint of women, people of color, gays, and other excluded groups. It illuminated limits in the classic texts never before considered important; it also made them relevant in new ways to new groups. It contested what had been a purely ethnocentric approach to culture; its partisans assaulted a host of long unquestioned claims and conventions, especially those concerning sexuality, gender, and mental health; and it is surely the case that their writings produced enormous debate and created many new interpretive possibilities. It is even possible to speak about a second Copernican revolution of philosophy, a "deconstruction" or "decentering" of Kant's transcendental subject, which meets the demands of a supposedly new epoch.

Postmodernism is an elastic concept; it describes an epoch robbed of certainties, all-embracing narratives, and transformative agents; it reflects an age in which qualitative differences between phenomena have seemingly been obliterated by the extension of what Marx termed the "commodity form." Whether the most important representatives of postmodernism ultimately provide a critique of this "condition" is an open matter. But the left-wing stance of its most dominant philosophers is indisputable. It is difficult to speak of a poststructuralist "school." But there are certain similarities with respect to the themes and the logic of argumentation among certain authors. Poststructuralism has sought to contest the continuing reliance on fixed structures or signs for interpreting theory and undertaking practice. It has constituted itself, whether purposely or not, as a tradition in its own right with its own intellectual predecessors. Especially given the self-professed individualism of its most important representatives, along with their annoying habit of appropriating the ideas of thinkers with very different epistemological premises, the intellectual origins of postmodernism becomes a matter of some importance. It is in terms of a tradition that the phenomenon is forged, and therein lies its authentic element.

The postmodernist enterprise has many sources. But its logic is probably best characterized by a form of "perspectivism" whose source undoubtedly derives from the writings of Frederick Nietzsche.[2] It was he, after all, who made the famous claim that "the subject is a fiction"[3] and thereby undercut any universal characterization of the individual. His primary philosophical categories of contention were obviously the *cogito* of Descartes and the transcendental subject of Kant. But the political object of his scorn was the language of the democratic citizen associated with both liberalism and socialism. Nietzsche feared the elimination of subjectivity, the unique moment of individuality, and genius in the name of equality. He despised what with religion had seemingly become a "genealogical" identification with the "herd," and he called for the individual to engage in a completely self-referential "transvaluation of values."[4] He associated knowledge exclusively with interest,[5] and he considered illusory any ethical stance with a universal or speculative referent for the formation of judgments.[6] It was, for Nietzsche, always a matter of exploding general categories and unexamined universal assumptions in the name of the lived experience. Indeed, the very attempt to generate a fixed and finished metanarrative was anathema precisely because it excluded the individual from participating in its construction.[7]

A new age of standardization, commercialization, and reification had made it necessary to articulate the concerns of subjectivity in a new way. Aphorism and montage, the assault on fixed notions of the real and "objective" forms of representation, would define the new enterprise. The way would open for each member of the audience to take an active part in the construction of any work. Subjectivity would dominate what had been considered "objective" reality, and individual concerns would define the "meaning" attributed to it. Boundaries between culture and politics, philosophy and science, art and criticism,[8] would subsequently appear as artificial

---

2. Friedrich Nietzsche, *The Will to Power*, ed. Walter Kaufmann, trans. Walter Kaufmann and R. J. Hollingdale (New York: Vintage, 1967), 267.

3. Ibid., 269.

4. Ibid., 156.

5. "It is our needs that interpret the world; our drives and their For and Against. Every drive is a kind of lust to rule; each one has its perspective that it would like to compel all the other drives to accept as a norm." Ibid., 267.

6. It is a condition defined by the weakness of the will in which "the 'good' and 'bad' man are merely two types of decadence: in all basic phenomena they agree." Ibid., 27.

7. Note the striking poststructuralist interpretation by Gilles Deleuze, *Nietzsche and Philosophy* (New York: Columbia University Press, 1983).

8. Instructive is the famous essay, "Uber Wesen und Form des Essays," in the first

as the moral categories by which individuals justified what was actually nothing more than their own will to power. The will indeed became the central philosophical concern. Anticipating the self-styled "politicians of the spirit" and the *politerats* of the modernist avant-garde, Nietzsche claimed that real change could only take place by making reference to this will and the terms in which its desires are expressed. A "new dawn" and a reinvigorated form of humanity, foreshadowed by Zarathustra and other "prophets" of the "superman," lay on the horizon, and the inability to deal with the implications of this new vision was the ultimate evidence of nihilism.

Martin Heidegger built on this claim. But he also thought that Nietzsche had compromised the radicalism of his message with his inability to overcome the strictures and assumptions of traditional philosophy. Nietzsche still maintained a conventional understanding of Being; he remained unable to grasp its "secret" or the "essence of nothingness" *(das Wesen des Nichts)* at its core; he still conceived of a connection between knowledge and interest, appearance and essence, thinking and being, idea and reality. This made a genuine self-mastery of the will impossible, and so, according to Heidegger, Nietzsche's thought evidences the very nihilism it sought to combat.[9] Nietzsche remains a representative, although the last great representative, of philosophical metaphysics.

Martin Heidegger sought a more radical stance. He believed it necessary to transvalue the notion of Being itself and thereby contest the entire tradition of Western philosophy beginning with Plato. All prior understandings of the concept rested on the possibility of its objectification or representation; as a consequence, the use of categories like "subject" and "object" became embedded within the very structure of Western thought. According to Heidegger, however, Being can never be made "present"; it eludes every possible form of objectification or categorization. "Being" is "there" only in the temporality *(Zeitlichkeit)* of an "existence" *(Dasein)* capable of asking after its own Being.[10] It reveals itself only through the singular experience generated by the most unique aspect of existence: the death which is "always mine" *(je meines)*. "Being," in short, is understood by Heidegger

---

pre-Marxist work by Georg Lukács, *Die Seele und die Formen* (Berlin: Luchterhand, 1971).

9. Martin Heidegger, *Der Europäische Nihilismus* (Pfülligen: Günther Neske, 1967), 30 ff.

10. Martin Heidegger, *Being and Time*, trans. John Macquarrie and Edward Robinson (New York: Harper and Row, 1962), 25–26.

as a function of an internal sense of time, and it makes itself felt through those moments of "anguish" *(Angst)* in which each feels the character of his or her finitude.

"Being," then must be grasped as a "Being-unto-death" *(Sein zum Tod)*. This makes it necessary for each "authentic" individual to contest every category, every form of organized experience, whereby "my" encounter with "my" most personal possibility is obscured, "my" uniqueness is threatened, and "my" desires are distorted. The public state of mind lacks intensity; its speech amounts to little more than chatter; its character is mediocre; it is defined by indifference to the inherently unique forms of experience. It is subsequently necessary to deny this public or common state of mind, this realm of all and yet no one, this world of *das Man*.[11] "Being" as my own, as "Being-unto-death," reveals itself not in the conventional representations of the public realm but in illuminated moments, snippets of artworks, everyday objects, and particular moods.[12] It breaks down logic and it escapes a common language. It always bears "my" imprint. What binds us is nothing more than the possibility of having that singular experience of Being, which is different for each. There is no grand narrative, no teleological purpose, no higher social value. Philosophy ceases to exist as an academic or abstract undertaking. Every universal, every "essence," every general claim is exploded in the concreteness of life: my impending death or the anticipatory stance *(vorlaufenden Entschlossenheit)* concerning its imminent "possibility." Nevertheless, just as Heidegger considered Nietzsche the "last metaphysician" and himself the prophet of a new philosophy, Jacques Derrida saw traces of traditional humanism in Heidegger's famous rejection of all "isms."[13]

Derrida called for a new philosophy, an explosion of metaphysics, predicated on a "deconstruction" of the language employed by philosophy itself. Derrida would retain the attack on "logocentrism" employed by Nietzsche and Heidegger. But he would radicalize it further or, better, make it more explicit by undermining the attempt to privilege reflection over intuition, the written word over the spoken, intentionality over contingency, the signified

---

11. Ibid., 166–67.

12. A more extended analysis of my views is provided in Stephen Eric Bronner, "Ontology and Its Discontents: Unorthodox Remarks on the Philosophy of Martin Heidegger," in *Of Critical Theory and Its Theorists* (Oxford: Blackwell, 1994).

13. Martin Heidegger, *Über den Humanismus* (Frankfurt am Main: Vittorio Klostermann, 1946).

over the signifier. The centered subject and the determinate object would finally collapse: the ability to privilege one stance over another, whether logically or normatively, would thereby become impossible, along with the rejection of all the major ideologies of this century and the past, including humanism.

Heidegger was seen by Derrida as providing Nietzsche with an ontological anchor for his metaphysics of the will. Insofar as Being serves as the foundation for existence, even if it never fully "presents" itself and even if it is grounded in "nothingness," postmodernists can claim that the concept still appears as an unnecessary remnant of absolutist thinking.[14] Better to consider this presence by its absence, make reference to it in every sentence and expression, only as what Jacques Derrida called a "line of erasure" or, ultimately, *le non-dit*.[15] The result is a particularly radical form of "the arbitrariness of the sign."[16] *Nothing* connects the original intention behind any signifier and the infinite possibilities for the signification of any given object. Coherence becomes impossible. Narratives subsequently collapse, along with hierarchical forms of thinking. Qualitative distinctions vanish. There is no "better" or "worse," except within arbitrarily constructed systems; there is actually only difference *(différance)*.

Subjectivity now escapes representation. It no longer makes sense for radicals to concern themselves with alternate foundations, absolute claims, or utopian institutions. It is not their function to judge between different possibilities or forward a positive program of their own. It becomes instead, according to Derrida, their "ethical-political duty" to illuminate the gap between logical argumentation and the intentions or desires informing it. They

---

14. "To save Nietzsche from a reading of the Heideggerian type, it seems that we must above all not attempt to restore or make explicit a less naive 'ontology,' composed of profound ontological intuitions acceding to some originary truth, an entire fundamentality hidden under the appearance of an empiricist or metaphysical text. . . . Rather than protect Nietzsche from the Heideggerian reading, we should perhaps offer him up to it completely, underwriting that interpretation without reserve; in a *certain way* and up to the point where, the content of the Nietzschean discourse being almost lost for the question of being, its form regains its absolute strangeness." Jacques Derrida, *Of Grammatology*, trans. Gayitri Chakravorty Spivak (Baltimore: Johns Hopkins University Press, 1976), 19.

15. The thought of writing the word *Being* "under a line of erasure" initially derives from Heidegger; see Jacques Derrida, *Of Spirit: Heidegger and the Question*, trans. Geoffrey Bennington and Rachel Bowlby (Chicago: University of Chicago Press, 1989), 52.

16. Derrida, *Of Grammatology*, 44 ff.

should preoccupy themselves with the "deconstruction" of reality, highlight the way in which any system of reference is constituted as a fabric of differences,[17] and expand the possibilities of signification and experience.

Derrida simultaneously rejects the possibility of either remaining within the limits of tradition or transgressing those limits. Both are predicated on a rejection of the "nonidentical" in favor of traditional assumptions of identity. These assumptions, culminating in the idea of "friendship," also inform all traditional notions of politics, though Derrida seems to forget that the very purpose underlying treaty-making in particular and decision-making in general presupposes a suspension of all concerns with empathy, friendship, and identity of feelings.[18] In any event, for Derrida, the philosophical point involves an attempt less to highlight any positive determination of what is "said," following Emmanuel Levinas,[19] than to hold open the process of "saying." Derrida is perhaps unique in putting matters quite this way. But, theoretically, the implications are the same as those generated by the majority of other postmodernist thinkers: everything becomes provisional, a matter of case-by-case determinations, and there is little sense of the obvious political and ethical dangers involved in the arbitrary definition or justification of concepts. For example, identifying law with right, Derrida is content to invoke a completely indeterminate and messianic "idea of justice"— revelatory in character and beyond experience or articulation—as a standpoint of criticism.[20] The similarity of his approach with the traditional positivist position of a legal thinker like Carl Schmitt, who also introduces a completely arbitrary notion of decision beyond immediate legal principles, simply never occurs to Derrida. It is apparently enough for him to liberate an inexpressible form of "desire," which speaks to justice, and reject the artificial ways in which reality has been constructed in order to repress it.[21]

Desire always escapes its formal definition; and if only for this reason,

17. Ibid., 27.
18. See Jacques Derrida, *Politics of Friendship*, trans. George Collins (New York: Verso, 1997).
19. Emmanuel Levinas, *Otherwise than Being or Beyond Essence*, trans. Alphonso Lingis (The Hague: Kluwer Academic, 1981); Jacques Derrida, "Violence and Metaphysics: An Essay on the Thought of Emmanuel Levinas," in *Writing and Difference*, trans. Alan Bass (Chicago: University of Chicago Press, 1978).
20. Jacques Derrida, *Force de loi* (Paris: Editions Galilee, 1997); also note the excellent discussion by Mark Lilla, "The Politics of Jacques Derrida," *New York Review of Books*, June 25, 1998, 36 ff.
21. Jacques Lacan, *Écrits: A Selection*, trans. Alan Sheridan (New York: Norton, 1977).

Jean-François Lyotard views the postmodern as an "incredulity toward metanarratives."[22] He suggests by this a skepticism toward all general claims, universal theories of history, and any view of society as a coherent totality with a fixed or stable "subject." The attempt to objectify the subject, according to this mode of thinking, necessarily flattens it out; the universal engulfs the particular; the attempt to thematize necessity leads to the constriction of freedom. Recourse to the metanarrative or the philosophical engagement with the "totality," in short, generates precisely the kind of homogenizing and utopian ambitions associated with totalitarianism. If Hegel said that "the whole is true," and Adorno responded with the statement that "the whole is false," Lyotard would rejoin with the claim that the whole is illusion and truth is always singular, partial, and disruptive.

The postmodern condition fosters a new sensitivity to the differences between individuals and groups even as it reinforces toleration of the "incommensurable."[23] Lyotard even believes it necessary to distinguish different "regimes of phrases" with their own rules in order to resist any "totalizing" impulse.[24] That would simultaneously make it possible to introduce multiple understandings for any given notion, such as justice.[25] The practical dangers of making and remaking "justice" as circumstances and desires dictate is never taken seriously. By the same token, theoretically, the need for either justifying the integrity of different realms or the type of rules appropriate to each is never articulated by Lyotard. And for good reason. If Kant is used as a paradigmatic example of such a procedure—if his description of the different realms of knowledge, metaphysics, and aesthetics is made possible only by defining each in relation to the others—then such an undertaking would obviously engage the postmodern author in the very type of "grand narrative" he or she should wish to avoid. It does not help to highlight the currently fashionable category of "critical difference" without articulating positive criteria for making judgments; it also does not help to emphasize the "critical distance" on reality offered by postmodernism without taking into account the notion of "reflection," embedded in

---

22. Jean-François Lyotard, *The Postmodern Condition*, trans. Geoff Bennington and Brian Massumi (Minneapolis: University of Minnesota Press, 1984), xxiv.

23. Ibid., xxv.

24. Jean-François Lyotard, *The Differend*, trans. Vlad Godzich (Minneapolis: University of Minnesota Press, 1988).

25. Jean-François Lyotard and Jean-Loup Thebaud, *Just Gaming*, trans. George Vandenabeelle (Minneapolis: University of Minnesota Press, 1985).

the idealist tradition, which fulfills exactly the same function.[26] Such procedures inevitably place the postmodern undertaking in contradiction with its own premises.

Postmodern logic inevitably privileges "desire," and in this vein "desire" undermines any practical referent for judging it. The entire purpose of the enterprise, perhaps most clearly expressed by Michel Foucault, is the affirmation of the self in the face of "dividing practices" and essentialist forms of "classification."[27] Repression is, following Nietzsche, genealogically structured.[28] It inherently reflects binary relations: black and white, female and male, straight and gay, sane and insane, normal and abnormal. Hegemony and subalternity subsequently rest on certain experiences and interests embedded in language and the knowledge it provides, or what Foucault termed *"epistèmes."* Consequently, the weaker party cannot resist the stronger, affirm himself or herself, by employing the dominant discourse. No categorical distinction is made between coercion and persuasion. Using language is a way of exercising power: there can be nothing "neutral" about reflexivity or concepts like justice and liberty.

It is again a question of making manifest what has been ignored in the name of "grand narratives," philosophical universals, and organizational hierarchies with their rules and regulations. The singular, the excluded, the forgotten logically become the preserve of postmodernists and poststructuralists. Insofar as recognition of the Other and knowledge about new forms of experience expands, in principle no less often than in practice, there is a certain legitimacy for this kind of cultural preoccupation. But the problems for political practice become readily apparent. No particular agency has privilege over any other; and with respect to organization, there is no logical way of justifying the imposition of discipline on any dissident member of any group: parliamentary rules of order become as authoritarian as the billy club. Spontaneity becomes the logical purpose of organization, even though lack of clear organizational rules can generate the most intense forms of authoritarianism. The most political expressions of the new trend have, for

26. See Nancy Fraser, *Justice Interruptus: Critical Reflections on the "Postsocialist" Condition* (New York: Routledge, 1998), 4 ff. and passim.
27. Michel Foucault, *The Order of Things: An Archaeology of the Human Sciences* (New York: Vintage, 1973), 125 ff.
28. Michel Foucault, "Nietzsche, Genealogy, History," in *Language, Counter-Memory, Practice: Selected Essays and Interviews*, ed. Donald F. Bouchard, trans. Donald F. Bouchard and Sherry Simon (Ithaca: Cornell University Press, 1977).

better or worse, been profoundly influenced by the anarchists' emphasis upon localism and autonomy. It is thus only logical that, where various poststructuralist thinkers should have emphasized the need for "micropolitics," Foucault sought to substitute the "specific" for the "universal" intellectual of both the bourgeoisie and the working class.[29]

In the poststructuralist view, political activists should deal with problems emanating from "where their own condition of life and work situates them."[30] Women must primarily speak for women, gays for gays, even as intellectuals must make use of their disciplinary knowledge to solve the particular problems of their "subject position." Intellectuals should commit themselves to the particular groups with whose unique discourses and experiences they, as individuals, are intimately familiar. Each social movement must retain its own distinct "intellectuals" in order to further those particular demands ignored by organizations with more universal aspirations. Genuine interaction is subsequently seen as taking place less between strangers in a public sphere than between "brothers" or "sisters" of any group whose members share a common experience.

Immanent criticism of the sort employed by Kant, Hegel, Marx, and the Frankfurt School is useless. The subaltern must develop its own forms of discourse with its own *epistèmes*, or assumptions for providing experience with meaning, which are closed to the Other. Genuine politics cannot take place through a consensual "dialogue"; it must instead explode the discourse. The basic metaphor of poststructuralism would become one of battle rather than conversation.[31] The point is to alter existing power relations in order to affirm any given subjective desire. And such affirmation occurs continuously. Desire takes varied forms. There is no single identity for a single person. Each person is a conglomerate of sites: color, ethnicity, class, sexual orientation, and so on. Each site projects a certain desire and a possible form of identification. The affirmation of subjectivity takes place in the multiplicity of "sites" wherein a multiplicity of repressed desires becomes manifest. Each projects a new experience of reality, and therein lies the prospect of liberation. Nevertheless, the moment of emancipatory possibility— the moment of "desire"—is always chained to its context.

---

29. Michel Foucault, "Intellectuals and Power," in *Language, Counter-Memory, Practice*; and Foucault, "Truth and Power," in *The Foucault Reader*, ed. Paul Rabinow (New York: Vintage, 1984).
30. Ibid., 68.
31. Paul Rabinow, introduction to *Foucault Reader*, 6.

Criticism from the "outsider" loses its value, questions concerning the adjudication of differences between groups are never faced, and the supposedly cosmopolitan respect for "difference" surrenders in favor of a new parochialism. Richard Rorty builds upon this stance. In the process, however, he surrenders the "responsibility to otherness" emphasized by Derrida along with the revolutionary radicalism of Foucault. His "pragmatism" inflates even as it tempers the "antiessentialist" character of his poststructuralist enterprise.[32] There is no need for "first principles." Inquiry is predicated on nothing more than the individual curiosity or subjective interests informing what Rorty calls "conversation." No epistemological "starting points" or discursive presuppositions exist for dealing with others. The self is a network of beliefs, desires, and emotions with nothing behind it and no substrate behind its attributes. The moral force of our convictions is "inseparable from understanding ourselves as the *particular* people we are," writes Rorty, and he goes on to argue "that the moral force of such loyalties and convictions consists *wholly* in this fact, and that nothing else has *any* moral force."[33]

Liberalism and, arguably, socialism can receive a "circular justification" with respect to the advantages they provide, though, according to Rorty, it is impossible to provide a philosophical legitimation of their basic principles. Points of universal ethical reference disappear. Rorty is, in this regard, initially willing to draw the radical practical implication of poststructuralist theory. Although he is nominally concerned with expanding the voices engaged in a social "conversation," his thinking is ultimately fueled by a particularist politics based on "ethnosolidarity" and a "civilized indifference" to others. Preoccupied with single issues rather than the formation of any broader forms of ideological solidarity or practical organization,[34] Rorty also considers it time to trade in the grand metanarratives of the intellectuals for "popular narratives." This indeed mirrors a certain phony intellectual slumming when it comes to "popular culture." Criteria for distinguishing between genuinely valuable "popular narratives" and simple prejudices or

---

32. Richard Rorty, *Consequences of Pragmatism* (Minneapolis: University of Minnesota Press, 1982).

33. Richard Rorty, "Postmodernist Bourgeois Liberalism," in *Objectivity, Relativism, and Truth: Philosophical Papers* (Cambridge: Cambridge University Press, 1991), 200.

34. "Either we attach a special privilege to our own community, or we pretend an impossible tolerance for every other group." Ibid., 202.

cultural trash, on one hand, and the innovations of popular culture, on the other, are, of course, never made explicit.

Postmodern intellectuals must surrender their totalizing ambitions. It is no longer up to them to "legislate";[35] their responsibility is now to build upon the insight that truth is a social construct, particular to a particular group with a particular set of experiences. Such a stance involves a hypocritical form of self-denial on the part of the intellectual. "Engagement" is reduced to the symbolic or existential gesture of the "person" in search of an identity whose own "I" is, nonetheless, always in doubt. The "experience" of reality takes precedence, and for this reason judgment always becomes both tentative and dogmatic: tentative with respect to the discursive justification of its claims, dogmatic with respect to the legitimacy of asserting them.

The fear of dealing seriously with the possibility of "falsifying" claims, which Karl Popper first introduced as an intrinsic part of the scientific method, is striking in this regard. Such a stance not only renders any practical encounter with established notions of "science" fruitless, because postmodernist criticisms have little to do with what actually occurs in the laboratory, but it also undermines the possibility of dealing with genuinely radical movements of "popular science" in the postcolonial world.[36] There exists, in any event, a marked difference between the demands for justification, which poststructuralists apply to their opponents, and their own refusal to articulate criteria with which to legitimate their positions. The inability to distinguish between persuasion and coercion indeed becomes mirrored in the inability to distinguish between forms of argument and particular claims. The arbitrary use of citations by thinkers with very different epistemological assumptions,[37] the postmodern dismissal of what Louis Althusser termed the *problématique* underpinning a given philosophical or political undertaking, has helped bring a profound epistemological confusion into their own works in particular and the progressive political project in general.

---

35. Zygmunt Bauman, *Legislators and Interpreters: On Modernity, Postmodernity, and Intellectuals* (Ithaca: Cornell University Press, 1987), 21 ff., 120 ff.

36. Meera Nanda, "Of Prophets Facing Backwards: Problems of Postmodern Critiques of Science in Postcolonial Societies," Ph.D. diss., Rensselaer Polytechnic Institute, 1998.

37. See Derrida, *Of Spirit: Heidegger and the Question*;Jean-François Lyotard, *Heidegger and "The Jews,"* trans. Andreas Michel and Mark Roberts (Minneapolis: University of Minnesota Press, 1990).

Postmodernists would surely respond by noting the lack of foundation for any type of genuinely epistemological inquiry. And without "foundations," epistemology supposedly loses its justification.[38] Even if epistemology lacks absolute justification, however, its various forms of expression might still harbor qualitatively different practical implications. These demand normative judgment. If the drive toward systematic thinking is seen as totalitarian, and all ethical justifications for action are termed illusory, then rendering a reasoned judgment becomes impossible. The abdication of ethical judgment thus turns into a principle of judgment.

Various partisans of poststructuralism are content with substituting the emphasis upon "difference" for the notion of critique inherited from modern idealism. They are essentially unconcerned with "ethics" because of its inevitable reliance on logical categories, epistemological assumptions, and ontological foundations.[39] Other poststructuralist thinkers, however, have noted the unsettling characteristics of this trend, and they have sought to deal with it. They have emphasized the importance of "tearing off the mask of illusions; the recognition of certain pretenses as false and certain objectives as neither attainable nor, for that matter, desirable."[40]

But that is simply inadequate. Critique or deconstruction is always the easy part; positive commitment and reconstruction are more difficult. And, as the positive concerns slip away, there is no place left for freedom to confront license, for the universal to confront the particular, for the idea of right to confront the stirring of desire, or for a common language with which to make sense of the world. Inquiries have been made into what Derrida has called an "ethics of ethics" predicated on a certain sensitivity underpinning the "relation to the Other."[41] Perhaps because he identifies discourse with reality, however, he has never even marginally articulated the character of that sensitivity and the nature of that relationship.

Nowhere is there a sense that people are involved in real activities, struc-

---

38. Sources for the postmodernist assault on epistemology are usually seen, for better or worse, in Theodor W. Adorno, *Against Epistemology—A Metacritique: Studies in Husserl and the Phenomenological Antinomies*, trans. Willis Domingo (Cambridge: MIT Press, 1985), and particularly the early work by Paul Feyerabend, *Against Method: Outline of an Anarchist Theory of Knowledge* (London: New Left, 1975).
39. Note the discussion by Honglim Ryu, "The Politics of Ethical Discourse," Ph.D. diss., Rutgers University, 1994, 167 ff.
40. Zygmunt Bauman, *Postmodern Ethics* (Oxford: Blackwell, 1993), 3.
41. Derrida, *Writing and Difference*, 111.

tured by real institutions and agendas, and that they must often make choices between available options. Regulative ideals for informing such choices are never provided; positive ends disappear as surely as the process by which their value might be ascertained. Ethics remains negative or deconstructive. But this is not "ethics." It merely introduces the term while withdrawing its content and purpose, which, incidentally, is precisely what occurs with the idea of justice. A self-referential ethics, an ethic unconcerned with providing positive criteria for making "practical" decisions or rendering normative judgments, is no ethic at all.

Such a stance can help make sense of aesthetic experiences and existential concerns with authenticity. But what is progressive in the cultural or existential realms need not prove progressive in the realm of politics, and vice versa. It is unnecessary to endorse the primacy of literary representation, or "socialist realism," to note the irrationalist and reactionary possibilities evidenced by purely self-referential forms of aesthetic theory when transferred into the realm of politics. There is indeed a case to be made that the possibility for genuinely engaging in new forms of aesthetic experience radically increases within a democratic political order and, furthermore, that expanding the range of experimentation is among the purposes of such an order. But thinkers like Nietzsche and Heidegger clearly did not agree. They equated democracy and equality, justice and "humanity," with decadence and mediocrity, the impersonal and the inauthentic. They were unconcerned with institutions, and they opposed the progressive political movements of their time. They obliterated the line between freedom and license. And that, indeed, can only benefit the powerful.

Most postmodernists side with the struggles of the excluded and the chastised. But they lack criteria to decide upon the legitimacy of the protest. Their preoccupation with "gaming" the rules of justice occurs without reference to any positive, or universalist, articulation of what justice might involve. Their encounter with Marxism occurs without reference to its teleology, its political economy, its notion of agency, or the political traditions on which it is based.[42] Their validation of desire is linked with an assault on utopia, and their antiessentialism logically generates a rejection of "rights." The popularity of postmodernism among a broad stratum of intellectuals in

---

42. Jacques Derrida, *Specters of Marx: The State of the Debt, the Work of Mourning, and the New International*, trans. Peggy Kamuf (New York: Routledge, 1994).

the United States during the 1970s and 1980s was indeed a philosophical reflection of the dissolution of the Civil Rights Movement and the collapse of the Poor People's Movement envisioned by Reverend Dr. Martin Luther King Jr.

Progressive forces have been on the defensive ever since. It is certainly not all the fault of postmodernism. But the post-1968 strategy clearly needs revision. Fragmentation has grown amid the new preoccupation with subjectivity. Arbitrariness has been fueled by the reliance on difference, the assault on universalism has propagated simple self-interest, and the rejection of grand narratives has made it impossible to thematize an increasingly complex and interdependent economic, social, and political order. Too much intellectual and practical work has been invested, too many cultural gains have been made, for postmodernists simply to discard poststructuralist thinking in the name of a new political orientation. It is little wonder that intelligent and politically concerned representatives of this tendency should have sought ways to temper the exaggerated attack on "essentialism" and to overcome the practical problems that their own theories helped generate. Thus, although Enlightenment values were initially considered an "obstacle" in understanding the identity politics of the new social movements,[43] certain thinkers began to maintain that postmodern logic leads to "an awareness of the complex strategic-discursive operations implied by [the] defense" of such values.[44]

Postmodernism becomes a way, in short, of attempting to reconstruct the Enlightenment heritage on a new "antiessentialist" and "nonuniversalist" basis.[45] But what this enterprise actually involves is never made clear. The dialectical sophistry of using anti-Enlightenment arguments to foster Enlightenment practice was never taken seriously. It was the same with the reasons why, putting the matter crudely, Enlightenment values should have traditionally been embraced by progressive and anti-Enlightenment by reactionary movements.[46] Practical concerns were also ignored. It simply re-

---

43. Chantal Mouffe, "Radical Democracy: Modern or Postmodern?" in *Universal Abandon*, ed. Andrew Ross (Minneapolis: University of Minnesota Press, 1988), 53.

44. Ernesto Laclau, "Politics and the Limits of Modernity," in Ross, *Universal Abandon*, 72.

45. Ernesto Laclau and Chantal Mouffe, *Hegemony and Socialist Strategy: Toward a Radical Democratic Politics* (London: Verso, 1985).

46. For a more complete discussion of the Enlightenment and its political heritage and its connection with contemporary political theory, see Stephen Eric Bronner,

mains unclear how, whatever the vague though enthusiastic commitment to rights, the liberal rule of law can be conceived without making reference to universals. How philosophical particularism might conflict with the requirements for a broader organizational unity on the left, or the normative institutional prerequisites for sustaining democratic and socialist institutions, is never confronted forthrightly.

A somewhat more metaphysical attempt to deal with the tensions between poststructuralist "antiessentialism" and the Enlightenment heritage occurs in the writings of Judith Butler. She rejects the basic opposition between "contingency" and philosophical "foundations."[47] Precisely because every foundational, universal, or totalizing narrative legitimates a dominant social interest, according to her line of reasoning, the claim itself is always contingent, and the point is to recognize it as such. But that is made possible only by recognizing the existence of a foundational or universal claim in the first place. A category like "woman" may, for example, hide the differences between various women. It remains necessary to retain the general category as a point of reference, however, in order to highlight the existence of contingent and particular women. The general category is thus introduced even though its "absolute" character is denied; it remains "open." The category is introduced only so that it can be dislodged, invalidated, or ignored later as circumstances dictate. The universal serves as a straw man, and support for it lacks any conviction. Nevertheless, it illuminates the way in which poststructuralism has come full circle.

Many poststructuralists now identify themselves with the institutional framework of liberal democracy. Richard Rorty, Judith Butler, and others have recognized that such an order alone makes it possible to challenge "hegemonic" forms of discourse and to foster diversity. And viewing liberalism as the foundation for pluralism, as the tradition ranging from John Locke to Lord Acton to Sir Isaiah Berlin already noted, makes perfect sense. To argue this from a poststructuralist perspective, however, creates a number of problems for the original theoretical undertaking. Liberal democracy is inherently based on "essentialist" premises; and, whatever the progressive

---

"The Great Divide: The Enlightenment and Its Critics," *New Politics* 5, no. 3 (Summer 1995): 65 ff.; also note the reply by Loren Goldner, "Renaissance or Enlightenment?" and my rejoinder, "Politics or Utopia?" *New Politics* 6, no. 1 (Summer 1996): 137 ff., 146 ff.

47. Judith Butler, *Gender Troubles: Feminism and the Subversion of Identity* (New York: Routledge, 1992).

intentions of various supporters of identity politics, not every form of particularism furthers liberal or democratic values. The practical necessity of embracing liberal values confronts the lack of any theoretical legitimation for them. The contradiction is glaring. And because it is irresolvable, some have chosen to believe that the best option is to sidestep the problem. Thus, the need to engage in what Gayatri Spivak originally called "strategic essentialism."[48]

In other words, poststructuralism must presuppose in practice what it denies in theory. And therein lies the most apparent political weakness of the approach. It has often been noted that this putatively radical theory has been unable to analyze the various imbalances of power under capitalism. But this has less to do with neglect than with an epistemological inability to thematize *any* phenomenon. It is the same with issues of conviction and program; typically, in his *Specters of Marx*, Derrida calls for a "new International" without confronting any of the traditional ideological, organizational, or political problems, let alone the new ways in which internationalism has been transformed and international politics can be pursued. The inability to present positive alternatives in a serious way is not a correctable flaw within an otherwise viable philosophical position. More is involved than the cynical and despairing rejection of political action by figures like Jean Baudrillard, who, finding that history has culminated in an undifferentiated and inert mass, advises us simply to "accommodate ourselves to the time left to us."[49] Deconstructive theory in general, critical of all grand narratives, unwilling to thematize institutions, and incapable of privileging any particular position on any particular issue, is also incapable of projecting the normative or institutional vision for contesting any system.

Only by providing positive convictions can a philosophy exhibit its political validity. This problem, indeed, goes to the core of the postmodern project. It is insufficient simply to call for recognition of any particular interest without reference to universal norms; cultural prejudices are inherent in this kind of political stance. But the universal is precisely what was sacrificed in the name of the particular during the 1970s and 1980s, and, as a conse-

---

48. Gayatri Chakravorty Spivak, *In Other Worlds* (New York: Routledge, 1989).
49. Jean Baudrillard, "The Year 2000 Has Already Happened," in *Body Invaders: Panic Sex in America*, ed. Arthur Kroker and Marilouise Kroker (Montreal: New World Perspectives, 1988), 35–44; also see Douglas Kellner, *Jean Baudrillard: From Marxism to Postmodernism and Beyond* (Cambridge, U.K.: Polity, 1989).

quence, the moral high ground held by the left during the Civil Rights Movement and the early struggles against the Vietnam War was clearly lost. Poststructuralist forms of "strategic essentialism" will surely not help in recovering it. They give no clue regarding when it is necessary to privilege universalistic against particularistic claims. The relativism and emphasis on particular "experience," which originally gave the method its philosophical power, are neither denied nor embraced. They are simply left in a strange form of limbo.

The contradiction between theory and practice now exists for postmodernism as surely as it did for the socialist labor movement when Eduard Bernstein chastised its leaders for preaching a revolutionary Marxist theory while engaging in a purely reformist practice. And the response to this current situation must take the same form. It is high time to end the equivocations. Let the postmodernist critics of Enlightenment values either keep their radically subjectivist form of theory and, in the manner of Nietzsche and Heidegger, transform the notion of praxis to meet their theoretical beliefs or else come to grips with political reality, recognize the needs of existing forms of progressive action, and draw the theoretical consequences.

This must, in the first instance, involve differentiating between relativism and pluralism. Both notions militate against the idea that any single truth will show the way into paradise; and, arguably, both call the notion of utopia into question. But pluralism presupposes certain universal conditions or institutions for exercising it as well as the ability of individuals to make judgments about its character. Relativism assumes, by way of contrast, that a judgment or a claim or an emotional attitude is what it is and lacks the need for any objective referent to validate it for others. Those, like Richard Rorty, who refuse to consider relativism a "real" problem simply turn their back on the destructive impact it exercises upon contemporary political discourse. Sir Isaiah Berlin, himself no friend of universalist pretensions, put it well when he wrote,

> Intercommunication between cultures in time and space is only possible because what makes men human is common to them, and acts as a bridge between them. Our values are ours, and theirs are theirs. We are free to criticize the values of other cultures, to condemn them, but we cannot pretend not to understand them at all or to regard them simply as subjective, the products of

creatures in different circumstances with different tastes from our own, which do not speak to us at all.[50]

During the Enlightenment, the "engaged intellectual" sought to contribute to the creation of pluralistic institutions and justify critique. Such engagement, however, did not preclude the formulation of those broader universal prerequisites for the constraint of arbitrary power without which the expression of subjectivity becomes impossible. Our planet harbors diverse customs and even more diverse possibilities for existential satisfaction. But the corrective for philosophical dogmatism is not an uncritical subjectivism skeptical of reason. It is instead a new willingness to thematize the past and forge a positive notion of political ethics capable of dealing with the structural imbalances of power and offering solutions to the problems facing us.

---

50. Isaiah Berlin, "The Pursuit of the Ideal," in *The Crooked Timber of Humanity: Chapters in the History of Ideas*, ed. Henry Hardy (New York: Vintage, 1992), 11.

14

◇━━━◇

The Radical Imagination:
Aesthetics, Spontaneity, Utopia

> Truth is inseparable from the illusory belief that from the figures of the
> unreal one day, in spite of all, real deliverance will come.
>
> Theodor Adorno

1 795: Robespierre had fallen two years before, and the Reign of Terror had ceased. The French Revolution, embattled at home and under siege from abroad, had been transformed from a parliamentary regime into an authoritarian triumvirate. Its radical democratic project had already been compromised, but Napoleon had not yet become, in the famous words of Hegel, "the world spirit on a white horse." Not just the bourgeoisie but humanity itself seemed to have lost its great hope for liberation. Yet, somehow, it was only fitting that Friedrich Schiller should have published his extraordinary *Letters on the Aesthetic Education of Man* during that same year. His new aesthetic vision would preserve in the imagination what politics had squandered in deed; his utopian image of cultural transformation would compensate for the failure of politics.

The need for a similar compensation appeared during the 1950s when it finally became clear to virtually all progressives that the emancipatory promise of the Russian Revolution had been betrayed. Social democracy was content with reaching a postwar accord with capital, and the majority of thinkers in what would become the major trends of the postwar period resigned themselves to the passing of utopia. Existentialists, critical theo-

rists, and later postmodernists were generally content to secure the unqualified primacy of subjectivity against the intrusions of a reified world. Most
embraced a cautious, defensive, left-liberal political posture, without an
agent, without a vision, without an overriding commitment to the radical
imagination. But there were also some who sought to forge a more radical,
emancipatory reaction against the totalitarian perversion of utopia. Their
respect for the integrity of the individual would prove no less genuine than
that of their more establishmentarian democratic opponents. Many of them
were unorthodox Marxists, former Trotskyists, and disillusioned communists. They, too, sought to compensate for the concrete failure of the revolution by reclaiming the sense of utopian possibility, recasting the notion of
engagement, inventing a liberated form of social organization, and providing a new understanding of agency, without teleological certainty, without
a mass base, and without an existing model.

Initially published in 1955, *Eros and Civilization* by Herbert Marcuse can
be seen as an attempt to compensate for the collapse of revolutionary politics, in general, and the institutional degeneration of the Soviet Union, in
particular,[1] by positing a primarily aesthetic vision of utopian emancipation.
Marcuse had always been influenced by Schiller, and this work illustrates
the fact. His vision is predicated on an anthropological break with "the reality principle" and its capitalist variant known as the "performance principle";[2] its utopian content is defined by a new respect for what Schiller had
understood as "play"; its aim is an erotically reconfigured humanity, or
what Schiller would have termed a new "aesthetic shape" for men and
women, with a new ethical "sensibility" repulsed by suffering; its critical
confrontation with the existing order rests on the rejection of "false needs"
and the "surplus repression" generated by the patriarchal family, the
church, the hierarchical division of labor, the state, and the media. Its radicalism is expressed in the visionary conquest of death and the "tyranny of
becoming over being." Its concern is with securing the enjoyment of a private life uninhibited by guilt. This utopia is indeed constructed upon the
most radical promise of art, the promise of Eros against Thanatos, which is
"attained and sustained fulfillment, the transparent unity of subject and object; of the universal and the individual."[3]

---

1. Herbert Marcuse, *Soviet Marxism: A Critical Analysis* (New York: Columbia
University Press, 1958).
2. Herbert Marcuse, *Eros and Civilization: A Philosophical Inquiry into Freud*
(New York: Vintage, 1962), 135.
3. Ibid., 34 ff., 110, 109.

To claim that the privilege accorded "play" in this emancipated order exhibits infantile regression is to miss the point; it does not matter that the abolition of the "performance principle" coupled with the transformation of the entire body into an erogenous zone, what Freud termed "polymorphous perversity," might result in the eradication of the ego.[4] Other standards, qualitatively different standards, are in operation. This utopia is, in keeping with Schiller, a "beautiful illusion" (schöner Schein). It is incapable of being realized if only because creating an emancipated society of this sort already presupposes the existence of emancipated individuals. The ability of subjects to even imagine unfettered freedom is, after all, precisely what advanced industrial society denies. Nevertheless, the challenge is made in what is surely the most influential work by Herbert Marcuse, One-Dimensional Man (1964).

Many of its themes were previously articulated in other works by other members of the Frankfurt School. Given the lack of translations before the 1970s, however, One-Dimensional Man was virtually the only work of critical theory available in the English-speaking world, and it was quickly translated into numerous languages, with the same extraordinary impact. Its theses were clear-cut. Advanced industrial society is absorbing all forces of opposition and obliterating the "subjective" conditions for conflict between classes, as well as between the individual and society, just as the "objective" reality of exploitation and injustice is intensifying. The extraordinary technological possibilities generated by advanced industrial society are increasingly being turned toward regressive ends. The "culture industry" is intent upon bringing about a "closing of the political universe."[5] Radical ideas are losing their emancipatory character in the very process of becoming popular, the ability to engage in critical reflection is diminishing, and a decline is occurring in what Marx termed the "material level of culture." What is called "thinking" now exists merely to make the prevailing system more efficient and raise technical means over normative ends. Individuals in advanced industrial society consequently find themselves adapting to the existing order rather than developing the capacity for critical judgment.

Thus, where Hegel could speak of the "unhappy consciousness" incapable of adapting to the constraints of his time, Marcuse highlighted the tri-

---

4. Erich Fromm, The Revision of Psychoanalysis, ed. Rainer Funk (Boulder: Westview, 1992), 111 ff.

5. Herbert Marcuse, One-Dimensional Man: Studies in the Ideology of Advanced Industrial Society (Boston: Beacon, 1964), 19 ff.

umph of the "happy consciousness."[6] The Other is, in short, threatened with integration and disempowerment. Residues of radicalism now lie only within "marginal groups" extrinsic to the functioning of the current order: women, minorities, students, and the inhabitants of the colonized world. Marcuse believed they might still generate a "new sensibility" predicated on the rejection of a vapid materialism and a stultifying notion of progress.

Prophetic with respect to the future role of the new social movements but still clear about the need for an active proletariat in bringing about radical change, Marcuse never developed a way of linking their interests with those of the working class. Skeptical about institutional politics, without any organizational ideas for sustaining the movement, he had as little sense of political program as the *enragés* of Paris. But his thinking anticipated the spirit of 1968 with its concern for alienation, its bohemian contempt for conformism, and its profoundly critical quality. *One-Dimensional Man*, in all these ways, inspired the movement and its most provocative slogans: "Power to the imagination!" and "Be realistic! Demand the impossible!"

This existential moment of politics became manifest in the writings of Marcuse, who had studied with Heidegger and closely followed intellectual currents in France. Whatever Marcuse's criticisms of Sartre's early writings,[7] his more critical stance on the Soviet Union, and his somewhat more nuanced views on revolution in the non-Western world, many of his concerns overlapped with those formulated by Sartre. Most fundamentally, indeed, both believed that material freedom had produced a spiritual impoverishment of the individual. Both identified freedom as, only and exclusively, a freedom of the subject; especially in the case of Sartre, this basic contention sharply contradicted his more dogmatic proclamations and his political misadventures. There was a sense that freedom was not being exercised. This unrelenting emphasis upon freedom, indeed, made Sartre's work a source of inspiration for the rebels of 1968 beyond his own political miscalculations.

His early masterpiece, *Being and Nothingness* (1939), highlighted the subjectivity of the subject in what was becoming a seemingly administered world. The individual is unique and alone. "Nothing" justifies his or her "being." As long as an individual acts, he or she is alive; thus, human exis-

---

6. Ibid., 56 ff.
7. Note the superb review of *Being and Nothingness* in Herbert Marcuse, *Studies in Critical Philosophy*, trans. Joris De Bres (Boston: Beacon, 1973), 174.

tence is always unfinished. The individual as a "being for-itself" "lacks" the fullness of a thing or a "being in-itself." He or she is therefore inherently incapable of fulfilling his or her personal "project," and in this sense "man is a useless passion."[8] At the same time, however, the ability to act with a purposive self-consciousness is precisely what makes a person human. Action is ontologically considered by Sartre a derivative of freedom and a product of choice: "It is freedom which is the foundation of the true, and the rigorous necessity that appears in the order of truths is itself supported by the absolute contingency of a creative free will."[9]

The foundation of individuality denies itself: "existence" precedes "essence." Each individual is contingent and "superfluous" *(de trop)*.[10] It is up to individuals to take responsibility for their actions—or, better, for defining themselves—within any given "situation." There is no universal subject, there is no subject of history, there is no God. There is nothing to support the existence of the individual and nothing that links a person with others. And that is precisely what makes "anguish" the most singular experience in which one becomes aware of one's freedom.[11] The concrete individual precedes the universal categories used to validate him or her. The need for self-definition is neither artificial nor organic; it is inscribed within the very experience of existence. And this concreteness was precisely what made Sartre's brand of existentialism so appealing. He may have engaged in a rather half-hearted attempt to relate his existentialism to humanism. Nevertheless, his irony is never sharper than when he speaks about those who choose to understand the world as a place where each hates everyone else, but "as individuals, naturally, not as men."[12]

Concrete existence and the "lived experience" are the genuine matters of inquiry: everything else is metaphysics or science. Sartre concerned himself, from the very first, with creating a "doctrine of action" for the "man who makes himself."[13] He steadfastly refused to submerge individuality beneath either the liberal citizen or the collectivist man of the people. Sartre's subject

---

8. Jean-Paul Sartre, *Being and Nothingness: An Essay on Phenomenological Ontology*, trans. Hazel Barnes (New York: Philosophical Library, 1956), 615.
9. Jean-Paul Sartre, "Cartesian Freedom," in *Literary and Philosophical Essays*, trans. Annette Michelson (New York: Collier, 1962), 195.
10. Sartre, *Being and Nothingness*, 84.
11. Ibid., xlv, xlviii, 29.
12. Jean-Paul Sartre, *Nausea*, trans. Lloyd Alexander (New York: New Directions, 1964), 117.
13. Sartre, "Cartesian Freedom," 237.

is constantly faced with the possibility of denying his or her responsibility for self-definition and engaging in "bad faith" *(mal foi)*.[14] This attitude is, in the first instance, a personal matter. It is an attitude, a way of existing in the world, an evasion of what one really is thinking and what one really is doing. Sartre has no use for an "inner certainty," a legacy of Protestantism, which lacks any objective referent for action: thus, it is a collaborator in one of Sartre's novels who provides a particularly glaring example of "bad faith" when he states, "A man must have the courage to act like everybody else in order not to be like anybody."[15]

Contesting bad faith involves a refusal to see oneself as an Other. It means accepting one's faults and the possibility of changing them. The Other is the "thief" of the subject's possibilities. Potentiality is the province of the subject, not the Other, and it is precisely from the condition of Otherness in the eyes of other subjects that any given person, concerned with his or her "authenticity," wishes to emerge. The Other has its own history in terms of philosophy generally and phenomenology more particularly.[16] But Sartre's conception marks an important philosophical contribution. His work highlights the position of the outsider. It calls upon the individual to accept responsibility for his or her choices in an absolute way. Subjectivity becomes a form of self-definition, and it is as real for the Jew, who must affirm his Jewishness, as for the woman living in a sexist world, as for the peasant of color engaging in terror as a response to imperialism.

Authenticity is, in the first instance, basically a matter of personal integrity: the point is not to become one of those who "succeed in hiding from themselves . . . acts of conduct which are objectively discoverable, which they cannot fail to record at the moment when they perform them."[17] But it inevitably becomes a matter of the isolated individual affirming certain existential and practical connections with others like him or her. The existential moment of loneliness remains, but against an abstract metaphysical understanding of the universal subject, the "authentic" individual constantly renders his or her subjectivity more specific and more concrete. The way in which this view anticipates the perspectives of those once considered "marginal groups" cannot be overestimated.

---

14. Sartre, *Being and Nothingness*, 43.

15. Jean-Paul Sartre, *The Age of Reason*, trans. Eric Sutton (New York: Bantam, 1968), 118.

16. Note the seminal study by Michael Theunissen, *Der Andere* (Berlin: Walter de Gruyter, 1981).

17. Sartre, *Being and Nothingness*, 54.

After all, for Sartre, it was always a matter of recognizing the Other as a subject in his or her own right. Reciprocity and equality were the goals of authentic activity, and it was with this ideal that Sartre sought to overcome the contradiction between identity and liberal assimilationism. The fight against prejudice, no less than the fight against exploitation, was seen by him as a part of the same quest for universal liberation. Thus, ignoring the potential for conflict between two very different ideological dynamics, Sartre could write, "The authentic Jew who thinks of himself as a Jew because the anti-Semite has put him in the situation of a Jew is not opposed to assimilation any more than the class-conscious worker is opposed to the liquidation of classes."[18]

Engagement was the issue: its content and its determinations were relevant only insofar as they were open to reflexive justification. Individuals must take responsibility not only for themselves but for the world in which they live and the problems associated with it. But unfortunately, those who must "make" themselves, who must assume responsibilities for the actions they undertake, often find themselves in "situations" not of their choosing. That is particularly the case for the oppressed, the exploited, and the powerless: there is a sense in which the emphasis upon the absolute responsibility of the individual veils the capitalist ideology of laissez-faire. The concrete analysis of human experience, which highlights the singularity of existence, becomes abstract insofar as the qualitative differences between contexts for action lose their specificity within the category of a "situation." "Freedom" is rendered concrete at the price of "necessity" becoming abstract.

Sartre sought to resolve this philosophical deficiency of *Being and Nothingness* in his unfinished *Critique of Dialectical Reason* (1956). This work, perhaps more than any other, philosophically prepares the way for the explosion of 1968. It fuses Marxism with existentialism by providing historical materialism with an ontological foundation in the freedom of the individual. The "lack" experienced by the individual is now translated into the existential sense of "scarcity" *(rareté)* against which any genuine commitment to "freedom" struggles.[19] But these struggles occur within a context created by groups that are themselves composed of individuals. Marxism can no longer remain content with "general" statements or claims; it must

18. Jean-Paul Sartre, *Anti-Semite and Jew*, trans. George J. Becker (New York: Schocken, 1948), 150.
19. Jean-Paul Sartre, *Critique de la raison dialectique* (Paris: Gallimard, 1960), 201.

articulate the specificity of action. That is the purpose behind *Critique of Dialectical Reason*; its intention is, "without being unfaithful to Marxist principles, to find mediations which allow the individual concrete—the particular life, the real and dated conflict, the person—to emerge from the background of the general contradictions of productive forces and relations of production."[20]

The *Critique* makes room for terror; it has a place for the party; it allows for discipline. But its "progressive-regressive" method militates against the Stalinist "liquidation of the particularity"; it contests the pseudodialectical attempt to "reabsorb man into the idea"; and it resists any causal or reductive analysis of action. It provides a stunning interpretation of the storming of the Bastille; it offers a new political sense of the tension between intentions and consequences; above all, however, it illuminates the subjugation of subjectivity by the institutions of advanced industrial society and the attempt to contest the unconscious forms of obedience they inspire *(serialité)* through reflection and an ongoing struggle even against organizations like the vanguard party, which supposedly serve the oppressed themselves.[21] It may confuse "alienation" and "objectification"; it is weak on institutional solutions; and it surely romanticizes the idea of political struggle. But this work also generates a view of individualism beyond simple egoism, engagement beyond dogma, and politics beyond institutional action. With the *Critique*, indeed, Sartre comes full circle in anticipation of 1968 and the rise of the new social movements: the individualist unimpaired by necessity, who later embraced the Communist Party on "realist" grounds, would now place a new premium on the spontaneity of the masses.

The emphasis on spontaneity was part of the radical project from the very beginning. There is indeed a point of convergence between anarchism and Marxism beyond their divergent views on historical development, the state, the political party, and the primacy of the working class. With its emphasis on the creation of workers' councils and a radically experimental vision of everyday life, as well as its concern with the abolition of alienation and hierarchy, this trend within Marxism developed its own tradition of political theory. It was probably initiated in this century by Rosa Lumexburg and Leon Trotsky and their notions of "proletarian self-administration" and

---

20. Jean-Paul Sartre, *Search for a Method*, trans. Hazel Barnes (New York: Vintage, 1968), 57.
21. 21. Ibid., 258.

"permanent revolution"; it received expression in the writings of figures like Victor Serge and others who identified with the dream of "soviet" rule and the mutiny of the Kronstadt sailors against the authoritarianism of the Communist Party in 1921;[22] it extended to the left wing of the Dutch Communist Party grouped around figures like Hermann Goerter, Anton Pannekoek, and Henriette Roland-Holst;[23] it found intellectual support in the preoccupation with "socialization" and councilist forms of democracy on the part of Karl Korsch and Otto Rühle.[24]

But this tradition probably received its most forceful postwar articulation in the writings of Cornelius Castoriadis, who, along with a few other intellectuals like Claude Lefort, founded the vibrant sect known as "Socialism or Barbarism," which lasted from 1949 until 1965.[25] Castoriadis was born in 1922 in Constantinople, spent most of his life on the extra-parliamentary left, and taught at the École des Hautes Études en Sciences Sociales before he died in 1998. Initially a member of the Communist Youth, he joined the Trotskyist Fourth International before deciding to form his own organization. Its public was made up of "old-style ultra-left groups: Bordigists, Council Communists, a few anarchists, and some offspring of the 1920s German Leftists."[26] It would unequivocally oppose both the Soviet Union and Western imperialism in the name of an "autonomous socialism" based on the self-rule of factories by workers or what, in 1968, was called *autogéstion*. But more than that, it also sought to "repudiate the capitalist model in all domains and in all its implications."[27] The emphasis placed by Castoriadis on "autonomy" was indeed unyielding: it was defined as a conscious domination over the unconscious, both psychologically and socially, which

---

22. Victor Serge, *Memoirs of a Revolutionary*, trans. Peter Sedgwick (New York: Oxford University Press, 1963), 70–156.

23. Note the critique directed against the tendency they exemplified by V. I. Lenin, "Left-Wing Communism: An Infantile Disorder," in *Selected Writings*, 3. vols. (Moscow: International, 1971), 3:345 ff.

24. Karl Korsch, *Revolutionary Theory*, ed. Douglas Kellner (Austin: University of Texas Press, 1977), 11 ff. and 194 ff.; Otto Rühle, *Baupläne für eine neue Gesellschaft* (Hamburg: Rowohlt, 1971).

25. Cornelius Castoriadis, "Socialism or Barbarism," in *Political and Social Writings*, 3 vols., ed. and trans. David Ames Curtis (Minneapolis: University of Minnesota Press, 1988).

26. Cornelius Castoriadis, "The Only Way to Find Out if You Can Swim Is to Get into the Water: An Introductory Interview" (1974), in *The Castoriadis Reader*, ed. and trans. David Ames Curtis (London: Blackwell, 1997), 5.

27. Ibid., 7.

implied a commitment to reflexivity as well as the subordination of all coercive activity and institutions to the conscious control of the public.[28] Democracy would ultimately take a radical turn; it would become an unending enterprise directed at everyday life.[29]

Consciousness is seen as confronting an artificially constructed set of ideological and institutional constraints upon action. Antonio Gramsci, interestingly enough, had already recognized what was at stake. This communist and "Western Marxist" would ultimately serve less as an influence on communist thought, or the critical theory of the Frankfurt School, than on a radically different tradition of Marxist structuralism whose importance in the United States would become particularly pronounced in the late 1970s. Gramsci realized that society was not neatly divisible into an economic "base" and a derivative "superstructure," as orthodox Marxists liked to claim. He also understood the importance of ideology and class consciousness in bringing about the revolution. He saw how various traditions of "subalternity," which produce passivity and a denial of subjectivity, undermine the ability of the working class to rule as a class and administer society through democratic organs like the soviets. If proletarian self-administration, the empowerment of subjects, is therefore the ultimate aim of the revolution, then the working class must engage in a "counterhegemonic" struggle against the ruling institutions and ideas of society.[30] Combating "subalternity" and "hegemony" would indeed demand a new "organic intellectual" and a willingness to recognize the possibility of different "national paths" to communism, given the unique history and peculiar cultural traditions of different nations and regions.

Gramsci still gave primacy to the role of class. Perhaps more than any other Marxist thinker, however, he sensed the practical and theoretical limits of the concept. He recognized its lack of applicability to a host of institutional phenomena and modes of subjugation. Transclass issues like cultural identity, the importance of existential concerns for political action, and the

---

28. Cornelius Castoriadis, "Marxism and Revolutionary Theory" (1964–65), in *Castoriadis Reader.*

29. This is precisely how the thinking of Castoriadis was appropriated by the students of 1968 and his most famous disciple, Daniel Cohn-Bendit; see Bendit, *Obsolete Communism: The Left-Wing Alternative*, trans. Arnold Pomerans (New York: McGraw-Hill, 1968).

30. Antonio Gramsci, *Selections from the Prison Notebooks*, ed. and trans. Quintin Hoare and Geoffrey Nowell Smith (New York: International, 1971), 245 ff. and passim.

need for a counterhegemonic struggle on the part of the subaltern would all play a profound role both in his thinking and in the legacy of his thought.

Later thinkers associated with the new social movements would discount the primacy he placed on class and his own view of the counterhegemonic struggle as being necessarily organized by a vanguard party. But they appropriated his belief in the unique discourse of the subaltern and the need for battle rather than conversation. They also embraced his belief that intellectuals must maintain an organic connection to the mass base of the movement; intellectuals should commit themselves to the particular group, if not the class, whose experiences they share as individuals. There is indeed the assumption, especially absent common projects or organizing principles like class, that these groups will have to forge a counterhegemonic stance in the name of their own existential and practical interests.

Gramsci became a point of theoretical departure for future theorists who would have to contend with new forms of conflict between classes and groups as well as within the groups themselves. Louis Althusser and his followers of the 1960s, building on Gramsci, sought to place a new epistemological spin on the multiplicity of concerns and standpoints arising on the left.[31] Engaged in combating dogmatism within the French Communist Party, seeking to emphasize the objective basis for a new tolerance, Althusser became the most important representative of Marxist "structuralism." Often mistakenly identified with positivism, but actually quite critical of the materialism developed by Engels and Kautsky, his thinking ran counter to the Hegelian and antiscientific humanism of the young Marx.[32] Althusser's aim was to transvalue the scientific basis of Marxism by transvaluing the definition of science.

He identified "science" with any set of rules capable of making a given object or interest "visible." In his view, different objects and interests simply require different methods of inquiry. Classical political economy is subsequently no more true or false than Marxism: what counts is the "specific

---

31. Louis Althusser, *The Future Lasts Forever: A Memoir*, ed. Olivier Corpet and Yann Moulier Boutang, trans. Richard Veasey (New York: New Press, 1993).

32. Louis Althusser, "On the Young Marx," in *For Marx*, trans. Ben Brewster (New York: Vintage, 1969); also note "On the Evolution of the Young Marx," in *Essays in Self-Criticism*, trans. Grahame Lock (London: New Left, 1976).

difference of the object" of concern and the guiding interest of the subject.[33] There is no hierarchy of "truth," and there is no causal determination. Anticipating the "poststructuralist" turn of figures like Foucault, arguing against Engels by claiming that "the lonely hour of the last instance never comes,"[34] Althusser sought to contest transhistorical or dogmatic notions of truth. He understood ideology as the set of practices, prejudices, and values that uncritically "reproduce" existing forms of ideational and material "production" and thereby interfere with the ability to render them "visible."[35] He would sharply differentiate ideology from "science."

Ideology shows its relevance only with respect to particular configurations of truth. Feminism need not serve as an "ideology" in relation to Marxism because it has a different constitutive object of interest; its practitioners need not interfere with inquiries into class issues. The converse situation, Marxism in relation to feminism, is no different: its practitioners need not interfere with questions dealing with gender by raising issues of class. The Hegelian notion of a mediated totality is thereby reconfigured into a "whole" whose mechanical interactions are subsumed within it and defined by it. Or, to put it another way, whereas Marxism can make class relations "visible" through its categories and race theory can illuminate race relations, feminism can perform the same function with respect to gender relations. Complementarity exists: new connections can be made between these three objects of interest, interpretive relations can be drawn and redrawn, and new theoretical traditions can arise, like "Marxist feminism."

Innovations of this sort are not seen merely as the contingent choices of particular actors. Quite the contrary. The subject effaces itself in relation to the object. Even the choice of inquiry, or the object of transformative action, is seen less as the arbitrary decision of a fully conscious subject than the result of a certain "overdetermination" upon an "agent" by a complex of both social and unconscious factors.[36] Transcendence vanishes. The structuralism of Louis Althusser has nothing to say about the future; it can only

---

33. Louis Althusser and Etienne Balibar, *Reading Capital*, trans. Ben Brewster (London: New Left, 1975), 78.

34. Louis Althusser, "Is It Simple to Be a Marxist in Philosophy?" in *Essays in Self-Criticism.*

35. Louis Althusser, "Ideology and Ideological State Apparatuses," in *Lenin and Philosophy and Other Essays*, trans. Ben Brewster (New York: Monthly Review, 1971).

36. Louis Althusser, "Contradiction and Overdetermination," in *For Marx.*

look back on an "overdetermined" past. No less than for the "science" of Hegel, which it so self-consciously sought to oppose, the owl of Minerva can spread its wings only at dusk.

Ernst Bloch saw the matter differently. He considered the speculative moment, the "anticipatory consciousness" of emancipation, to be the foundation of both radical theory and radical practice. Born in Ludwigshafen in 1885, an early philosophical representative of the modernist avant-garde, his ultraradicalism would lead him to oppose the Popular Front and, tragically, support the Moscow Trials.[37] Bloch went east following World War II, and, experiencing the disillusionment attendant upon the revelations of Stalin's crimes by Khrushchev at the Twentieth Party Congress of 1956, he fled to West Germany in 1961 and taught philosophy at the University of Tübingen until his death in 1977. Nevertheless, in keeping with one of his central ideas, his work is not invalidated by the political miscalculations of his life.

Bloch's *The Spirit of Hope* (1918) was published while the stench of the trenches was still fresh and the possibilities of workers' councils were in full bloom. This work fused an eschatological interpretation of Marx with elements of a then pervasive "life philosophy," Kantian teleology, and a certain religious fervor. The "grounding" for his conception of utopia would come later, in his encyclopedic *The Principle of Hope* (1959), with its explosive view of Being as unfinished and intent upon realizing the always elusive "not-yet" existent. An intimation of a harmonious "subject-object unity," which must be understood more as the real beginning than as a Hegelian form of closure,[38] is seen as underpinning historical experience in its "nonidentity." Human existence inherently "juts beyond" its context. Ideas are not exhausted by the repression conditioning their origins. They are not reducible to the "position" of their authors or the interests of any particular class, race, or sex. They retain their own dynamic; and, from those that are ignored no less than from those whose emancipatory character is perverted, there develops what Bloch termed an "underground history of the revolution."

Fantasy and recollection merge. Traditions stand in need of utopian transvaluation. Emancipatory impulses can be gleaned from religion and the the-

---

37. Ernst Bloch, "Jubiläum der Renegaten," in *Politische Messungen, Pestzeit, Vormärz* (Frankfurt am Main: Suhrkamp, 1970).

38. Ernst Bloch, *Subjekt–Objekt: Erläuterungen zu Hegel* (Frankfurt am Main: Suhrkamp, 1962).

ology of forgotten revolutionaries like Thomas Münzer,[39] from the canvases of expressionist painters like Wassily Kandinsky, and from a tradition of utopian philosophy whose roots reach back over Marx to the romantics and the visionaries of the Renaissance to the mystics of the Middle Ages and the generally unrecognized radical legacy of classical antiquity. Utopian anticipations of the "best life," spurred by the imagination, resist all dogmatic forms of stage theory or all unilinear notions of history.

Bloch's utopia does not inhabit the land of what Samuel Butler called *erewhon*, which is *nowhere* spelled backwards, but rather exists in an intricate relation with the world of power, injustice, and poverty. As Bloch put the matter in his famous phrase, "Man does not live by bread alone, especially when he doesn't have any."[40] Utopia exists unconsciously in the minds of lovers, each with an idea of what the "best" relationship should be; it occurs whenever ethics contest interests; and it inspires any commitment to radical social change. Utopia exists in every "moment" of the totality, and perhaps each moment is always ready to burst its "realistic" confines. Causal explanations of society are therefore inherently limiting. Tensions exists not only between the whole and its dynamic parts but also between these parts themselves. They are ultimately incommensurate: the attempt to fully realize the utopian possibilities of one moment will inherently impinge upon another. Thus, what Bloch ultimately termed the "world experiment" cannot be realized *en toto*.

Utopia must remain utopian. Utopia becomes dangerous in the attempts to realize its content. It has justified repression in the present by pointing to the future. It has legitimated the separation of means from ends. It has led us to underestimate reforms and it has made us blind to reality. It has been imbued with mysticism; and, especially when understood in ontological terms, it has become difficult to separate the "false" forms of utopian thinking from the true. It is also no longer possible to talk about an agent for realizing the oldest dream of humanity. But the invocation of utopia makes us realize that what we have is not necessarily what we want and what we want is not necessarily all we can have. It makes us conscious of what divides us in order better to understand the impulse that unites us. It restores a sense of what "humanity" involves. It bequeaths a healthy respect for the

---

39. Ernst Bloch, *Thomas Münzer als Theologe der Revolution* (1921; Frankfurt am Main: Suhrkamp, 1972).
40. Ernst Bloch, *Erbschaft dieser Zeit* (Frankfurt am Main: Suhrkamp, 1973), 403.

past, and it explains why the classics have become classics. Above all, however, it makes clear that, if we concern ourselves only with what is "pragmatic" or "possible," the transformative moment—the moment of prefiguration—will vanish. Those are the circumstances under which commitment withers, along with the possibilities attendant upon the exercise of freedom.

PART IV

EMPOWERING THE OTHER

15

The Logic of the New Social Movements

New social movements have defined the terrain of oppositional politics in the United States for more than a quarter of a century. They mark the self-emancipation of the Other, the return of the repressed. Centered around issues of identity, self-determination, and the contestation of prevailing norms, the new social movements have had a genuine impact on society. They have given rise to new institutionally oriented transnational interest groups, international conferences, and even—sometimes—international legislation. A grudging respect is now given to the most diverse traditions, and few any longer consider the meaning of progress as self-evident. The cultural self-understandings of minorities and the possibilities for the exercise of autonomy, freed of parochial religious controls and communal prejudices, have clearly expanded. New concerns with human rights, new attempts to confront the previously unquestioned cultural dominance of white European males, and a new sense of ecological danger to the planet have indeed proved global.

New social movements now preoccupy social and political theorists all over the world. An explosion in the literature has kept pace with the unprecedented growth in new identities, new concerns, and new grievances. Advocates of the new social movements, especially in the United States, have appropriately taken credit for bringing the excluded somewhat into the mainstream and transforming the customs and culture of modern America. It is often forgotten that until the 1960s, Jim Crow ruled in much of the

United States and discrimination against women and homosexuals was an accepted part of everyday life. The new social movements created a new public sphere or, better, a broad network of self-conscious constituencies, each with its own community organizations, publications, lobbying groups, resources, and interest groups. They brought the dirty little secrets of even the most liberal society into the public arena: racial prejudice and Eurocentrism, sexism and homophobia, torture of animals and the despoliation of a shared world.

The new social movements have helped liberate subjectivity from its stultifying institutional definitions, and they have furthered multiplicity by calling into question the forms of identity inherited from a bygone age. Many of their theorists have learned much from critical theory, existentialism, and postmodernism. Even when these traditions are not mentioned explicitly, their themes come to the forefront. The new social movements sought to contest instrumental reason and traditional notions of power associated with the state. They broadened the notion of oppression and highlighted cultural and ideological issues. But this undertaking often became exaggerated and extravagant. As such issues were ripped from their anchoring in the economy and the state, for example, representation itself often became the object of inquiry, and dogmatic notions of identity and consciousness arose that were divorced from any material notion of self-creation. It is a mistake, however, to judge the social movements from their most extreme participants. Their political logic deserves consideration, as well as the way in which their claims to unique vantage points, ever more particular and specific forms of identity, challenge individuals to create their own biographies and move beyond any simple reduction to material interest.

Diversity has assumed a value in its own right, and a shift has taken place from the more traditional politics concerned with matters of distribution to a new preoccupation with recognition. Politics has become less a matter of changing institutions than of changing the minds and values of people. And, in a way, this development makes perfect historical sense. Existing political parties were unwilling to acknowledge and express the legitimate concerns of what became known in the 1960s and 1970s as the new social movements. Thus, they followed a different, noninstitutional path.

Politics took on a new immediacy: the real action was now seen as occurring less in established institutions than in the initiatives undertaken at the grass roots. Activism seemingly broke out everywhere, and in keeping with a radical spirit of community, "participation" became the catchword of the left. The attempt to change everyday life was often greeted with skepticism. But they have made clear how much it matters whether a black youth can claim his civil rights were violated, a young woman can have an abortion legally, a gay couple can adopt a child. Still, if partisans of the new social movements can claim credit for the successes in transforming the culture of everyday life, they must also accept some degree of responsibility for the institutional setbacks of the 1980s and 1990s. It is indeed necessary to consider whether the virtual identification of progressive political practice with the practice of the new social movements is still viable.

No one standpoint or party can any longer make universal identity claims within a world increasingly defined by difference and individuation. New social movements have broken the monopoly over "politics" exercised by political parties, constituencies motivated by distributional concerns, and institutions like the state. Thus it is not surprising that the new social movements should have originated in the United States, with its peculiar institutional structure, its weak political parties and strong interest groups, its liberal individualism and voluntary associations, its lack of a genuine socialist tradition and ideological preoccupation with class consciousness. All these factors contributed to generating a "new" conception of politics during the 1960s and especially in its aftermath.

Movements in the West were inspired by the anti-imperialist revolutions of the Third World: these uprisings generated revolutionary hopes for some, sympathy for the victims of imperialism in ever more, and a general assault on the traditional assumptions underpinning Western hegemony. The possibility of a genuine revolution never existed anywhere among the major nations of the Western world. Thus, it only made sense that a liberal-socialist emphasis upon political reform should have coexisted with a far more radical "counterculture" imbued with utopian themes. It was in the counterculture that the spirit of resistance and nonconformism, experimentation and fantasy, found its new home. But this produced problems and contradictions: it became fashionable to inflate liberal reformism through radical rhetoric and deflate the most radical cultural choices by viewing them simply as "different."

There is, of course, a certain logic to this development. A common purpose and a reinvigorated liberalism with universalist assumptions and liberal–socialist aspirations initially informed the Civil Rights Movement. It fused a number of seemingly diverse concerns, and soon enough, the Civil Rights Movement allied itself first with the struggle against the Vietnam

War and then with the Poor People's Movement. But with the dissolution of the "movement" into a set of discrete interests, attendant upon the assassination of Dr. Martin Luther King Jr., in 1968, the whole dissolved into its parts. New suspicions arose in theory concerning the manner in which the particular forms of oppression experienced by people of color, women, and gays were being veiled by universalist categories and concerns. The emphasis on identity and particularism is less a product of the 1960s, or the original Civil Rights and antiwar movements, than of the 1970s and 1980s, when the era of radical protest was over.

But that does not change matters: new social movements empowered the Other. They fostered a new awareness of what was nonwhite, nonmale, and contrary to the notion of progress in advanced industrial society. To speak of a "new awareness," however, only dramatizes both the nature of the problem and the character of the response. Racism and sexism and a rampant disregard for nature are nothing new and, in principle, should always have been recognized as crucial issues of concern. In the predominantly white and masculinist culture, however, this was generally not the case. Liberals and social democrats essentially saw racism and sexism as anachronistic prejudices in the process of being eradicated by general forms of enlightenment. Orthodox Marxists and communists considered them subordinate to the question of class and open to solution only "after" the revolution. Conservatives either saw no real problem at all or viewed such prejudices as so deeply embedded that political action could not resolve them without disrupting the prevailing customs and mores. All of them, moreover, essentially identified progress with economic growth and the development of technology.

The new social movements, by contrast, dealt forthrightly with otherness. They highlighted what would become known as "institutional racism," patriarchy, and the costs of "progress." Often building on the arguments of existentialists, critical theorists, and poststructuralists, they highlighted new forms of solidarity, skeptical attitudes toward accepted assumptions, and rejections of those who would privilege one "standpoint" over another. The new social movements introduced new existential forms of self-identification and solidarity; in the process, they gave cultural issues an expanded and directly political connotation. Their intellectual representatives subsequently interpreted prejudice in terms far more radical and substantive than those employed by traditional social scientists. Indeed, by making public what were previously understood as basically private concerns, the new social movements engaged in a fundamental redefinition of political theory.

Modernity has taken on a new look. It no longer can be identified simply with what Max Weber termed the "iron cage" of bureaucracy, which assumes an increasing emphasis upon the normal and the standard; it must also be associated with the unleashing of the Other. Modernity generates difference as well as conformism, experimentation as well as alienation, and a sense of uniqueness to complement feelings of anomie. The other side of increasing bureaucracy and commodification is indeed a new dynamic of fragmentation, an emphasis upon increasingly particular and specific forms of identity, that informs the new social movements.

What was previously understood as class consciousness became reinterpreted in a more subjectivist and yet more essentialist form. Natural attributes would serve as the source of solidarity rather than a purely historical result of a particular production process. This situation made it impossible for these movements to distinguish between politics and culture, and some of their most important theoreticians call upon activists to concentrate less on "the politics of politicians" and "power politics" than a somewhat vaguely defined "creative politics" or "art of politics." Their most radical supporters contest the need for rigid organization, expertise, and "professionalism." They reject establishmentarian notions of progress and the conventional, or "straight," lifestyle.

New social movements thereby evidence a certain contempt for what conservatives in the 1960s called "the silent majority." But this contempt, if it was ever real, is also tempered by strong sentiments for the excluded, the ignored, the oppressed. In this regard, for better or worse, the new social movements stand within a long tradition of populist thinking on the American left. Interestingly enough, these movements also highlight the enduring legacy of what are fundamentally premodern problems for modern politics. Thus, in the best sense, the new social movements view modernity as an unfinished enterprise.

Racism, patriarchy, homophobia, and the instrumental domination of nature still constitute unresolved problems. But there is a way in which all predate the emergence of modern capitalist society. All have an anthropological component, and all are irreducible to the demands of any given system. It is not merely the present but the past that needs rectification; it is not a matter of changing only current policies but also ingrained habits and assumptions. It becomes difficult to say where ideological work ends and practical politics begins. They blend in a unique manner. That is why, with the new social movements, terms like *reform* and *revolution* lose their determinate character. Distinctions within the new social movements continue to exist, but they take a different form. It is better to speak of the tensions between an extrainstitutional and an integrationist, a "grassroots" and a bureaucratic, a "fundamentalist" and a "realist," tendency.

Tensions of this sort become immediately apparent in the long history of struggles undergone by African Americans. Socialism once held a certain attraction for many within the African American community during the first decades of the century. But the prejudice exhibited by so much of the white working class and the rural traditions of many in the black community, coupled with the general weakness of the socialist movement in the United States, tended to undermine its allure. These same factors, in combination with the populist legacy, enhanced the appeal of nationalism. Its advocates have often been weak on political and economic programs. Nevertheless, their emphasis on the pervasiveness of racism and the need for a new form of solidarity generated new interest in Africa and a new concern with the establishment of a black identity.

In the South of the United States during the 1950s and 1960s, a burgeoning Civil Rights Movement organized through the churches and committed to integration employed pacifist forms of resistance and the universalist assumptions of a liberal society to contest the exclusion and discrimination experienced by black people throughout the United States. Its leadership would soon link criticism of the political system with a criticism of its foreign policy, especially the Vietnam War, and the economic plight of poor people. This radical vision of a morally reinvigorated American society with a new commitment to political equality and economic justice, if not a new institutional form with which to sustain the movement over time, was the legacy of Dr. Martin Luther King Jr.

Even before King's death, however, many blacks were wary of the important role played by whites in the Civil Rights Movement, and the identity of the movement became an issue for groups ranging from the Student Nonviolent Coordinating Committee to the Nation of Islam. Indeed, if pacifism was called into question, so was the role Christianity played in the black community. "Black pride" and "black power," a new concern with the African heritage, became issues of profound salience as Eurocentrism and "white-skin privilege" came under attack. Attempts were made to link the struggles undertaken by people of color in the United States with those in the former colonial territories.

The revolutionary upsurge in the Third World has receded, but such cultural concerns are still strong. In fact, whatever its failings on the institutional level, black nationalism has only grown with the triumph of conservatism in the 1980s and the abandonment of the broader liberal vision by white society. Its emotional allure and symbolic power have helped assert the existence of an African American constituency, and it has shed new light on the plight of people of color within the global community. The question for the future will surely involve the conflict over whether assimilation or separation, nationalism or internationalism, universalism or particularism, will be privileged in political terms.

The feminist movement faces a similar ideological choice. It is increasingly becoming a practical question with regard to which value will assume ideological primacy: "equality" or "difference," compromise or sectarianism, organization or grass roots, class or gender, internationalism or parochialism. "Either/or" is obviously a limited proposition. But the usual reference to "both/and" does not help much either. It remains a matter of which receives priority over the other in what context. This translates into the following practical dilemma: Insofar as the women's movement insists upon equality, which makes it more acceptable in a liberal society with competing interests, it will obviously sacrifice to some degree its radical and nonconformist spirit. If the women's movement insists upon emphasizing its anti-institutional and ideological posture, on the other hand, its politics will tend to become ever more symbolic and marginal to serious political action. This tension still reflects basic fissures within the movement. There is even a sense in which it is more meaningful to consider the women's movement less as a monolithic entity than as an aggregate of several different organizing strands.

Groups initially organized around a single attribute of sex, race, or sexual orientation. Feminism from the mid-1960s to the mid-1970s, for example, sought to bring all women together "as women," and its proponents employed a vision of society with women on top and men on the bottom as the model for all politics, sexual or otherwise. But sexuality and race eventually split the movement into its radical and liberal wings, and different feminist groups and visions multiplied. The quest for an ever more particular identity resulted in ever greater forms of ideological and organizational fragmentation: women who are black and lesbian and working class, for example, found themselves torn with respect to identity in a situation where none of the original feminist groups were able to meet their existential needs. For the new social movements in general, according to this logic of fragmentation, it only makes sense that a new organization should appear with an ideological and practical interest in perpetuating its own autonomy. The practical implications generated by this logic of identity have fostered distrust within the "the left" even as "the right" has been able to define it as a set of "special interests."

The collapse of communism and the abandonment of traditional liberal programs, coupled with the political triumph of conservatism, intensified what had already been an ongoing splintering of progressive forces. Many looked to the environmental movement, the emergence of political parties like the German Greens, as offering a ray of hope. Its concerns with the survival of the planet and the pollution of natural resources are moreover often seen less as particular, or identified with a given group, than universal in character. The instrumental exploitation of nature, the obsession with growth, the alienation of modern life, and the price paid for progress are also not merely incidental issues. A new form of what Ulrich Beck termed "ecological enlightenment" has surely illuminated the "risks" inherent in turning the world into a laboratory in which the most unthinkable catastrophe can result from the most minuscule bureaucratic decision.

As the history of environmental organizations suggests, however, the environmental movement remains a particular interest in a world of competing interests. Its emphasis on limiting growth and "sustainable development" are looked on with suspicion by those without jobs, a constituency often concentrated in the ghettos as well as on the periphery. Class and race, in short, come into play when considering the ecological vision of environmentalists and the debate over economic growth. Ideas concerning the ability of industry to regulate itself, or foster environmental policies capable of reversing the damage, also now seem incredibly optimistic, given the devastating impact of deregulation on the environment. Especially in the United States, whatever the central role of ecology in envisioning a livable future, its implications call for consideration within a more general context cognizant of the interplay of interests and the structural imbalances of power in modern society.

The new social movements have had genuine success in mobilizing people and bringing numerous "private" forms of oppression into "public" consciousness. They have radically transformed everyday life for the better. To uncritically valorize their tactics, or to turn necessity into a virtue, however, is foolish. The new social movements, their ideology and their tactics, evidence limits as well as contributions. Any new form of progressive theory with progressive aims must confront the debilitating competition between them over increasingly scarce resources and the upward distribution of wealth and power engineered over the last three decades of the century. It must deal with the manner in which even the most progressive interest groups gain a stake in maintaining their own autonomy and privilege the concerns of their particular membership. It must face the possibility that the politics of identity and the existing logic of fragmentation have become self-defeating. All of this, however, is part of a broader concern: it is time for political theory to view the passing of the 1960s with something more than nostalgia.

It is necessary to look at history in a more, not less, universal way: almost all forms of political theory generated over the past two hundred years are complicit in their dismissal of non-Western cultures. The world has generally been viewed through the lens of a tiny fraction of humanity. Africa, Asia, and Latin America have never really been part of the discussion. No wonder new demands for recognition in the aftermath of World War II should have arisen from those who were neither white, Christian, nor Western. New spiritual values, new existential forms of self-identification, and new national hopes would become intrinsic elements in the struggle against imperialism and colonialism. These would indeed become apparent in the writings and influence of diverse political figures like Mahatma Gandhi, Frantz Fanon, and Che Guevara.

World War II transformed the three great continental mass movements. Arguably of even greater international significance was the impetus it provided for what would become the liquidation of the colonial empires of Belgium, Britain, France, Holland, and other Western nations. This process of decolonization indeed transformed the globe. It began with the independence of India in 1947 and the communist victory over the forces of Chiang Kai-shek in China in 1949. But it gained force in Vietnam with the defeat of French forces at Dienbienphu, the drama involved with the Algerian Revolution, the tragic death of Patrice Lumumba in the Congo, and the Cuban Revolution of 1960. The anti-imperialist struggle generated an explosion of revolutionary enthusiasm, a genuine sense of shame among many intellectuals in the imperialist nations, and an assault on the traditional assumptions underpinning Western hegemony. It brought attention to the obvious: economic progress along the Western model has produced untold misery for a great portion of the globe.

With the passing of more traditional economic and political forms of imperialist exploitation, however, it soon enough became a matter of the ways in which the newly liberated nations would understand themselves in relation to their own oppressed constituencies as well as to the world of their former masters. Various partisans of "postcolonial theory" have, in this regard, sought to reinstate the experiences of those excluded from Western culture, and even their own, without necessarily insisting upon the return to a premodern past. This new trend has been marked by an increasing concern with the cultural, the noninstitutional, and the existential moment of liberation. As a consequence, especially given the seeming lack of interest in the various traditions of imperialist theory, other crucial issues have fallen by the wayside: the fragility of governmental systems, the organizational problems with respect to social justice, and the normative prerequisites for maintaining a democratic order. These problems constitute part of the imperialist legacy. Coming to terms with it is, indeed, perhaps the most difficult challenge facing political theory in the future.

16

Race: Reflections on the African American Heritage

The problem of the twentieth century is the problem of the color-line.

W. E. B. Du Bois

The United States was populated by immigrants. They came from many countries and they spoke many languages, and each had his or her story. Some were the victims of war and famine, others, the subjects of religious or political repression; and almost all were poor. They came willingly, looking for a better life for themselves and their families, and they saw America as a land of opportunity. It was true of the Irish, the Swedes, the Germans, the Italians, and the Jews. It was true of every group except those from Africa. They too came from many countries and spoke many languages. Each of them also had a personal story. Many had endured war and famine, others had surely experienced religious hatred and political repression; and almost all were poor. But there was a difference. They did not come willingly, and, if only for this reason, they never saw America as the land of opportunity.

Slavery and, perhaps even more important, "Jim Crow" laws mark the shared experience of African Americans. Slavery took people from many lands, with many languages and the most divergent cultures, and gave them a sense of commonality predicated upon the color of their skin. It turned this one factor among many into the essence of their commonality. Slavery cost its victims their languages, their cultures, and their families as well. It also cost them their formal equality and the recognition of their cultural contributions to civilization. Jim Crow laws served to secure this situation following the abandonment of Reconstruction in 1876. African Americans could only feel themselves incorporated within a society that excluded them. It is no wonder that W. E. B. Du Bois should have spoken about the "double consciousness" incorporated by the African American. No concept more adequately highlights the tensions and political problems associated with overcoming the rigid juxtaposition between integration and separatism.

Du Bois was one of the great intellectuals of the century, and his influence extends beyond any single discipline.[1] The scope and quality of his scholarly undertakings, which continued unabated until his death in Ghana in 1963 at the age of ninety-six, made his work seminal for any number of fields beyond black history, ranging from urban sociology and American history to anthropology and the philosophy of racism. The works themselves tell the story: there is his doctoral dissertation from Harvard, "The Suppression of the African Slave Trade" (1896), his empirical study, entitled *The Philadelphia Negro* (1899), his most famous work, *The Souls of Black Folk* (1903), his classic *Black Reconstruction in America* (1935), *The Negro* (1939), with its bold African perspective, and his unfinished *Encyclopedia of the Negro*. In conjunction with all of this, he was also a teacher and an activist. There is no question about his role in shaping the idea of a black culture and its legacy for America. His influence on African American political theory and practice was decisive.

W. E. B. Du Bois was a child during Reconstruction, a young man during the resurgence of the Ku Klux Klan, an established figure during the famed Harlem Renaissance, an avowed antifascist during the war, a consulting delegate at the founding of the United Nations, a supporter of the Soviet Union during the cold war, a prophet of the Civil Rights Movement, and an exiled sage when a new cluster of states arose in Africa during the 1950s and 1960s. The question is whether a common theme, beyond the obvious concern with black politics and identity, can unite such manifold activity; and here there is much debate. Most of his supporters suggest that his thinking evolved. Other more daring critics view his idea of the "talented tenth," whatever his later qualifications of the concept in terms of the "guiding hun-

---

1. David Levering Lewis, ed., *W. E. B. Du Bois: A Reader* (New York: Holt, 1995); also note the balanced study by Arnold Rampersad, *The Art and Imagination of W. E. B. Du Bois* (Cambridge: Harvard University Press, 1990).

dredth" of the race,[2] as indicative of his "elitist" perspective on the possibilities of bringing about change in the African American community.[3] Nevertheless, even though Du Bois himself would rarely mention the idea after World War I, it would seem that his notion of the "double consciousness" is the key concept for understanding his political theory.[4]

Du Bois dealt squarely with what it meant to be an American of African descent, and this allowed him to assume a unique position. It called for maintaining the tension between both sides of what is generally considered the opposition between assimilation and separation, equality and difference, class and race, universality and particularism, Americanism and Africanism. The idea of "double consciousness" placed him in opposition to both the assimilation of reformers like Booker T. Washington and the racial separatism of populist leaders like Marcus Garvey. It enabled Du Bois sometimes to emphasize the need for integration, as a cofounder of the National Association for the Advancement of Colored People (NAACP), and edit its magazine, entitled *Crisis*, even as it also allowed him to highlight the contributions of his people as well as the need for separate, if interconnected, forms of racial self-education.

Writers like Richard Wright and James Baldwin would pick up the idea of "double consciousness." And for good reason. The concept speaks to a situation in which most political organizations of African Americans are no longer committed simply and unambiguously either to integration or separatism, the modern or the premodern, the American present or the African past. The question is whether the tension and uncertainty within the notion of "double consciousness" can ultimately make for a coherent black politics in the future. Its antithetical elements deserve more attention. This indeed makes it necessary to consider the thinking of Du Bois' two most prominent opponents, Booker T. Washington and Marcus Garvey.

When he died in 1915, at the age of fifty-nine, Booker T. Washington had

2. Du Bois' statement on the "talented tenth," from *The Negro Problem* (1903), and his revision of the concept, in a memorial address given in 1948, are reprinted in Henry Louis Gates Jr. and Cornel West, *The Future of the Race* (New York: Knopf, 1996); also see Joy James, *Transcending the Talented Tenth* (New York: Routledge, 1997).

3. See Adolph L. Reed Jr., *W. E. B. Du Bois and American Political Thought: Fabianism and the Color Line* (New York: Oxford University Press, 1997).

4. Note the section on the "double consciousness" in W. E. B. Du Bois, *The Souls of Black Folk*, ed. David W. Blight and Robert Gooding-Williams (Boston: Bedford, 1997).

lost the enormous standing he had earlier achieved. His fame had grown in what was effectively a counterrevolution against the radical changes promised by Reconstruction. Sympathy for blacks was on the wane, equality was under assault, and universal suffrage in the South and elsewhere was being effectively chipped away by poll taxes, literacy tests, and physical intimidation, until legitimate political organization within the existing system of interest groups had become impossible. Political parties lost their interest in pressing the claims of former slaves; the courts turned their backs; the Ku Klux Klan was on the rise; and an ideological assault upon the "carpetbaggers" and "radicals" of the years following the Civil War was under way in academia no less than in the early films of Hollywood, like *Birth of a Nation* by D. W. Griffith.

Washington sought to contest racism in a period of reaction. But there is little sympathy for him now. He is perhaps still embraced by the right for his doctrine of black self-help as well as his opposition to unions and any other form of mass mobilization. Progressives and the more militant, however, generally consider him a collaborator or even an Uncle Tom. And there is a certain legitimacy to that view. Washington was not a tragic figure, and he did not play a subversive game of subservience. His important "Atlanta Exposition Address" of 1895 resonates with sincerely believed clichés.[5] It calls upon blacks to "make friends" with whites and on "people of all races" to work together in building a "new South." The problem lies not with the words, of course, but with the reality. Washington's message simply assumed that whites would reciprocate the gesture of good will made by blacks, despite the lynchings and other racist practices brought to light by progressive muckrakers and courageous organizers like Ida Wells. His accommodationism contradicted the life experience of most black Americans, and his educational perspective was narrowly practical rather than political.

Washington wanted jobs for his people; caricaturing the most crude forms of economism, however, he maintained that political equality for whites and blacks must await the attainment of economic equality. There is a question whether any other politics was possible in the face of the unremitting violence and prejudice faced by African Americans at this time. But there is also a sense in which Du Bois was correct in his famous criticism of Washington, which led him to form the NAACP. Washington simply mis-

5. The speech is reprinted in Booker T. Washington, *Up from Slavery: An Autobiography* (New York: Doubleday, 1901).

read the primacy of politics and, as a consequence, supported a reformist strategy under circumstances in which the achievement of even genuine economic reforms was effectively impossible. His pragmatism was ultimately unpragmatic; it ignored the need for a political vision capable of mobilizing a genuinely mass base. Washington was indeed ultimately the intellectual representative of a small black professional and bourgeois caste capable of dominating a black society hermetically sealed from the broader world of whites.

Booker T. Washington was still read in white schools in the United States in the 1950s and the early 1960s. The case of Marcus Garvey was very different.[6] Born in Jamaica in 1887, an immigrant to the United States in 1916, he was a great speaker, like Booker T. Washington; and, also like him, he was neither a theorist nor a scholar in the traditional sense. But for Garvey, accommodation and integration were unconscionable. He would unequivocally insist upon separatism until his death in 1940. Unfortunately, however, Garvey would become defined by what he so strenuously opposed.

The blatant racism of the last quarter of the nineteenth century produced the foundations for two very different responses. If it fostered an emphasis upon purely economic issues among some, if it resulted in fear and a retreat from mass mobilization among certain segments of the black community, it also created the felt need for a new form of solidarity and a mass politics predicated on separatism. Blacks fleeing racism in the South were ushered into ghettos in the North. The unwillingness of either the white liberal bourgeoisie or the white working class to forge any kind of meaningful alliance with African Americans created a situation in which the stance of Washington was no more or less pragmatic than that of Garvey. His Universal Negro Improvement Association, a staunchly nationalist alternative to the NAACP, sought to fashion a new solidarity based on race. Thus, he would maintain that his organization "believes in the social and political physical separation of all peoples to the extent that they promote their ideals and civilizations, the privilege of trading and doing business with each other. It believes in the promotion of a strong and powerful Negro nation in Africa."[7]

---

6. Judith Stein, *The World of Marcus Garvey: Race and Class in Modern Society* (Baton Rouge: Louisiana State University Press, 1986); Rupert Lewis, *Marcus Garvey: An Anti-Colonial Champion* (Trenton, N.J.: Africa World Press, 1988).

7. Marcus Garvey, "Speech to the Second International Convention of Negroes" (1921), in *The Nationalism Reader*, ed. Omar Dahbour and Micheline R. Ishay (Atlantic Highlands, N.J.: Humanities Press International, 1995), 302.

Garvey was a charismatic personality who, like Sabbatai Sevi, the "false Messiah" of the Jews,[8] called upon his people to take their possessions and leave for the promised land. He stood disgraced, convicted of mail fraud and other crimes, when he died in 1940 at the age of fifty-three. But he serves as an important symbol for many African Americans, and during his lifetime he had significant support and an impact on the everyday life of the black constituency. Few more starkly emphasized the need to retrieve the culture and history of Africa for American blacks. Garvey envisioned a proud and self-sufficient black nation, and he sought to strengthen the international bonds between people of color. But his organization was neither a party nor an interest group; its demands were vague and uncertain. His racialism also ignored the heterogeneity and class divisions among people of color, as well as the complex of other factors relevant to nationalism. Garvey was content to outline the hardships suffered by Negroes in different parts of the world to promote his stance that there is no other place for them but Africa. "Africa for the Africans" was his slogan, and it serves as a clue to the failure of his enterprise. Just as he refused to recognize the difference between a nation and a continent, and just as he refused to consider the existence of multiple tribal and familial loyalties within either, he rejected any possibility of a "double consciousness." He refused to accept the idea that African Americans are, after all, still Americans.

Political theory does not simply stop when it reaches national or racial or cultural boundaries. African American political theory is not somehow isolated from ideological tendencies manifest in Western political movements. In a sense, the ideological logic employed by both Washington and Garvey is not as "new" as the social movements they wished to represent. Accommodation to the existing cultural milieu, rejection of political mass mobilization, and a belief that noneconomic reforms will prove attractive only to a small elite are all cardinal beliefs of European reformism. Garvey, for his part, shared the existential and organicist assumptions of European advocates of integral nationalism, and his preoccupation with quasi-military parades, the cult of the leader, and racialist notions of cultural superior-

8. Ironically, the study of Sabbatai Sevi and the enormous influence his vision exerted nearly five hundred years ago offers much to an understanding of the "new social movements" in our own time; see Gershom Scholem, *Sabbatai Sevi: The Mystical Messiah*, trans. R. J. Zwi Weblowsky (Princeton: Princeton University Press, 1971).

ity show a certain similarity with the ideas of a burgeoning European fascism.

For different reasons, neither Washington nor Garvey offered a genuine politics of reform nor a vision capable of contesting political inequality, economic imbalances of power, or the cultural plight of the African American. Whereas Booker T. Washington began a line of development that eventually extended to Thomas Sowell, along with any number of other contemporary neoconservative intellectuals opposed to affirmative action and supportive of "black capitalism," Garvey heralded the separatism of Louis Farrakhan and the Afrocentrism of figures like Leonard Jeffries. Nevertheless, Garvey also influenced figures of a different moral and political caliber.

Malcolm Little was born in 1925. He was the son of a Garveyite whom Malcolm believed had been killed by whites under suspicious circumstances. Malcolm became a street hustler and spent time in jail, where he learned about the Nation of Islam led by the Honorable Elijah Muhammad. After he left jail he joined the Black Muslims, abandoned his slave name for the letter X, and became their most prominent representative. Renowned as an orator, Malcolm X became the leader of the New York mosque, and he preached a separatist doctrine and a morality of puritanical virtue. He was genuinely shocked when it became apparent that Elijah Muhammad had engaged in illicit sexual affairs and when rumors of financial mismanagement surfaced.

But the fact is that Elijah Muhammad was becoming increasingly jealous of Malcolm X. Upon being forced out of the movement in 1963, when he spoke about the "chickens coming home to roost" immediately following the assassination of President John F. Kennedy, Malcolm X traveled to Africa and Europe. He met with various revolutionaries, and in Mecca, where he encountered blue-eyed Muslims with light skin, he ultimately reached the conclusion that Africa was less a racial than a geographical term and that Islam could not be understood in racialist terms. He returned to the United States intent upon forming alliances with whites willing to cede prominence to blacks, concerned with human rights and—perhaps most important— with forging closer connections with people of color everywhere.[9] His autobiography is indeed representative of black men who lift themselves beyond the miseries and superficialities of ghetto life, take their destiny in their hands, and confront white society with unmitigated anger. Malcolm X was

---

9. *The Autobiography of Malcolm X* (New York: Grove, 1965).

ferocious in his commitments and his hatreds but also reflective and self-critical. He was genuinely complex, both personally and politically, and his ideas were still fragmentary and unformed when he was assassinated in 1965 by members of the Nation of Islam.[10]

Toward the end of his life Malcolm X showed a new tolerance for Martin Luther King Jr., and there is a sense in which he was moving toward a more universalist position. Both leaders posed a threat to the existing establishment. Both sought a new foreign policy toward the former colonial nations, disinvestment in racist regimes like that in South Africa, and an expanded role for the United Nations. Malcolm X, for his part, even sought to bring the matter of racism in America before the General Assembly. But revisionists who ignore the profound differences between them perform a disservice to both. Martin Luther King Jr. spoke with the biblical eloquence of the preacher, whereas Malcolm X spoke the fiery language of the street. The former was a Christian who gained his fame in the South, whereas the latter found Islam in jail and an audience in the North. The former sought integration, as a moral imperative, and the latter derived a belief in segregation from his idea of "black revolution."

Both were advocates of human rights, but whereas Malcolm X understood this in terms of an uncritical support for national self-determination and an unwillingness to criticize those from different cultures,[11] King employed it with reference to the individual contesting the state in the antinationalist terms of liberalism and socialism. Neither was sure about the organizational form a new movement should take. But King was clear about his values and his program. Malcolm X never really defined either the political meaning of "black power," which often gave rise to the most absurdly radical rhetoric in conjunction with the most reformist goals,[12] or the terms under which unity with whites should prove possible. He indeed stands more as a cultural icon than as a genuinely political visionary.

Others looked at matters differently. C. L. R. James sought to show the genuinely international significance of the values underpinning the Enlightenment and the French Revolution.[13] A. Jennings Randolph, editor of *The*

---

10. *Malcolm X Speaks: Selected Speeches and Statements*, ed. George Breitman (New York: Merit, 1973).

11. Note the concluding letter in *Malcolm X Speaks: Speeches, Interviews, and a Letter by Malcolm X*, ed. George Breitman (New York: Merit, 1973).

12. See Stokely Carmichael and Charles V. Hamilton, *Black Power: The Politics of Liberation in America* (New York: Vintage, 1967).

13. C. L. R. James, *Black Jacobins: Toussaint L'Ouverture and the San Domingo Revolution* (New York: Vintage, 1963).

Masses, worked tirelessly for the creation of black unions and campaigned for alliances with white workers throughout his long life. George Padmore and a host of others worked with the communists, who, for better or worse, stood in the forefront of efforts to battle racism and secure the freedom of African Americans.[14] These socialist thinkers and activists are generally seen as either underestimating the cultural dimension of African American life or believing it could simply coexist with overriding organizational dictates or broader systemic concerns.[15] But there is also something involved that is deeper than organization or clarity of programmatic commitment. None of these explicitly socialist and communist activists and intellectuals were able to make use of the religious institutions in which a majority of everyday black people were engaged,[16] to create a new form of political symbolism, or to fashion a moral imperative with resonance for both whites and blacks.

The Reverend Martin Luther King Jr. dealt with these needs and, navigating his way toward a universalist and class-based movement of the poor and disenfranchised, became the guiding force in what would become the Civil Rights Movement and the Poor People's Movement. Born in 1929, the son of a minister, he grew up among the insular elite of the black community in Atlanta. He was precocious and received his doctorate in 1955 from Boston University with a dissertation on Paul Tillich, a Christian socialist whose work fused the Protestant dissident tradition with Kant and Marx. These intellectual strains would find their way into King's thinking as well.[17] He is perhaps best remembered for his towering oratory, his notion of nonviolent civil disobedience, and his moral posture. There is no question that he captured the moral high ground in a way other leaders could only envy. In keeping with the philosophy of Gandhi, King sought to appeal to the conscience

---

14. The growing disillusionment with the communists is expressed with intelligence and poignancy in the great novel by Ralph Ellison, *Invisible Man* (New York: Random House, 1952), and in the classic contribution of Richard Wright to the famous collection entitled *The God That Failed,* ed. Richard Crossman (New York: Bantam, 1965).

15. See Manning Marable, "Why Black Americans Are Not Socialists," in *Speaking Truth to Power: Essays on Race, Resistance, and Radicalism* (Boulder: Westview, 1998).

16. See David J. Garrow, *Bearing the Cross: Martin Luther King and the Southern Christian Leadership Conference* (New York: William Morrow, 1986); Taylor Branch, *Parting the Waters: America in the King Years* (New York: Simon and Schuster, 1988).

17. Martin Luther King Jr., *Stride toward Freedom: The Montgomery Story* (New York: Harper and Row, 1958).

of his opponents as well as his followers. Nevertheless, there is still more to his radical legacy.

Using the media of the very system King sought to transform and employing the institutional power of the black Baptist Church, following Kant and Marx, he showed how a critique based on positive principles could challenge a supposedly liberal nation to live up to its self-professed ideals. Influenced by the tradition of the NAACP and W. E. B. Du Bois, though unambiguously liberal in his politics, he offered an alternative to the thinking of both Booker T. Washington and Marcus Garvey. King placed fundamental primacy on political rights and, without equivocation, condemned separatism.[18] Subordinating intuition and questions of identity to universal norms, highlighting integration and ultimately generalizable class interests, he showed the profound connection between Enlightenment values and any genuinely progressive mass movement.

His classic "Letter from a Birmingham Jail" was a radical and cosmopolitan response to those who thought the Civil Rights Movement was "going too fast" and opposed the idea of outsiders seeking to change the South.[19] It emphasizes the need to distinguish between just and unjust laws, or "positive laws" and the "rule of law," in order to justify nonviolent civil disobedience. His belief that dissidents must accept punishment for breaking the law, inspired by the example of Mahatma Gandhi, was part and parcel of Kantian moral philosophy. But it is too often forgotten that the achievement of political equality, which was underscored by the passage of the Civil Rights Act of 1964 and the monumental Voting Rights Bill of 1965, was only the first step. In the spirit of Kant, Marx, and Du Bois, King next sought to connect his movement with the struggle against the Vietnam War. He became a champion of the United Nations, and he called upon the United States to institute a new foreign policy with respect to the Third World. Following the creation of new bonds between the civil rights and antiwar movements, he sought to fashion a new movement, which became known as the Poor People's Movement."[20] It called for genuine urban renewal, nationalization of certain industries, and a guaranteed annual wage. King had be-

---

18. Martin Luther King Jr., *Where Do We Go from Here: Chaos or Community?* (New York: Harper and Row, 1967).

19. Martin Luther King Jr., *Why We Can't Wait* (New York: Harper and Row, 1964).

20. Gerald D. McKnight, *The Last Crusade: Martin Luther King Jr., the FBI, and the Poor People's Campaign* (Boulder: Westview, 1997).

come a democratic socialist by the time of his death, and his new Poor People's Movement stood clearly within the tradition of the Popular Front. It could have turned into just another interest group, or it could perhaps have served as the basis for a new political party. Its future was already uncertain when King was assassinated in 1968 while addressing a garbage workers' strike in Memphis.

Both the Civil Rights Movement and the Poor People's Movement have now disintegrated. The former was, arguably, a victim of its own success, and the unfulfilled possibilities projected by the latter were undermined by the combination of a concentrated ideological and political assault of elites from above and the growing fragmentation attendant upon an embrace of identity politics from below. King has become a national symbol, but the importance of his philosophical legacy can no longer be taken for granted. His genuine legacy lies in the unequivocal commitment to certain Enlightenment values, the logic of his political development, and the radicalism of his concrete demands. Many from the right and the left still criticize the work of his last years, given the growth of identity politics among his own followers, the vacillation of white liberals, and the lack of support from the political establishment. But there was probably no figure in the last half of this century who so fully incarnated a commitment to a genuinely radical reformism.

Martin Luther King sought a new connection between theory and practice. He was indeed the only major American political activist of the postwar world whose movement linked the old and the new left. His movement, grounded in local communities, forced the federal government to take action against the racist laws upheld by any number of states, and it contested communitarian values in the South by invoking the critical universalist values of the liberal and, later, socialist traditions. King saw the connection between the Declaration of Independence and the call for freedom incorporated in slave songs. He was not some pragmatist incapable of understanding the moral sources of political action and unwilling to affirm the values in which he believed. He was also not the precursor of a tepid postmodern particularism incapable of questioning its relativism and unwilling to thematize the whole. King challenged the totality with an emancipatory vision intent on transforming the state, the economy, foreign policy, and the existing culture. He offered a concrete vision with which to transform the landscape of American society, and as an old participant in the Civil Rights

Movement once told me, perhaps even more important, he was unafraid to bring out the best in his followers.

In the aftermath of the Civil Rights Movement, African Americans have entered the mainstream of life in the United States. Lynching and the more noxious expressions of racism have become a thing of the past, and when singular events occur, they are condemned all across the political spectrum. African Americans now constitute a genuine voting bloc, and, especially in local and state elections, their representatives have entered the corridors of power in a manner previous generations would have considered unimaginable. A relatively small yet vital black bourgeoisie is also emerging in the United States. Perhaps even more important than all of this, even if only for public consumption, a "color-blind" ideology committed to individual rights and "fair play" has become embedded in the political discourse. Nevertheless, by the same token, racism in everyday life obviously continues.

National policies for African Americans are still dependent upon coalitions with white liberals; and, given the assault upon the welfare state, or what Frances Fox Piven and Richard Cloward have called "the breaking of the American social compact," feelings of betrayal have become common and warranted. If it is true that a black bourgeoisie is on the rise, it is also true that the transition to an "information society" has been particularly hard on African Americans: there are still ghettos, and there are still qualitative differences between black and white workers with respect to any number of economic indicators. In addition, we are also witnessing the marked growth of a black *Lumpenproletariat*.[21] Where such substantive inequality exists, the "color-blind" perspective can serve reactionary interests by calling for the abolition of various policies targeting the plight of poor African Americans and seeking to make the playing field more level.[22]

It no longer makes sense to consider America a "white supremacist" state. For working-class and poor African Americans, however, economic racism reinforces the social racism generated by longstanding "cultural attitudes" and feeds into the desire by capitalists, whether conscious or unconscious, to maintain political divisions among workers and the poor. There are ways in which questions of race and class intersect even though the one remains irreducible to the other. This indeed only complicates a situation in which

21. Frances Fox Piven and Richard A. Cloward, *The Breaking of the Social Compact* (New York: New Press, 1997), 131 ff. and passim.
22. See Dinesh D'Souza, *The End of Racism* (New York: Free Press, 1995).

blacks, culturally deprived of their own past and intent on rediscovering it, remain stranded in the nation of which they nevertheless remain an integral part.

Under these circumstances, it is easy to see racism as nothing more than a function of power; and because blacks as a group are relatively powerless, one might think that, by definition, they cannot be racist. But this is faulty logic, and it ignores the political component of the problem. The ideology of the oppressor can be internalized by the oppressed, and it can thereby profoundly affect their struggle for freedom and equality. The terms in which racism is understood will, in short, have an impact upon the attempts to abolish it. Racism is not reducible to economic or political interest. But it serves capital by dividing working people; it is politically self-defeating and morally debilitating. It has become a matter of linking the struggle against the imbalances of power associated with racism to the struggle against the economic imbalances of power associated with capitalism.

Major figures within the African American tradition, particularly Du Bois and King, always knew this, and they ultimately recognized the need for coalitional white support. Especially during the last two decades of the twentieth century, however, such support has been lost in large measure. The collapse of the "movement" and the reactionary upsurge of the 1980s undermined the political organization of the poor as well as the legislation they both need and deserve. Certain prominent tendencies within the African American movement have contributed to this trend by surrendering the moral terrain gained since the death of Martin Luther King Jr. Demagogues and nationalists have indeed employed fiery rhetoric without a program of markedly generalizable appeal and simple old-fashioned guilt without a sense of the backlash it generates.

Race has always been a questionable concept, and, scientifically or "biologically," it has little basis in reality. Its "organic" understanding has been historically associated with conservative and even fascist traditions. It has traditionally been employed to abrogate individual and class responsibility and to assault the rule of law. Things do not change when purportedly left-wing proponents of "critical race theory" call upon blacks to engage in "jury nullification" and vote their racial conscience, rather than observe legal rules, when sitting in judgment of any black on trial for any crime. Such logic suggests that the criminality of a racist legal system invalidates the punishment of any black criminal. It thereby excuses one crime by making reference to another, and it is derivative of a victim-based logic in which, given the assumption that "whites" are all powerful, blacks become defined by what they oppose. This kind of stance is also an insult against the working-class victim of a thief, the female victim of a rapist, or any victim of a killer. With its attack on the very possibility of impartial judgment, indeed, what results is a reactionary assault on the rule of law, and the notion of guilt and innocence, in the name of particularist ideals.

Such an attitude is designed for failure: failure for the most oppressed African Americans, who must make basic life choices under the most difficult conditions, and failure in terms of any possible alliance between African American and white or Hispanic or women or gay workers. The need for such an alliance, once again, has become a seminal concern within much of African American political theory. The character of the alliance may mean something different for Du Bois and for Garvey, for Malcolm X and for King, and even for Cornel West and for Adolph Reed. But therein lies the challenge. African American politics is in a state of limbo; it is caught between assimilation and separatism, radical rhetoric and substantive timidity, the social demands for equality and the cultural demands for difference. It is now a question of highlighting what each of the most significant figures in an undervalued and multifaceted tradition can contribute toward clarifying the values appropriate for a new cosmopolitan politics.

17

◆══════◆

Sex: Gendered Experiences

F eminism has unquestionably been the most influential new political philosophy in the last quarter of the twentieth century; certainly within academia, as bell hooks has noted, it has moved "from the margin to the center."[1] Just as the clash between assimilation and separatism deeply influenced the thinking of people of color, however, the battle over equality and difference has pervaded the women's movement. The political development of the two movements was the same. It was, again, by first securing the conditions of equality that possibilities for the expression of difference multiplied. Suffrage was the key for both movements; and in the case of women, it made possible the transformation of formerly private issues—abortion, incest, and spousal abuse—into matters of public policy. Feminism is not the exclusive possession of the American women's movement, and especially in the United States, it is perhaps necessary to consider the contributions from elsewhere. But it is true that the struggle for suffrage in the United States, which began with Margaret Fuller in the 1820s, took on new life in the 1860s with the creation of women's clubs for the pursuit of various social reforms and, often, self-education. In the same vein, although female suffrage was achieved in the United States in 1919, the creation of a self-consciously "feminist" movement seemed necessary to make

---

1. bell hooks, *Feminist Theory: From Margin to Center* (Boston: South End, 1984); useful background works also include Judith Grant, *Fundamental Feminism: Contesting the Core Concepts of Feminist Theory* (New York: Routledge, 1993); Ursula I. Meyer, *Einführung in die feministische Philosophie* (Munich: Deutsche Taschenbuch, 1997); Rosemarie Putnam Tong, *Feminist Thought: A More Comprehensive Introduction* (Boulder: Westview, 1998).

good on the possibilities offered by public life and to forge a new voting bloc. Indeed, whatever the rhetoric, women were not successful in forging this kind of unified political bloc.

Questions regarding the emancipation of women were always connected with broader progressive movements, built on Enlightenment principles, which wished to contest the political constraints and the economic exploitation of modernity. Mary Wollstonecraft sought to extend the rights of the French Revolution to women;[2] also, quite clearly, the attempt to employ liberal and socialist principles in dealing with the oppression of women was a matter of major concern for Harriet Taylor and John Stuart Mill.[3] Anarchists like Richard Godwin and utopian socialists like Charles Fourier linked the ability of women to expand their life experiences with the very idea of an emancipated order. Marx and especially Engels indeed saw the domination of women as anthropologically underpinning the division of labor in capitalist society, the bourgeois family as an artificial and hypocritical contrivance, and capitalism itself as inhibiting the creation of an order predicated on the gender-neutral assumption of *The Communist Manifesto* in which "the free development of each is the condition for the free development of all."

It is of some consequence that *The Origins of the Family, Private Property, and the State,* by Frederick Engels, and *Woman under Socialism,* by August Bebel, the leading political figure of the German Social Democratic Party after the turn of the twentieth century, should have figured among the most popular works of socialist literature. These works were informed by the sexual mores of the Victorian era. Yet, in contrast with what is commonly assumed, and against the prejudices of many socialist and communist followers, Engels and Bebel did not consider work in the home "nonproductive" and irrelevant when compared with productive activity in the factory. This was only so for capitalism, which was seen as valuing only what is bought and sold. Both works were indeed predicated on the assumption explicitly stated by Bebel: "There can be no liberation of mankind without independence and equality of the sexes." Such thinking emphasized the need for solidarity with working women and considered them comrades in a common fight against capitalism; it viewed the family and the secondary

---

2. Mary Wollstonecraft, *A Vindication of the Rights of Women*, ed. Carol H. Poston (New York: Norton, 1975).

3. John Stuart Mill, "The Subjection of Women," in John Stuart Mill and Harriet Taylor Mill, *Essays on Sex Equality*, ed. Alice S. Rossi (Chicago: University of Chicago Press, 1970).

status of women as historical rather than natural phenomena; and it offered a theoretical position with which to analyze and overcome women's plight. Indeed, when reflecting upon the publication of *Woman under Socialism*, Clara Zetkin wrote years later: "It was more than a book, it was an event—a great deed!"[4]

Important figures in the labor movement who were concerned with the plight of women are often dismissed from contemporary feminist discussions in the United States. They are identified with socialism, communism, and Marxism. But that view is a mistake: it ignores their contributions to the feminist movement and the way in which their thinking illuminates the different forms the movement took. The general ignorance about the career of Clara Zetkin offers a case in point. She was, after all, the predominant voice of socialist feminism for an entire generation, and, outside the United States, she remains a symbol of the struggle for women's rights. Born in Mainz in 1857, the child of liberal bourgeois parents, Clara Zetkin first became famous for a speech given during the founding congress of the new socialist international of 1889. A fiery speaker, an intimate friend of Rosa Luxemburg and Karl Liebknecht,[5] she too placed primacy on the creation of a revolutionary class consciousness among workers. She was a major force in the achievement of women's suffrage in Germany, and, in accordance with the requirements of proletarian "self-administration," she was fundamentally concerned with the equal participation of women in running society. Thus, confronting the collapse of social democracy in 1914, she could write: "When the men kill, it is up to us women to fight for the preservation of life. When the men are silent, it is up to us to raise our voices on behalf of our ideals."[6]

Less a theorist than a publicist and activist, who sat on the executive boards of numerous unions, Zetkin served as the editor of *Gleichheit* (Equality) from 1892 to 1916. This journal, which had a circulation of 125,000 before the war, became the primary organ of the feminist left within the social democratic movement: it steadfastly rejected entering into coalitions with "bourgeois" women, which was precisely the same position

---

4. Clara Zetkin, *Selected Writings*, ed. Philip S. Foner (New York: International, 1984), 78.

5. Note Zetkin's beautiful obituary following the assassination of these two great political figures, "Rosa Luxemburg and Karl Liebknecht," in *Selected Writings*.

6. Clara Zetkin, "To the Socialist Women of All Countries," in *Selected Writings*, 116.

taken by American radicals like Emma Goldman, and it emphatically opposed the creation of an independent women's movement. Zetkin's political stance on women was no different, in principle, from the position articulated by other leaders of the far left with regard to coalitions with bourgeois forces on any number of other issues.

There should be no misunderstanding: Zetkin did not forget the unique needs of women in the name of class concerns, and she did not ignore "difference" in the name of "equality." Zetkin sought an independent caucus for women within the socialist movement, an idea later embraced by the communists, and she was aware that the voice of women needed an institutional form of expression. But she could also write that "in the atmosphere of the materialist concept of history, the 'love drivel' about a sisterhood which supposedly wraps a unifying ribbon around bourgeois ladies and female proletarians, bursts like so many scintillating soap bubbles."[7] There is indeed a sense in which her feminism was less an autonomous position in its own right than a crucial element within a broader worldview informed by internationalism, class politics, and a vision of revolutionary transformation.

It was the same with Alexandra Kollontai. The most prominent feminist within the communist movement, which she would serve faithfully until her death in 1952 at the age of eighty, Kollontai had originally worked as an organizer in the socialist labor movement. A proponent of free sexuality and abortion, a champion of health and day-care services for working mothers, and a leading advocate of equal wages and the entry of women into the labor force, she was basically in accord with Zetkin in her belief that "the struggle to achieve political equality for *proletarian women* is part and parcel of the overall class struggle of the proletariat; when it becomes an independent militant aim, it eclipses the class objectives of women workers."[8] Kollontai fought in the revolution of 1905, like Rosa Luxemburg, and she highlighted the intrinsic connection between the development of radical feminism and that of other radical currents within society.[9]

---

7. Clara Zetkin, "What the Women Owe to Karl Marx," in *Selected Writings*, 96.

8. Alexandra Kollontai, "International Socialist Conferences of Women Workers" (1907–16), in *Selected Articles and Speeches*, trans. Cynthia Calile (New York: International, 1984), 41.

9. Alexandra Kollontai, introduction to "The Social Basis of the Women's Question" (1908), in *Selected Articles and Speeches*, 27.

Kollontai was also a leading figure on the left wing of the socialist movement, an outspoken opponent of World War I, an articulate supporter of the communist revolution, an architect of social welfare in the Soviet Union under Lenin, and an ambassador and diplomatic adviser for the Soviet Union under Stalin. It is still not clear how this old Bolshevik survived the purges, especially considering that she became an important member of the left-wing Workers' Opposition of the 1920s, constantly criticized the prudery of the Communist Party, and identified herself with the construction of a utopian order built upon the abolition of the nuclear family. Indeed, with respect to the role of women, her stance never really changed: it highlighted the class basis of feminism, the commitment to socializing domestic work, and a notion of emancipation beyond the purely institutional.[10]

> The lack of provision for millions of mothers, and the lack of concern for young children on the part of society, is the cause of the present bitter conflict over the incompatibility of female professional labor and motherhood, a conflict which lies at the heart of the whole problem of motherhood. . . . Social measures, including comprehensive maternity insurance provision for young children, must be implemented as they will enable the woman *to fulfill her natural calling without abandoning her professional obligations, without losing her economic independence, and without withdrawing from active participation in the struggle for the ideals of her class.*[11]

Other feminists within the socialist labor movement, however, offered a more "revisionist" worldview. Their most important representative was undoubtedly Lily Braun.[12] Born in 1865, daughter of a military family with aristocratic pretensions, she was a free spirit; from the time of her youth, she struggled against repressive social conventions. Bebel's *Woman under Socialism* influenced her decision to join the labor movement, and her trajectory followed that of many comrades on the party "right": she surrendered a class standpoint and a vague notion of revolution for a more embracing populism and the struggle for clear-cut reforms. Lily Braun called for coalitions of women from all classes without party affiliation. She also initially supported the German cause in World War I. Her lack of concern with

---

10. Alexandra Kollontai, preface to "Society and Motherhood," in *Selected Articles and Speeches*, 110.

11. Ibid., 107.

12. Lily Braun, *Memoiren einer Sozialistin*, hrsg. Elisabeth Fetscher (Munich: Piper, 1985).

class politics or internationalism opened the way for particularism and a new form of interest-group politics for those concerned with seeking their national, religious, or gender identities.

Nothing better demonstrates the changes in consciousness than the often misunderstood conflict between the left and the right in international socialism on the "woman's question." The irony is unmistakable and rarely acknowledged. Clara Zetkin would become the most famous feminist in the labor movement even though she privileged an international revolutionary class standpoint and later, attendant upon her entry into the communist movement, gave unquestioned primacy to the party; indeed, tragically, when she died in 1933 she had become little more than a mouthpiece for its policies. By contemporary standards, her stance could actually be viewed by many feminists as conservative. As for Lily Braun, her reputation drifted into obscurity following her death at the age of fifty-one. But her position anticipates what is now often identified with "radical" feminism, although in fact it involved a rejection of international revolutionary class action in favor of feminist reforms and a preoccupation with the interconnection between private and public forms of sexism. It is striking that what was once considered the radical view has now become conservative, and what was once considered conservative is now seen as radical.

There is surely a sense in which this change is justified. It is predicated on a very different understanding of radicalism. The standpoint has shifted. And there is no figure more responsible for the change than Simone de Beauvoir. Born in 1908, a rebel against the constraints upon self-expression imposed by her family, she came to know Jean-Paul Sartre and his friends while a student at the École Normale Supérieure. Always concerned with the effects of sexism, a partisan in all the major events of the postwar period, it was only when she joined the Mouvement de la Liberation des Femmes, in 1971, that she actually participated in an organization concerned purely with feminist issues. It was also only around the same time that she surrendered her belief that socialism would solve the problems of feminism.[13] Nevertheless, by the time she died in 1986, it was clear that Beauvoir had established both an existential and a political rationale for a feminist "movement."

Beauvoir was at the center of French intellectual and public life for nearly

---

13. "Interview with Beauvoir: Ich bin Feministen," in *Simone de Beauvoir heute,* hrsg. Alice Schwarzer (Reinbeck: Rowohlt, 1991).

six decades. She was the lifelong companion of Jean-Paul Sartre. Many modern feminists have castigated her supposed subordination to him, her refusal to publicly admit her lesbian affairs, and various other aspects of her private life. But this is all historical revisionism in the worst sense of the term. The philosophical and political *problématique* for her major works undoubtedly came from Sartre; she too concerned herself with the moral imperatives of action, the tragic conflicts between intention and consequence, and the responsibility of the individual for his or her choices. Admiration and love, however, need not stand in the way of reasoned reflection. Her writings were clearly informed by a feminist spirit and her own massive erudition. Her extraordinary diaries, whatever their particular misjudgments of certain people and political events, incorporate the spirit of her age, and her novels like *The Blood of Others* (1945) and *The Mandarins* (1954), which won the Prix de Goncourt, provide a remarkable insight into the cultural atmosphere of the postwar period in which they were written. *The Second Sex* indeed remains the single most influential work for the international development of feminism.

Originally published in 1949, when a backlash against feminist reforms was under way both in Europe and the United States, it sought to provide an understanding of women and their subjugation from a phenomenological perspective. Its elegant and wide-ranging introduction states the overriding problem clearly: Women have been defined purely in relation to men and not as autonomous beings.[14] Transcendence is the province of man: he employs his intellect, exercises power, and manifests the potential to transform his situation. Woman, by contrast, is condemned to immanence: she is identified with her body, suffocates under patriarchal relations, and is placed in a position of subservience against her will. Man, in this way, is the subject and woman is the Other: "Woman does not entertain the positive belief," she could write, "that the truth is something *other* than what men claim."[15] Women experience an unchosen subjugation. But they can either accept or reject their condition. Anticipating what would later become the differentiation between "sex" and "gender," viewing "woman" as made rather than born, Beauvoir opposed biological determinism of any sort.[16] She also believed in the mutability of patriarchal oppression. It thus became incumbent

14. Simone de Beauvoir, *The Second Sex*, ed. and trans. H. M. Parshley (New York: Vintage, 1989), 599 ff.
15. Ibid., 612.
16. Ibid., 3 ff.

upon women to demand inclusion in what are traditionally considered male pursuits and to reject their relegation to the kitchen and the nursery.

The Second Sex is primarily an attack upon the manner in which women are socialized. It assumes an ontological foundation, the unconditioned freedom of the individual, for understanding women and the repression they experience. The freedom of women is compromised by arbitrary and prejudicial constraints, created by a male society, that deny them subjectivity. In phenomenological terms, however, the relation between subject and Other is, by its very nature, a struggle for dominance undertaken in the name of self-affirmation. It takes a combination of self-consciousness and respect for that consciousness by the Other to suspend the battle. And so, in keeping with Sartre's existential definition of love,[17] De Beauvoir insisted upon the treatment of women as subjects in their own right. This, in turn, would generate the demand for a broader institutional commitment to political equality and economic independence. Indeed, whatever her self-identification as a woman and her identification with women as women, the philosophical stance of Simone de Beauvoir was predicated on the right of women to express themselves as individuals.[18]

Beauvoir sees no place for "difference," in the sense of women retaining certain "essentialist" attributes or forms of logic. But it is simply unfair to condemn her for calling upon women to enter a "male" society: especially if women constitute the Other, they necessarily participate in the production and reproduction of the world. Her lack of concern for the "feminine" and for maternity is also less a function of her unconscious identification with "maleness" than of the gender-neutral presuppositions underpinning her phenomenological outlook. Changing the oppressive conditions faced by women, she knew, would require a common identity among women. Asserting the link between women "as women," just as for blacks or proletarians, would indeed begin for Simone de Beauvoir with the ability to say "we."

This identity would become generated at the grass roots. A new social movement formed, and it gained a particular impetus in the 1960s and the 1970s. Decentralized in character and antibureaucratic in style, often revolutionary in its rhetoric and radical in its cultural demands, it created the preconditions for political action. The public sphere produced by the wom-

---

17. Jean-Paul Sartre, *Being and Nothingness: An Essay on Phenomenological Ontology*, trans. Hazel Barnes (New York: Philosophical Library, 1956), 364 ff.; Beauvoir, *Second Sex*, 642 ff.

18. Beauvoir, *Second Sex*, 627 ff.

en's liberation movement, in fact, is still exemplary among antiauthoritarian movements and reminiscent of the "workers' world" generated by social democracy in the early part of the century. This feminist public sphere includes novels, poetry, and plays dealing with women; it involves magazines, presses, and various popular illustrations of women's lives; it encompasses academic departments, the scholarly research on women across disciplinary boundaries; it incorporates health clinics, rape counseling, and a host of other services; it speaks to festivals, public meetings, and demonstrations; it also embraces the activities of funding agencies, interest groups, and the like.

The feminist public sphere is an extraordinary phenomenon, and it grew out of the women's liberation movement of the 1960s and 1970s. Inspired by the belief that "sisterhood is powerful,"[19] generated from the exploitation of women in everyday life, it had a profound impact on the general perception of women and their roles. Some of its proponents may have mistakenly seen women as a "class," which they constitute by virtue of their control over the production of "use values" in the home,[20] but most radical feminists recognized the transclass character of their attempt to bring women together, and most Marxists understood that all production under capitalism occurs in terms of exchange. The new feminist public sphere empowered a generation of women and made it possible for them to take control of their lives. It served to combat the set of institutional and ideological relationships by which men exercise power over women. To this extent, whatever its lack of traditional political organization, women could conceive of their grassroots movement as "political" or as an articulation of what Kate Millett termed "sexual politics."[21]

In the most radical terms, which received expression in concert with the emergence of the various other movements of 1968, feminist politics was not simply concerned with historically specific grievances or prejudices. Liberal works were content to deal with these concerns.[22] Radical feminists instead sought to overturn the anthropological foundations of women's oppression in patriarchy and child rearing. All the symbols of male power,

19. Robin Morgan, *Sisterhood Is Powerful: An Anthology of Writings from the Women's Liberation Movement* (New York: Vintage, 1970).
20. Margaret Bentson, "The Political Economy of Women's Liberation," *Monthly Review* 21, no.4 (September 1969): 16.
21. Kate Millett, *Sexual Politics* (New York: Avon, 1971).
22. Betty Friedan, *The Feminist Mystique* (New York: Dell, 1963).

instantiated in forms ranging from etiquette to advertising to sports and social interaction, stood in need of transformation. "The personal is political"
became the dominant slogan of the movement, because the political response against sexism demanded the introduction of new cultural norms
and a reaction against the dominant socializing process. Power was thereby
loosened from traditional, rigorously institutional, "political" definitions,
and autonomy became identified with a set of existential needs for liberation
denied by male society. These were the terms in which sexual politics were
waged by the most spirited intellectuals in the movement.

But this attempt to transform everyday life in a revolutionary fashion
soon came into conflict with the more "practical" or integrationist elements
within the movement. The point was not that radicals like Kate Millett or
Shulamith Firestone were opposed to the struggle for reproductive rights,
efforts to gain equal wages for women, and a host of other legislative demands. Quite the contrary. It was, for them, merely a question of engaging
in a critical form of solidarity; it had become clear that "there exists a
wholly different reality for men and women."[23] The struggle must seek the
revolutionary transformation of patriarchy and the conditions under which
birthing and child rearing are the province of women alone.

The organizational vehicle for such a revolution, its institutional aims,
and even its mass base were never defined. Pragmatists were quick to point
this out. Many of them liked the emphasis upon a uniquely feminist form of
experiential reality, and some even highlighted the belief that nurturing and
maternal thinking are essential qualities of women. As far as the pragmatists
were concerned, however, the style of the radicals no less than the indeterminate character of their goals endangered the possibilities for meaningful
reform. The loose organizational structure and anti-institutional predilections of the movement were seen as simply interfering with the translation
of demands into legislation by its "interest groups."

Other feminist activists with an eye on greater political efficacy called
upon women to organize in a more "professional" manner. Already in
1912, Lucy Bruns, Crystal Eastman, and Alice Paul had helped found the
Congressional Union, which was reorganized in 1916 as the National Woman's Party. It became known for its commitment to a national amendment
for women's suffrage, its militant tactics of picketing and hunger strikes,

---

23. Shulamith Firestone, *The Dialectic of Sex: The Case for Feminist Revolution*
(London: Women's Press, 1979), 151.

and its insistence upon holding the party in power responsible. Figures like Crystal Eastman called upon unions and existing socialist parties to seek equal employment opportunities and equal pay for women.[24] Their efforts indeed extended to issues of birth control, free sexuality, maternity pay, housework compensation, and an Equal Rights Amendment, which was first introduced in Congress in 1923.[25] Activity of this sort indeed helped shape a new women's agenda.

This earlier feminist agenda was originally informed by a radical, vanguardist spirit.[26] There was a sense that these organizing efforts were in advance of the base or, at least, adequately reflected its general concerns. World War II, however, marked a break. The organized movement subsided as men returned from the fighting, women were forced out of jobs, and radicals put their energies into the civil rights movement and then fighting against the Vietnam War. With an all-encompassing mass movement on the rise, activity at the base overtook the activity of "professional" activists. Soon enough, however, lobbyists and politicians again began to translate the specific grievances of women into policy on a score of issues, from abortion and equal pay to harassment and day care to opening male-only schools and activities to women. The success of such efforts to transform the condition of women and the climate in which they lived, and the use of the state to do so, was remarkable. The political landscape was changed in less than a generation. But there was also something lost. The tension between radicals at the grass roots and professionals in the halls of state and national assemblies indeed became ever more intense.

Bureaucratic dynamics know neither sex nor race nor class. They would prove no different for the women's movement than for any other. Organizational regulars increasingly called upon women at the base to eliminate the radical rhetoric, the antihierarchical values, and the utopianism, which had helped inspire the movement in the first place. Dealing with political institutions in capitalist democracy would call upon feminists, in the same way as others with grievances, to transform their long-range ideals into short-term

24. See Susan Craig, " 'Freedom Is a Large Word': The Life and Politics of Catherine Crystal Eastman," Ph.D. diss., Rutgers University, 1999.

25. For a contemporary view of the problems associated with such an enterprise, see Jane Mansbridge, *Why We Lost the ERA* (Chicago: University of Chicago, 1986).

26. Nancy Cott, *The Grounding of Modern Feminism* (New Haven: Yale University Press, 1987).

demands. Nonradicals believed it necessary to "balance" personal with social issues and the "politics" with the "vision" of the movement. Utopian radicalism would, according to the "liberal" analysis, leave the women's movement "isolated in a splendid ideological purity, which gains nothing for anyone."[27]

Of course, if the point is to build bridges with men and other radical movements, other paths present themselves for feminists. A major thinker and historian of the women's movement, Sheila Rowbotham opposed the reformist trend. A student of the English historian E. P. Thompson, influenced by a variety of anarchist and Marxist sources, Rowbotham was committed to furnishing women with a tradition and highlighting the connections between their struggles and those of other revolutionary movements.[28] Rowbotham became a seminal figure in the international women's movement of the 1970s. She was involved with the struggle for abortion rights and any number of other issues. Nevertheless, with the image of 1968 looming in the background, she could still write,

> It is not enough to struggle for particular reforms, important as these are. Unless we understand the relationship of the various elements within the structure of male-dominated capitalism, we will find the improvements we achieve are twisted against us, or serve one group at the expense of the rest. . . . One group of women can be bought off at the expense of another, young women against old, middle class against working class. If we are ready to settle for a slightly bigger bite of the existing cake for a privileged section we will merely create gradations among the underprivileged. We will not change the context in which women are inferior.[29]

Rowbotham was aware of the ways in which lobbying groups and transclass forms of organizing would inevitably sacrifice the interests of working women for middle class or bourgeois women. Aware of the precapitalist

---

27. Jo Freeman, *The Politics of Women's Liberation: A Case Study of an Emerging Social Movement in Relation to the Policy Process* (New York: McKay, 1975).

28. Sheila Rowbotham, *Hidden from History: Rediscovering Women in History from the Seventeenth Century to the Present* (New York: Pantheon, 1973), and *Women, Resistance, and Revolution: A History of Women and Revolution in the Modern World* (New York: Vintage, 1974).

29. Sheila Rowbotham, *Woman's Consciousness, Man's World* (Middlesex, Eng.: Penguin, 1973), 122–23.

character of women's oppression[30] and seeking to link the assault on patriarchy with capitalism, she placed particular emphasis upon linking issues of gender with those of class and race without sacrificing the identity claims or integrity of any particular group. She indeed foresaw the importance of "translating the experience of one group to another without merely annexing the weaker to the stronger."[31] Indeed, even as the 1980s began, Rowbotham consistently warned against "accepting one way of organizing for socialism and another for feminism."[32]

The connection between feminism and socialism seemed almost self-evident.[33] Women have always been a central component of the labor force,[34] and it has indeed become possible to speak about the "feminization of poverty."[35] Women have predominated in the substitution of part-time for full-time labor, office and clerical employment, and in jobs consistent with the household and familial burdens they traditionally bear. These kinds of jobs are particularly difficult to organize. But whatever the ways in which gender oppression has affected the division of labor, the inability of socialist movements to capitalize on this part of the labor force has hurt them. Regrettably, those who are relegated to the lowest-wage jobs, especially women of color, have stood outside the organizing efforts of the labor movement.[36]

Complicating the matter further, however, is the way in which the concern with class confronts the logic of solidarity informing the new social movements, in general, and feminism, in particular. New social movements have primarily been built on a transclass understanding of identity, and, if only for this reason, the terms for bringing about such an alliance remain undefined. Rowbotham anticipated, far more clearly than most, the issues of a left plagued with a multitude of identity claims under circumstances in which interest groups have seemingly become the substitutes for political parties of the oppressed and disenfranchised. But she never articulated the

30. Ibid., 117.
31. Ibid.
32. Sheila Rowbotham, "The Women's Movement and Organizing for Socialism," in Sheila Rowbotham, Lynne Segal, and Hilary Wainwright, *Beyond the Fragments: Feminism and the Making of Socialism* (Boston: Allyson, 1981), 39.
33. Juliet Mitchell, *Women's Estate* (New York: Vintage, 1973).
34. See Rosalyn Baxandall, Linda Gorden, and Susan Reverby, eds., *American's Working Women* (New York: Vintage, 1976).
35. Barbara Ehrenreich and Frances Fox Piven, "The Feminization of Poverty," *Dissent* (Spring 1984).
36. Donald Sassoon, *One Hundred Years of Socialism: The West European Left in the Twentieth Century* (New York: New Press, 1996), 657 ff.

terms in which an alliance of forces could be brought about. Opposed to separatism and clear about the importance of revolutionary tradition for a revolutionary movement, Rowbotham could not foresee the fragmenting dynamics fostered by unique identity claims within the feminist movement or the power they would gain as the conservative counterrevolution of the 1980s entered full swing.

Feminists grew sensitive to the ways in which the particular voice was in danger of being lost as a result of challenges to the "false universals" of liberal feminism and what came to be considered by women of color and lesbian feminists in the mid-1970s the Eurocentric and white character of the women's liberation movement. Feminism would indeed become a terrain of often explosive cultural contestation. This was already the preeminent concern of the speech by Audre Lorde, which she delivered in 1979 at a panel discussion, titled "The Personal and the Political," for the Second Sex Conference in New York. "The Master's Tools Will Never Dismantle the Master's House" blasts the academic and conformist currents of feminism. The article insists on highlighting the differences in race, sexuality, class, and age among women. Community is based on difference, in her view, and ultimately, "divide and conquer must become define and empower." Audre Lorde, indeed, calls not merely for the toleration of difference but for a new emphasis on the mutuality between women and a new vision of interdependence.

At issue here is not the more extreme formulations associated with the most radical elements within the women's movement. Every mass movement has had its sectarian wing and the equivalent of slogans like "sex is rape" or "imperialism is penetration." They are less interesting for their avowedly feminist "perspective" than for the ways in which they take metaphor for reality and surrender the ability to distinguish between qualitatively different forms of action. This fits into a distinctively postmodernist perspective on the struggles of women for empowerment and emancipation.

A new concern with difference would develop in the 1980s. It would move beyond the traditional preoccupation with the differences between men and women, hierarchically structured by patriarchy, and would instead concentrate both upon the creation of a "higher" feminist sensibility and the differences among women themselves. Inspired by a belief in the ultimate mutability of the human character, a psychological perspective indebted to Sigmund Freud and Jacques Lacan, and a postmodernist concern with the discursive creation of reality, this new stance would privilege the power of the imagination. Indeed, quite consciously, it would confront the political realm and the anthropological legacy of sexism in aesthetic and utopian terms.

The initial aim was to show the manner in which women were excluded from philosophy and the ways in which neutral concepts such as subject and object, justice and liberty, were actually gender biased. The exclusion of women from the canon of political thought, which begins with Plato and Aristotle, justified a redefinition of the discipline and of its core concepts.[37] Insofar as the concepts were defined by men, moreover, it might also mean a rejection of the attributes associated with the *homo politicus, homo oeconomicus,* or *homo rationalis.*[38] Obsessions with power, logic, and individual autonomy must be contested by women intent on affirming their contempt for power, their "feelings," their closeness to nature, and their sense of female community.[39] Such a stance, of course, is "essentialist" in the worst sense, and it not only excludes women from engaging in instrumental political debates but also keeps them from making use of many faculties and parts of their characters. Nevertheless, if the confrontation with an inveterately male-oriented world is the purpose, then it is necessary to contest a situation in which "the whole is false."

Postmodern feminism rejects history, metaphysics, and teleology: history is the male-dominated realm of power; metaphysics rests upon the transcendental, gender-neutral subject; and teleology presupposes a human project whose coherence can no longer be taken for granted. It is possible to distinguish between the "historically real" situation of women as oppressed subjects and the "philosophically real" situation in which equality exists[40]—the two can even be juxtaposed with one another; but this would produce an immanent critique of society. The more radical and politically indeterminate forms of feminism prefer to begin with a more encompassing confrontation with reality launched in terms of what Cornelius Castoriadis called "the imaginary." The mutability of language, its ability to construct and deconstruct "the real," is seen as making it the site of feminist resistance. And without taking the matter of reification into account, authentic feminist re-

---

37. See Susan Moller Okin, *Women in Western Political Thought* (Princeton: Princeton University Press, 1992).
38. Meyer, *Einführung in die feministische Philosophie,* 136 ff.
39. Janet Biehl, *Rethinking Ecofeminist Politics* (Boston: South End, 1991).
40. Charlotte Annerl, *Das neuzeitliche Geschlechterverhältnis* (Frankfurt am Main: Suhrkamp, 1991), 155 ff.

sistance ultimately becomes equated with the creation of a feminist "language." Luce Irrigary indeed makes this the fundamental aim of her "ethics of sexual difference."[41]

The assumption is clear: the terms in which men and women are linguistically defined become the terms in which they define themselves. It is therefore necessary to explode the reigning rules of presentation and argumentation. Precisely because these rules define the ways in which women think, however, their critique will lack its own positive form of expression. It must take place within the prevailing forms and thereby its immediate possibilities will necessarily be curtailed: the new language must make way before a new feminist form of speech in which female possibilities, drives, instincts, and emotions are privileged. A way must be opened for the unconscious to inform speech acts: fragments, epigrams, poetry, emotional assaults on the patterned and the logically constructed, come to the fore.

A new feeling, or what Italian feminists call *affidamento*, becomes a matter of crucial importance; and it, in turn, presupposes a sharp differentiation of women from men in terms of what constitutes religion, economics, politics, and the like. New possibilities for the mother–daughter relationship make themselves felt; new self-understandings of the body appear in terms of a more intensive form of what Freud termed "polymorphous perversity." The female imaginary opens elements of the unconscious, female speech presupposes female culture, and the new culture provides the basis for a more complete social and anthropological transformation.

The moment of truth lies in the attempt to highlight the need for what Flaubert called "sentimental education." There is a sense in which social and political education involves more than ratiocination or knowledge of traditions. It can also involve a self-conscious concern with a radically new style of conduct, and here perhaps customary language is inadequate—what Marcuse once called a "new sensibility" in which aggression, cruelty, and vulgarity are no longer tolerated. There is nothing inherently foolish about attempting to create new ways of feeling, new social relationships, new forms of economic interaction, or a new means of expression for a new movement. The problem with the utopian vision offered by Irrigary is the way in which it is compromised by her directly political analysis.

Many feminists have noted the ways in which Irrigary ignores the racial

---

41. The following derives from the assortment of writings included in *The Irrigary Reader*, ed. Margaret Whitford (Oxford: Blackwell, 1991).

and class differences among women, which play such an important part in feminist attempts to reinterpret political economy to meet the real situation of women,[42] and the way her arguments rest on binary relationships. But the problems run deeper: they express a profound lack of connection between theory and practice. Her radical antiliberal utopian theory, indeed, ultimately grounds itself in liberal and totally conventional assumptions. She assumes the "rights" of women predicated on their human dignity: the right to pursue their own identity; the right to a specific mother–daughter relationship; the right to discover feminist traditions; the right to financial equality; the right to reciprocity; and the right to the status of the citizen. That is all fine and good. But there is no sense of how this fundamentally liberal discourse impinges upon her calls for a genuinely new feminist language, a radically different form of feminist economics, and an alternative feminist science. It does not help to suggest that they are part of the "imaginary" and therefore unrealizable. Irrigary's flight of the radical imagination, woefully indeterminate in terms of what it actually projects, combines with a political stance that barely takes a step beyond Mary Wollstonecraft.

Of course, it is possible for feminists to suggest that the gender-neutral discourse is merely an ideological cover for male interests, in the same way that it is possible for Marxists to claim that the human or universal discourse is an ideological cover for class interests. Such a stance ultimately creates a position in which any discourse must prove reducible to gender class interests. The social contract is a case in point: yet it makes little sense to speak about "contracting" into society, because from the time of Hobbes, the creation of the social contract has been a merely hypothetical construct, and as for neglect of the body, the liberal subject has always been metaphysical in character.[43] Liberal principles never make reference to any particular subject precisely because the subject underpinning them is either implicitly understood as universal or explicitly defined as transcendental—and in either case, indeterminate. That is why Enlightenment rationalism, in general, and liberalism, in particular, have been accused of ignoring the emotions, the sentiments, and the experiences of real individuals. The emancipatory power of liberalism, however, derives from its very lack of empirical qualification and the ability of the aggrieved to contest existing forms of inequal-

---

42. Note the classic work by Charlotte Perkins Gilman, *Women and Economics* (New York: Harper and Row, 1966).

43. Carole Pateman, *The Sexual Contract* (Stanford: Stanford University Press, 1988), 19 ff. and 38 ff.

ity by making reference to an inherently unrealized and purely metaphysical notion of reciprocity. In Hegelian terms, sexism is a product not of the liberal idea but of the system claiming to have realized it.

Whether this transforms feminism into an offshoot of liberal or socialist political theory is an irrelevant question: the reliance on universal precepts by the women's movement occurred from the very beginning, and it is also playing a role in the present. Political discrimination, inadequate health care for women, economic exploitation of women, war crimes against women, justified in the name of religion and custom—the dogmas of a premodern world—have generated a new global women's movement.[44] It is based primarily not on some postmodernist notion of "difference" but on the discourse of rights and the traditional feminist commitment to equal participation; not on particularism or a relativistic form of multiculturalism but on an internationalism whose roots in the women's movement reside in the pacifism of women like Bertha von Suttner.[45] It is based not on flights of fancy concerning an ill-defined feminist economy or vaguely aesthetic notions of a feminist language but on the legacy of socialist ideas and a concern on the part of figures like Clara Zetkin and Alexandra Kollontai with the exploitation of poor women and working mothers.

There are many trends in the contemporary women's movement, and it is no longer appropriate to conflate feminism with any particular political organization or movement in the manner of the 1970s. In the wake of the overriding conservative backlash, which has also had a deep impact upon women,[46] much of "radical feminism" has either isolated itself in "women's studies" or identified itself with obscurantist and particularist forms of postmodernism. Both lead away from a self-consciously political practice. The question is now whether the new feminist movement of the next century will choose to recognize the greatness of its political legacy. Indeed, looking backward and pointing forward, the genuine radicalism of feminism exists in its self-identification as an ineradicable part of what is still an international project concerned with extending the goals of liberalism and socialism.

44. Charlotte Bunch and Niamh Reilly, *Demanding Accountability: The Global Campaign and the Vienna Tribunal for Women's Human Rights* (New Brunswick, N.J.: Center for Women's Global Leadership, 1994), 33 ff.
45. Jutta Landa, "Progress in Peace: Bertha von Suttner," in *Vienna: The World of Yesterday, 1889–1914,* ed. Stephen Eric Bronner and F. Peter Wagner (Atlantic Highlands, N.J.: Humanities Press International, 1997).
46. See Elinor Burkett, *The Right Women: A Journey through the Heart of Conservative America* (New York: Scribner, 1998).

18

Nature: Ecological Visions

A ll the major political traditions expressive of modernity have identified progress with the domination of nature because their understandings were fashioned in accordance with the empirical and positivistic assumptions of the "natural" sciences. Modernity can itself be philosophically defined by the rejection of the cosmological outlook and the construction of nature and the natural into the Other of progress and development. More is at stake than recycling or even saving this or that species. Oceans are becoming sterile, soil infertile, air unbreathable, and weather unstable. A new project is involved, and it is predicated upon reconsidering the notion of progress and understanding nature as more than an object of domination defined in purely "scientific" terms. The ecological vision has its roots in a premodern understanding of the connection between humanity and nature; in the modern context, it derives from a romantic rejection of the industrial revolution. Ecology and environmentalism stand in reciprocal relationship to one another: "Environmentalism is ecology in practice, and ecology is environmentalism in theory."[1] The theory and the practice converge in their attempt to reclaim the all-encompassing Other, to reappropriate a lost element of human experience, and to grant a new privilege to nature.

Whatever the importance of Ralph Waldo Emerson and Henry Thoreau, it has been particularly difficult to comprehend the radicalism of this idea, especially in the United States, because of the glaring lack of familiarity with

---

1. Manuel Castells, *The Information Age: Economy, Society, and Culture* (Oxford: Blackwell, 1998), 2:113.

the tradition of speculative philosophy. The hegemonic liberal tradition always understood society as a contract between individuals intent on pursuing their labor without intervention from the state or religious institutions. Nature essentially dropped out from the very beginning. Descartes had severed mind from body, spirit from nature, and the human from the animal. In keeping with Francis Bacon and Isaac Newton, no less than René Descartes,[2] Hobbes and Locke increasingly saw nature as atomic, inert, and reducible to its constituent empirical parts. Rousseau, perhaps most notably, tried to reverse the trend. But he never developed a genuine philosophy of nature: the "natural" served merely as the critical point of reference for confronting an amoral notion of "progress" and a profoundly decadent form of "civilization." With Kant, of course, it was a different matter. Viewing nature as a "metaphysical-dynamic" entity[3]—a view that is rarely acknowledged—he is generally praised for relegating its empirical manifestations to the object domain of the mathematical faculty and the province of "pure reason." The result was yet another expression of the dualism for which Kant's philosophy is justifiably famous. But the dualism was quickly forgotten: the mainstream was content to understand nature in purely instrumental terms. Ecological theory simply vanished until, many would argue, it was too late.

The way was clear for positivists like Auguste Comte and Henri de St. Simon to explain the workings of society using the criteria of the natural sciences and for social Darwinists like Herbert Spencer, William Graham Sumner, and most recently Ayn Rand, with her emphasis on the "virtue of selfishness," to transfer an insistently amoral evolutionary doctrine concerning the "survival of the fittest" into the normative arena of society. And so, as positivism paved the way for the "behavioral revolution" of the social sciences in the 1950s, social Darwinism buttressed the growing belief in biological racism during the 1890s and early 1900s. Engels preferred "dialectics" to either social Darwinism or the biological notions of racism being fostered in the labor movement by Eugen Dühring; it was with these concerns in mind that he wrote his enormously popular treatise on nature, which was known as the "Anti-Dühring," wherein he called anti-Semitism the "socialism of imbeciles." In keeping with positivism, however, he sought

2. Franz Borkenau, *Der Übergang vom feudalen zum bürgerlichen Weltbild: Studien zur Geschichte der Manufakturperiode* (Paris: Alcan, 1934).
3. Immanuel Kant, *Metaphysical Foundations of Natural Science,* trans. James Ellington (Indianapolis: Bobbs-Merrill, 1970).

to ground his "scientific socialism" in the "dialectical laws" of nature. The identification of nature with the "scientific" categories used to comprehend it, which defined technological progress, became secure in the eyes of both its proponents and its enemies.

Ecologists and the advocates of an environmental politics are intent upon breaking this connection. Such an undertaking, however, involves more than a simple rejection of the Western tradition. It involves rediscovering a neglected part of the classical heritage or what Ernst Bloch termed the "Aristotelian left."[4] Grounded in Aristotle's categories of dynamism and potentiality, a cosmological vision of nature flourished in North Africa while Europe was plunged in the Dark Ages. This view rests on the idea of a *vivis naturae*,[5] a living nature, with its own subjectivity and its own logic. A dynamic life force, or *natura naturans*, preserved from what has been objectified in theory and practice, is seen as underpinning its empirical expressions, or *natura naturata*. Such a standpoint inherently challenges an instrumentally based technology and the more "successful" development of science in its empiricist and positivist forms. Its most important thinkers include relatively forgotten figures like Plotinus, Avicenna, Averroës, Joachim di Fiore, Tommaso Campanella, Giordano Bruno, Baruch Spinoza, and F. W. J. Schelling.

All of them influenced the writings of Ernst Bloch, and, indeed, he has appropriately been called the "Marxist Schelling."[6] Both he and the great idealist philosopher considered nature alive rather than inert, a source of intersubjective action rather than a composite of atomic parts, dynamic rather than simply empirical, and a subject in its own right rather than a dead object.[7] It is fair to say that Schelling anticipated the modern notion of an ecosystem, though he had no sense of its being endangered. But it was Bloch who considered the liberation of nature a precondition for an emancipated order: freedom could only mean the unique forming and shaping of matter, which, in keeping with Hegel and Marx,[8] depended upon the recog-

---

4. Ernst Bloch, *Das Materialismusproblem: Seine Geschichte und Substanz* (Frankfurt am Main: Suhrkamp, 1972), 479.

5. Ernst Bloch, *Vorlesungen zur Philosophie der Renaissance* (Frankfurt am Main: Suhrkamp, 1972), 51.

6. Jürgen Habermas, *Philosophische–politische Profile* (Frankfurt am Main: Suhrkamp, 1973), 147 ff.

7. F. W. J. von Schelling, *Ideas for a Philosophy of Nature*, trans. Errol Harris and Peter Heath (Cambridge: Cambridge University Press, 1988).

8. Alfred Schmidt, *The Concept of Nature in Marx*, trans. Ben Fowkes (London: New Left, 1971), 89 ff.

nition that what was being transformed was not merely nature but ourselves.

Genuine progress involves not merely resolving the most profound conflicts between people as a way of furthering the sense of humanity but also overcoming the even more profound conflicts between humanity and nature. It may be true that the reified character of nature, which is highlighted by modern science and technology, is inscribed within it as the *natura naturata*. But the emphasis on the *natura naturans*, the elemental spirit of nature, provides an alternative way of viewing the phenomenon and a critical perspective on its purely instrumental usage. Emancipation will subsequently involve less a reassertion of the nonidentity between subject and object than a commitment to a new subject-object unity predicated upon the recognition of nature as a subject in its own right. Precisely because the *natura naturata* is ineradicable, however, full recognition of the potential within nature is impossible, and the "achievement" of utopia remains utopian.

This mode of thinking rejects a line of development which, as Theodor Adorno once stated, "leads from the bow and arrow to the atomic bomb." It contests a form of alienation deeper than what Marx defines as the separation of workers from their products, their friends, and the development of their own potential. It contests the alienation of ourselves from our world by contesting the transformation of nature into a commodity: it projects what Marcuse termed a "pacification of existence" by resurrecting the concern with quality against quantity and condemning the sacrifice of the *natura naturans* no less than the despoliation of the *natura naturata* in the pursuit of profit. Ecology indeed contests an unqualified commitment to technological development, and it is little wonder that an emphasis on small groups and local production should inform what Murray Bookchin originally termed "social ecology."[9]

This stance seeks to combine anarchism and a certain understanding of socialism, community, and labor, with ecology serving as the bridge between them. It is indeed the case that anarchism, with its romantic heritage and its traditional contestation of "civilization," has always evidenced a certain affinity for an ecological consciousness. Its critique of progress, its inclusion of the "wild" as a necessary corrective for an overbearing anthropocentrism,[10] extends toward the productivism embraced by the followers of

9. Murray Bookchin, *The Philosophy of Social Ecology: Essays in Dialectical Naturalism* (Montreal: Black Rose, 1995).

10. John Clark, "A Social Ecology" in *Capitalism, Nature, Socialism* 8, no. 3 (September 1997).

Marx. There is also a sense of the global character of ecological devastation. But the anarchist critique is carried on in populist terms: it focuses on "corporate power" rather than capital, which obviously prevents employing existing businesses to further ecological aims, and its antihierarchical stance undermines the ability to create necessarily huge transnational organizations or work within existing international institutions to develop and implement ecological programs. All of this puts anarchism at odds with socialism: it remains unclear how the new combination of community and labor should actually manifest itself as a new revolutionary subject, and it is also unclear how tensions might be resolved between the environmentalist concern with an ecologically sustainable economy and the traditional policies of growth on which workers depend.

In the same vein, the conflict between "deep" ecology and "shallow" ecology is real. Different understandings of organizational struggle, and even rationality, come into play. The two positions also proceed from fundamentally different assumptions. The issue at stake is whether the ecological struggle must contest the status quo as a totality or whether it can employ technology and the state to mitigate the current devastation of the planet. The first stance fits with the more ambitious aspirations of both "deep ecology" and the new social movements.[11] Indeed, if the notion of progress and technological development employed by the status quo is called into question, then it only follows that the demand should arise for a "new science," whether from feminists or ecologists or both.[12]

Carolyn Merchant deals with many of these issues.[13] Her vision of a matriarchal golden age in which nature and culture were unified is surely suspect as a critical reconstruction of the history of nature. But she legitimately criticizes the traditional positivistic model and advances a new "holistic" perspective. There is nothing neutral about mathematical formalism, according to Merchant, and its limits become evident in its mechanical equation of the whole with the sum of its parts. Nature must instead be seen as alive, and its parts must be considered in their interconnection. All living

---

11. Bill Devall and George Sessions, *Deep Ecology: Living as If Nature Mattered* (Salt Lake City: Peregrine Smith, 1985).

12. Susan Griffen, *Woman and Nature: The Roaring inside Her* (New York: Harper and Row, 1978); Sandra Harding, *The Science Question in Feminism* (Ithaca: Cornell University Press, 1986).

13. Carolyn Merchant, *The Death of Nature: Women, Ecology, and the Scientific Revolution* (New York: Harper and Row, 1980).

things are seen as having rights, necessitating new priorities for science and production. Merchant still understands ecology as a way of extending the principles inherited from the democratic revolutions of the last centuries. The ecological vision does not constitute a rupture with history. For her, it must instead demand a reorientation or redirection of progress.

That is an enormous project. But it is not enough for many proponents of "ecofeminism." The idea was first introduced by Françoise d'Eaubonne's *Feminism or Death* in 1974,[14] and it has much in common with "deep ecology."[15] Its argument basically proceeds from the assumption that there is an inherent link between the exploitation of nature and the oppression of women. Both are seen as occurring within a patriarchal context in which diverse experiences and sentiments are homogenized within a certain instrumental or male understanding of science. Its anthropocentric assumptions ascribe usefulness only to what aids a technological form of domination that is self-serving for men and simultaneously self-defeating for the planet. It makes more than analogical sense, for ecofeminists, to speak of the "rape" of nature, and it is also logical that they should emphasize a recognition of the rights of other species, value nature in its own right without respect to use, and reject the assumptions concerned with securing a higher standard of living at all costs.

There is much that is useful in the positions advocated by deep ecology and ecofeminism. The skeptical attitude toward progress is seminal for the development of a critical perspective. The attempt to preserve nature and natural beauty from the incursions of the commodity form is of paramount importance. The willingness to consider a new role for acupuncture and herb therapies threatens the knowledge monopoly of groups like the American Medical Association even as it empowers the sick by expanding their options. The response to the horrifying torture of animals, which takes place far more for profit than for scientific research, is itself a matter of human dignity and has roots in Jewish law.

But it is counterproductive to talk about forced population control and the purifying quality of diseases and natural catastrophes.[16] Whatever the

14. A fine overview is provided by Rosemarie Putnam Tong, *Feminist Thought: A More Comprehensive Introduction* (Boulder: Westview, 1998), 246 ff.

15. See Jim Cheney, "Ecofeminism and Deep Ecology," *Environmental Ethics 9,* no. 2 (1987): 115–45.

16. Luc Ferry, *The New Ecological Order,* trans. Carol Volk (Chicago: University of Chicago Press, 1992).

links between women and nature through childbirth and subsistence work under conditions of economic underdevelopment, it is also illusory to believe that this should provide women with a privileged insight into nature and non-Western women with a more natural and intuitive knowledge about nature than Western women.[17] It is similarly naive to speak of integrating spirituality or magic into science, identifying nature with a goddess, or generally responding to Max Weber by seeking to "reenchant the world."[18] Science thereby loses its integrity and becomes nothing more than a particular cultural perspective among others.[19] Under such circumstances, no possibility exists for challenging repressive religiously sanctioned customs in terms of critical reflection or scientific rationality. Ecofeminist and deep ecological views rarely consider the benefits women might derive from technology or civilization. Antisecularist critics also never explain just how women are to dissociate themselves from "male" culture, and they refuse to illuminate the costs of retreating into what is actually a quite typically "male" romantic communion with nature. Ecofeminists and deep ecologists offer no marginally realizable program, no analysis of structural constraints, and, essentially, no politics.

André Gorz has, by way of contrast, insisted upon the need for a new form of "ecological realism."[20] Born in 1924 in Vienna, among the most important thinkers of the French student movement of 1968, his work was profoundly influenced by both Castoriadis and Sartre. A believer in the ultimate goal of workers' self-management who later distanced himself from Marxism and socialism,[21] he would ultimately champion a radical reduction of work. The liberation of workers from work is part of a utopian tradition within French socialist thought going back over Paul Lafargue to Charles Fourier, and it is likely to become a fundamental element in any progressive program for the next century.

Gorz places undue stress on local organizing and autonomous action

17. Maria Mies and Vandan Shiva, *Ecofeminism* (London: Zed, 1993).

18. Mary Daly, *Gyn/Ecology* (Boston: Beacon, 1978); Irene Diamond and Gloria Feman Orenstein, eds., *Reweaving the World: the Emergence of Ecofeminism* (San Francisco: Sierra Club, 1990).

19. Sandra Harding, *Is Science Multicultural?: Postcolonialisms, Feminisms, and Epistemologies* (Bloomington: Indiana University Press, 1998).

20. André Gorz, *Ecology as Politics*, trans. Patsy Vigderman and Jonathan Cloud (Boston: South End, 1980), 11 ff.

21. André Gorz, *Adieux au prolétariat: Au delà du socialisme* (Paris: Editions Galilee, 1978).

from below as against the need for macrosocial forms capable of organizing basic needs.[22] But his emphasis on the reduction of work fits squarely into an ecological vision in which nature no less than civilization is endangered by an unqualified commitment to growth. It is no longer enough to refrain from consuming more, according to this standpoint; it is time to start consuming less.[23] More to the point, it is time to reconsider what is being produced, what is being consumed, and how. Gorz indeed is insistent that "the struggle for different technologies is essential to the struggle for a different society."[24]

But it is arguable that the society is already different. Ulrich Beck has made this even more radical argument.[25] Modernity has changed not into its opposite but into a new form with a new guise in which "risk" has taken on a wholly new meaning. The illusions of the past appear in an existentially and technologically restructured present. There is no escape from modernity, and there is no such thing as "postmodernity." It may be that the "bastions of rationality in which the technical sciences used to operate are collapsing—but we are moving in, we must live in them."[26] Beck's thinking assumes the need to refashion the Enlightenment and the older industrial form of modernity, with its unilinear understandings of progress and unqualified commitment to technology, in order to deal with an ecologically imperiled order. Thus, he can write, "Those wishing to understand modernization as an increasingly autonomous process of creating the new must also count on modernity becoming old. The other side of this aging of industrial modernity is the establishment of a risk society. This concept defines a phase of development of modern society in which new dynamics of social, political, ecological, and individual risks are called forth and confront the institutions of control and security in industrial society."[27]

The ecological stance assumed by Beck, among the most important con-

---

22. André Gorz, *Paths to Paradise: On the Liberation from Work,* trans. Malcolm Imrie (Boston: South End, 1985), 63 ff.

23. Gorz, *Ecology as Politics,* 13.

24. Ibid., 19.

25. Note, for a more extensive analysis of this important thinker, Stephen Eric Bronner, "Ecology, Politics, and Risk: Considerations on the Social Theory of Ulrich Beck," *Capitalism, Nature, Socialism* 6, no. 1 (March 1995): 67–86.

26. Ulrich Beck, *Ecological Enlightenment: Essays on the Politics of the Risk Society,* trans. Mark Ritter (Atlantic Highlands, N.J.: Humanities Press International, 1995), 19 ff. and 147 ff.

27. Ulrich Beck, *Die Erfindung des Politischen* (Frankfurt am Main: Suhrkamp, 1993), 35.

temporary sociologists and the author of the classic *Risk Society*, revolves around the idea of a "risk calculus." This concept is itself predicated upon the belief that ignorance grows in concert with knowledge and that it is therefore necessary to privilege caution and safety when dealing with technological change. Therein lies the check upon unqualified growth and the uncritical belief in "progress." It is now necessary to proceed with a sense of the disastrous implications latent within any form of technology as well as the "organized irresponsibility" of contemporary bureaucracies in which the smallest decision can produce untold destruction, as in the case of Chernobyl, and each bureaucrat seeks to avoid responsibility for any decision. Yet Beck is no Luddite. He has little use for antitechnological prejudices or any other romantic assumptions defined in relation to an antiquated industrial capitalism. The risk society is capable of generating scientific possibilities as well as ecological dangers.

Rejecting those who take their stand either for or against progress, noting how doubt is the "inside ally" for any future reformation of science, Beck maintains that the advances of science have demolished the assumptions and certainties usually associated with scientific rationality. It makes no sense to differentiate between theory and its application; interests are considered materially driven, and form is identified with substance. New "reflexive" forms of modernization are seen as being forced to address ecological problems and other issues relating to the quality of life. Technological development and the preservation of nature can, in short, no longer be considered mutually exclusive concerns. Beck's critique of modernity is indeed undertaken with an eye on its most radical possibilities.

Revolution is now being incorporated into the system. Or, better, modernity has become a "subpolitical 'system of revolution' without a revolutionary subject, program, or goal."[28] It is less a matter of changing technique than of changing the conditions in which technology is pursued. Thus, with a utopian twist, Beck can write, "Technicians must free themselves from economic domination in order to free society from alienated forms of technical domination. It may sound paradoxical: freedom of technology and social liberation from technology may coincide. Or, in other words, the radicalization of modernity—technique as *l'art pour l'art*—can simultaneously create the preconditions for solving the systemic problems of directing, controlling, and democratizing technology."[29]

---

28. Ulrich Beck, *Politik in der Risikogesellschaft* (Frankfurt am Main: Suhrkamp, 1991), 39.
29. Ibid., 188.

It remains somewhat unclear to what extent the critique of "organized irresponsibility" is accurate when, especially in the private sector, corporations still link pay and benefits and stock options with the expansion of profits: it is also, arguably, less a matter of avoiding decisions in the corporate world than of competing over the possibility of making them and having the power to disavow them when they produce poor results. It is surely true that the new society is one in which a socializing of scientific decision making should become more democratic. Nevertheless, Beck evidences a profound lack of concern with organizational arrangements when it comes to these new forms of decision making, the incentives driving the new pursuit of technology, and the status of the scientific method itself.

Herbert Marcuse addressed this matter directly. He claimed that the formal methods of science were implicated in the oppressive and repressive manner in which they were employed. The issue is not merely one of socializing science, or even democratizing decision making, but rather of transforming the meaning of science itself. Science must be conceived in terms of a new aesthetically informed receptivity to nature, which is devoid of the "reality principle" and its ethic of productivity. It is a matter of exploding a situation in which "scientific-technical rationality and manipulation are welded together into new forms of social control. Can one rest content with the assumption that this unscientific outcome is the result of a specific societal *application* of science? . . . The general direction in which it came to be applied was inherent in pure science even where no practical purposes were intended, and . . . the point can be identified where theoretical Reason turns into social practice."[30]

This view is very much in accord with the anthropological critique of civilization offered by critical theory. Its power lies in its immediacy, but the question is whether external pressures and constraints inform the internal dynamics of science with respect to research followed and projects undertaken. This stance rejects the rigorous separation of facts from values: It provides values for a form of scientific engagement generally considered value-neutral.[31] It envisions a new science informed by the new erotic possibilities of a liberated aesthetic whose concerns, in keeping with Kant and

---

30. Herbert Marcuse, *One-Dimensional Man: Studies in the Ideology of Advanced Industrial Society* (Boston: Beacon, 1964), 146.

31. Jürgen Habermas, "Technology and Science as 'Ideology,' " in *Toward a Rational Society: Student Protest, Science, and Politics,* trans. Jeremy J. Shapiro (Boston: Beacon, 1970).

Schiller, include an attack upon the reification of nature. It offers, in short, a new way of solidifying the connection between aesthetic and scientific experience.

Linking aesthetics and science can prove enormously fruitful for social theory. But the issue here is not simply social theory. New notions of science must illuminate what scientists do in the laboratory. It is simply not enough to inveigh against bourgeois materialism for being implicated in capitalist production and patriarchal oppression without introducing an alternative set of criteria capable of falsifying claims. Indeed, if only the invocation of utopia provides the foundation for a critique of the status quo, to remain content with its purely abstract delineation leaves the status quo intact.

"Politicizing" science is not the same thing as challenging the projects and purposes scientists pursue and embrace. Totalitarianism has shown the dangers in refusing to differentiate between forms and practices of scientific action: talk of "male" science is as foolish as talk about "Jewish" science. An external theory of nature cannot, and should not, make claims about the internal demands of scientific practice, and vice versa. Political theory can help explain the conditions under which scientific changes take place and the material reasons why any given science is employed for any given set of aims. But it cannot have the last word regarding the validity of any given scientific formulation.

Aesthetics is no substitute for science: it remains necessary to distinguish between different spheres of inquiry. Unless that occurs, unless boundaries are introduced, a mishmash will result in which metapsychological and anthropological sentiments intrude upon debates over methodology even as concerns over the philosophical status of nature displace political attempts to formulate programs and perspectives capable of informing action. Technological rationality retains its logic, manifests it in different ways in different disciplines, such as physics compared with chemistry, and harbors any number of contradictory social implications. Thus, it makes little sense to identify science or technology simply in terms of a single category like reification. A critique undertaken from such a standpoint will necessarily prove indeterminate.

We cannot recover what reification has lost by regressing to pre-technological conditions to some prior unity irrelevant to the contemporary world. The solution is neither a return to the primitive, qualitative, and natural, nor a speculative leap into a "new age" and a whole "new technology." On the contrary, the critical concept of totality aids in identifying the *contingency* of the existing technological system, the points at which it can be invested with new values and bent to new purposes.[32]

Growth no longer guarantees a rising standard of living for everyone, even in the short run; it may actually produce a general worsening of living standards in the long run. The most economically advanced societies have indeed been undermining the health of the planet for decades and letting the economically weakest nations suffer the most immediate and severe consequences. It therefore only makes sense that older forms of industrial growth should now be encountering not merely ethical resistance but physical limits, as well. Rudolf Bahro, whose critique of "actually existing socialism" became legendary in the 1970s, was correct in insisting that "the idea of progress in general must be interpreted in a radically different way from that to which we are accustomed. . . . Per capita consumption of raw material and energy, per capita production of steel and cement, are the criteria *par excellence* of a totally alienated progress."[33]

The depletion of nature is inscribed within a system predicated on the quest for profits of individual firms without concern for the broader needs of their class, their society, or their planet. The major social democratic economist, Karl Polanyi, had indeed already argued before the close of World War II that the capitalist market was intent on ruining the natural preconditions for its functioning.[34] There remains no reason why capitalist industries should concern themselves with ecological issues unless they are forced to do so. But the situation was no better under "actually existing" socialism, in which a bureaucratic apparatus, preoccupied with rapid industrial growth and beholden to the short-term interests of industrial sectors, lacked democratic accountability and avoided ethical responsibility for the disastrous ecological consequences of its policies. The industrial system of production and reproduction, which has been inherited from the nineteenth century, must itself become the object of scrutiny.

Nature currently exists as a point of departure for capital but not a point

---

32. Andrew Feenberg, *Critical Theory of Technology* (New York: Oxford University Press, 1991), 178.
33. Rudolf Bahro, *The Alternative in Eastern Europe*, trans. David Fernbach (London: New Left, 1978), 263.
34. Karl Polanyi, *The Great Transformation: The Political and Economic Origins of Our Time* (Boston: Beacon, 1944), 130 ff.

of return.[35] And the effects of this situation are dramatic. A situation may be emerging in which the traditional contradictions of overproduction, which essentially deal with the valorization of capital and class antagonisms, are simultaneously generating a "second contradiction" of underproduction with respect to the possibilities inherent in the general exchange between humans and nature.[36] The first contradiction deals with "exchange value," the second with "use value." The tension between exchange value and use value has a long history among the critical economists of Western Marxism.[37] Such a stance makes clear the importance of contesting the treatment of nature, which is obviously not produced as a commodity, as if it were a commodity. The philosophical emphasis upon "use value" raised by ecological theory seems inherently to foster a concern with the "autonomy of society"; it might well project issues beyond those of the technico-productive system by contesting the central aim of social life, "the unlimited expansion of rational mastery."[38]

But this radical possibility has not been translated into a genuine political vision. Looking beyond the current technico-productive system is utopian unless its fundamental contradictions are being taken into account. And contemporary ecological movements have not been able to resolve them. It has historically been the case that, "just as green reforms don't necessarily imply red reforms of the production relations, red reforms (e.g., full employment policies and wealth redistribution) don't necessarily imply green reforms of the productive forces."[39] The tension between these concerns has even made itself felt in "green" political parties. Only in Germany has the Green movement wielded any real power, although smaller organizations have been active elsewhere in Europe and the Americas with differing degrees of success. The environmental movement is alone among social movements in having organized itself not merely as an interest group but as a

---

35. James O'Connor, "Capitalism and Nature," in *Natural Causes: Essays in Ecological Marxism* (New York: Guilford, 1998), 123.

36. Note the seminal essay by James O'Connor, "The Second Contradiction of Capitalism," in *Natural Causes*.

37. Isaak Illich Rubin, *Essays on Marx's Theory of Value*, trans. Milos Samardzija and Fredy Perlman (1928; Montreal: Black Rose, 1973); Roman Rosdolsky, *The Making of Marx's "Capital"* (London: Pluto, 1982); Karl Korsch, *Karl Marx* (New York: Russell and Russell, 1938).

38. Cornelius Castoriadis, "From Ecology to Autonomy," in *The Castoriadis Reader*, ed. and trans. David Ames Curtis (London: Blackwell, 1997), 240, 247.

39. James O'Connor, "Ecological Socialism," *Capitalism, Nature, Socialism*, no. 33 (March 1998): 53.

political party. Nevertheless, many still wish to maintain its original status as an "antiparty party" while working within the system.[40]

But that has essentially proved impossible. Green political organizations, whether as interest groups or as parties, experience the same pressures as others. Insofar as the ecological party insists upon its anti-institutional and strict ideological posture, its politics will become ever more symbolic and marginal to the formation of policy. Insofar as it seeks access to institutions and transforms itself into a lobbying organization or an interest group or a party, however, it tends to dilute the ideological dynamism from which its mass constituency initially drew inspiration. It undercuts the original attempt to view environmental politics as a kind of "celebration," a form of "healing," an "inner revolution," and a form of "counter-power."[41] The question is whether the movement should remain a mainstay of the counter-culture; indeed, everywhere, this has led to a profound conflict between its "pragmatist" and "fundamentalist" factions.

Pragmatists like Joschka Fischer turned the German Greens into a genuine electoral force and an alternative to the Social Democratic Party in the late 1980s and 1990s. But their electoral victories came at the cost of what were once seen as the unique characteristics of the movement: its rejection of hierarchy in favor of "rotation" of offices; its rejection of traditional organization in favor of decentralized decision making; its rejection of growth in favor of the small and the beautiful; its rejection of the industrial in favor of the agricultural; its rejection of the "system" in favor of an alternative "lifestyle"; and its rejection of "militarism" in favor of an unwavering pacifism. The pragmatists still highlighted ecological concerns. But they proved willing to compromise on most issues concerning the status of the welfare states, took a more "reasonable" position on foreign affairs, and basically soft-pedaled ideological commitments other than those concerning the maintenance of civil liberties. Given their growth and parliamentary status, indeed, it was with shock and dismay that they witnessed the rebellion of the Fundamentalists in 1998. Their fight over the platform of the party called upon Germany to radically decrease gasoline consumption, withdraw from the North Atlantic Treaty Organization, and abolish the army. This development almost wrecked the ability of the party to serve as an accept-

40. Petra Kelly, *Thinking Green: Essays on Environmentalism, Feminism, and Nonviolence* (Berkeley, Calif.: Parallax, 1994), 37.
41. Ibid., 39–40.

able national coalition partner in what would become the "Red-Green" victory over Helmut Kohl and the Christian Democrats in 1998.

The ecological movement must now consider itself part of a larger enterprise. Growth and ecological sanity cannot be viewed as mutually exclusive, and in deciding upon priorities, ecological activists must take into account the needs of other movements. It would be irresponsible to call upon the formerly colonized world to turn away from "development," because the preoccupation with raising the material standard of living is distinctly Western;[42] environmental destruction is most rampant in the economically underdeveloped nations within the world economy.[43] More to the point, most people, especially in the underdeveloped nations, live not a life of consumerism but a life of deprivation and even starvation, as most people did in most places before the twentieth century. The attack on growth undermines any serious possibility of linking environmental struggles with those of working people and people of color: it is indeed the source of a sectarianism whose roots run deep in the environmental movement.[44]

The struggle against "bad" technology must stand in some coherent relation to the development of "good" technology, and mitigating further damage to the environment must occur in conjunction with the introduction of measures capable of fostering genuine alternatives for what is traditionally understood as growth. It is no longer possible to rigidly divorce attempts to make capital internalize environmental costs from calls for radical changes within the workplace and the abolition of debilitating labor.[45] The degree to which the less radical concern is privileged over the more radical, indeed, will probably depend less upon the strength of the ecology movement than on the political power generated by an alliance among progressive forces.

Ecology can help build an alternative to the sectarianism of identity politics and the rigidity of old-fashioned class perspectives. Its concern with the undemocratic determination of "progress" and growth, the alienation of modern production, speaks to the most radical preoccupations of both democracy and socialism. Its interest in eradicating air pollution, protecting

42. Serge Latouche, *In the Wake of the Affluent Society: An Exploration of Post-Development*, trans. Martin O'Connor and Rosemary Arnoux (London: Zed, 1993).

43. Daniel Litvin, "Development and the Environment," *Economist*, March 21, 1998, 65.

44. Mark Dowie, *Losing Ground: American Environmentalism at the Close of the Twentieth Century* (Cambridge: MIT Press, 1995).

45. James O'Connor, "Technology and Ecology," in *Natural Causes*, 208.

the oceans, confronting global warming, securing the ozone layer, and preserving the multitude of species from the rapacity of modern capitalism has already helped give internationalism a new connotation and a new purpose. Ecology has turned the emancipation of nature into the precondition for the emancipation of people and, in the process, projected the need for a new sense of planetary life.

19

◦━━━◦

The Forgotten:
Anti-Imperialism, Nationalism,
Postcolonialism

Western imperialism generated its Other in the anti-imperialist struggles, which shook the world in the aftermath of World War II. These movements sought to emphasize the incommensurability between the colonized and the colonizer, and their understanding of national self-determination was predicated on a desire to articulate the specific attributes of a given cultural community. Indeed, given the self-proclaimed universalism of the imperialists, it only makes sense that these movements should have been skeptical about Western notions of democracy. Nationalism was important for the anti-imperialist undertakings in the colonial territories precisely because it could incorporate indigenous traditions and, in response to Western notions of modernity, give the preimperialist past a utopian glow. Ideological preoccupations of this sort, however, obviously helped inhibit economic and political development. Thus, the basic tension with anti-imperialist and postcolonialist thinking.

Imperialism had been a topic of interest in Europe since the beginning of the twentieth century, and in the popular imagination, its racial justification went back over Rudyard Kipling and his notion of "the white man's burden" to the ugly pamphlet of Thomas Carlyle entitled "The Nigger Question." Imperialism also had its critics: John Hobson, the teacher of John

Maynard Keynes,[1] opposed what he considered a "parasitic" outgrowth of capitalism in favor of a more rational and distributive use of the surplus capital intended for export abroad among domestic workers;[2] Rosa Luxemburg saw the existence of precapitalist territories as a safety valve for the continuation of capitalism, which explained why investment occurred despite its tendency toward overproduction, and she believed the fight against one necessarily called for a fight against the other;[3] Joseph Schumpeter saw imperialism as part of an inherently irrational legacy of precapitalist life, which would disappear as the calculable and instrumental rationality of capitalism gradually became internalized in the populace at large;[4] Karl Kautsky and Rudolf Hilferding despaired of a world divided into spheres of influence under the control of a few great powers, a form of "ultra-imperialism";[5] and, more recently, Hannah Arendt understood imperialism as the product of "superfluous" men whose domestic support derived from an alliance between capital and the "mob."[6]

None of these thinkers was particularly illuminating about the effects of imperialism on the colonized population: in the Western world, prior to World War II, this would remain more the preserve of novelists like Joseph Conrad, André Malraux, André Gide, Jakob Wassermann, Anna Seghers, and Bruno Traven. The economic and political theorists were basically content to analyze imperialism, and their interpretations were rarely connected with any positive organizational or ideological contributions to an anti-imperialist politics. Lenin was an exception, and surely this helps explain his enormous impact on what came to be known as the Third World. Even with respect to his notion of imperialism as the "last stage of capitalism," however, he employed a fundamentally Eurocentric frame of theoretical reference; and again, his ultimate concern was less the particular situation of

---

1. With respect to the aftermath of World War I, in this regard, note the superb study of 1919 by J. M. Keynes, *The Economic Consequences of the Peace* (New York: Penguin, 1988).

2. John A. Hobson, *Imperialism* (Ann Arbor: University of Michigan Press, 1971).

3. Rosa Luxemburg, *The Accumulation of Capital*, trans. Agnes Schwarzschild (New York: Monthly Review, 1968).

4. Joseph A. Schumpeter, *Imperialism and Social Classes*, trans. Heinz Norden (New York: A. M. Kelly, 1958).

5. Karl Kautsky, "Ultra-Imperialism," *New Left Review*, no. 59 (January–February 1970): 41–46.

6. Hannah Arendt, *The Origins of Totalitarianism* (Cleveland: Meridian, 1958), 123 ff.

people in a given territory than the manner in which their struggle would further the internal development of communism. Already in the early 1920s, a particularly gifted Indian protégé of Lenin, Manabendra Nath Roy, suggested that it was time to abandon the complex class analysis employed by his teacher and view the anti-imperialist struggle from the standpoint of non-Western conditions and non-Western ideas. This heretical stance would, indeed, ultimately lead to his ouster from the Communist International.

Others, like José Carlos Mariátegui, arguably the major representative of Marxist thought in Latin America and the founder of the Peruvian labor movement, struggled to maintain this idea.[7] Although profoundly influenced by a variety of Marxist and non-Marxist thinkers ranging from Luxemburg and Lenin to Croce and Sorel, he sought to emphasize the importance for revolutionary action of traditions associated with the eighteenth-century rebel and author, Tupac Amaru, and others. He wrote an important defense of Marxism. But he also sought to infuse it with other traditions. This great and forgotten revolutionary activist, who lived much of his life physically impaired and died in 1930 at the age of thirty-six, looked back to the Incas for a source of communal solidarity in the same way that Marx mentioned the peasant *mir* (communal organization) as the basis for revolutionary possibilities in Russia. In his most famous work, *Seven Essays in the Interpretation of Peruvian Reality* (1928), he essentially sought to cast class politics in populist terms. Mariátegui anticipated many of the ideas associated with contemporary anti-imperialist thinking. But tensions inevitably arise between his emphasis upon grassroots action and communist notions of organization, populist concerns and class interests, the ideas of Europe and the traditions of those who suffered the most at its hands. Nevertheless, with more sensitivity and balance than many of those who came later, he represents perhaps the most authentically socialist commitment to national self-determination.

Nationalism would become an end unto itself in 1943, when the Communist International was liquidated to hasten the formation of a second military front and the allied invasion of Normandy. It had been fifteen years since Stalin first institutionalized the idea of "socialism in one country." But

---

7. Note the essays by Mariátegui collected in *Marxism in Latin America from 1909 to the Present: An Anthology*, ed. Michael Lowy, trans. Michael Pearlman (Atlantic Highlands, N.J.: Humanities Press International, 1982), 28 ff.

from the beginning, he meant it only for the Soviet Union. Other communist movements and nations would still have to follow orders. As for noncommunist movements for national self-determination, they were given little chance of success. National self-determination really took on a life of its own only after World War II. Britain had emerged from the conflict economically and militarily shattered, France and the rest of Europe as well, and anti-imperialist movements took advantage. Ho Chi Minh called for an independent Vietnam in 1945, and barely a year later, the Philippines was granted independence by the United States. India finally broke free from English rule in 1947, and in 1948, Israel fulfilled the Zionist vision of Theodor Herzl with the creation of its independent homeland for Jews in 1948. A year later Indonesia gained independence from the Netherlands and Mao Tse-tung introduced the People's Republic of China.

The Bandung Conference of 1955, organized by Gamal Abdel Nassar of Egypt, Jawaharlal Nehru of India, and Tito, sought to create a neutral space between the West and the East. The cold war generated the need for new regional forms of association among the nonaligned nations, along with the notion of a Third World. This undertaking was basically acceptable to the Soviet Union, whose foreign policy generally involved support for anti-imperialist struggles directed against the United States. Interestingly enough, however, this single-minded emphasis upon anti-imperialism often meant surrendering the spirit of Leninism. The USSR's earlier insistence that it serve as the model for these fledgling states faded in favor of a position in which it primarily sought strategic allies in the cold war.[8] The Soviet Union, in short, became less involved in determining the character and future of "socialism" than in strengthening its national interests.

Fearful of international repercussions, for example, Stalin urged the Chinese communists to reach an agreement with Chiang Kai-Shek in the immediate aftermath of World War II. It is also no wonder that, in Cuba, the communists should initially have condemned Castro's legendary attack on the Moncada barracks in favor of a more reformist strategy, centered around the urban proletariat, and a "national democratic front." Every communist party in Latin America, with the possible exception of those in Peru and Chile, took this position, as did the Communist Party of the United States. Thus, although various versions of Marxism-Leninism were appro-

---

8. Richard Lowenthal, *Model of Ally?: The Communist Powers and the Developing Countries* (New York: Oxford University Press, 1977).

priated by anti-imperialist movements seeking national self-determination, communist parties generally opposed the use of revolutionary tactics, even if they later sought to lay claim to their successes.

Leninism respected the quest for identity, the attempt to radically differentiate the anti-imperialist movement from its racist and exploitative antagonist. And this was part of the struggle from the very beginning. It also offered the idea of an emancipatory alternative to the status quo. The new society its advocates projected, after all, would be the radical counterpart to the racism, exploitation, and egoistic individualism of "bourgeois society." More than that, it might even provide a utopian alternative to the Western idea of civilization. The "new man" was originally a literary notion whose emergence coincided with the modern idea of utopia in the works of thinkers like Sir Thomas More and Campanella. But it was embraced in the theoretical writings produced by the early-twentieth-century avant-garde. It also played a profound role in communist thinking, especially during the "heroic years" from 1918 to 1921, when everything seemed possible.[9] This utopian notion was subsequently picked up by many of the most radical thinkers and activists of the anti-imperialist struggle. Thus, Che Guevara could write,

> Man dominated by commodity relationships will cease to exist. . . . Man will begin to see himself mirrored in his work and to realize his full stature as a human being through the object created, through the work accomplished. Work will no longer entail surrendering a part of his being in the form of labor-power sold, which no longer belongs to him, but will represent an emanation of himself reflecting his contribution to the common life, the fulfillment of his social duty.[10]

The idea of the "new man" is intertwined with the idea of revolution. A genuinely radical social transformation not only transforms "objective con-

---

9. Even in 1924, it was still possible to write that under communism, "man will become immeasurably stronger, wiser, and subtler; his body will become more harmonized, his movements more rhythmic, his voice more musical. The forms of life will become dynamically dramatic. The average human type will rise to the heights of an Aristotle, a Goethe, or a Marx. And above this ridge new peaks will rise." Leon Trotsky, *Literature and Revolution*, trans. Rose Strunsky (Ann Arbor: University of Michigan Press, 1971), 256.

10. Che Guevara, "Building New Men," in *Twentieth-Century Political Theory*, ed. Stephen Eric Bronner (New York: Routledge, 1997), 276.

ditions" but also liberates the masses from the reactionary habits and sentiments of the past. A better world lies on the horizon, one devoid of the exploitation and individualism associated with advanced industrial society.
The new revolutionary societies born of anti-imperialist struggles must
overcome the commodity form and the old divisions generated by imperialism and replace them with new forms of utopian solidarity. Indeed, such
was the vision painted by Che Guevara in his famous essay on the future of
the Cuban Revolution, "Building the New Man."

A dramatic figure consumed by revolutionary zeal, Guevera played a crucial role in Castro's seizure of power.[11] He was in charge of revolutionary
firing squads exacting justice without meaningful trials; he caused havoc in
his stint as minister of economics; he angered radicals in the Organization
of African States by suggesting a leading role for Cuba in the African revolution; and he died the martyr's death he assuredly sought as a guerrilla in the
highlands of Bolivia among a peasantry whose language he could not speak.
A romantic halo hovered over Guevara, however, and he had little use for
the traditional communists of his time, with their unbending reliance upon
the urban proletariat as the vehicle for revolutionary action in the former
colonial nations. He was indeed widely identified with a new ultravolunta-
rist theory of guerrilla warfare, grounded in the peasantry, which essentially
radicalized the military elements already implicit in Lenin's vision of the
vanguard party.[12]

No more than Lenin, of course, was Guevara able to articulate any plausible connection between the authoritarian state of the present, which ultimately stifles creativity as it fosters conformism, and the utopian society,
with its "new man" of the future. They were both surely internationalists in
a way other authoritarian thinkers of African or Asian or Islamic "socialism" were not. But institutional questions still vanish, and issues dealing
with the preconditions for any genuinely democratic order are still post-
poned until "later."

Others in Latin America and elsewhere, of course, did things differently.

---

11. See Jon Lee Anderson, *Che Guevara: A Revolutionary Life* (New York:
Grove, 1997); and *The Che Guevara Reader*, ed. David Deutchman (New York:
Ocean, 1997).

12. Che Guevara, "Guerrilla Warfare: A Method," in Lowy, *Marxism in Latin
America*. An enormously popular tract of the 1960s, which offers a concise sum-
mary of this theory, was also provided by a former political disciple of Guevara; see
Regis Debray, *Revolution in the Revolution?* trans. Bobbye Ortiz (New York:
Grove, 1967).

"Liberation theology" has had a profound impact in certain economically disadvantaged areas; its fusion of materialism with grace, struggle with a vision of God's kingdom, has undoubtedly inspired action by the "lowly and the insulted."[13] Liberation theology highlights the oppression of women, and it is directed toward the peasantry. Its partisans have aided the struggles of the dispossessed and the disenfranchised. Marked by intellectual nobility no less than exceptional bravery, they are generally profound opponents of authoritarianism and champions of equality and internationalism. But liberation theology has little to say about political power, and its symbolism is relevant only for those initially committed to Christianity. Even its radical priests depend upon the ecclesiastical establishment, and its communitarian message undermines the personal character of salvation promulgated by Christian orthodoxy. Its internationalism is truncated, and its commitment to republicanism is often uncertain. There is a sense in which this child born of the marriage between Christianity and Marxism suffers from the philosophical weakness of both: it offers teleological faith without material foundations, seeks substantive equality without making reference to any particular institutional arrangements, and shrouds the particular in the veil of the universal.

But for all that, liberation theology is an innovative development. It speaks to the ways in which traditions can combine to form new ones. The formerly colonial world places its stamp on the past. There is even a "subtradition" of Latin American Leninism whose supporters, whether reticent or enthusiastic, are committed to republicanism. This was the case with many in Nicaragua. But the most powerful representative of this trend was surely Salvador Allende. Allende attempted to combine mass politics with vanguardism and a modern form of Leninism with a commitment to democratic socialism; it ultimately cost him his life once liberals abandoned his

13. Note the seminal work for this tradition by Ernst Bloch, *Atheism in Christianity: The Religion of the Exodus and the Kingdom*, trans. J. T. Swann (New York: Herder and Herder, 1972). Also of interest in what has become an immense literature are James H. Cone, *The God of the Oppressed* (New York: Orbis, 1997), Leonardo Boff, *The Path to Hope: Fragments from a Theologian's Journey*, trans. Philip Berryman (New York: Orbis, 1993); and Gustavo Gutierrez, *A Theology of Liberation: History, Politics, and Salvation*, ed. and trans. Sister Caridad Inda and John Eagleson (New York: Orbis, 1988). On the background, note Christian Smith, *The Emergence of Liberation Theory: Radical Religion and Social Movement Theory* (Chicago: University of Chicago Press, 1991); and Michael Lowry, *The War of the Gods: Religion and Politics in Latin America* (New York: Verso, 1996).

coalition in the Chilean crisis of 1973. In this vein, the *Canto General* of Pablo Neruda, among his greatest poems, offers an extraordinary phenomenological approach to the history of oppression and struggle for freedom in the Americas. The emphasis upon democracy has, indeed, only grown in the last decade of the twentieth century. The former president of Brazil, Fernando Cardoso, a democrat and a socialist, coauthored *Dependency and Development in Latin America* while in exile from the military clique ruling his nation. Appalled by the authoritarian logic and the failure of the communist-leaning forms of revolution, Jorge Castaneda has also rightly insisted on the introduction of a "democratic imperative" and the importance of "reformulating nationalism" from the perspective of a new regionalism in the continents where imperialism once reigned.[14]

All this, however, is not as simple as it sounds. Admittedly, Mustafa Kemal Ataturk fashioned a staunchly nationalistic republican revolution in Turkey following the collapse of the Ottoman Empire in the aftermath of World War I. But the Turkish case was relatively isolated. Intent on warding off the expansionist designs of both the Soviet Union and the Western powers, Ataturk sought to create a secular society whose democratic norms made Islamic worship voluntary. He maintained that Islam had decayed under religious dogmatism, and he sought to reinvigorate it with the spirit of rational inquiry and a Western notion of the individual. Islam was seen as having its place within a common civilization whose different elements might yet nurture one another. There is clearly a cosmopolitan element within the thinking of Ataturk. But he was also aware of the need for an antidote to the alienation and anomie that modernization would introduce. Thus, rejecting both communism and religion, he embraced nationalism.

Various other anti-imperialist movements would attempt to blend modern ideologies like nationalism or socialism with premodern beliefs. Traditionalism and modernization, rejection and appropriation of the "West," found their way into anti-imperialist struggles from the very beginning. There is indeed a sense in which it should have been obvious: nations under precapitalist conditions, economically exploited and also threatened with the eradication of their culture, will only rarely prove able to look forward without simultaneously looking backward.[15]

---

14. Jorge G. Castaneda, *Utopia Unarmed: The Latin American Left after the Cold War* (New York: Vintage, 1994).

15. The matter becomes even more complex, given that "modern nations and all their impedimenta generally claim to be the opposite of novel, namely rooted in the

Mohandas Gandhi made full use of this insight.[16] A republican educated in England as a lawyer, and cognizant of the benefits attendant upon the liberal rule of law, Gandhi articulated a vision of India composed of decentralized village communities infused with a religious ethic of nonviolence and sacrifice. His famous employment of nonviolent civil disobedience expressed, for him, "the root of Hinduism"; Gandhi indeed characterized violence as a Western import. Nonviolence became the logical form of opposition to English colonialism even as it created a seemingly plausible connection between means and ends for an Indian movement intent upon national self-determination. Nonviolence seemed to provide a way of avoiding the problems created when emergent democratic states lack democratic cultural foundations.

Gandhi's belief in nonviolence was both moral and instrumental. It was the same with the precapitalist values and symbols he employed, like the spinning wheel, which is still inscribed on the Indian flag. His imagery of village life, reminiscent of Russian anarchists like Kropotkin and Tolstoy, was surely useful in contesting the power and ideological underpinnings of British imperial rule. Beyond the anti-imperialist struggle, however, Gandhi undoubtedly anticipated the detrimental effects modernization would have on traditional culture in what would remain, for the foreseeable future, a traditional society. And so, although he stood opposed to the existing caste system, he obviously believed that highlighting the religious acceptance of poverty might help provide stability under conditions in which it would remain a fact of life for most Indians, again, for the foreseeable future. Nevertheless, for all that, Gandhi maintained a commitment to reason and the primacy of the dialogue in determining the veracity of claims and adjudication of grievances.

---

remotest antiquity, and the opposite of constructed, namely human communities so 'natural' as to require no definition other than self-assertion. . . . [But] just because so much of what subjectively makes up the modern 'nation' consists of such constructs and is associated with appropriate and, in general, fairly recent symbols or suitably tailed discourse (such as 'national history'), the national phenomenon cannot be adequately investigated without careful attention to the 'invention of tradition.' " Eric Hobsbawm, "Inventing Traditions," in *The Invention of Tradition*, ed. Eric Hobsbawm and Terence Ranger (New York: Cambridge University Press, 1983), 14.

16. Dennis Dalton, *Gandhi: Nonviolent Power in Action* (New York: Columbia University Press, 1993); Ved Mehta, *Mahatma Gandhi and His Apostles* (New Haven: Yale University Press, 1993); *The Essential Writings of Mahatma Gandhi*, ed. Raghavan Iyer (Delhi: Oxford University Press, 1991).

His philosophy, including his famous notion of *satyagraha*, is more complex than many would care to think.[17] Gandhi consistently defended a form of ethical pluralism predicated on a belief in the many-sidedness of all phenomena *(anekantavada)* and the fragmentariness of all human understanding. All judgment, political or otherwise, is seen as provisional, along with the criteria for comprehending existence and its "truth" *(satya)*. All that really remains fixed is the existential responsibility of the individual, whose most decent attributes are tolerance, selfless devotion to the common good, and the commitment to search for ever more complete understandings of an inherently incomplete truth.[18] There is no absolute rule of judgment capable of eliminating moral conflicts. Precisely for this reason, Gandhi sought to unify means and ends in action. This led him to identify himself with the masses of the impoverished in order that reason might "be strengthened by suffering." The willingness to undertake suffering and accept the legal consequences for an act of resistance instills a sense of purpose, undermines egoism, and strengthens the genuine "power of the self" or the "soul force" *(satyagraha)*. Violence always presupposes a dogmatic belief in the correctness of a particular stance, and in this regard it inherently undermines the search for truth and self-realization or enlightenment. Thus, nonviolence ultimately goes hand in hand with the embrace of *satyagraha*.

Whatever his extraordinary legacy, however, Gandhi was working at cross-purposes. He was smuggling a religious element into a secular state; and, although he sought an India hospitable to both Hindus and Moslems, his own religious tradition and preference remained clear. The concrete implications of what, in fact, became the partition of a subcontinent undermined the spiritual content of his message, and from the perspective of more secular figures like Jawaharlal Nehru and Rabindranath Tagore his emphasis on religious traditionalism and precapitalist symbols subverted an assault on poverty and religiously sanctioned understandings of caste. Nevertheless, whatever their skepticism, even they paid their obeisance on numerous occasions to the distinctive precapitalist character of Indian culture and the new nationalism.

---

17. Note the fine discussion by Manfred Steger, "Peacebuilding and Nonviolence: Gandhi's Perspective on Power," in *Peace, Conflict, and Violence: Peace Psychology for the Twenty-first Century*, ed. Dan Christie, Richard Wagner, and Deborah Winter (Englewood Cliffs, N.J.: Prentice-Hall, forthcoming).

18. Mahatma Gandhi, *An Autobiography: The Story of My Experiments with Truth* (Boston: Beacon, 1993).

Both Nehru and Tagore, and especially Tagore, have been miscast in the Western imagination as spiritualists or simple followers of the mahatma. In fact, Nehru was a modernizer of the first order and, after his fashion, an internationalist who played an important role at the Bandung Conference of 1955. As for Tagore, who received the Nobel Prize for Literature in 1913, he was intent on condemning inequities outside the "narrow domestic walls" of his own society, and his own intellectual roots drew on the Hindu, the Muslim, and the British cultures.[19] Both Nehru and Tagore refused to reject Western notions of science, and Nehru, in particular, looked to the "dynamic element" of modern life. The simplistic identification of the Third World with an atavistic and particularist worldview is a Eurocentric fiction.

Gandhi, Tagore, and Nehru all sought a modern national community beyond the interests of any particular caste or creed. The ultimate success of their vision seems likely despite the governmental crises, the communalist demagoguery, and the religious rioting of the 1990s. India is a functioning democracy; it is a secular state separate from its hundreds of ethnic groupings and sects in which, following the vision of Nehru, the attempt is still made to keep social identities outside the political arena. But the price for the new state was high. Indeed, given the fierce Hindu and Muslim nationalism existing within the original anti-imperialist movement,[20] it remains questionable whether any program could have prevented the partition of 1948 in which untold thousands lost their lives and Gandhi met his death, at the hands of a Hindu fanatic, at the age of seventy-nine.

Decolonization is seen by many thinkers as an inherently violent process. According to Frantz Fanon,[21] in fact, it pits two incompatible forces and two mutually exclusive worldviews against one another. Dialogue with the racist is worthless: even if it were possible, it would be demeaning. During the high point of anti-imperialism, however, it was considered basically impossible because the interests of the colonizer and the colonized were seen as

19. Rabindranath Tagore, *The Religion of Man* (New York: Macmillan, 1931), 101 ff. Note also *Selected Letters of Rabindranath Tagore*, ed. Khrishna Dutta and Andrew Robinson (Cambridge: Cambridge University Press, 1997), which was published on the fiftieth anniversary of Indian independence, with a superb foreword by Amartya Sen.
20. Christophe Jaffrelot, *The Hindu Nationalist Movement in India* (New York: Columbia University Press, 1997).
21. Lewis R. Gordon, *Fanon and the Crisis of European Man* (New York: Routledge, 1995); Irene L. Gendzier, *Frantz Fanon: A Critical Study* (New York: Grove, 1986).

starkly opposing each other. Representatives of the colonized natives found themselves asking, "What is left of the colonized at the end of this stubborn effort to dehumanize him? He is surely no longer an alter ego of the colonizer. He is hardly a human being. He tends rapidly toward becoming an object. As an end, in the colonizer's supreme ambition, he should exist only as a function of the needs of the colonizer, i.e., be transformed into a pure colonized."[22]

The only way in which it is possible for the colonized to assert his or her subjectivity and manifest his or her solidarity with others, according to Fanon, is through violence. Violence is no longer merely a means, whose use should be minimized, but is now considered an act of catharsis on the part of the native. Decolonization ultimately implies violence because it calls for replacing one "species" of man with another. Violence alone is capable of obliterating the settler and affirming the existence of the native. It alone can give natives their dignity, strengthen their sense of self, and affirm their solidarity with their community. And that community does not include the collaborationists among the colonized, the "national bourgeoisie," or its allies seeking to import the civilization of the imperialist.

Fanon was no friend of bourgeois nationalism; in his view, it can produce only "an empty shell, a crude and fragile travesty of what might have been."[23] The nationalist phase of the revolution, generated in the cities, must become "spontaneous" in the countryside. The domestic bourgeoisie is ultimately no less the enemy than the imperialist intruder. Revolution must grip the masses, and for this to occur, violence must generate its own dynamic. Only then will the broader masses realize that they can attain freedom only at the risk of their lives. Violence thus assumes a cathartic quality; it is a "cleansing force." Indeed, for the native incapable of escaping what Fanon called "the fact of blackness," it has its own justification.

Born in Martinique in 1925 and a soldier in North Africa during World War II, for which he received the Croix de Guerre, Frantz Fanon ultimately received a degree in psychiatry from the University of Lyons and returned to Algeria in 1952. His activities as the chief resident at a government psychiatric hospital, where he worked until his tragic death in 1961 at the age of thirty-six, were surely useful for the case studies on the psychological ef-

---

22. Albert Memmi, *The Colonizer and the Colonized*, trans. Howard Greenfield (Boston: Beacon, 1965), 86.
23. Frantz Fanon, *The Wretched of the Earth* (New York: Grove, 1961), 156.

fects of imperialism so important to his various scholarly endeavors. Progress showed him its Janus face: it was not the agents of progress who would prove revolutionary but rather the flotsam discarded by progress: the petty-bourgeois intelligentsia, the *Lumpenproletariat*, and, above all, the peasantry. Indeed, from first-hand experience as well as from theoretical reflection, Fanon concluded that the starving peasant instinctively recognizes the value and legitimacy of violence.

> For him there is no compromise, no possible coming to terms; colonization and decolonization are simply a question of relative strength. The exploited man sees that his liberation implies the use of all means and that of force first and foremost. . . . Colonialism only loosens its hold when the knife is at its throat, no Algerian really found these terms too violent. The leaflet only expressed what every Algerian felt at heart: Colonialism is not a thinking machine nor a body endowed with reasoning faculties. It is violence in its natural state, and it will yield only when confronted with greater violence.[24]

No possible community of interest unites the white working class in the imperialist national territory and the peasant of the colonial territory.[25] Without a communist international or an unflinching belief in the capitalist notion of "competitive advantage," there is little to bind together the black and brown victims of imperialist oppression, numbering in the hundreds of millions, with the few million white workers still relatively privileged in their degree of exploitation. Marxism needed redefinition to meet the needs of the native under colonial rule: exploitation deriving from the "organization of production" would have to make way in the name of a far broader "organization of oppression." Fanon indeed was crucial in giving a new cultural understanding to what were previously political and economic notions of both revolution and oppression.

Others had led the way. Gandhi looked to the spinning wheel. Leopold Senghor took the matter much further in his theory of "negritude." He called upon the colonized peoples of Africa to harness their inner and tactile qualities against the abstract and rational forms of cultural hegemony exercised by the imperialist West. Making use of vintage racist images, Senghor spoke about substituting tactile sensualism for the Greek *logos* and a statement like "I feel, I dance the Other; I am" for the Cartesian claim, "I think;

---

24. Ibid., 281.
25. Frantz Fanon, *Toward the African Revolution* (New York: Grove, 1968).

therefore I am."[26] The intuitive and the instinctive confront the reflexive and the complex. The "communal" and the "organic" oppose the "atomistic" and the "mechanical." Interestingly enough, whatever the Afrocentric commitment to "socialism" or the Islamic rejection of imperialism, the attacks on the principles of the Enlightenment remain remarkably similar to those of a reactionary and primarily Catholic nineteenth-century Western counter-Enlightenment. This new postcolonial stance is, indeed, most often defined by what it most radically opposes. It often endorses racialized categories by simply reversing the valuation they are assigned.

Chinua Achebe better illuminates what is at stake in the final chapter of his famous novel, *Things Fall Apart*. The main character, Okonkwo, is found hanging from a tree. The district commissioner reflects: it would seem that "the story of this man who had killed a messenger and hanged himself would make interesting reading. One could write a whole chapter on him. Perhaps, not a whole chapter but a reasonable paragraph, at any rate."[27] The district commissioner feels that he can conclude every important aspect about Okonkwo's life just by looking at the man's corpse. The native's past personal history becomes irrelevant, along with the history and culture of every other African with whom the imperialists interact. The colonialist deems his subject's history worthless. Indeed, with the deliberate suppression of precolonial cultures, it only makes sense that the colonized should now fight to have their differences recognized and form an identity of their own, separate from the one assigned them by the West.[28]

Eurocentrism creates the world in its image. It presents itself as universalist but is in fact particular. Edward Said makes this clear in his famous statement that neither the Orient nor the Occident is simply "there."[29] Terms like *Orient* and *Occident* are not primarily geographic designations: they have an ideological and existential character, and they presuppose a particular binary way of looking at the world. This worldview indeed is built upon hegemonic foundations. The Orient was "orientalized" in the Western popular media and its academic presses. The negative image of the Arab in par-

---

26. Leopold Sedar Senghor, *On African Socialism*, trans. Mercer Cook (New York: American Society of African Culture, 1964), 72 ff.

27. Chinua Achebe, *Things Fall Apart* (New York: Fawcett Crest, 1994), 208–9.

28. Gareth Griffiths, "The Myth of Authenticity," in *The Postcolonial Studies Reader*, ed. Bill Ashcroft, Gareth Griffiths, and Helen Tiffin (New York: Routledge, 1995), 241.

29. Edward W. Said, *Orientalism* (New York: Vintage, 1979), 4.

ticular, or non-Western peoples in general, obviously justifies Western domination. Orientalism is, however, not simply part of a Western plot to hold down the "Oriental" world. It is more than that: it is also an idea through which Western cultural and political hegemony legitimates itself to itself.[30]

Western identity is itself defined by the way it relates to the East. The Orient has helped to define the West as its contrasting image, idea, personality, and experience. Orientalism becomes a "style," a mode of dealing with what the West supposedly is not, a way of ideologically controlling the Other. It puts the West into a whole series of relationships with the Orient—or any other non-Western construct—without ever losing the upper hand. The superiority this false construct of the Arab provides the Western analyst makes it possible to ignore the manner in which non-Western peoples relate to the West; and many believe that only one response is possible. Indeed, just as Jean-Paul Sartre argued after World War II that Jews should no longer rely on the platitudes of liberalism or humanism[31] but rather should organize around a specific identity, the "Arab" or the native must explode the popular stereotype.

Trinh T. Minh-ha has described the way in which the West places everyone else in a "one-place-fits-all 'other' category."[32] Contrary to the conventional narratives of European and Western interpreters of imperialism, however, a new discourse has been developed in which the narratives of those with first-hand experience in organizing and struggling against imperialism are employed as primary sources in their own right. This new "postcolonial" discourse has opened new avenues for those seeking to understand the dimensions of rebellion and identity; it has contributed to a multiculturalist worldview in which each experience of a given culture is given its legitimacy. Nevertheless, it suffers from a postmodernist refusal to offer criteria for justifying claims and providing positive alternatives to dominant stereotypes.

Postcolonialism is a disparate enterprise, and its authors do not constitute a single school or ideology. They offer signposts on a treacherous road to liberation, and they oscillate within a constantly swirling discourse: oral history, memoirs, poetry, music, and literature. Proponents of postcolonialism work from the assumption that the cultural effects of imperialism linger and

30. Ibid., 12 ff.

31. Jean-Paul Sartre, *Anti-Semite and Jew*, trans. George J. Becker (New York: Schocken, 1948).

32. Trinh T. Minh-ha, "No Master Territories," in Ashcroft, Griffiths, and Tiffin, *Postcolonial Studies Reader*.

that the struggle for identity still exists in this era of fallen empires. Those in the former colonial nations must still discard the identities and stigmas assigned to them by their oppressors. But this is only the first step. The black peasant woman must cope not only with the racial and economic implications of her condition as a member of her culture but with the sexual oppression she experiences within that culture. "Hybridity" also complicates the matter of identity. What results from the postcolonial enterprise is a recognition that identity is always in flux and that its determination involves a process predicated upon an ongoing breakdown of groups; it is always a matter of acknowledging what Gramsci originally called the "subaltern,"[33] listening to the "voice" of the forgotten, and recognizing that his or her discourse is not our own.

The problems with the new mode of discourse lie less with what is said than with what is not. It is surely the case that women forced to wear the veil, along with those subject to a host of other premodern prejudices, need and deserve their own voice. But there is little comment when it comes to the institutional guarantees with which their voices can be heard. It is precisely those without a voice who most require the institution of the republican idea and the notion of civil liberties, whether these are Western constructs or not. Introducing them will obviously serve as an affront to certain forms of theocratic thinking and the legitimacy of premodern customs precisely because these new institutional forms make possible new self-chosen, rather than inherited, forms of identity. It is the same with notions of African socialism. And the problem is less that it is a bastard construct than that it avoids either differentiating between cultural and political norms or giving primacy to the one over the other. India has hundreds of religious sects with very different values and norms; each deserves "recognition." But leaving the matter at that is a recipe for chaos. Such recognition can occur only through the existence of a liberal democratic state whose own demands for a form of "civic faith" will intrude on the demands raised by particular identity claims. Especially a nation still mired in "postcolonialism," following the insights of Hobbes, must stand beyond the cultural interests of all in order to secure the cultural freedoms of each.

A new postcolonial theory cannot ignore the organizational arrange-

---

33. Antonio Gramsci, "History of the Subaltern Classes: Methodological Criteria," in *Selections from the Prison Notebooks,* ed. and trans. Quintin Hoare and Geoffrey Nowell (New York: International, 1971), 52 ff.

ments, and the philosophical assumptions underpinning them, in the name of cultural identity. There is a reason why it is always the despots and the dictatorial cliques who embrace relativistic notions of national self-determination and cultural identity, and it is the dissidents concerned with civil liberties who demand the introduction of republican institutions. The identification of the revolutionary or anti-imperialist state with its populace is as spurious as the identification of race with the interests of all those who fall under the category. It is less a matter of developing a strategy for the "postcolonial" enterprise in terms of "discursive formations," or engaging in fruitless debates about whether the Other can adequately voice the otherness of the subaltern,[34] than of facing the challenge of constructing innovative liberal institutions and offering socialist and internationalist values for the emancipation of the once colonialized world. Empowering the subaltern, indeed, is possible only when the radical imagination confronts the realities of political power.

---

34. Gayitri Chakravorty Spivak, "Can the Subaltern Speak?" in *Marxism and the Interpretation of Culture*, ed. Cary Nelson and Lawrence Grossberg (Urbana: University of Illinois Press, 1988).

Epilogue

◆———◆

Ethical Choices, Progressive Politics, and the Challenges of Planetary Life

CRITIQUE AND THE END OF HISTORY

The new millennium actually began in 1989. The crumbling of the Berlin Wall brought to a close what Eric Hobsbawm called "the short century."[1] It started with a world war generated by competing imperialist powers, which produced the conditions for yet another cataclysm, and it bore witness to atrocities never before imagined. The disgust for the ideas held responsible should have come as no surprise. Small wonder, then, that the twentieth century should have ended with "the grand narratives" invalidated and with "philosophy, which once seemed obsolete, continu[ing] to exist because the moment to realize it was missed."[2] This view is the last and most ruthless contestation of the young Marx, who envisioned the proletariat as having no goals of its own to realize,[3] and a future

---

1. Eric Hobsbawm, *The Age of Extremes: A History of the World, 1914–1991* (New York: Vintage, 1994), 5.

2. Theodor W. Adorno, *Negative Dialectics*, trans. E. B. Ashton (New York: Seabury, 1973), 3.

3. Karl Marx, "Letter to Arnold Ruge, September 1843," in *Writings of the Young Marx on Philosophy and Society*, ed. and trans. Loyd D. Easton and Kurt H. Guddat (New York: Doubleday, 1967), 214–15.

revolution that, in keeping with the promises of the idealist tradition, would prove capable of fulfilling the idea of freedom. It constitutes the immanent critique of historical teleology, and it dramatically reflects the real situation in which progressive politics finds itself.

Only now, in an increasingly multicultural world, is capitalism becoming a genuinely global phenomenon, and a progressive response can no longer presuppose its connection with any emancipatory ideals. There is no escaping this planetary context; to put it another way, there is no "outside." Utopia can perhaps still inspire action, and it remains a crucial category for political theory, but the image recedes behind the attempt to conceptualize it. The absolute idea of emancipation has given way before regulative ideals, incapable of ever being fully realized, contesting repression within the existing context. These ideals are primarily liberal, socialist, and internationalist. They derive from the progressive heritage of the past. Nevertheless, if they are to resist being reduced to purely polemical usage in the present, their most radical implications need reconstruction from the perspective of a critical political theory.

Words like *critique* and *critical* are used all the time. But the political commitment to their implications is often lacking. Genuine critique is the product of an ethical decision: it requires, at a minimum, resisting a complete capitulation to what *is* in the name of what *should be*. There is no absolute foundation for such a decision. The link between ideas and action, theory and practice, can no longer be taken for granted. Political aspirations seem predetermined, whether consciously or unconsciously, and new ideas of emancipation remain abstract or without institutional referent. Indeed, with utopia tamed, it might even appear that history is at an end.[4]

Hegel had already envisioned this possibility when he saw the idea of freedom as having realized itself in a constitutional monarchy with a capitalist economy. Existential questions regarding individual morality and the meaning of existence would continue; reforms would continue; and even conflict would continue. People would not necessarily find themselves "happy"; it might prove necessary to extend the benefits of liberal universalism to previously excluded groups; national rivalries and wars of aggression would

---

4. Francis Fukuyama, "The End of History?" *National Interest*, no. 16 (Summer 1989): 3–18. A more extended response is provided in Stephen Eric Bronner, *Moments of Decision: Political History and the Crises of Radicalism* (New York: Routledge, 1992), 125 ff.

remain part of the human drama. Nevertheless, the framework for action would be set.

Narrow economic calculation and simple attempts to satisfy increasing national consumer demands now seemingly define social action; preoccupation with the administrative solution of increasingly technical problems of the state and the national economy have rendered ideology obsolete. Thinking has apparently become "one-dimensional." Fanatical movements may cling to the past, class war might yet break out, authoritarianism still exists, a devolution of power is taking place, and nations like Indonesia could splinter into smaller units. But there should be no misunderstanding: "It is not necessary that all societies become successful liberal societies, merely that they end their ideological pretensions of representing different and higher forms of human society."[5] The question for those committed to the new is whether other possibilities, even if they are only speculative, present themselves beyond the liberal capitalism of the nation-state.

A critical theory of politics must confront this situation directly. It cannot invoke the need for faith in some indeterminate socialist alternative, recycle fascist predictions about the failure of democracy, or indulge in the old-fashioned longings for a "new man." Those times are over. It must illuminate the clash of conflicting interests, the existence of qualitative differences within the status quo, and—perhaps above all—a new normative perspective with which to resist parochialism and provincialism. It must begin to reconstruct the traditions appropriate to its purposes in the light of new conditions. The new always stands in some positive relation to the old: otherwise, indeed, it would not be new.

ETHICAL CHOICES

Looking back to the teleological, or "redemptive," dogmas of the past for inspiration can only prove self-defeating. It is no longer possible to believe, like the old-fashioned proponents of orthodox Marxism, that the emancipated future is appearing as present. A philosophy of history no longer anchors theory and practice; its agents have all proved inadequate to the tasks set for them. The normative purposes of political theory have been cast into doubt; ontology cannot retrieve them, and science is concerned with facts

5. Fukuyama, "The End of History?" 13.

rather than values. Political theory has become dependent upon an ethical decision concerning its purpose. And such a decision can only prove contingent: it is easy enough to retreat into what Thomas Mann called a "power-protected inwardness."

There is nothing intrinsically or self-consciously "political" about political theory. It can remain self-consciously ahistorical, collapse the future into the present, forget the unfulfilled ideals born of compromised traditions, and bemoan the lack of alternatives. Traditional political theorists have often dealt with the canon in the same way that literary theorists schooled in the "new criticism" have approached literary texts and artists infatuated with the idea of *l'art pour l'art* have evaluated paintings. Postmodernist thinkers have consistently substituted the discussion of domination for a confrontation with power. It has indeed become fashionable to sacrifice the historical and the institutional for the psychological and the aesthetic—and still insist upon the political character of the given inquiry. Luxuries of this sort, however, are not available to a genuinely critical theory of politics; it must, again, evince a concrete character and a reconstructive intent.

Critique can no longer afford to turn its back upon the workings of power or the positive values underpinning its emancipatory enterprise.[6] It has become unrealistic for even the most devout adherents of the Frankfurt School to insist on the "great refusal" or the simple "nonidentity" of subject and object. The radicalism of this stance has been squandered: its uncompromising rejection of the "system," with its indeterminate slogan proclaiming that "the whole is false," has already been incorporated into mainstream academia and the culture industry. Employing categories of this sort has turned critical theory into a form of pseudocritique and resulted in dialectical paralysis.

Connecting critical theory with a certain set of public aims[7]—highlighting its commitment to liberal ideals of institutional governance, socialist notions of economic justice, and internationalist perspectives for dealing with transnational problems—is the only way to reinstate its radical character. Critical theory must recall, in keeping with Hegel, that new ideas of political emancipation will necessarily remain abstract without an institutional refer-

---

6. See Theodor W. Adorno, "Resignation," in *Critical Models: Interventions and Catchwords*, trans. Henry W. Pickford (New York: Columbia University Press, 1998).

7. Note the more extensive discussion in Stephen Eric Bronner, "Points of Departure: Sketches for a Critical Theory with Public Aims," in *Of Critical Theory and Its Theorists* (Oxford: Blackwell, 1994).

ent. In short, once again critical theory must become political: it must project an egalitarian global order, one that is sensitive to cultural differences but in which a restructuring of economic power complements an ever expanding realm of democratic action.

Critical political theory must address the question of practice in new ways. It must still steer between materialism and metaphysics. It can no longer accept the existence of prefabricated revolutionary agents like the proletariat any more than the illusory comforts of an analytic philosophy whose ideas stand outside of history and beyond any concern with action. A critical theory of politics needs to focus upon the *transformative* moment in which ideas might influence action, the *interface* between ideas and action: the structures and the constraints, the institutions and the movements, the customs and the norms with which it is possible to inhibit or expand the autonomy of citizens. Indeed, without a willingness to envision ideas in action, political theory loses its ability to fashion meaningful distinctions between institutions or to formulate the complex struggles facing the exploited and disenfranchised.

INSTITUTIONAL DETERMINATIONS

"Truth," wrote Hegel, "is concrete." And it becomes concrete only through the introduction of qualifications and "mediations." Without recourse to such qualifications, judgment becomes impossible, and critique inhabits "the night in which all cows are black." Lacking reference to the complex institutional forms in which it becomes manifest, the idea of freedom remains abstract. There are serious structural differences between democracies with one-party regimes, two-party systems in which the winner takes all, and various forms of proportional representation. Each has a different impact on the ability of the disadvantaged to gather information, coordinate their efforts, present their demands, challenge the manner in which priorities are set, and render institutions democratically accountable. Each harbors a different likelihood for engaging in war. Each has a different impact on the exercise of freedom and, in terms of radicalizing perhaps the best existing definition of cosmopolitanism, the ability of its citizens to feel at home everywhere and garner the benefits of hospitality.[8]

---

8. Immanuel Kant, "Perpetual Peace," in *Political Writings*, ed. Hans Reiss (Cambridge: Cambridge University Press, 1970).

Setting up a rigid dichotomy between representative government and despotic regimes, whether fascist or communist, is necessary but not sufficient: it makes a qualitative difference for the life choices faced by individuals whether there is public control over investment, full employment, free child care, national health insurance, a progressive tax policy, and a genuine commitment to public education and the extension of public knowledge,[9] along with a host of other social services. Ideological, political, and economic power are distributed in fundamentally divergent ways. And the need for a critical perspective on this complex reality remains: it is indeed striking that the triumphant "liberal" capitalist state should have reverted to the most draconian policies of the free market upon the collapse of the alternative with which it previously had to compete.

Monarchy, dictatorship, fascism, and representative democracy of various types are all possibilities for a capitalist economic system at particular times and under specific circumstances. The state is not an indeterminate monolith. Identifying it with bureaucracy, bureaucracy with alienation, and alienation with the "commodity form" in order to trumpet a rarefied and noninstrumental understanding of politics simply does not help matters.[10] A critical theory of politics must take seriously the different opportunities for social change, different interests, and different possibilities for enacting policy under different forms of government. Whatever the phenomenological character of the state, its various institutional incarnations must be shown capable of privileging different interests, norms, and forms of action. It makes little sense simply to inveigh against bureaucratic institutions in the abstract or the epistemic assumptions of instrumental reason in general: the quality of everyday life along with the most basic health issues and life expectancy are profoundly influenced by the impact of structural imbalances of power and provincial prejudices.[11]

A direct connection exists between the level of intervention by the state and the possibilities for participatory action in a liberal polity. Attempts to limit the impact of the state upon economic affairs have historically been connected with attempts to constrain the development of an organized poli-

---

9. Note the fine study by Elizabeth A. Kelly, *Education, Democracy, and Public Knowledge* (Boulder: Westview, 1995).

10. Blandine Kriegel, *The State and the Rule of Law*, trans. Marc A. LePain and Jeffrey C. Cohen (Princeton: Princeton University Press, 1995), 112 ff.

11. Richard G. Wilkinson, *Unhealthy Societies: The Afflictions of Inequality* (New York: Routledge, 1998).

tics from below; the attack on the interventionist state in the 1980s in the United States clearly occurred in concert with an assault on unions as well as the legislative advances made by minorities and other previously excluded groups. Certain policies are obviously also more conducive to furthering the organizing abilities and material demands of working people than others. The ability to make distinctions of this sort and generate institutional mediations between the universal and the particular is the stuff of any genuinely dialectical perspective: Hegel already considered the ability to comprehend increasingly complex phenomena as the hallmark of intellectual progress.

A single suit can no longer be made to fit all sizes. The market is useful in indicating consumer preferences, eliminating inefficiency, and creating incentives for investment; and the state can mitigate its inequalities by securing a safety net for working people. One implicates the other. The future projects not merely a mixed economy, however, but a mixed society. There remains a basic choice to be made between the old communitarian notion of the culturally homogeneous "people's state" *(Volksstaat)* and the liberal state composed of citizens with diverse customs and beliefs seeking to determine their destiny peacefully under the liberal rule of law *(Rechtsstaat)*. Other choices, however, also remain: universalism and particularism, internationalism and nationalism, globalism and localism, centralization and decentralization, planning and individual initiative, the rights and responsibilities of citizens, are all part of political life in the new planetary context. The *proportionate role* each plays will have a real impact on society.

The issue of the interventionist state is not simply technocratic, a matter of balancing the efficiency of the market with the inefficiency of bureaucratic organizations or balancing profits and costs. Ideals are at stake in terms of the normative purposes given policies and interests serve. These increasingly disappear from the administrative discourse,[12] and it is incumbent upon a critical theory of politics to restore them: this was indeed the aim of critical theory in the first place. For such an undertaking to prove effective, however, clarity is necessary with respect to the goals it wishes to serve and the traditions with which it wishes to align itself. The unqualified critique of the totality ultimately generates little more than an "antipolitical politics." The liberal state is not an inflexible abstraction, just as socialism is no longer a predetermined form of economic organization. Future struggles will revolve around determining the connections between them as well

---

12. See Antonia Grunenberg, *Der Schlaf der Freiheit* (Reinbeck: Rowohlt, 1997).

as the ways in which differences of degree can turn into differences of kind within the seemingly same republican model.

THE BATTLE FOR DEMOCRACY

Truly radical democrats never considered the republic the fulfillment of democracy. Its appeal derived merely from the accountability of its institutions and its ability to guarantee the rights of individuals and enable them to participate in the life of their communities. Radical ideas of democracy have always been motivated by the vision of humanity taking control of its destiny. Popular participation in decision making is an irreplaceable component of this vision; and, as the proponents of communitarianism have shown, it can take various forms. But the workers' council or "soviet" is its most radical institutional expression. Anarchists and anarcho-Marxists surely exaggerated its virtues: the councilist vision cannot deal with the market; it lacks institutional mechanisms necessary to guarantee the rights of individuals; its belief in the willingness of people to actively participate in all the decisions of their community is simply naive. There is also something profoundly antihistorical and even dogmatic about mechanically seeking to transplant a vision of the 1920s into the 1990s. Nevertheless, with these reservations in mind, Ralph Miliband was correct in refusing simply to identify democracy with republican institutions:

> It is not only political arrangements which need sustained and convincing criticism, but also the exercise of arbitrary power in all walks of life in factories, offices, schools and wherever else power affects people's existence. The notion that the battle for democracy has already been won in capitalist democratic systems, save for some electoral and constitutional reforms at the edges, simply by virtue of the achievement of universal suffrage, open political competition and regular elections is a profoundly limiting and debilitating notion which has served conservative forces extremely well, and which has to be exposed and countered.[13]

---

13. Ralph Miliband, "Reflections on the Crisis of Communist Regimes," in *After the Fall: The Failure of Communism and the Future of Socialism* (New York: Verso, 1991), 13.

Liberal republicanism spoke to the process of democratic decision-making without bothering overly about participation. Councils or soviets, by way of contrast, were usually long on participation and short on institutional cohesion. And so, generally, the republic and the council were seen as standing in opposition to one another. But this view is unjustifiably rigid. Just as the accountability of institutions is strengthened by the existence of an informed and active public, so is a feeling of empowerment necessary for participation. Critical political theory must begin speculating about the possible connections between the republic, the council, and a set of burgeoning transnational institutions. Such an undertaking is possible, however, only by projecting the inherently liberal vision of a democratic order in which, whatever the variations, citizens can arrive at their decisions without the influence of prejudice or the constraints deriving from material self-interest.

Such a view presupposes a socialist notion of material equality and an international perspective: without these qualifications liberty remains a purely abstract enterprise. It assumes the willingness to render various nonpolitical institutions like capital more accountable and to foster new multicultural forms of participation through the creation of "secondary associations."[14] All of this, however, depends upon imagining the possibilities for new organizational arrangements within the liberal state. The much-vaunted end of the state is indeed as illusory as the end of history:[15] the liberal republican state will take its new place within the new international planetary arena, just as painting took its new place within a reality dominated by first photography, then film, and then television.

International organizations will still employ the governmental forms, and they will appropriate the liberal principles inherited from the republican nation-state: a complex federalism will become the hallmark of a new international order, and subsidiarity, the principle whereby decisions capable of being made by more decentralized institutions are made by them, will appear as one of its guiding principles. States are necessary to mediate the connection between individuals and their world as surely as cities and towns are necessary to mediate the connection between individuals and their nations. The state is in danger of being swamped less by political demands

14. Joshua Cohen and Joel Rogers, *Associations and Democracy* (New York: Verso, 1995).

15. Jean-Marie Guehenno, *The End of the Nation-State*, trans. Victoria Elliott (Minneapolis: University of Minnesota Press, 1995).

from below than by economic trends from above, such as the rise of a global criminal economy, multinational corporations, and new international lending organizations.[16]

There are no organizational tricks to avoid the bureaucratic petrification of even the most radically democratic institutions. Centralized power is an unavoidable element of modern life, and it confronts the longings for self-determination by the populace, what Benjamin Barber has called the "passion for democracy."[17] In absolute terms, this conflict harbors no solution. The liberal ideal inherently fosters a *creative friction* between the institutional poles of politics; and critical political theory must explore the ways in which the interplay between bureaucracies and their constituencies, accountability and participation, extend the democratic possibilities of civil society.

CIVIL SOCIETY

Civil society has a long tradition within political theory, going back to Aristotle.[18] Liberals and Hegelians initially identified it with the market. Civil society was the realm apart from the state in which private interests would predominate. But this reduction was already questioned by Alexis de Tocqueville. In his writings about America it became abundantly evident that purely instrumental and egoistic assumptions could not explain the participation of the individual in "voluntary associations," ranging from bowling leagues to social movements or interest groups, let alone account for the role of the church in everyday life or the host of prejudices intertwined with everyday life. With the onset of the twentieth century, civil society was increasingly seen as the basis for "community" and the host of moral values associated with "civic virtue."

Politicians and revolutionaries now ignore the institutions of civil society at their peril. Such institutions logically served as the focal point of discussion following the collapse of communism and the attempts to emancipate

---

16. Manuel Castells, *The Information Age: Economy, Society, and Culture* (Oxford: Blackwell, 1998), 3:134 ff.

17. Benjamin R. Barber, *A Passion for Democracy: American Essays* (Princeton: Princeton University Press, 1998).

18. Note, for a general overview, John Ehrenberg, *Civil Society: History, Politics, Theory* (New York: New York University Press, 1999).

civil society from the intrusions of an authoritarian state. The purpose of the liberal revolutions of 1989 was indeed to reinvigorate the sphere in which consensus is freely forged, differences are openly expressed, and recognition for the individual is discursively secured.[19] With the conservative assault on the interventionist state in the 1980s, however, civil society had already become a matter of renewed interest in the United States and Western Europe. Communitarians sought to foster participation through voluntary associations, to emphasize the need for "authority," and to combat state regulation. Even critical thinkers like Jürgen Habermas called upon new social movements to preserve the "life-world" of shared experiences, constituted by cultural reproduction and socialization, from bureaucratic reification and "internal colonization."[20] Nevertheless, the concept was fundamentally abstracted from international developments in communications and technology pertaining to the interplay between states and peoples.

Civil society was understood as militating against both the state and the economy. It was seen as embracing a set of institutions and practices, like religion and voluntary associations, that fall under neither politics nor economics. Even in these terms, however, a rigorous definition of civil society has become a matter of contention. It is generally understood by making reference to the following categories:

(1) Plurality: families, informal groups, and voluntary associations whose plurality and autonomy allow for a variety of forms of life; (2) Publicity: institutions of culture and communication; (3) Privacy: a domain of individual self-development and moral choice; (4) Legality: structures of general laws and basic rights needed to demarcate plurality, privacy, and publicity from at least the state and, tendentially, the economy. Together, these structures secure the institutional existence of a modern differentiated civil society.[21]

Whether this understanding actually justifies an autonomous view of civil society is, of course, another matter. The state and the market obviously influence the activity of voluntary associations, the possibilities for developing "public opinion," the degree of privacy, and the law. International insti-

19. Axel Honneth, *The Struggle for Recognition: The Moral Grammar of Social Conflicts*, trans. Joel Anderson (Cambridge, U.K.: Polity, 1995).
20. Jürgen Habermas, *The Theory of Communicative Action*, trans. Thomas McCarthy (Boston: Beacon, 1987), 2:356 ff.
21. Jean Cohen and Andrew Arato, *Civil Society and Political Theory* (Cambridge: MIT Press, 1992), 346 ff.

tutions and multinational corporations, however, also increasingly affect the once relatively self-contained character of civil society. Culture industries obviously intrude upon it, along with the new possibilities for travel, and an increasingly sophisticated educational system clearly manifests the potential to foster curiosity about the Other.

"Civil society" is an inherently reified notion. It is not an autonomous sphere of life but is, rather, profoundly affected by the state and the market. Plurality, publicity, privacy, and legality secure nothing at all. They are themselves secured by political institutions, economic arrangements, and—above all—movements, whose members make use of them. It is indeed questionable whether civil society is anything more than a heuristic concept covering a set of incommensurable associations and institutions: it makes more sense, from a political perspective, to consider the manner in which its movements and institutions articulate their concerns.

Civil society frames the interplay of interests; it serves as the battleground within which those interests first gain recognition. The real question involves, again, less the character of the concept than the character of these interests. Those endemic to movements generated within civil society must prove neither purely calculable nor purely institutional: otherwise they would fall into the sphere of the market or the state. Their grievances must somehow resist being defined in those terms. And this involves more than the quaint preoccupation with "civic virtue," or moral consensus, associated with so much of communitarian thought. Their interests can prove explosive. They often threaten to overturn traditional values and unravel the social fabric. There is, in short, a profoundly radical quality to the issues with which the new social movements of civil society have concerned themselves: subalternity, hegemony, and identity.

THE INVERSION OF POLITICS

New social movements have rendered political a host of cultural issues previously considered unpolitical and, simultaneously, rendered unpolitical the majority of distributive concerns traditionally identified with the political.[22] They highlight a new form of what Anthony Giddens calls "life politics"

---

22. Ulrich Beck, *The Reinvention of Politics: Rethinking Modernity in the Global Social Order*, trans. Mark Ritter (Cambridge, U.K.: Polity, 1997), 132 ff.

intent on liberating the repressed possibilities of the individual from outworn traditions and petrified forms of conduct. Their members are no longer primarily concerned with political parties and state institutions and markets or the role they play in adjudicating grievances, organizing interests, and stabilizing democracy.[23] Old distinctions between left and right are seen by many as having lost their salience.[24] New social movements resist the need for rigorous worldviews in favor of a soft humanism. They make their "subpolitics" in the streets by employing new forms of coalition building, protests intent on "blocking" entrenched interests, and new forms of publicity in raising new demands. The status quo must now face the decentralizing demands of the new social movements, with their new set of postmodern and "postmaterialist" agendas.

Institutional issues collapse into the preoccupation with everyday life, politics blends into culture, and bureaucratically organized "interest groups" become identified with the movements whose concerns they institutionally express.[25] Modernity is seen as fostering individualization even as it generates ways of undermining it through bureaucracy and the commodity form. New ecological threats to the planet intensify the self-critical tendencies within every facet of what has been called the "risk society." A new mentality, concerned less with dogma than with a basic humanism, makes itself felt among the new social movements: it is seemingly no accident that the more recent expressions of nonviolent revolution, which extend from the triumph of "people power" in the Philippines to the assault on communism in Eastern Europe, should have been unmistakably influenced by the 1960s. The freeing of individual needs becomes the new object of emancipatory concern for a new form of "reflexive" modernity.[26]

For all that, however, there is nothing inherently progressive about the new social movements. The largest of them embrace a reactionary religious fundamentalism. They oppose freedom with respect to lifestyles, and they

23. Ibid., 142 ff.
24. Anthony Giddens, *Beyond Left and Right: The Future of Radical Politics* (Stanford: Stanford University Press, 1994). For an alternative argument, which is far more persuasive, see Norberto Bobbio, *Left and Right: The Significance of a Political Distinction*, trans. Allan Cameron (Chicago: University of Chicago Press, 1997).
25. Beck, *The Reinvention of Politics*, 94 ff.
26. Ulrich Beck, "The Reinvention of Politics: Towards a Theory of Reflexive Modernization," in Ulrich Beck, Anthony Giddens, and Scott Lash, *Reflexive Modernization: Politics, Tradition, and Aesthetics in the Modern Social Order* (Stanford: Stanford University Press, 1994).

explicitly reject secular humanism. It is simply arbitrary to identify "social movements" with a certain political tendency and forget about those of a reactionary sort ranging from the Christian Coalition to the militias and the Islamic Brotherhood. Terms like *left* and *right* indeed remain essential precisely in order to distinguish between social movements themselves. The new social movements are not only, or even primarily, concerned with "postmaterialist" values. Many do not inherently oppose growth, and they are not always fundamentally composed of middle-class constituencies.[27] Voting rights and day care are not postmaterialist concerns; ecological devastation threatens the planet; and the interests of working people are enmeshed with the activities of many new social movements.

A "capacity for self-organization" may define the new politics. But it is illusory to suggest, with Ulrich Beck, that the "prevailing objective constraints have begun to crumble." Quite the contrary. Attempting to understand the politics of the new social movements without reference to organizations, institutional arrangements, and attendant imbalances of power is self-defeating. Not only powerful corporations but also grassroots movements will take the form of "interest groups" in the American political contest. It does not matter whether the interest group is constituted by women, people of color, or gays. It is, indeed, dangerous to ignore the dynamics of bureaucracy described by Max Weber.[28]

Every organization seeks to maximize the interests of its constituency, and interest groups with smaller constituencies with detailed agendas, and great economic resources, will fare far better than large constituencies with broad programs and less economic power. Each also gains a vested interest in maintaining both its own autonomy and the fragmentation of progressive forces, less because of any prior commitment to the liberation of subjectivity than because of the self-perpetuating dynamics of bureaucracy. It is naive to uncritically celebrate the proliferation of ever more groups, which supposedly encompass multiple and increasingly particular forms of oppression, without recognizing the institutional dynamics of interest groups or the fragmenting logic of identity politics within the market economy. Particularist agendas, ideologically justified and organizationally reinforced, turn the whole of progressive forces into less than the sum of its parts. New social

27. Habermas, *Theory of Communicative Action*, 2:392 ff.
28. Max Weber, *Economy and Society*, ed. Guenther Roth and Claus Wittich (Berkeley: University of California Press, 1978), 941 ff., 956 ff., 1111 ff., 1158 ff.

movements will indeed sooner or later have to deal critically with the ideologies inspiring them and begin to contemplate the need for new bureaucratic alliances in order to affect the determination of who gets what, when, and how.

PLURALISM AND INTERESTS

New social movements may consider themselves innovative insofar as they focus on what were previously understood as nonpolitical issues. But there is a sense in which the primacy of the "nonpolitical" has been part and parcel of the American political system from the very beginning. Constitutional limits on state power, checks and balances, made the United States a beacon for political dissidents throughout the twentieth century. Its fragmented political system with its weak political parties, its single-member congressional districts in which the winner takes all, created a favorable institutional context wherein the new social movements could organize themselves and their interests could receive articulation. "Pluralist" thinkers of the 1950s and early 1960s, in fact, saw the ability to generate a multiplicity of "private" interests in public ways as the primary institutional safeguard against totalitarianism and the defining characteristic of American democracy.[29] Nevertheless, they tended to denigrate questions dealing with class politics and institutionally reinforced imbalances of social and economic power.

Pluralism institutionally expresses what has been called "the end of ideology."[30] It begins with interests and the "interest group," which itself is generally defined as a mechanical aggregation of shared individual concerns, takes center stage. Political mobilization occurs through the "interest group," whose primary goal is the translation of demands into legislation and the gaining of private benefits from public resources. Commitment to any particular group can be motivated by either moral or material interests. But those who share a common concern on any given issue will find them-

---

29. David Truman, *The Governmental Process* (New York: Knopf, 1951); Robert A. Dahl and Charles E. Lindblom, *Politics, Economics, and Welfare: Planning and Politics in Economic Systems Resolved into Basic Social Processes* (New York: Harper, 1953); Robert A. Dahl, *Who Governs?: Democracy and Power in an American City* (New Haven: Yale University Press, 1961).

30. Daniel Bell, *The End of Ideology: On the Exhaustion of Political Ideas in the Fifties* (New York: Collier, 1961).

selves in disagreement on another. Extending support for any particular issue and engaging in constantly shifting coalitions are the strategies generally pursued by interest groups. This makes "success" dependent upon an efficient bureaucratic structure, resources, effective leaders, commitment to a particular set of goals, and willingness to accept "partial" victories. Interest groups almost spontaneously embrace the "rules of the game"; and, almost by definition, they pursue a politics of reasonable compromise or "mutual adjustment."[31]

Pluralism is a modern, technocratic expression of liberalism. Procedures take precedence over substantive ends, interest groups turn structural into instrumental problems, and various institutional filters tend to determine what becomes an "issue" in the first place.[32] Politics thereby becomes depoliticized; it turns into a function of what David Truman called "specialized experiences and selective perceptions." The sheer multiplicity of groups, along with the existence of overlapping loyalties, supposedly weakens the power of any particular group and any particular ideology. "Potential" interests may always loom on the horizon. But, clearly, legitimate interests are only those recognized within an overriding consensus. Or, putting it another way, problems are recognized as such only when they become problems for the mainstream. The built-in parochialism of this standpoint indeed initially made things difficult for nontraditional constituencies concerned with fostering racial justice, sexual equality, and a critique of technological progress.

Democracy is understood by pluralists as a complicated interplay between elites and masses or between "autonomy and control."[33] Many pluralists oppose increased participation by the base because their principal agent for political action, the interest group, must make use of political professionals whose concerns and style are very much at variance with "the grass roots." Interest groups routinize the romanticism inspiring the initial creation of the mass movement, and they also have an interest in maintaining their autonomy. They inherently seek to perpetuate themselves and privilege the issue with which they are concerned beyond any calls for a broader organizational unity.

---

31. Charles E. Lindblom, *The Intelligence of Democracy: Decision Making through Mutual Adjustment* (New York: Free Press, 1965).

32. Peter Bachrach and Morton S. Baratz, *Power and Poverty: Theory and Practice* (New York: Oxford University Press, 1970).

33. Robert A. Dahl, *Dilemmas of Pluralist Democracy: Autonomy vs. Control* (New Haven: Yale University Press, 1982).

Pluralism surely underestimates the difficulties in the process whereby "potential" interest can become legitimate. It ignores qualitative differences between them. It seeks to disempower any single faction, even if it should constitute the great majority of those without "property," in the name of preventing the centralization of unaccountable power or political authoritarianism. It dampens the spirit of democratic mobilization. But it also illuminates how the American system has been able to preserve democracy and hinder structural reform at the same time. Pluralism highlights the inherent tensions between any bureaucratic interest group and the mass base it claims to represent far better than the uncritical advocates of identity politics. Its assumptions help explain the workings of the system and the lack of a broader unity between progressive organizations. Its logic clarifies the ways in which interest groups break down ideological coherence, undercut the creation of consistent platforms, generate a discourse of otherness predicated on concrete interests, and thereby "cut across" the most profound "cleavage" of the production process: class.

THE OTHER AND ITS DISCONTENTS

The discourse of otherness has, globally and locally, led to a political dead end. The fragmentation of the left is obvious for anyone with eyes to see: particular interests are increasingly obscuring common needs. And it has given rise to much discussion. But there should be no misunderstanding: the issue is not simply the "inclusion" of the Other into the liberal state, the "recognition" of the Other, or the ability to "exercise" constitutional rights in order to learn from the Other.[34] It is rather a matter of identifying the terms in which a certain unity of the exploited can take place against prevailing inequities, a new perspective could be developed in order to contest particularism, and—finally—a new sentiment might be generated capable of fostering the will to appropriate contributions from diverse cultures in a new way.

These are the genuinely radical questions and, in the first instance, the difficulty in dealing with them derives from current ideological tendencies that employ existential categories to address social and political problems.

---

34. Jürgen Habermas, *Die Einbeziehung des Anderen: Studien zur politischen Theorie* (Frankfurt am Main: Suhrkamp, 1997), 128 ff., 154 ff., 237 ff.

A critical theory of politics must highlight the difference. From an existential perspective, or an ontological position, each is Other to someone else regardless of gender or color or sexual orientation: woman can be Other to woman and male person of color Other to male person of color. In political or social terms, however, otherness becomes defined from the perspective of groups and thereby takes on a binary, more narrow, and arbitrary form: just as woman is Other to man, so is black to white, gay to straight, and the Orient to the Occident. The Other becomes the excluded; it inherently connotes oppression and exploitation.

A stance of this sort excludes the possibility of being simultaneously dominant and Other insofar as it mechanically distinguishes the "markers" of identity and it refuses to determine which is paramount in what setting. No criteria are provided for determining whether a male person of color is subaltern to a woman worker and, in practical terms, whose interests should take primacy when they conflict. Consequently, too often the introduction of the Other generates a form of conceptual violence in which reason is sacrificed to personal "experience." The Other fragments: the possibility for building solidarity between groups flounders on the reef of multiple discourses, multiple identities, and multiple organizations intent on privileging their multiple constituencies.

Karl Marx believed that capitalism would ultimately eliminate all classes other than the bourgeoisie and the proletariat. Certainly premodern prejudices and racism would divide the working class and inhibit its revolutionary development. But, for all that, Marx would still have probably agreed with market advocates like Milton Friedman and Joseph Schumpeter that the logic of the market, or the "commodity form," would introduce a new mind set guided by a fundamentally instrumental rationality. Each of these thinkers held a certain unilinear understanding of historical development. Also, in a way, each underestimated the structural impact premodern ideas could have in modern society. There can be little doubt that prejudice against any group undermines the ability of its members to sell and buy "labor power" on the market: it subverts the ability of certain individuals to act as producers and consumers; it denigrates them as citizens; and it intrudes upon their autonomy.

Capitalism can accommodate a variety of solutions to issues dealing with racism, sexism, and ecology. Movements have been able to introduce formal equality in any number of ways, to close the income gap between black and white members of the "middle class," and to reorganize the nuclear family;[35] certain incentives have even been used to guide the creation of technology capable of dealing with threats to the ecological health of the planet. But there is no need to believe that such developments are the necessary outcomes of capitalism or modernity. Other outcomes are equally possible. Ideological commitments and material interests, such as "creationism" and the gun lobby, can perpetuate premodern attitudes. New social movements must now decide whether the quest for material equality, an institutional expansion of democracy, and internationalism are intrinsic elements of their enterprises. Only with the ethical decision to make such issues part of the agenda in the first place does it become essential for them to consider their connection with class concerns.

Mechanical attempts to connect them are doomed to failure, and not merely for epistemological reasons. The new social movements privilege recognition, and class politics aims at redistribution. It is possible to envision a "bivalent" conception of justice incorporating both without privileging either: "participatory parity" might then be gained through the distribution of equal resources among groups and the creation of cultural conditions for assuring mutual esteem among them.[36] But movements concerned with recognition are usually ideologically organized in transclass terms with an eye on particular interests, which are often endangered by broader and more universal forms of political mobilization; redistributive movements, on the other hand, usually respond to the production process and maintain a commitment to generalizable interests. This incommensurability is rarely taken into account, and, if only for this reason, the transformative moment in such bivalent theories tends to vanish: they offer no way of confronting the divisions between new social movements and class movements in practice.

Terms of judgment are also lacking when issues concerning redistribution and recognition conflict. American unions accommodated and benefited from segregation during the 1920s and 1930s, and in numerous cases, separatist arguments were forwarded in order to raise issues dealing with the oppression of particular groups. It is possible to demand "critical support" for the one or the other. But the terms in which such support should be determined are never articulated. The same problems arise when it is a matter of choosing whether class or identity, redistribution or recognition, must

---

35. Stephanie Koonz, *The Way We Really Are: Coming to Terms with America's Changing Families* (New York: Basic Books, 1997).

36. See Nancy Fraser, *Justice Interruptus: Critical Reflections on the "Postsocialist" Condition* (New York: Routledge, 1997).

take priority. Attempts to produce a "bivalent" conception of justice—one that refuses to offer conditions for privileging either class or identity, the cosmopolitan or the provincial, the liberal or the communitarian, unions or interests—are of interest only from the purely metaphysical standpoint. They shatter once political events come into play.

A brief look at the conflicts that occurred in the Ocean Hill–Brownsville neighborhood of Brooklyn in 1968[37]—a situation that anticipated the collapse of the New Left—offers an illustrative case in point. A group of self-selected representatives of a primarily black community sought control over both the choice of teachers and curriculum in its schools. This would, of course, have set a precedent for current demands by the Christian Coalition to determine what is taught and who teaches in white reactionary localities. In any event, the teachers' union led by Albert Shanker, with a heavily Jewish clientele, resisted what it saw as an incursion into its control over the work process. The old civil rights coalition exploded: blacks became pitted against Jews, community against unions, identity against class. It is easy to say in retrospect that just a bit of compromise on both sides would have settled the issue. Given the heightened tensions, however, such a compromise was impossible. It was necessary to privilege one side and one set of values over another. It was a moment of decision.

Enough fine thinkers have remained content simply to insist upon the need to embrace both universalism *and* particularism, community *and* labor, interest groups *and* unions, identity *and* class. But this is to pretend that profound differences of material, ideological, and bureaucratic interest are relatively minor. It is to ignore the manner in which they are not merely mechanical, or instrumental, but rather take on a life of their own. The quest for "recognition" or affirmative action can, as is the case with certain trends within the African American and women's movements, generate a demand for "redistribution." But there is no reason that it must. Nationalism or parochialism will not somehow "dialectically" turn into internationalism and cosmopolitanism. The criterion for privileging either identity or class in a given situation is the extent to which highlighting the one would speculatively allow for furthering the concerns of the other: the anti-Semitism fostered in Ocean Hill–Brownsville would, in this vein, have rendered any form of sustained and interracial class action impossible. Support for the unions would, at least in principle, have allowed for the possibility of raising community concerns in the future.

---

37. Maurice R. Berube and Marilyn Gitell, eds., *Confrontation at Ocean Hill–Brownsville: The New York School Strikes of 1968* (New York: Praeger, 1969).

Marx and his socialist followers surely underestimated the contributions made by separate transclass organizations, and the labor movement has been most culturally retrograde where the emphasis on redistributive demands was most exclusive. By the same token, however, cultural self-expression in terms of identity claims has often exacerbated political disunity among workers, thereby strengthening capital. Indeed, this is precisely what explains the current paradoxical situation in which cultural and political progress by previously neglected groups has accompanied an overriding economic assault upon workers and the welfare policies of an interventionist state.

The new social movements have been unable—and, more important, unwilling—to address this contradiction. Trapped within a particularism of their own making, intent on identifying cultural with political issues, the ideology of the new social movements inhibits their conceptual encounter with a class-based economy. Embracing a logic of fragmentation and insisting upon an ever greater specification of transclass identity claims, they find it ever more difficult to develop a unified response to the structural inequities of a system in which serving the economic interest of capital is still the precondition for serving all other economic interests. The extent to which gender and race become "wedge" issues is the extent to which cultural matters supersede economic concerns. It has indeed become a matter of contesting what has appropriately been called the "law of displacement," whereby symbolic concerns substitute themselves for material issues.[38] The disenfranchised and exploited ever more surely find themselves fighting over form while forgetting about content. For all that, however, content retains its salience. Now more than ever, critical political theory must begin to refocus on capitalism with an eye on the ideological and organizational values necessary to contest it.

GLOBALIZATION AND CAPITALISM

Globalization is perhaps the most widely discussed and least understood phenomenon of the last quarter of the twentieth century.[39] It has been iden-

---

38. Russell Jacoby, *Dogmatic Wisdom: How the Culture Wars Divert Education and Distract America* (New York: Doubleday, 1994), xii.

39. Useful introductions to the concept are provided by Ulrich Beck, *Was ist Globalisierung?* (Frankfurt am Main: Suhrkamp, 1997); Saskia Sassen, *Globalization and Its Discontents* (New York: New Press, 1995); and Malcolm Waters, *Globalization* (London: Routledge, 1995).

tified with new forms of communication, new transnational fiscal institutions, new modes of capital accumulation, new types of modernization, and more esoteric concerns. In general, however, social scientific analysis of globalization has been remarkably impoverished because the requirements for a political response to its more debilitating effects rarely surface. It is indeed probably best to consider the phenomenon in the following way:[40] the global system as it exists at the end of the twentieth century is not synonymous with global capitalism, but the dominant forces of global capitalism are the dominant forces in the global system; its building blocks are the transnational corporation, a still-evolving transnational capitalist class, and the wasteful culture of consumerism; consequently, any serious internationalist effort to further liberal socialism must target all three.

It is true enough that there is nothing automatic about globalization:[41] not all firms are transnational, many are local and regional, and policies enacted by local and regional institutions, influenced by local and regional expressions of the public sphere, can inhibit the globalization process. But it is also true that old geographical designations are increasingly losing their validity: it will make ever less sense to speak of North and South. What will remain is a planet punctuated by "black holes" of social exclusion. Extreme poverty is no longer spatially constrained in the manner of times past:

> It comprises large areas of the globe such as much of Sub-Saharan Africa, and impoverished rural areas of Latin America and Asia. But it is also present in literally every country, and every city, in this new geography of social exclusion. It is formed of American inner-city ghettos, Spanish enclaves of mass youth unemployment, French *banlieues* warehousing North Africans, Japanese Yoseba quarters, and Asian mega-cities' shanty towns. And it is populated by millions of homeless, incarcerated, prostituted, criminalized, brutalized, stigmatized, sick, and illiterate persons. They are the majority in some areas, the minority in others, and a tiny minority in a few privileged contexts. But, everywhere they are growing in number, and increasing in visibility, as the selective triage of informational capitalism, and the political breakdown of the welfare state intensify social exclusion.[42]

40. See the excellent essay by Leslie Sklair, "Social Movements and Global Capitalism," in *The Cultures of Globalization*, ed. Fredric Jameson and Masao Miyoshi (Durham: Duke University Press, 1998).

41. Ralf Dahrendorf, "Anmerkungen zur Globalisierung," in *Perspektiven der Weltgesellschaft*, hrsg. Ulrich Beck (Frankfurt am Main: Suhrkamp, 1998), 41 ff.

42. Castells, *The Information Age*, 3:164–65.

Capitalism has undergone a profound internal development: industrialism has been pushed to the margins of the world order, and a new form of global "informationism" has taken its formerly privileged position: telecommunications is conquering time and space; global financial networks are supplanting localized sources of capital; labor is becoming individualized and decentralized, thereby rendering collective bargaining ever more difficult; and working people are being polarized by the conflict between skilled labor and a generic form of expendable labor.[43] Traditional organs of popular resistance have been decimated, if not entirely broken, and utopian solutions have lost their mass appeal. Deindustrialization, coupled with the new mobility of multinational capital, has drastically weakened national unions, and class-specific parties are a thing of the past in advanced industrial societies. It is impossible to presuppose the will to resist, let alone the existence of class unity, in any meaningful form. The left is on the defensive, and contesting the power of capital has lost most of its existential appeal.

Interest in identity or "culture," however, does not obliterate the "inverted world" of capitalism and its structural imbalances of power.[44] Workers are still primarily a "cost of production." Technology still threatens jobs even as it offers the prospect of greater prosperity and leisure.[45] Investment still fuels employment, and capitalists must still reinvest at least part of their profit for research and development in order to produce more efficiently and ward off competitors. Appropriate levels of investment in the present still require the likelihood of appropriate profits in the future. Should instability exist, should workers make exorbitant demands, or should any set of circumstances arise in which profits are threatened, investment will slow or cease. Workers thus remain dependent upon the unaccountable actions of capitalists whose decisions are determined more by private advantage than any consideration of the public good.[46]

Economic laws may still produce the collapse of the capitalist system. But few any longer believe such a result is "inevitable," and contemporary radicals are no longer willing to develop a politics predicated on that assump-

---

43. Ibid., 3:342 ff.

44. Karl Marx, *Capital: A Critique of Political Economy*, trans. Samuel Moore and Edward Aveling (New York: International, 1967), 1:71 ff.

45. Note the discussion by Henry Pachter, "The Right to Be Lazy," in *Socialism in History: Political Essays of Henry Pachter*, ed. Stephen Eric Bronner (New York: Columbia University Press, 1984).

46. Joshua Cohen and Joel Rogers, *On Democracy: Toward A Transformation of American Society* (New York: Penguin, 1983), 47 ff.

tion. Independent social or economic trends no longer offer much hope. When the welfare state was still relatively unchallenged, for example, Jürgen Habermas and Claus Offe developed their argument that commodification was giving way to "decommodification."[47] Capitalism was seemingly undermining its own assumptions; and, in the future, labor power would increasingly withdraw from the market. But this prophecy has been contradicted by the drastic decline of unions during the 1980s as well as the trend toward "privatization" advanced by a triumphant conservatism. It is no longer even possible to presuppose the existence of a "welfare" state, let alone the future elimination of labor's dependence on market uncertainties: Franklin Delano Roosevelt or Leon Blum look more radical than ever in the light of the most recent conservative onslaught. The patronizing attitude with which so many radicals thought of such figures in the 1960s and 1970s, the sense that all this was "just" liberalism or "just" social democracy, makes even less sense now in a new planetary context than it did when economic growth more or less automatically guaranteed an improvement in the lives of working people.

THE QUEST FOR UNITY

There is an obvious pressing concern for "democratic coordination" among progressive forces.[48] And this is true both globally and locally. Such coordination can involve unifying interest groups, each intent on preserving autonomy, in single-issue coalitions. In lieu of other effective forms of political organizing, of course, these undoubtedly have their place. Given the sheer number of coalitions battling for resources, however, it remains enormously difficult to sustain interest and commitment. Embracing this form of politics uncritically also puts off dealing with a situation in which bureaucratically organized groups have an institutional interest in autonomy and the social movements they represent are enmeshed in an ideological politics of frag-

47. Habermas, *Theory of Communicative Action*, 2:374 ff.; Claus Offe, *Disorganized Capitalism*, ed. John Keane (Cambridge: MIT Press, 1985), 101–28. For a critical discussion, see Adam Przeworski, *The State and the Economy under Capitalism* (London: Harwood, 1975), 73 ff.
48. The associative and public presumptions for "democratic coordination" are discussed, from the standpoint of a discourse ethic, in Joshua Cohen, "Deliberation and Democratic Legitimacy," in *The Good Polity*, ed. A. Hamlin and B. Petit (Oxford: Blackwell, 1989).

mentation. Critical political theory must confront issues of this sort more directly: it is necessary to highlight the liberal and socialist values underpinning any creative reconstruction of progressive politics and the urgency of formulating a new internationalist perspective for the future.

Unity is the precondition for any assault on capital and authoritarian political institutions. But self-interest is not as glaringly obvious or readily identifiable as many would like to believe. Not all individuals working with existing interest groups or social movements have an interest in rendering capital accountable, and not all working people have an interest in embracing policies with respect to race and gender. It is simply foolish to expect fragmented and diverse constituencies simply to rally around an arbitrarily determined list of prefabricated legislative proposals, most of which are the products of the liberal and socialist traditions anyway, and then reject the ideological struggle by making reference to an outworn rhetoric of American nationalism.[49]

Such "pragmatic" thinking remains mixed in simple coalition politics, and it ignores the problems associated with this traditional strategy. Its understanding of group interests, capitalism, and the prerequisites for unity is also impoverished. Material interest offers merely the prospect of tactical unity: interest groups will always prove susceptible to the moral economy of the separate deal, and without an ideologically motivated base, this instrumental undertaking will politically produce, at best, a degenerate version of the Popular Front or a weak attempt to recreate the Democratic Party of the 1960s. It is impossible to ignore the way in which, internationally and domestically, the power of capital rests on the ideological and organizational divisions among workers. It is also necessary to confront, ideologically and organizationally, the lack of solidarity or, better, the unwillingness to embrace the ideological implications without which political unity becomes impossible.

Nothing happens ex nihilo: it is necessary to begin where the most radical organizational possibility ended for furthering the idea of freedom. The current situation, in which political parties are losing their character and progressive interest groups are under attack, makes it necessary in the United States to reconsider the unfulfilled promise of the Civil Rights Movement and the Poor People's Movement it spawned. These movements were fueled

---

49. See Richard Rorty, *Achieving Our Country: Leftist Thought in Twentieth-Century America* (Cambridge: Harvard University Press, 1998).

by idealism. Both harbored a strong liberal commitment to "rights"; and, if the Civil Rights Movement retained a certain socialist sensibility, the Poor People's Movement was clearly an attempt to provide the substitute for a social democratic labor movement. A new *mass association* hovered between its constituent interests and a new political alternative to the Democratic Party in the United States when Martin Luther King met his death in 1968.

A bit more than twenty years later, Eastern Europe, galvanized by the catalytic efforts of small groups of intellectuals, unionists, and concerned citizens, witnessed the effect of various national mass associations in the overthrow of communism. Neither in the United States nor in Eastern Europe, other than in the Czech Republic, would they survive. What had been true for the Poor People's Movement and the Rainbow Coalition was also true of the Civic Forum in East Germany. These mass associations were unable to sustain themselves without turning into new political parties or lobbying associations capable of influencing existing political parties. Yet they fostered the creative friction, discussed earlier, between the need for bureaucracy and the demands for participation. They also projected a politics intent on working both inside and outside existing institutions.

It is simply irresponsible for progressive undertakings in political theory to avoid what Lenin called the "organizational question" and refuse to speculate upon the preconditions for a new movement. Any such organization will be composed of diverse interest groups, and the concerns of each of them must obviously receive adequate and fair representation. This alone makes it necessary for each of its component groups to transcend their own particularism. Especially in the current ideological context, however, such an undertaking will call for legitimation in more than purely instrumental terms. Only with the prior acceptance of an ethical commitment to confront the workings of capitalism does it make sense to speak about general organizing principles and ways of overcoming "cross-cutting cleavages" of race and sex without forgetting their importance.

Class is naturally what these cleavages are cutting across, and in the process it is being obliterated, both analytically and politically. A critical theory of politics must reinstate the category not in order to remain orthodox or true to socialist or communist traditions but simply because conditions of class exploitation still exist, both globally and locally. There is no avoiding the obvious: class structures cannot be contested in the absence of class politics. And class politics requires class values. The question revolves around the meaning of class in the modern era. It can no longer be predicated on historical teleology, viewed as one "variable" among others, or grounded in the "objective" underpinnings of "science." Class must instead be primarily understood as a transformative concept: the category with which to define the common concerns of working people within each of the new social movements without privileging the demands of any.[50]

THE CLASS IDEAL AND PROGRESSIVE POLITICS

Marx fused the empirical, structural, and speculative—or political—notions of class in his teleological theory. He believed that capitalist society would empirically generate a steadily growing industrial proletariat, structurally defined by the sale of its labor power, which would politically view itself and its party as the only agent capable of creating a new socialist order.[51] But this unity of the empirical, the structural, and the speculative has been shattered. The industrial proletariat no longer provides an adequate correlative for the working class; those "selling their labor power" include even wealthy executives; and the teleological foundations for class consciousness have collapsed. Empirical notions of class have become too narrow, the structural view appears woefully indeterminate, and class solidarity has lost its "objective" foundation.

Only an ethical emphasis upon the ideal of class unity can demarcate the common interests of those working people divided in separate interest groups seeking to contest the imbalances of power in the capitalist economy. Such a stance breaks with orthodoxy but not with tradition: highlighting the ethical moment of class unity provides the same immanent critique of Marx that Marx launched against Hegel and Hegel used against Kant. The class ideal confronts the "objective" perspective offered by "scientific socialism" with an ethical claim, teleological guarantees with contingency, and the primacy of the economic with the primacy of the political. It projects "class" less as a prescribed attribute of production than a speculative category necessary for making sense of its effects.

The *class ideal* is an inherently critical concept with positive, or recon-

---

50. Note the more complete discussion contained in Stephen Eric Bronner, *Socialism Unbound* (New York: Routledge, 1990), 161 ff.
51. Ibid., 10 ff.

structive, underpinnings. It has nothing in common with the new ways of "thinking" offered by Nietzsche, Heidegger, and Derrida, which share a fascination with what amounts to little more than revelation, and it is instead boldly logocentric and universalistic. The class ideal specifies the structure of the modern production process, along with its two major actors, and it challenges the "inverted world" of capitalism in which working people are treated as the object and capital as the subject of its activities. It contests the arbitrary use of power, and it insists upon the need to establish a plausible connection between means and ends. It critically appropriates the contributions of the new social movements and the participatory concerns so prominent in the anarchist tradition. Nevertheless, its principled commitment to public aims is framed in terms of the values associated with liberalism, socialism, and internationalism. It therefore builds upon the principled commitment to public aims and the major influences upon progressive politics: liberalism, socialism, and internationalism.

Turning class into a primarily ethical notion, subordinating its economic to its political meaning, is a radical move. This does not involve simply forgetting about the empirical or structural elements of "class." But it does call for privileging the normative purpose of class analysis rather than simply engaging in empirical or structural investigations for their own sake. It highlights the need to resurrect the link between class analysis and class action. The class ideal speculatively projects the possibility of socialist practice and the preconditions for its success. Its metaphysical character thus retains a materialist purpose. Indeed, following Rousseau, the category seeks "to unite what right sanctions with what is prescribed by interest, in order that justice and utility may in no case be divided."[52]

The class ideal is, like all regulative ideas, a philosophical tool whose critical power and political efficacy are completely contingent in an already disenchanted world. The class ideal cannot provide the existential self-confidence, the clear-cut sense of purpose, or the ability to command sacrifice of religious ideologies. But its lack of certainty, its inability to guarantee the realization of its judgments, reflects the real situation on the left. It would be disingenuous to artificially recreate the sense of certainty associated with times past. The left is on the defensive in practice, and it would only be self-defeating to deny this in theory.

---

52. Jean-Jacques Rousseau, "The Social Contract," in *The Social Contract and Discourses*, trans. G. D. H. Cole (London: J. M. Dent, 1973), 165.

Progressives must confront the current political *identity deficit* without illusions. Nothing any longer "inevitably" predetermines their success or even acceptance of the class ideal. Their undertaking rests on postulates rather than ontological foundations. It must assume a certain notion of the individual subject, and it must militate against treating individuals as a cost of production. It must thus presuppose a certain principled commitment to the dignity of the subject as well as the capacity for reflection upon which any possibility for democracy or ethical judgment is based. It must indeed still aim to subordinate an alienated history made behind the backs of people, or what Hegel called the "cunning of history," to the democratic will of the international community.

Progressives should also recognize that the freedom of the subject is irreconcilable with any regime and any system. An inherent tension exists between organizational demands and individual desires no less than, especially under conditions of scarcity in which nature is endangered, the social needs for efficiency and the individual concerns with creativity. It is, in short, impossible to deny the asymptotic relationship between regulative ideals and the world in which they function. The idea that socialism constitutes nothing more than an emancipatory alternative to the given system is a fiction. Those committed to progressive politics will have to deal with a situation in which the welfare state remains a capitalist state, investment remains in private hands, and reforms are possible only if their costs do not overly threaten the existing accumulation process or an acceptable rate of profits for the capitalist class. They will have to face the reality in which it will remain much easier for elites than for the poor to organize themselves, define the agenda, unify on issues, gain access to information, and raise funds for political purposes. They will also have to recognize that some institutions and policies surely foster individual autonomy better than others and contest the unnecessary constraints on liberty. A new progressive movement must prize the self-conscious attempt to expand the arena of individual choice. Thus, the need for a criterion of political judgment.

This criterion will have little "scientific" or ontological justification; its legitimation can derive neither from the fact that it exists prior to politics nor from the fact that it stands embedded within the organic tradition of a community. Instead, the justification for this criterion should prove at once logical, historical, speculative, and political: logical insofar as any emancipatory order presupposes its existence; historical insofar as it confronts past forms of political practice with its emancipatory purpose; speculative insofar as it provides a critical vantage point for judging the emancipatory quality of any given proposal; and political insofar as it informs an organizing principle to contest the substantive and formal structures of repression. *The principle of democratic accountability* meets these needs: democracy is logically impossible without it; the bureaucratic petrification of the communist and socialist movements are contested by it; reforms and institutional changes gain their normative value from it; and any organizational attempt to move beyond the fragments on the left presupposes it.

The principle of democratic accountability is derived from the liberal rule of law, and it speaks to the constriction of arbitrary power. Though liberalism need not generate socialism or a confrontation with the inequities of the capitalist production process, it is impossible to consider socialism without reference to its liberal foundations. The proponents of the new social movements were correct in demanding that the elimination of racism, sexism, and the like not be left to a truncated dialectic of history or await the creation of a classless society. Contesting capital and democratically determining public priorities, from the vantage point of the class ideal and what might be termed "liberal socialism," is possible only under conditions of interclass unity. Such unity presupposes a respect for formal democratic values and procedures with respect to the Other. Precisely because it has become impossible to rely upon teleology, within the existing constraints, a new progressive movement must prefigure the emancipatory outcome it seeks to realize.

The old verities have passed into the mist of history: the end no longer justifies the means. Revolution has lost its self-evident emancipatory content, and it is no longer possible to assume that reforms will somehow "evolve" in an uninterrupted fashion or culminate in socialism: a new approach toward these conflicting political strategies has become necessary. Excluding from "socialism" anything other than a revolutionary assault on the existing accumulation process and the state is self-defeating: the infantile romanticism, which shuts its eyes to the terrible implications of revolution, is simply a form of dogma. But there is also a reformist dogma. Its partisans identify politics with their particular organization, success with their legislative activities, and freedom with the liberal status quo. They embrace compromise, though their clientele will always foot the bill; they trumpet their "reasonableness" to ward off potentially more radical action from below; they lay claim to "pragmatism" when ideological issues are raised; and they always ignore the alienation and the political disillusionment they foster.

Revolution has lost its teleological priority: it is no longer the "categorical imperative" with which to judge the value of any given political engagement in the present.[53] The only justification for revolution is a context in which the principle of accountability is completely lacking and in which a mass sentiment is palpably directed against palpably corrupt institutions. In the same vein, however, the meaning and value of a reform depends upon the conditions in which it is instituted. As much as any new progressive movement must make reference to institutions and legislation, its ideology must highlight the need to bring people into the streets, raise expectations, and expose the inherently unfinished character of freedom.

There is a sense, however, in which any new progressive movement must appear far more modest than that of the old. There are no longer the great demonstrations or the red flags flying everywhere on the first of May. There are no longer the seemingly invincible proletarian parties of times past. All of this might appear in a new form, and a critical political theory must work for that possibility. But the existing conditions of political fragmentation and ideological confusion are impossible to avoid. History has gone its own way, and socialism has lost its objective foundation. Thus, strangely enough, the speculative use of the class ideal for progressive politics ultimately becomes justified on materialist grounds.

INTERNATIONALISM AND THE COSMOPOLITAN SENSIBILITY

The "world" looked different in the last century, and it will, perhaps, look even more different in the next. Incredible explorations of outer space and remarkable parapsychological investigations of the inner mind will take place. Maps will change. Some nations will disappear and others will emerge. Old battles within and between nation-states will overlap with new conflicts between regional institutions and between regional institutions and the United Nations. The culture industry will extend its reach, diversify its products, and still render all forms of "authentic" national or ethnic culture fit only for the museum, the parade ground, or the hidden restaurant. Old-fashioned disparities between wealth and poverty will change; it will seem ever less useful to focus on purely national issues. People will ever more surely be called upon to make sense of their world in terms of a planetary

53. Georg Lukács, "Tactics and Ethics," in *Political Writings, 1919–1929*, ed. Rodney Livingstone, trans. Michael McColgan (London: New Left, 1972), 3 ff.

life. But that will be no easy task. Such an endeavor offers new challenges for political theory in the twenty-first century: it calls for inaugurating a new internationalist perspective informed by liberal-socialist values and a new view of the "canon" infused with a cosmopolitan sensibility.

Internationalism still offers something fresh. Perhaps that is because it has always been taken far less seriously by progressive movements than their partisans would care to believe: The First International saw its undertakings subverted by ill-fated calls for decentralization; the Second International had no effective sanctions for combating the pursuit of national interests by its members; and the Third International obeyed the commands of the Soviet Union.[54] The contradiction is glaring: whereas an earlier international labor movement with strong ideological claims lacked the institutions necessary for the democratic resolution of grievances and effective pursuit of policies, today, progressives find themselves without a genuinely internationalist movement and with a set of essentially bourgeois international institutions whose claims on the loyalty of citizens is incomparably weak.

There should be no misunderstanding: globalization is not internationalism.[55] Quite the contrary. An internationalism informed by liberal-socialist values, in fact, harbors the only viable progressive response to the globalizing social and economic trends of our time: transnational organizations are increasingly evidencing their bureaucratic interest in becoming autonomous from their member states; economic oligarchy, managerial authority, and class formation are already occurring on a transnational plane; cultural styles and information are no longer confined by national borders. It will become increasingly necessary for international organizations to guarantee rights in the administrative state, the sovereignty of territory, collective identity, and perhaps even the democratic legitimation of the nation-state.[56] Unfortunately, however, the "subjective" response to an ever more surely "objective" situation is lacking on the part of the exploited and disempowered. Their experience is obviously situated in time and space: they have also, for better and for worse, been socialized in the most divergent cultures. The

---

54. Michael Forman, *Nationalism and the International Labor Movement* (University Park: Pennsylvania State University Press, 1998).

55. Daniel Singer, Whose Millennium? Theirs or Ours? New York: Monthly Review, 1999, pgs. 186ff.

56. Jürgen Habermas, "Die postnationale Konstellation und die Zukunft der Demokratie," in *Die postnationale Konstellation: Politische Essays* (Frankfurt am Main: Suhrkamp, 1998), 105 ff.

particular is an ineradicable element of the universal, just as the ethnic is of the national and the national is of the international: the question is what value the particular retains from an internationalist perspective.

There is nothing "risky" about the new postmodern interpretations of cosmopolitanism and internationalism: no serious expression of either ever simply wished to liquidate the particular. It simply misses the point to talk about "pluralizing" cosmopolitanism in a postmodernist fashion, to qualify it with nationalism, or to "root" it in local traditions. These new interpretations simply pander to the political advocates of identity politics and blunt the critique—traditionally and legitimately—leveled by cosmopolitanism against the parochial, the confined, and the nationalistic.[57] Fashionable academic standpoints of this sort ignore internationalist traditions, and they refuse to consider the political impact their watered-down views might have on building commitments for burgeoning transnational movements and institutions. They also have little to offer for those who would move beyond purely formalistic views on internationalism or those comfortable postmodern and communitarian positions in which a lukewarm tolerance is extended to all cultures and the world is turned into a set of competing cultural ghettos.

In forging an alternative understanding of cosmopolitanism, there is perhaps more to be learned from the great modernist movements of the early twentieth century than from the politics of the labor internationals. Impressionism, postimpressionism, fauvism, cubism, expressionism, dada, and surrealism all self-consciously sought and used influences from Africa, Asia, and Latin America. Writers like Gide, Hesse, Malraux, and Tagore fused North and South and, often in spite of their own personal prejudices, brought to Europe a new cosmopolitan sensibility. But the left has grown more cautious as the right has grown more bold. Contrasts are necessary; challenges to the accepted Western frame of reference and encounters with intellectual traditions from diverse continents capable of contesting one another must be embraced not merely for the sake of "diversity" but in order to generate something new and appropriate to the emergent forms of planetary existence.

Otherwise progressive political forces are still enthralled by ethnic and nationalist sentiments while internationalism has been appropriated as a self-serving ideology by the bosses of the multinational corporations and the

---

57. Bruce Robbins, "Actually Existing Cosmopolitanisms," in *Cosmopolitics: Thinking and Feeling beyond the Nation*, ed. Peng Cheah and Bruce Robbins (Minneapolis: University of Minnesota Press, 1998), 2 and passim.

technocrats of the new transnational organizations. The irony of this situation is readily apparent. And costly, too. For in the present context, reinvigorating the ethical appeal of socialist beliefs in economic justice and liberal republican ideals will ever more surely depend upon reclaiming and reconstructing internationalism. Its modern postcommunist expression inherently presumes the liberal principles of reciprocity and, if internationalism is to have any meaning for the victims of imperialism, their economic empowerment as well. It must also effectively refer to the host of new transnational problems: human rights, regional imbalances of economic power, and the pollution of the planet. It is unnecessary to speak about a "grounding." Internationalism must, however, be infused with a new cultural attitude or sensibility. Indeed, as long as the notion is not inimically opposed to the benefits of discourse, it makes sense to speak of the need for a new form of "sentimental education."[58]

Cosmopolitanism completes and gives purpose to what Kant termed the "unwritten code" of constitutional liberalism and, logically, to socialism as well. Its sensibility projects an ethic with substance. It obviously embraces human rights. But it also demands more. It seeks the existence of political and economic conditions in which each can feel at home everywhere, each can enjoy the culture of the other, and each can move beyond what he or she thought were the limits of everyday experience. The *cosmopolitan sensibility* inherently contests the provincial and the limited. It celebrates a situation in which intermarriage, deracination, multilingual societies, and an intensified individualism are breaking down traditional forms of religious authority and those atavistic notions of "community" embraced with nostalgia by conservatives, communitarians, anarchists, and many postmodernists. It projects what has appropriately been termed a "melange effect."[59]

Suffocating walls of tradition are crumbling along with established understandings of community.[60] The issue is not whether the Other should be dealt with by forgetting differences in the fashion of the humanist or, whatever this means, *through* our differences.[61] An internationalism infused with

---

58. Richard Rorty, "Human Rights, Rationality, and Sentimentality," in *Truth and Progress: Philosophical Papers* (Cambridge: Cambridge University Press, 1998), vol. 3.

59. Jan Nederveen Pieterse, "Der Melange-Effect," in Beck, *Perspektiven der Weltgesellschaft*, 87 ff.

60. Uma Narayan, *Dislocating Cultures: Identities, Traditions, and Third-World Feminism* (New York: Routledge, 1997).

61. Kwame Anthony Appiah, "Cosmopolitan Patriots," in Cheah and Robbins, *Cosmopolitics*, 111.

a cosmopolitan sensibility presumes a certain capacity for empathy on the part of all individuals, beyond the constraints imposed by their race, gender, or "situation." It assumes the existence of cultural differences, and, from a critical standpoint, it celebrates the creative friction between the particular and the universal. It also assumes that politics cannot answer every existential question posed by life; and if it insists upon treating religious institutions like any others, it has nothing to say about genuine "religiosity" or issues like the existence of God.

New developments in the formation of an international civil society provide the material foundations for this new cosmopolitan sensibility. A new infrastructure of mobility and communication between peoples has generated new interests and new forms of curiosity. The loss of an absolute alternative to the status quo has also brought with it the loss of an absolute Other. The Other is no longer as foreign as it once was, and it will undoubtedly become even less so. The term itself borders on the anachronistic. Changes of this sort call for a new attitude beyond liberal and socialist commitments, an attitude simultaneously political and aesthetic, which will inspire citizens to search for ways of making their own culture comprehensible to others rather than using it as a form of security and exclusion.

THE CONTOURS OF PLANETARY LIFE

The past never entirely disappears: it will surely continue as a *residue* of nostalgic hopes, if not simply outworn prejudices, and a substitute for utopia. The secular problems of the coming age are complex, and those who cling to the past will cling to it all the more fanatically. The cosmopolitan sensibility is not enough: empowerment of the Other, of the immigrant, not merely in his or her own community or the state in the abstract[62] but within each of the innumerable Other communities, is increasingly becoming the only way to guarantee the recognition of his or her civil rights. The cosmopolitan sensibility must be secured through institutional and normative commitment. Without protection by the class ideal, without the formal liberal commitment to reciprocity and a socialist emphasis on material equality, it becomes just another justification for commodification and "McWorld": a manifestation of globalization, arguably, even more dangerous for Western democracy than fundamentalism.[63]

62. Habermas, *Die Einbeziehung des Anderen*, 143.
63. Benjamin R. Barber, *Jihad vs. McWorld* (New York: Times Books, 1995).

An internationalism inspired by a cosmopolitan sensibility should prove to be a theme for political theory in the next century precisely because it offers the most appropriate way of confronting globalization and other problems associated with what is rapidly becoming a new form of planetary life. Concern with the plight of people of color around the world has expressed itself in various ways relating to the structural inequities between North and South. A global women's movement has clearly emerged, with international conferences and international lobbying groups within the major transnational organizations. Ecological issues, in particular, require greater international collaboration, not less: they call for a strong international legal order to deal with acid rain, global warming, pollution of the seas, destruction of vegetation, and protection of animals and rare species. Various groups like Amnesty International, Greenpeace, and Medicine without Frontiers have gained force in an *international civil society* whose inhabitants are drawn ever closer by the information revolution and by conditions that call for them to stress human rights over particularism and equality over difference.

Trends within labor are creating similar needs. The contradiction between the increasing mobility of capital and the fixity of labor is becoming ever more pronounced. Immigration, intermarriage, religious pluralism, and a world culture are undermining national identities, along with the logic of fragmentation implicit within modernization itself. An increasingly hybrid labor force is, in short, increasing the heterogeneity within, and decreasing it between, particular nations.[64] And so, no less than on the domestic plane, classes and movements must coordinate their concerns in international terms. The political question for the next century is whether progressive political forces will prove capable of fighting for their interests within the new international institutions on the planetary stage.

Nationalism is still the ideology of our time. Entrenched bureaucracies of the nation-state still have an interest in perpetuating it. Outdated notions of national sovereignty and self-determination, atavistic traditions and customs, still have visceral appeal. It is a matter of generating new internationalist commitments to new institutions and the explicit attempt to fulfill the cosmopolitan possibilities projected by the technology of the future.

Organizations like the United Nations can alone adjudicate between con-

---

64. Nigel Harris, *National Liberation* (Reno: University of Nevada Press, 1990), 284.

flicting national claims, and legitimate concerns regarding the imbalances of power within these institutions will not change that. But practice seeks its expression in theory. The original connection between republicanism, national self-determination, and internationalism has been lost.[65] A critical theory of politics must reconstruct it in terms of a new speculative posture: support for national claims should ultimately rest on the degree to which they potentially facilitate the empowerment of international institutions predicated on liberal principles and socialist notions of economic justice. That these ideals might conflict says nothing about their validity. Ethics offers no formula for success: its desire for consistency is always thwarted by the conflicting pressures of reality.

Especially in this age of globalization, with its changes in migration patterns and the palpable need to ensure equitable wages as well as transnational standards of health and safety, critical political theory must forward a radical international vision of the liberal-socialist state. It alone can counter what is becoming an increasingly rigid disparity of wealth, power, and misery not only between continents but within continents, not only between regions but within regions, not only between states but within states, not only between cities but within cities.

Globalization has created the need for an international version of the New Deal. The future of such an enterprise depends upon the creation of a reinvigorated transnational labor movement with socialist values. It demands new institutions in which to operate, new transnational courts of justice with the ability to impose sanctions, and perhaps even new political parties of a transnational character in which citizens of different nations can vote in any number of national elections. Globalization has made it incumbent upon advocates of progressive politics to call for new controls on the movement of capital and a stable system of pegged exchange rates, curtailment of the debt-enforcement powers associated with the World Bank and the International Monetary Fund, and a commitment to rising wages and high employment. Growth directed toward repairing and protecting the environment should, indeed, become part of the next internationalist agenda on human rights.[66]

With the close of the cold war, it has perhaps finally become possible to

65. Micheline R. Ishay, *Internationalism and Its Betrayal* (Minneapolis: University of Minnesota Press, 1995).
66. Joanne Barkan, "The Old Welfare State in the New Age of Competition," *Dissent* (Winter 1995): 71 ff.

speak about a genuine "international community" and a new view of intervention in which national sovereignty has lost its absolute character: the international community under the aegis of the United Nations has increasingly taken upon itself the responsibility of calling for the introduction of human rights within states. New possibilities of "plural citizenship" and coordinated forms of proportional "refugee burden sharing" among nations also present themselves as possible solutions to some of the pressing problems connected with the new form of planetary life.[67] Support for developments of this sort is not necessarily required by discourse ethics or even as a consequence of the supposedly latent universal elements within new social movements,[68] let alone by some variant of "strategic essentialism." It is, instead, a practical prerequisite for any attempt to resist what has become a new transnational capitalist offensive.

Reforms of global magnitude presuppose the political power to enforce them: transnational organizations with teeth. Left at a purely administrative or technocratic level, internationalism will fail and the weakest will suffer the most. Even while fashionable theorists decry totalizing standpoints and fasten their eyes on particularist concerns, the need grows for an articulation of the liberal form, the socialist commitment, and the cosmopolitan substance of internationalism in the next century. This new internationalism will not prove reducible to any set of national claims or loyalties. It is not patriotism writ large any more than the family is the ethnic group writ small. It will neither simply abolish nor simply extend past ways of thinking about political history. It must instead reconfigure our understanding of human development into a form that is very different from the currently fashionable social history and oral history inspired by localism, community, and identity. This new internationalism calls for making sense of the past by viewing it through a universal lens. And there should be no mistake: "Universal history does not suppress the histories of individual nations, but tries to understand them as contributions to history in general. Just as one loses sight of the history of Sardinia after that kingdom fought for the unity of Italy, so the histories of Belgium, Holland, and Luxembourg will soon have

---

67. Peter H. Schuck, *Citizens, Strangers, and In-Betweens: Essays on Immigration and Citizenship* (Boulder: Westview, 1998), 217 ff., 282 ff.

68. See George Katsiaficas, "The Latent Universal within Identity Politics," *New Political Science*, nos. 38–39 (Winter–Spring 1997): 79 ff.

a merely provincial interest, and even the histories of greater countries will be submerged in the history of the development of the Common Market."[69]

The claim that only nationalism can grip the hearts of citizens is nonsense; the partisans of Judaism, Islam, and the Catholic Church know better. Enormous sacrifices, including often sacrifices of national identity, actually took place in all three of the internationals that marked the modern labor movement. Internationalism has its own history, which extends from Grotius and Kant to Paine and Marx, from Jean Jaurès and Rosa Luxemburg to Dag Hammerskjöld and Martin Luther King Jr. It is to be found in music and the arts as surely as in transnational developments like slavery and colonialism. Economic, political, and cultural conditions demand the reappropriation of a new internationalist legacy in which democracy and equality are understood less as the possessions of this or that nation than as elements of a planetary project.

A new moment of decision, an ethical choice grounded only in the hatred of any arbitrary prejudice or exercise of institutional power, looms on the horizon. An untapped potential exists within the strivings of humanity for a better world. It becomes evident in the utopian visions of the radical imagination, the cooperative undertakings launched against political intolerance and economic injustice, and the often unrecognized cosmopolitan impulses of everyday people manifest in their attempts to escape parochial constraints on their lives. A palpable need exists to articulate principles and ideas capable of creating more than an additive unity between groups, informing a general project of progressive forces, building a new sense of solidarity, and offering new cultural visions of emancipation for a new world. But this calls for confronting history rather than forgetting it. Only by engaging the radical traditions of the past can new forms of theory begin to contest the world of the next millennium, in which it will surely still be the case, as Bertolt Brecht wrote, that "there are some who live in darkness, and others who live in the light; and one sees those in the light, while those in the darkness disappear."[70]

---

69. Henry Pachter, *The Fall and Rise of Europe: A Political, Social, and Cultural History of the Twentieth Century* (New York: Praeger, 1975), xi.

70. These are the closing lines of the film version of "The Three-Penny Opera," by Bertolt Brecht, published in *Gesammelte Werke* (Frankfurt am Main: Suhrkamp, 1967), 2:497.

Index

ecosystems, 267
Eisner, Kurt, 118
emancipatory interest, 2, 148
Encyclopedia of the Negro (Du Bois), 234
engagement, 145, 212
Engels, Frederick, 130, 248, 266
enlightenment, 180
Enlightenment values, 201–2, 242–43
environmentalism, 230, 265–80
equality: formal, 52; substantive, 31
Equal Rights Amendment, 257
Erfurt Program (1889), 98
Eros and Civilization (Marcuse), 207
ethics, 199–200, 335; and choice, 301–3
Etzioni, Amitai, 21
Evola, Julius, 123
existential hopelessness, 44
existentialism, 146, 154–69
Existentialism and Humanism (Sartre), 167

Falange, 114
family values, 64, 66
Fanon, Frantz, 291–93
Farrakhan, Louis, 124, 239
Fasci di Azione Rivoluzionaria (Fascists for Revolutionary Action), 115
Fasci di Combattimento (1919), 116
fascism, 22, 43, 84, 108–25; Carl Schmitt's conversion to, 58–60; engendered by liberalism, 181; as a political identity, 87–90, 116; relationship to capitalism, 177
feminism, 229–30, 247–64
Feminism or Death (Eaubonne), 270
Feuchtwanger, Lion, 119
feudalism, 57
Feuerbach, Ludwig, 175
Firestone, Shulamith, 256
First International, 69
flat tax, 24
Flaubert, Gustave, 167–68, 262
The Flies (Sartre), 167
Foucault, Michel, 8, 195–96

The Foundations of the Nineteenth Century (Chamberlain), 110
France, Anatole, 112
France under the Jews (Drumont), 112
Franco, Francisco, 74
Frankfurt School, 147, 170–86
freedom, 39; in anarchism, 68; of choice, 176; idea of, 29–30, 209, 303
free market, 65
Freikorps, 118
French New Right, 123
French Revolution (1789), 27, 130, 206
Freud, Sigmund, 260, 262
Frey, Gerhard, 123
Friedman, Milton, 64, 65, 316
Fromm, Erich, 149, 170, 183
"From the Rights of Man to Socialism" (Jaurès), 94
Frye, Northrop, 6
Fuller, Margaret, 247
fundamentalism, 125; religious, 311–12
Futurists, 115

Gadamer, Hans-Georg, 11
Gandhi, Mohandas, 241–42, 289–91, 293
Garvey, Marcus, 235, 237–39
Gaulle, Charles de, 155, 160
Gemeinschaft, 28
Gentile, Giovanni, 28, 29
German Group 47, 6
German imperialism, 59
German National Socialist Workers' Party (SNDAP), 119
German Red Army Faction, 70
German Social Democratic Party (SPD), 98, 248
Germany, 171
Gesellschaft, 28
The Ghost of Stalin (Sartre), 166
Giddens, Anthony, 310–11
Gide, André, 155, 331
Giscard d'Estaing, Valéry, 124
Gleichheit (equality), 249
globalization, 319–22, 330, 334–36

third way between socialism and capitalism, 105
Third World anti-imperialist revolutions, 225
Tito, Josip Broz, 46
Tocqueville, Alexis de, 19, 21, 46, 308; voluntary associations, 49
Toller, Ernst, 118
totalitarianism, 143; democrats response to, 4–5; expressed in Nazism, 121
"Traditional and Critical Theory" (Horkheimer), 176
traditionalism, 55
traditions, 7–13; legitimacy, 46
Treaty of Versailles, 87
Trinh, T. Minh-Ha, 295
Trotsky, Leon, 47, 130–31, 137; on Lenin's theories, 129
Truman, David, 314
truth, 56, 198, 217, 290, 303
Turgenev, Ivan, 70
Turkey, 288
"Twenty-one Points" (Lenin), 134

undistorted communication, 32–33
unitary democracy, 79–80
United Nations, 334–36
United States liberalism, 28, 30–31
Universal Negro Improvement Association, 237
utopia, 219

Vallès, Jules, 69
Valois, Georges, 112
vanguard organization, 138
vanguard party, 128–29, 134; identified with the state, 116

Vietnam, 284
Vietnam War, 64; opposition, 149, 183, 242
violence, 292
Vogelin, Eric, 56
Voltaire, 12, 26
voluntarism, 88
voluntary associations, 49, 52–53, 308
voting rights, 247
Voting Rights Bill of 1965, 242

Walzer, Michael, 44
Washington, Booker T., 235–37, 239
wealth, unequal distribution of, 53, 53n32, 63
Weber, Max, 27, 44, 271, 312
Weimar Republic, 87
welfare state reductions, 62–63, 66
Western Marxism, 171–75
"What Is to Be Done?" (Lenin), 128
Wilde, Oscar, 93
Wollstonecraft, Mary, 248
Woman under Socialism (Bebel), 248–49, 251
women's liberation movement, 229–30, 247–64
women's suffrage, 247
Workers' Opposition, 251
World War I, 72, 133; assault on liberal principles, 30, 43; great betrayal, 126; as total war, 108
World War II, 60–61, 231
Wright, Richard, 235

Zetkin, Clara, 133, 249–50, 252
Zinoviev, Grigory, 173
Zola, Emile, 112
Zurich Congress (1893), 70

About the Author

Stephen Eric Bronner is professor of political science and comparative literature at Rutgers University–New Brunswick. He is author of numerous scholarly and popular works as well as editor of a best selling text-reader, *Twentieth Century Political Theory*. He is a noted authority on critical theory, socialism, and continental politics and appears frequently as a media commentator in both the United States and Germany. He has received many distinguished teaching awards both locally and nationally and also received the Michael Harrington Book Award from the APSA Caucus for a New Political Science in 1994.